Pequot Library
SOUTHPORT, CONNECTICUT

A Gift in Memory of
Mrs. Sargent Eaton
from
Bridgeport House & Garden
Club
of Greater Bridgeport

The Dictionary of Roses in colour

The Dictionary of

ROSES

in colour

S. Millar Gault and Patrick M. Synge

Foreword by Frank M. Bowen

Photographs by Ernest Crowson

Published in collaboration with

The Royal Horticultural Society and The Royal National Rose Society

Michael Joseph
London

First published 1971
Reprinted 1975
Third Printing 1980

© Rainbird Reference Books Limited 1971

This book was designed and produced by
Rainbird Publishing Group Limited
36 Park Street, London W1Y 4DE
for Michael Joseph Limited, 44 Bedford Square,
London W.C.1

The text was set in Monophoto Baskerville 9/10 by
Jolly & Barber Limited, Rugby, England
The book was printed by
de Lange/van Leer N.V., Deventer, Holland
and bound by van Rijmenam N.V.,
The Hague, Holland

ISBN 0 7181 0911 2

Contents

Foreword

The Dictionary of Roses in colour is a companion volume to *The Dictionary of Garden Plants in colour* which, since its first publication in 1969, has been in such world-wide demand as to establish it as one of the most interesting and useful gardening books available today. There is a close resemblance in the arrangement, format and high quality of production of the two volumes which is not surprising in view of the fact that Patrick M. Synge, V.M.H. is joint author of both.

As Editor of The Royal Horticultural Society for twenty-four years until his retirement little more than a year ago, as author and as plant collector, Patrick Synge is so well known as to need no introduction from me. Many thousands of gardeners everywhere have gained inestimable pleasure from his efforts. In this volume, he has concentrated especially on the History and the species, 'old garden' and climbing roses. His co-author, S. M. Gault, M.B.E., V.M.H., has produced the 'modern' section, covering Hybrid Teas, Floribundas and modern shrub roses; and it is difficult to think of any man better qualified to undertake this task. A noteworthy and very unusual distinction is that both authors hold the Victorian Medal of Honour, the highest honour of The Royal Horticultural Society.

Millar Gault has been a professional horticulturist all his working life. After initial training in Scotland, his native country, he occupied with distinction several posts of increasing responsibility until in 1955 he was appointed Superintendent of Regent's Park and began the work that, in the succeeding fourteen years, set his mark on the landscape of Britain's Capital. With praiseworthy backing from the Ministry of Public Building and Works, he transformed Regent's Park from a well known into one of the world's finest city parks; and so developed and improved the already famous Queen Mary's Garden that today, with The Royal National Rose Society's own Display Garden and Trial Grounds at St Albans, it constitutes a mecca for rosarians from every country. If Millar Gault's final love is roses he, like Patrick Synge, also is a very knowledgeable plantsman as evinced by the many cultivars of shrubs, gladioli and other kinds, as well as roses, with which he has enlivened the exhibitions in The Royal Horticultural Society's fortnightly Shows, of plants submitted for awards. To the discerning observer, there has been a significant thread running through all his exhibits, namely, they are all potentially first class garden plants of their respective kinds. This characteristically sound, practical approach has enhanced the many years of devoted service which Millar Gault has given as a judge in all our country's foremost Horticultural Shows and as a member of Council of The Royal National Rose Society to which, since his retirement, he has been acting as Horticultural Consultant.

The cogent remarks on the value of good colour illustrations by Lord Aberconway in his Foreword to *The Dictionary of Garden Plants in colour* apply equally to this companion volume. It contains about five hundred and the original photographs were all taken by Ernest Crowson, one of the leading British photographers of flowers, working under the personal guidance of the Authors and using the same camera as much as possible. Roses in certain colour ranges – notably the reds and so called 'blues' – are notoriously difficult to reproduce absolutely true to life, but in this instance, it appears to me that the Authors' objective of a high general standard has been attained over a range of illustrations that, to the best of my knowledge, is unique in a rose book.

The text has benefited from being reviewed in draft for the two collaborating Societies by a small panel of well known rosarians and I warmly commend this Dictionary to all who are interested in roses for its wealth of practical and interesting information, the extraordinarily wide range of illustrations in colour and the pleasingly high quality of the whole production. My pleasure in so doing is enhanced because this is the first time that The Royal Horticultural Society and The Royal National Rose Society have together collaborated in such a venture and thus have illuminated the close and happy relationship between them that has persisted over many years.

FRANK M. BOWEN
President
The Royal National Rose Society
London, Great Britain. January, 1971.

Introduction

History of Roses:

their introduction and their raising

Roses have been cultivated as garden plants since very early times, yet it is surprising how little we really know about the origins of the ancestral plants which contributed to our present day roses. Records of breeding within the last hundred and fifty years are numerous and mostly reliable but earlier we must rely mainly on pictures, on early collectors' descriptions and often on the rather vague descriptions in the early herbals. In a much quoted verse, Walter de la Mare wrote truly:

> 'Oh, no man knows,
> Through what wild centuries
> Roves back the rose.'

Like lilies, roses have long been symbolic plants, treated with care and reverence and even the earlier representations are probably a long way from the wild species. The Minoans of the Middle Minoan period of Knossos in Crete knew roses and one has been found on one of the old frescoes of about 1600 BC reconstructed by Sir Arthur Evans' team. Most of these frescoes are highly stylized and it is difficult to attribute them to particular plants, particularly as the rose shown appears to be an aberrant specimen with six petals. Dr Hurst, however, has suggested that this may be a representation of *R.* × *richardii*, the rose of Ethiopian churches, long known as *R. sancta* and thought to be a hybrid of *R. gallica* × *R. phoenicia*. The roses that grow wild in Crete now are mostly forms of *R. canina*, the Dog rose or its near relative *R. corymbifera* and *R. arvensis*, but undoubtedly Crete at that period had trade with Egypt and Middle East countries and so one can only guess from where the Minoan form may have come. Sir Leonard Woolley in his excavations at Ur of the Chaldes in the Euphrates-Tigris valleys came across references to roses as well as vines and figs being brought back as part of the booty at the end of a campaign by King Sargon who is believed to have reigned from 2648 to 2630 BC, nearly five thousand years ago.

There are ancient Chinese paintings, some over a thousand years old, which show China roses quite clearly among their other flowers and the late Mr E. A. Bunyard, a great authority on old roses, identified these with some of the China and *odorata* roses which were introduced from China early in the nineteenth century but they do not show anything of the wealth of wild species roses from western China and the marches of Tibet.

There are about 150 recognised and described species of roses which range across the northern hemisphere from the Pacific coast of North America, south to Mexico and eastwards through northern Europe and North Africa, through northern Asia where there is by far the largest representation, through Siberia to the Himalayas, China and Japan, and south to the Philippines. The most tropical species is *R. clinophylla* from East Bengal and North India but it is rarely seen in cultivation. The majority of the others have been in cultivation, although the greater part of the introduction of Asiatic and North American species is derived from collections made within the last hundred and fifty years. Roses are not found wild in the southern hemisphere and there are no native ones in Australia, New Zealand or South America, although the introduced roses grow splendidly in some of these countries, particularly in New Zealand. This pattern of distribution is common to many other genera. They are primarily a genus of the north temperate regions and consequently nearly all are hardy in gardens in Great Britain and most of northern Europe and North America, although in parts of Canada and the colder northern states of the U.S.A., some require winter protection.

There is little reference to particular roses in classical Greek literature, except in such stylized phrases in Homer as 'the rosy-fingered Dawn', while Aphrodite is reported as embalming Hector's body with rose compounds. There are highly complimentary references to roses in the work of the poet Anacreon who lived about 600 BC, and some quotations from later writers which may have been taken from the much earlier writings of Sappho, whose poetry in the original, alas, has almost entirely been lost to us. Later there are references in Herodotus and Theophrastus, the pupil of Aristotle who, in the third century BC, was the first great naturalist writer and observer. The land of Greece has never lent itself to great gardening and the Romans were probably much better gardeners and had an easier climate for gardening with greater water supplies. They probably also had more leisure in which to appreciate their plants and certainly roses played a large part in their enjoyment of flowers. Roses would decorate their highly lavish feasts and chaplets of roses would be worn while a rose would be hung from the ceiling. To speak 'sub-rosa' became the accepted phrase for a confidential talk at the end of the banquet. In spite of this there are no contemporary pictures or accurate descriptions which enable us to identify with real certainty the roses they grew, although

Virgil gives us a clue to the autumn Damasks. It is presumed, however, that these were the roses we would now describe as Gallicas and probably Damask roses with a preponderance of *Rosa gallica officinalis* and the valuable Paestum rose, *R. damascena bifera* which grew round the Temple of Paestum, south of Naples, and had the most valuable quality of a second autumn flowering in addition to the summer flowering to which *R. gallica* was confined. Undoubtedly the Romans understood the art of grafting, and possibly also of budding, and hybrids between these forms may also have been grown and perpetuated by grafting on wild stocks. Whether any intentional hybridization took place we do not know.

Dr C. C. Hurst, to whose cytological researches we owe much of our recent knowledge of rose history, noted that *R. gallica* was also shown as a religious emblem by the Medes and Persians as early as the twelfth century BC and it may be that the species, if true wild species it may be, was found native in those areas. The dwarf form of *R. gallica* is usually described as native to southern Europe and extending into western Asia and to grow only 2–3 ft (0·6–0·9 m.) high with pink or crimson flowers, but I must confess that I have never found it growing wild and feel some doubt about these records. However, it finds a place in *Flora Europaea* with a very wide distribution. Dr Hurst adopted Miss Blackwell's later name of *R. rubra* for this, since the earlier Linnean description of 1753 referred to another rose close to *R. canina* and Linnaeus did not describe the commonly grown *R. gallica* till 1759, but Mr Gordon Rowley, one of our foremost systematic scholars on the taxonomy of the genus, has shown more recently that it is not necessary to adopt the name of *R. rubra* and that we may revert again happily to the use of *R. gallica*.

The Apothecary's Rose of Provins was undoubtedly *R. gallica officinalis* and in the thirteenth century this was grown round the town of Provins, south-east of Paris, which became the centre of a large rose perfume industry, used both as conserves and as dried roses, probably an early form of potpourri, for this rose is unrivalled for its scent and it had early been discovered that some of this could be preserved after drying the petals. This was erroneously known as the Red Damask rose for it is really a true *gallica*. The striped *R. gallica versicolor*, 'Rosa Mundi', supposedly named after Fair Rosamund, the beloved mistress of Henry II, was first recorded in the early seventeenth century and was obviously a sport from the red *gallica*, but when or where it arose is unknown. So its association with Henry II's Rosamund is very doubtful. It is still widely grown and wonderful hedges of it covered with flowers, as a buddleia or sedum is covered with butterflies, can be seen in several famous gardens. It stands well hard annual clipping and may be kept to a height of 3 ft (0·9 m.). It only flowers once, however. The Gallicas such as 'Cardinal de Richelieu' and 'Charles de Mills' were developed later, probably mostly in the middle of the nineteenth century although 'Tuscany' may be the same as Gerard's Velvet Rose recorded in 1596.

The Damask roses form a fairly homogeneous group closely allied to the Gallicas and their origin is undoubtedly very old. Tradition suggests that they owe their name to Damascus whence they were brought to Europe by the crusaders.

This may well be. Probably some came earlier to the Romans. We have no direct evidence either way. Again, Dr Hurst has produced some cytological evidence that the group has been derived from crosses, either natural or artificial, between *R. gallica* and *R. phoenicia* and *R. moschata* and he considered that the group showed some of their characters. They are distinguished by the strong spicy scent and looser growth than in *R. gallica* and their colours are mainly pinks and whites, without the sumptuous blue-purple of the *gallicas*. This is perhaps not surprising if we accept Dr Hurst's theory, for both the other supposed parents have white flowers. Some of the later raised Damask roses may also include *R. × centifolia*, the Provence Rose, in their parentage. Dr Hurst divided the Damask roses into two groups, the summer flowering single-season ones derived from *R. gallica* × *R. phoenicia* and the autumn Damask rose which was called *R. bifera* and derived from *gallica* × *moschata*. These two groups, however, are hardly apparent in the present-day Damasks, which are probably more mixed in their parentage. Both these groups were known in very early days, probably to the Romans and some were widespread. To the summer Damask roses belongs the York and Lancaster striped rose, distinguished from the striped 'Rosa Mundi' by the white instead of pale pink background colour of the flowers and the extra petals in its rather untidy semi-double flowers. Also here probably belongs the Holy Rose, *R. × richardii*, which was brought from the courtyards of holy places in Ethiopia and described by Richard in his *Flora of Abyssinia* of 1848 as *R. sancta*, a name which unfortunately had later to be rejected since it had been earlier used for quite a different rose. It is unlikely that it was raised in Ethiopia and Dr Hurst suggested that it may have been taken from Asia Minor by St Frumentius, an early Christian missionary of the fourth century, who was captured by the Ethiopians, taken to their capital of those times, Axum, and there had a long and profitable life, becoming bishop and secretary to the king. Dr Hurst thought that this might also be the rose of which the remains were found in Egyptian tombs of Upper Egypt of the period between the second and fifth centuries AD. These were sent to Kew and thence to Brussels where the rose authority of the day, Professor Crepin, identified them with *R. × richardii*. They had formed part of a garland.

The records of the autumn Damask roses were even earlier. In the tenth century BC, they were mentioned as growing in the island of Samos, flowering twice a year and being used in the cult of Aphrodite. These were probably the same roses as Herodotus later mentions growing in the gardens of Midas in Macedonia which were very sweetly scented and had 60 petals. Their attribution from this phrase to *R. × centifolia* is probably not correct. This was probably the autumn flowering rose of Paestum, so well known to the Romans and mentioned by Virgil as flowering twice a year. It is probably also the rose of the Pompeian frescoes. Another form of Damask rose is *R. damascena trigintipetala*, the rose grown in great quantities around Kazanlik in Bulgaria for producing Attar of Roses. The famous York and Lancaster rose was also a Damask and, with its flowers of white and red, was regarded as a symbol of reconciliation between the warring houses of York and Lancaster whose emblems the white and red roses had been.

The Damask roses have also given us the Albas and Dr Hurst concluded that $R. \times alba$ was a hybrid of $R. damascena$ with a form of $R. canina$ as the female parent. Dr Ann Wylie in her Masters Memorial lectures to the R.H.S. in 1954 suggested $R. gallica$ as the other parent. This agrees with the cytological evidence, the Albas being hexaploids and derived from the tetraploid *gallicas* and the *caninas* which are irregularly tetraploid to hexaploid. The *albas* are distinguished by flowering usually once only in the summer, by their strong scent, pink or pale blush-pink flowers, grey-green foliage and above all for their garden vigour and persistence. One of the loveliest of all is the pale pink 'Céleste' with its wonderful combination of flower and foliage. They are also distinguished by other enchanting and romantic names such as 'Maidens' Blush', 'Cuisse de Nymphe Emue', probably the same as 'Maidens' Blush', 'Belle Amour'.

Roses seem to have been well regarded in England even from Norman times and there is a story that William II, Rufus, when he wanted to enter a nunnery at Romsey to see the young Matilda, made the excuse to her aunt who was keeping her concealed there that 'he only wanted to admire the roses' and they may have been either Gallica or Damask roses. The red rose was regarded as the symbol of the passion of Jesus while the white rose was the symbol of Mary's purity and as such they feature in many early pictures. Germain Bazin, the Conservateur-en-Chef du Louvre, has shown us several in his fascinating book *A Gallery of Flowers*, in particular the details of the rose screen at the back of the German Martin Schongauer's picture, *Madonna in the Rose Bower*, probably painted in 1473. This shows a semi-double red rose, possibly $R. gallica officinalis$, and a semi-double white which looks like an *alba* rose. The author attributes the red rose to $R. canina$, the Dog rose, but I do not think this is correct. He shows also a detail of a basket of roses painted by Cranach in 1506. These are carried by a young boy who brings the roses to St Dorothy and he wears a chaplet of similar roses, showing both semi-double white and red ones of rather similar type to those painted by Schongauer. These were probably the common roses of the time and may also have been the common roses of the Romans and distributed by them over Europe, for they were great spreaders of good plants wherever they went. The Alba roses were much used by the great Renaissance painters and probably the shower of rose petals that Botticelli rained down over his Venus were Alba roses.

Although most people consider the Centifolias, the Rose des Peintres, or more prosaically, the Cabbage roses, as typical of the old roses, they were not in practice the oldest and arose towards the end of the sixteenth century probably from the autumn Damask crossed with an *alba* rose and thus contained four species, $R. gallica$, $R. phoenicia$, $R. moschata$ and $R. canina$. There are pictures by Jan de Heem and Jacob Walscappelle which show Centifolia roses early in the 17th century while in 1720 a Moss sport of a Centifolia rose appeared in the list of plants at the physic-garden at Leyden made by Boerhoave and later in 1730 $R. centifolia$ was shown in the magnificent illustrated catalogue of Robert Furber, *The Twelve Months of Flowers*. He was a nurseryman at Kensington but his catalogue illustrations engraved from paintings by P. Casteels, were so lavish that they are now prized as prints for decoration and many have been hand coloured. It was slow, however, to spread, possibly because young plants are not often very vigorous. These are primarily the roses of the Dutch flower pieces, large and luscious, seeming as if they had at least a hundred petals. Occasionally an *alba* is found also, or a Damask, but rarely a *gallica*. The Cabbage rose is nearly always sterile and most of the variants have arisen as bud sports.

The Moss roses also came as bud sports, mainly from $R. centifolia$, but in a few cases from a Damask rose. It is interesting to think of such an odd and seemingly artificial fantasy as the 'Chapeau de Napoléon' with its buds resembling a green mossy cockaded hat as having arisen by a chance mutation. The first old Moss rose is thought to have arisen in Holland early in the eighteenth century. Some of these show reversions to their parents and so betray their origins.

The old herbalists such as Clusius, Dodens, Gerard and Parkinson, were the first, however, to put down any systematic accounts of roses and they still knew comparatively few. Gerard only had 14 in 1597, while Parkinson, a much more reliable herbalist, in 1629 described 24. It was only towards the end of the next century that the number really grew and Miss Mary Lawrance in 1799 published her *A Collection of Roses from Nature* with 90 hand-coloured etchings. This was the first of the great rose books but it could not compare in quality with the really great rose books of the next century. She showed the first coloured plate of the 'Austrian Copper' and a very striking one it is too, one of the finest plates in the book and splendid for colour. She called it '*Rosa lutea* β *bicolor*, the Austrian Rose'. This is one of the earliest plates showing a yellow rose derived from $R. foetida$ which had long been known, probably having been cultivated by the Moors in Spain in the 13th century. Usually sterile, it yielded no progeny except this sport until the introduction of the semi-double Persian form, $R. foetida persiana$, in 1837 which played such a large part in the parentage of our present day roses. The only other yellow roses known in Europe were forms of $R. spinosissima$ and $R. hemisphaerica$ the yellow Sulphur rose of the orient which intrigued Clusius and later Redouté, who painted it so magnificently. Its large double sulphur-yellow flowers tend to droop but are beautiful. Unfortunately it is now a plant without vigour and very rarely flowers in Britain but may grow better in a warmer climate.

From America came early $R. virginiana$, St Mark's Rose, or in its semi-double form 'Rose d'Amour', which was introduced prior to 1640 when it was described by Parkinson, but in general American species did not play any great part in our rose history.

It was the contribution from China that made the great breakthrough and the first of these China roses only arrived in 1789, or according to some authorities 1792, although there is a doubtful record of a China rose grown by Philip Miller, presumably in his Chelsea Physic Garden, as early as 1752. The two new introductions were 'Slater's Crimson China' and 'Parson's Pink China', the first a garden rose rather than a wild one, was a real dark red, shrubby rather than climbing. It is said to have been brought from a Calcutta garden by the captain of an East Indiaman and given to Mr Gilbert Slater, a Director of the East India Company, who planted it in a greenhouse and flowered it two years later. 'Parson's Pink China' was introduced either in 1789 or 1793 according to various authorities and was also a shrub rose which will grow from 3 ft to 10 ft (0.9–3.0 m.) depending on condition. One account suggests that it was sent to Sir Joseph Banks, another that Mr Parsons of Rickmansworth had it and first flowered it four years after introduction. This may be the same rose as that known as 'The Monthly Rose' and if so it is still in cultivation. 'Slater's Crimson China' was thought to be extinct but was recently rediscovered in a Hertfordshire garden and also in Bermuda. The wild *R. chinensis*, with a single flower, was not collected till about 1884 when Dr Augustine Henry found it in Central China near Ichang. He described it as a climber with solitary single deep red flowers but sometimes with pink flowers. A few years after the first introductions two Hybrid China roses were introduced and these are known as *R. × odorata*, hybrids of *R. chinensis* and *R. gigantea*, a rampant climber. These were 'Hume's Blush Tea-scented China' sent in 1808 or 1809 to Sir Abraham Hume of Wormleybury from a nursery near Canton, again by an agent of the East India Company, and 'Park's Yellow Tea-scented China' introduced from the same Canton nursery in 1824 by J. D. Parks for the Horticultural Society of London.

Thus from China came the four ancestors which have contributed more than any others to our present roses for they brought the gene or genes for recurrent flowering, often described, although erroneously, as perpetual-flowering. This has contributed more than any other character to the present unbounded popularity of roses. Fortunately also they were easily propagated from cuttings.

About the same time *R. banksiae* in its double white form was sent from China in 1807 by William Kerr who was collecting for The Royal Botanic Gardens, Kew, and earlier in 1793 came *R. bracteata*, mother of 'Mermaid', but apart from this Chinese species have not contributed greatly to rose breeding as have the four garden Chinas discussed above. It was fortunate that these came at a time of intense rose interest which, at the early part of the nineteenth century, centred on France but quickly spread to England. The great grower was the Empress Josephine at Malmaison, near Paris, perhaps seeking solace from Napoleon's long absences on his campaigns, and the great artist was Redouté, an unrivalled partnership which led to the greatest book on roses we are ever likely to see, *Les Roses*, which was published in three large folio volumes between 1817 and 1824 after the Empress's death in 1814. These contained 170 plates of roses grown at La Malmaison and an accompanying text by Claude Antoine Thory. They were printed in colour and finished by hand. There is a superb copy in the Lindley Library of the Royal Horticultural Society in London. Redouté's paintings of roses have a grace and delicacy found in no other drawings of roses, although many artists have attempted them, and one can browse most happily through his volumes today and attempt to identify the flowers with the roses we know. Alas, many of them have been lost to us but some remain such as the *R. centifolia* of which there is an exceptional plate and the moss form of this is also included.

The collection of the Empress Josephine transcended nationalities. It is recorded that during the Napoleonic wars, roses for her, in particular the 'Parson's Pink China'

rose, were sent from England under a special free conduct and reached her safely. Her enthusiasm encouraged the fashion for growing roses and this in turn encouraged the nurserymen so that in the next century far more new roses were raised than ever before, especially in France, and some of these are still well worth growing. The appreciation of the individual plant for its own sake rather than solely for its effect in the landscape also accorded more with nineteenth-century gardening than it had with the broader landscape effects of the eighteenth century landscape architects.

The two next great advances making use of the recurrent flowering of the newly introduced China roses, however, took place outside Europe. In 1802 in the warm climate of South Carolina in the U.S.A. Champneys, an American nurseryman, crossed 'Parson's Pink China' rose with the Musk rose *R. moschata*. This was presumably the true *moschata*, a late-flowering loose shrub, rather than the vigorous white-flowered Climber which masqueraded so long under this name and has now been considered possibly a hybrid of the rose long known as *R. brunonii*, now regarded as a variety of *R. moschata* under the name *nepalensis*. *R. moschata* brought in two valuable characters, its late flowering, which combined with the recurrent flowering of the China rose, apparently a recessive character, to bring a much longer season of flower, and its unique musky sweet scent which is carried on the air. This gave him a rose which he called 'Champney's Pink Cluster' but it was summer flowering only and a diploid with only 14 chromosomes. Seedlings from this rose were raised by Philippe Noisette, a French nurseryman also living in South Carolina, and he selected one which he called the Old Blush Noisette rose. In 1814 he sent one of these to his brother, a nurseryman in Paris, who distributed it. It was called *R. noisettiana* and drawn by Redouté and became the parent of the Noisette roses. It also was more recurrent flowering than its parent. About 1830 this Blush Noisette was crossed with 'Park's Yellow China' rose, an *odorata* hybrid from *R. chinensis* and *R. gigantea* and these gave us the yellow Noisettes, which did not lead further, and the yellow Tea roses which are directly in the line of parentage of our present Hybrid Tea roses. Seedlings from these lead us to the lovely Climbers 'William Allen Richardson' and 'Maréchal Niel', still diploids and still grown in some old gardens and in the case of 'Maréchal Niel' as greenhouse Climbers. The phrase Tea rose is an odd one, but it is said to be derived from the scent of the bruised fresh tea leaf, not from that of the dried tea leaves which is all that most of us are familiar with. The first to be introduced was 'Hume's Blush Tea-scented China'.

The other advance occurred in the Isle of Réunion in the Indian Ocean, then known as L'Isle de Bourbon and a French colony. Roses were grown there as hedges but sometimes the kinds of roses were mixed. In 1817 a French botanist named Breon, there in charge of the Botanic Gardens, noted an unusual plant in a hedge of the Autumn Damask rose and 'Parson's Pink China' rose and his plant appeared to be intermediate between them. Seeds from it were sent to France to M. Jacques, royal gardener to the King Louis Philippe, near Paris, and among them was the first named Bourbon rose, 'Rosier de l'Isle Bourbon' which Redouté drew in 1824, a fine vigorous plant with bright rose-pink semi-double flowers and a good scent. Inter-crossing between this and its seedlings and the original Gallica and Damask roses produced a large and varied group many of which had increased their chromosome numbers being tetraploid with 28 chromosomes. These included such outstandingly lovely roses as 'Mme Pierre Oger', which is still widely grown and appreciated and appeared in 1878 as a sport from 'La Reine Victoria'.

The combination of 'Hume's Blush China' with the early Bourbons gave us our first pink Tea roses and the first of these, raised in 1833, was appropriately· called 'Adam', but unfortunately is no longer with us. Interesting diagrams tracing genetically the origin of these groups will be found in the report of the Masters Memorial Lectures given by Dr Ann Wylie to the Royal Horticultural Society and reproduced in their Journals for 1954 and 1955 and I am indebted to her for such a clear exposition of this subject.

The Bourbon roses were distinguished by their prickly stems and their rounded flowers with closely imbricated shell-like petals, characters which they passed on in some instances to the next great group, the Hybrid Perpetuals, which formed the larger proportion of the last century's roses. Hundreds of these were listed, most of which have now died out, but some famous ones and good garden plants such as 'Baron Girod de l'Ain' remain with us. These in-cluded ancestry from three main groups, the Bourbons, the Portlands which were early derivatives of autumn flowering Damasks and *gallica* roses crossed with 'Slater's Crimson China' and the Hybrid Chinas which came from *R. gallica* crossed with 'Hume's Blush Tea-scented China' rose. Al-ready we were getting far from the first generation hybrids towards the vast races of mongrels which we have today. M. Laffay in France was probably the greatest raiser of these about the middle of the last century and increased their size of flower greatly, but there were keen growers in England as well, such as William Paul whose nursery list far exceeded in numbers that of any rose grower today. His two books of 1848 and 1872 entitled *The Rose Garden* listed and described with enthusiasm a vast quantity, the majority of which could not be found today.

The Hybrid China roses were important in the history of roses and were derived from *R. gallica* and 'Hume's Blush Tea-scented China', the first appearing about 1815 and as a group there are several which are still worth growing. Apart from their part in the origin of the Hybrid Perpetuals, they have been mingled with other roses such as the Tea roses and the Multifloras and so have contributed both to our Polyantha and Floribunda roses and to the Hybrid Tea roses. The earliest of these was known as 'Brown's Superb Blush' but it has disappeared completely. The majority of the early ones were probably triploids and so sterile but later, about 1830, several fertile tetraploids occurred such as 'Malton' and 'Athalin', both now lost to us. From this mutation the path ahead became clearer, although they were mainly summer-flowering only owing to the dominance of the gene for summer flowering over that for recurrent flowering. Segregation in later generations, however, allowed the recurrent flowering characteristic to appear. By such small genetic changes, big changes in our roses of great garden importance can arise. These China roses usually grew

better in the warmer summer climate of Italy and the south of France than in Britain.

'La France' was raised by Guillot in France in 1867 and is generally considered either as the first Hybrid Tea rose or as the forerunner of them. According to Dr Wylie, and probab-ly rightly, its parentage is uncertain although this is generally given as the Tea rose 'Mme Bravy' and the Hybrid Perpetual 'Mme Victor Verdier'. 'La France' has large silvery-pink flowers with the pointed buds of a Tea rose and is re-current-flowering. It is still grown well at La Bagatelle, Paris. The bush is quite vigorous, about 3 ft (0·9 m.) high and a little more across. There is, however, some blue in the pink-ness of the flower, not a really clear colour. Unfortunately it has a low degree of fertility being a triploid. However, from this and other rather similar crosses, more seedlings were raised and some of these were fertile tetraploids such as 'Mme Caroline Testout', 'Lady Mary Fitzwilliam' and 'Mme Abel Chatenay'. This was parallel to the tetra-ploid developments in the Hybrid Chinas and Bourbons. All the early Hybrid Tea roses were whites, pinks or reds, and only later did the yellow colour appear.

This yellow came through the introduction of *R. foetida* as a parent but unfortunately it is mainly sterile. The French nurseryman Pernet-Ducher, however, was very persistent and made thousands of crosses using mainly the variety *persiana*, the semi-double form of *R. foetida*. The first really yellow Hybrid Tea rose was 'Soleil d'Or', a tetraploid. It was crossed back to *R. foetida* in the form of the Austrian Copper *R. foetida bicolor*, and the seedlings from this had very strong coloured, orange and deep yellow flowers but, like their parent, tended to be weak growers, very thorny and unduly susceptible to black spot, and without much scent. These characteristics have been modified over the years but the tendencies still remain. However they now form a large and important group of our modern roses. The early seedlings of this group were known as Pernetianas after M. Pernet-Ducher. The deep yellow still seems to remain a recessive character but even now we have incomplete knowledge of the inheritance of colour in roses and, like so many other long cultivated groups, their extremely hetero-genous (mongrel) character makes any assessment more difficult.

As we come into the present century the influence of two other species, both from the Far East, becomes apparent; *R. multiflora* in the Polyantha roses and thence through to the Floribundas; and *R. wichuraiana* in the Ramblers. *R. multiflora* itself has only rather small white flowers in clusters and the wild single form did not reach Europe till 1862 but long before that garden hybrids with *multiflora* ancestry had been sent from China. From these crossed with Hybrid Chinas came first some of the earlier Ramblers, especially some with dusky violet-purple flowers such as 'Veilchenblau', while in America, the 'Dawson' rose which played an important part in their breeding, had *R. multiflora* in its ancestry. From another group of *multiflora*, crossed with a dwarf pink China rose, probably the one known as 'The Fairy Rose' with rather dwarf shrubby habit and small pink flowers in clusters, came the Dwarf Polyan-thas and here again a French nurseryman, M. Guillot of Lyon, was the prime breeder. These dwarf roses were good garden plants for their long season of flowering and hardiness in growth, although they were not spectacular as have been some of the later developments. One of the best known was called the 'Orléans Rose' raised in 1909 and the parent of many sports.

In Denmark, starting from about 1910, a nurseryman, Poulsen, crossed these dwarf Polyanthas with Hybrid Teas to produce the Hybrid Polyanthas of which many present-day rose growers will remember 'Else Poulsen', a delightful pink, and 'Kirsten Poulsen', both introduced in 1924 from a cross between 'Orléans Rose' and a single red Hybrid Tea called 'Red Star'. They were much larger than the dwarf Polyanthas both in flowers and in stature and were widely grown. They were also crossed on to Hybrid Tea roses such as 'Ophelia' and thence, by many stages, has come the great development of all the Floribunda roses.

Rosa wichuraiana is a Japanese climber, though often spreading along the ground, distinguished by its vigorous growth, its glossy shining foliage and its large sprays of single white flowers. It is late flowering also, a characteristic which it has passed on to its numerous Rambler progeny, and which is a valuable garden character since it brings them into flower after the first flush of other roses is over. They have also inherited its lovely shining foliage, as well as its hardiness. Their only faults are a lack of scent and a single season of flower in most cases. From a cross between *R. wichuraiana* and a yellow Tea rose 'Shirley Hibberd', M. Barbier raised in 1900, the superb, almost evergreen 'Albéric Barbier', still in my opinion to be placed among the twelve finest Ramblers for any garden. Its vigour is only surpassed by the great 'Kiftsgate' form of *R. filipes*. Later the same French grower raised 'Albertine', another of my twelve top Ramblers, this time using a copper coloured Hybrid Tea rose, 'Mrs A. R. Waddell', as the other parent. In the U.S.A. *R. wichuraiana* was also popular as a parent and in 1901 Jackson and Perkins raised the famous 'Dorothy Perkins' by crossing it with 'Mme Gabriel Luizet', a Hybrid Perpetual with large pale pink flowers. As a garden plant it is far surpassed by later seedlings, 'Excelsa', 'Crimson Shower' and 'Sanders White', with better, cleaner flower colours and without its almost unavoidable propensity to mildew, but none of them have shared her vast popularity over so long a season, a vogue which clotted the gardens of the temperate world with a cloud of acrid sugar-pink about the middle of each July.

In North America also, another line of *wichuraiana* hybrids raised, by the firm of Brownell, from crosses with very winter-hardy Hybrid Teas, led to 'Dr W. Van Fleet', a lovely shell-pink climber, though only with a single season of flower. However from this came a recurrent-flowering sport 'New Dawn' which is undoubtedly one of the most popular free-flowering and desirable of climbing roses today, as well as figuring in the parentage of a large number of our most successful and popular roses.

During the last hundred and fifty years also the contribution of the great plant collectors to our roses has been large, particularly those working in China, Japan and the Himalayas. We have already traced the influence of the *chinensis*, *gigantea* and *odorata* stock in the development of modern roses and it has been gigantic, but also great has been the number of good climbing and shrub roses which have been introduced, although as yet they have played little part in the breeding programmes of the great rose firms.

Rosa bracteata came to us as a result of Lord George Macartney's mission to China in 1792. On his staff was Sir George Staunton, a keen collector, and he had two gardeners attached to him. They were fortunate in that the Imperial Chinese Court had moved north to Jehol for the summer and on the way there they were able to botanize in the hills by the Great Wall as well as journeying overland from Peking to Canton on the way back.

Rosa banksiae, as already mentioned, was first introduced by the Kew collector William Kerr, who lived in China from 1803–12, close to the famous Faté nursery gardens in Canton, a source of many good plants.

When Robert Fortune was sent to China by the Royal Horticultural Society in 1843 he was instructed among other plants to look for 'The Double Yellow Roses of which two sorts are said to occur in Chinese gardens exclusive of the Banksian'. The Society already had appreciable knowledge of Chinese garden plants from the exciting drawings sent home by Reeves. No record exists, however, of his introduction of these double yellow roses which would presumably have been *odorata* hybrids like the one previously introduced by Parks. The great French priest collectors such as David, Soulié and Farges did not introduce many living plants although roses were undoubtedly among their specimens. To Ernest Wilson, however, we owe the greatest number of valuable western Chinese roses, *R. moyesii*, a wonderful shrub rose both for its flowers and its hips, *R. davidii*, *R. multibracteata*, *R. willmottiae*, and climbers such as *R. filipes* and *R. rubus*. A little later Reginald Farrer sent his dainty Threepenny-bit Rose, *R. farreri* from South Kansu. He also sent from this expedition forms of *R. banksiae*, *R. hugonis*, *R. multibracteata* and *R. rubus* although he cannot claim to be the first introducer of any of these species. In Upper Burma he collected forms of *R. macrophylla* and *R. sericea*. Curiously George Forrest, perhaps the most voluminous and successful of all collectors, is not credited with any new roses. He was probably more interested in primulas and rhododendrons, but his description of *R. banksiae* in the Lashi-pa valley backed by the massive peak of Li-Chiang, gives a picture of a climbing rose as it should be allowed to grow. He wrote 'Can you imagine a rose mass a hundred or more feet in length, thirty feet high and twenty through, a veritable cascade of the purest white backed by the most delicate green, and with a cushion of fragrance on every side? One sight such as that, and it is only one of many, is worth all the weariness and hardship of a journey from England'.

From the Himalayas came more forms of *R. macrophylla* and *R. moschata* while from Afghanistan, the dowry of a boundary commission, came the lovely golden *R. ecae* named after the initials of the collector's wife, Mrs E. C. Aitchison.

After this brief interlude of travel we must turn again to breeding developments in Europe and the next important one was probably the raising of the Pemberton Hybrid Musks, 'Cornelia', 'Felicia', 'Penelope' and 'Vanity', still among the finest roses for our gardens, with their abundance of flower over such a long period. The Rev. Joseph Pemberton lived at a village in Essex called Havering-atte-Bower and had a long interest in raising roses which the duties of a country clergyman allowed him to indulge. His first introduction was 'Daphne' in 1912 and his last probably 'Felicia' in 1928. The incomparable 'Buff Beauty', probably also of his raising was introduced by his former foreman Bentall in 1939. They are all descended from the three species *R. chinensis*, *R. moschata* and *R. multiflora* through 'Aglaia', introduced in 1896 and 'Trier' of 1904. When 'Trier' was crossed with the pale Hybrid Tea 'Ophelia', it produced 'Felicia', while crossed with other roses has produced 'Moonlight' and 'Pax'.

Wilhelm Kordes of Germany is one of the great rose breeders of this century. Although a German by nationality, his first rose nursery was at Witley in Surrey before the first World War, during which he was interned. When he returned to Germany, he developed his famous nursery at Sparrieshoop and gave its name to an excellent and very vigorous pink shrub rose. To him we owe two very successful lines of breeding; 'Joanna Hill' and other Hybrid Tea varieties crossed with *spinosissima* forms which gave us, in 'Frühlingsgold' and 'Frühlingsmorgen', two of the finest large shrub roses in cultivation; and the Kordesii recurrent-flowering climbing and pillar roses which have added such bright reds and orange-reds to our gardens. To him we also owe 'Independence' ('Sondermeldung') which, owing to a mutation, carried a new pigment in roses, pelargonidin, which has been responsible for the bright orange-red in so many modern roses, a colour which has proved popular but one which may be harsh and difficult to fit into the garden. Perhaps his lovely and popular Floribunda 'Schneewittchen' ('Iceberg') will be more compatible with many gardeners.

Other raisers of most successful roses have included the vast Meilland establishment, at Antibes in the south of France, which has grown out of perhaps the most successful rose ever raised, 'Peace'. Harry Wheatcroft, in a recent book, estimated its sales at a hundred million. Indeed commercial rose growing has become big business, perhaps more than any other field of decorative horticulture. Other important raisers are Mathias Tantau of Germany, who gave us 'Super Star' ('Tropicana') and 'Duftwolke' ('Fragrant Cloud'); Pedro Dot of Spain, who gave us 'Nevada' and 'Mme Grégoire Staechelin'; McGredy's of Northern Ireland, who gave us 'Elizabeth of Glamis', 'Mrs Sam McGredy' and many others; Dicksons, also of Northern Ireland, who gave us 'Grandpa Dickson', one of the best pale yellow Hybrid Teas, and 'Dearest' one of the most charming pink Floribundas. From the U.S.A. came others from the firm of Jackson and Perkins, from where Mr Boerner raised 'Aloha' and 'Fashion'; from Herbert Swim of California who raised 'Sutters' Gold' and 'Pink Parfait'. From England, LeGrice has given us 'Allgold' and the well scented 'My Choice' while amateurs have also raised a few winners such as Mr Norman's 'Frensham' and 'Ena Harkness'; Mr Allen's 'Golden Chersonese', a new break; and Bertram Park's 'June Park'. From France recently MM. Delbard and Chabert gave us 'Altissimo' which I consider one of the best red Climbers. These are only a few out of the multitude that has been raised and put on the market in recent years.

The rose specialist societies have also played a considerable part in the encouragement of rose growing and, by their constant trials in the evaluation of the best varieties for garden purposes, have performed a most valuable service. The Royal National Rose Society (Great Britain) is now the biggest specialist flower society in the world as regards membership. It was the child of two clergymen famous in rose growing, Dean Reynolds Hole and the Rev. H. Honeywood D'Ombrain. Dean Hole's *A Book about Roses* was first published in 1869 and was the standard book on the subject for many years with over twenty editions. In 1858 Dean Hole also organized the first National Rose Show held in England at St James' Hall in London. This show was transferred to the Crystal Palace in 1860, so large was the attendance. The Rose Society was founded in 1876 at a meeting in London when Hole became its first President and D' Ombrain its first Honorary Secretary, a powerful team which stayed together for twenty-six years in the running of the Society with the aid of Mr Edward Mawley as Joint Honorary Secretary. In 1916 another great rosarian, Mr Courtney Page, became Joint Honorary Secretary and sole Secretary in 1917. He died at the age of 80 in 1947 still serving the Society. On his death, Mr Edland, his deputy, became the first fully paid Secretary and remained until his death a few years ago in 1964. This period saw the establishment of the new trial grounds and offices at Bone Hill, near St Albans, probably the most comprehensive trial of roses anywhere in the world. Roses, however, perform differently under different conditions and the same ones are not always the best in different countries so most valuable trials and collections have been established at other centres and judging is held there. These include the lovely grounds on the hillside overlooking Florence in Italy, the truly splendid park at Bagatelle, the great park outside Madrid and another outside Orléans. International rose awards are now given at Rome, Madrid, Paris, Geneva, The Hague, Lyon, Orléans, Belfast, Japan and New Zealand. The American Rose Society is a very active body that also holds trials in different parts of the U.S.A. as well as holding conventions and publishing a monthly bulletin. The International Registration Authority for roses is the American Rose Society which publishes the standard descriptions in conjunction with Messrs J. Horace McFarland under the title *Modern Roses*. The last published, which has been used extensively in the nomenclature of roses in this book, is *Modern Roses 7* and it contains many thousands of names. It is very desirable to have one standard list of names for all to follow as has been widely recognized by recent International Horticultural Congresses who have been instrumental in appointing the International Registration Authorities.

The main emphasis of the national rose societies has been towards the encouragement of the Hybrid Tea and Floribunda roses, and undoubtedly these are the most popular. So much interbreeding, however, has gone on that the dividing line between these and also between the Floribundas and the Shrub roses has become indistinct. This is a natural process but perhaps a new classification is required now. Such classifications are admittedly imperfect and artificial and there will always be borderline cases, but they are necessary.

So the cult and development of roses has grown far since the days of the Greeks and Romans, even since the days of the sixteenth and seventeenth century herbalists. What of the future? We can be fairly sure that the enthusiasm will not diminish. The spate of new varieties is likely to continue but I hope may become more varied. Probably breeding for size of bloom and brightness of orange-scarlet flame colours, which has been such a feature of recent years, will show progressively fewer spectacular advances, outstanding show plants as they are. I anticipate that raisers will become more adventurous in their use of other species, so far only a very small proportion have been used, and also in their raising of roses which will be good garden shrubs and climbers with a long season of flower. The popularity of shrub roses, even though some of them only flower once, is increasing. They make such a great spectacle when they flower, even if it is seasonal, and I foresee more attempts to combine the old with the new and bring a longer flowering season to some of our old dusky purple beauties. Even so the words of Dean Hole when he inaugurated the National Rose Society will always remain true, 'He who would have beautiful roses in his garden must have beautiful roses in his heart'. On the continuing enthusiasm of so many rests the future of the rose as a garden plant.

Cultivation

It is fortunate for lovers of roses that their favourite plant will grow on most soils, exceptions being a bog or other badly drained area, or where the so called soil is bare, hungry chalk. Few are so fortunate as to be able to site their garden in deep fertile medium loamy soil with unimpaired drainage, open to full sunshine but not too exposed to cold winds from north and east. Family matters generally have to be considered; even the Royal National Rose Society, when it moved to its present headquarters at St Albans, had to give precedence to such matters as staff availability, banking and postal facilities. The result is that, as has been shown there, roses can be grown in what is basically little more than a gravel bed, although it has one advantage, that of drainage, one of the essentials in rose growing. Roses do not like their roots to be kept in a permanent state of saturation. It can, I think, be taken for granted that commercial growers who have to earn a living from their roses, will, as a matter of course, choose land that is reasonably suitable as a growing medium for their valuable crop. I suppose that most people who visit such establishments do so mainly to see the roses when in flower and therefore do not see the preparatory work carried out previously. Here of course, powerful tractors pulling a plough replace the spade for the preliminary cultivation and digging which I regard as essential. I have heard of roses being grown without digging but I have not yet seen a commercial grower who dispenses with digging or ploughing and I have certainly never done so myself. On the other hand I do not think it is really necessary to go to the other extreme of trenching 3 ft (0·9 m.) deep with a triple sandwich of farmyard manure, as a filler, between the slices of soil. This is an unnecessary waste of manure and labour, both expensive in these days (unless you like the exercise, many do, but in moderation).

Having established that deep ploughing is still thought necessary by commercial growers, they also find it necessary to enrich it with farmyard manure, plus fertilizers. This, so far as I am concerned, has been common practice for many years and I was greatly comforted to find, on a visit to Shardlow Hall, Derbyshire, England, in 1969, that nutritional trials on roses there confirmed that this is still good practice. This is a Ministry of Agriculture Centre where many experiments connected with roses are carried out and in the nutritional trials already referred to, striking results were shown which emphasized the value of organic matter in the soil, particularly when aided by nitrogen and potash. Roses in plots which did not receive organic matter, compared badly. Much has been written over the years about soils in connection with roses and other crops and as I am not a soil scientist, there seems little point in adding a further contribution, especially as I believe the physical texture of the soil is of the greatest importance. Much may be done to improve texture, always provided drainage is good. Heavy soils can be improved by the use of stable manure if obtainable. If not, garden compost, spent hops, old straw, chopped bracken and peat, in short any organic material, plus a dressing of gypsum, worked into the surface soil to improve tilth will help.

Light soils will be improved by farmyard manure of a heavier type; cow and pig manure, or abattoir manure, strong smelling, even malodorous materials which must be deposited quickly under a cover of soil, particularly in urban areas. Compost, from any form of animal or vegetable waste, when properly made is of tremendous value. Peat is now the universal source of organic matter and is easier to obtain and apply in town gardens. Dried composts or sludges are obtainable from some Municipal Authorities. These sometimes require to be 'pepped up' in potash content. Sewage sludge from industrial areas can be dangerous as it could contain chemicals which may inhibit plant life. Few gardeners will grow roses on a scale sufficient to warrant the employment of tractor drawn implements, therefore the incorporation of organic materials, particularly bulky ones can best be carried out by digging. I am not yet convinced the earthworm is more efficient in this respect than the spade or the digging fork in heavy soil. Depth of cultivation depends to some extent on the nature of the subsoil; to bring up inert clay, chalk or gravel is likely to do more harm than good. Better results will be obtained by breaking it up and at the same time incorporating some organic material, but leaving it *in situ* with the more fertile top soil above. A good dressing of organic matter should be added to the top soil in such a way as not to interfere with planting, and this may well be augmented with a dressing of coarse hoof and horn meal, an ounce (28 g.) or so to each square yard; this is slowly available to the plants over a considerable period. Roses for display are frequently grown in beds cut out on the lawn. If on heavy soil, these are better raised some 7 inches (18 cm.) above the general level to afford better drainage, particularly in winter. If, on the other hand, the soil is light, this is unnecessary and may well be harmful in hot, dry weather. Where grown in borders, if at all possible, the whole area should be cultivated manually or mechanically. Few things give more disappointment than planting good roses in an ill-prepared site such as just taking out a hole, pushing the plant in, hoping it will do well. There is always room for hope but in such cases, it pays a poor dividend. Many measures can be advocated and discussed to improve soils of different types. These can be found in many books on gardening and advice can be obtained from the two great Societies who are collaborating with this book. In particular they can give advice regarding soil tests which a commercial grower would normally have carried out but which might not be worth while for growing just a few roses, if you get your soil into good physical condition and supplement this with a well balanced fertilizer. There are some proprietary ones available, specially compounded for roses.

When rose beds have been carefully prepared before planting, little if any further feeding should be required the first year, although I always think mulching is desirable, but should if possible be carried out before the soil gets dry. April is probably the best month before the roses have grown sufficiently to suffer much damage. Much of my rose growing having been done in a public garden, I have found peat the best material for this purpose. Many rose lovers find the aroma of the roses more salubrious in conjunction with peat than with farmyard manure or even spent hops, unless exceptionally well weathered. Another difficulty arises as these materials attract worms, which in turn attract birds, who with eager energy scatter them all over the grass; very good for the grass no doubt, but no good for the roses or the mower. Lawn mowings also have drawbacks, especially if the grass has been treated with a selective weed-killer which does not impair a crop of annual meadow grass amid the roses. I do not despise leaf mould, if easily obtainable, but this also can produce a varied crop according to the type of woodland from which it comes. Some leaves can also have quite a high lime content, though possibly not enough to be harmful, but this risk does not arise with peat.

In the second and supplementary years, roses will show their appreciation of feeding by a better performance especially as by this time, there should be sufficient fibrous roots to benefit, provided plenty of moisture is also available, either naturally or provided by irrigation. Feeding formulae are in good supply. Many people have their own, indeed some commercial growers make them available and good proprietary mixtures are obtainable, specially compounded for roses. Some are based on Tonks formula (parts by weight: 12 superphosphate (P); 10 potassium nitrate (N & K); 2 magnesium sulphate; 1 iron sulphate; 8 calcium sulphate; applied 3–4 oz (85–113 g.) per square yard (0·8 square m.)) long looked upon favourably, almost revered (being based on the ashes of a cremated rose plant) by many good growers. I have always found the general purpose fertilizer John Innes Base (parts by weight: 2 hoof and horn, $\frac{1}{8}$ in. (3 mm.) grist, 13% N; 2 superphosphate of lime, 19–23% P_2O_5; 1 sulphate of potash, 50% K_2O) useful, especially when supplemented by Kieserite in the same proportion as sulphate of potash to provide magnesium. Applied after pruning, 2–3 oz (57–85 g.) per square yard (0·8 square m.); a further dressing can be applied after the roses have been dead-headed for the first time. The best results are likely to be obtained by observing your roses as each season differs climatically; if soft growth predominates in a wet season, a dressing of a high potash mixture may be just the thing and fish manure with added potash is excellent. In August, a dressing of sulphate of potash helps to ripen young wood and bring the trees through the winter months in good condition.

Foliar feeding has become popular in recent years as an additional method of improving crops. In my view it should not be used as a substitute for good cultivation but to augment it in an endeavour to attain perfection. Some reputable growers have found this extra assistance of value in bad seasons, especially after a difficult spring, and also if plants have been checked by sudden drought or some other cause. Proprietary foliar feeds are on the market and they seem to be the most satisfactory method unless you like to experiment. 'Do-it-yourself' formulae are available. Some are also available which are not incompatible with the insecticides and fungicides used for spraying, thereby cutting down some of the time required, one of the arguments used by those who do not favour this technique. I understand that breeders also find foliar feeding of some value when their seedlings tend to exhaust the limited amount of compost in which they are grown. If roses are well mulched, little cultivation will be required as most weeds should be smothered. However if weeds do appear, very shallow hoeing or use of a special weed-killer such as Paraquat will dispose of them. Care, great care must be taken when applying Paraquat or proprietary mixtures based on it, to ensure the liquid does not touch the roses, their leaves, stems or roots.

Suckers are generally easily recognized by experienced growers but frequently cause some concern amongst beginners who do not recognize them as emanating from the stock on which the rose is growing. They are most easily seen when they occur on standard stems, where they are easily rubbed off, if noticed when young. When growing from the roots, as they are apt to do on standards budded on *rugosa*, they should be traced back to the original point of growth and pulled off, not cut or pruned, as this simply results in renewal, frequently in greater strength. Good nurserymen clean off suckers before sending out their plants but mistakes can occur, especially if in one of these modern establishments they are travelling along a conveyor belt. Therefore, inspect before planting and remove cleanly with a sharp knife any knob on the roots.

Recognition, as mentioned, sometimes puzzles newcomers to rose growing. Rugosa suckers should not be difficult as this stock is seldom used for bush roses, but very frequently for standard and half standard roses which may be planted amongst other bush roses in beds. These suckers may appear some distance away from the standards and thus cause confusion but are generally just under the soil and can be traced back for removal when recognized. The leaves are light green, rounder in form and wrinkled, quite distinct in fact, especially amongst roses with dark green or bronze-tinted leaves.

There are stocks which unless roots are damaged by deep hoeing or using a spade amongst the roses, practices which I deprecate, will produce very few if any suckers, but some strains of *R. canina* are apt to do so. Again, these are lighter in colour than most roses, with narrower leaflets, sometimes more numerous also, and generally traceable to a point under the knob which occurs where the rose was budded onto the stock.

Dead-heading where a number of roses are grown can be a major operation but many people find it a pleasant task, taking them in and around their roses. It is very necessary with hybrid teas, floribundas and recurrent flowering shrubs and climbers, unless in some cases you value the hips more. Occasionally, as with 'Golden Wings' that beautifully recurrent shrub, the early flowers can be removed for a time, the later ones, if left, will add a crop of hips to extend the season even further. Some floribundas, soon produce an abundance of hips which delays the next crop of flowers. I am glad to see that the practice of cutting off dead flowers right back to a strong bud, in order to produce another strong shoot is now being dropped in favour of removal to the first leaf, with the result that new flowers come along much more quickly and that, after all, is what is required for colour in the garden.

Disbudding is not essential unless particularly choice blooms are required for exhibition purposes or for the commercial flower market. Generally a better and more extended garden display will be obtained by allowing the flowers to develop naturally. Those who require special blooms for exhibition generally find disbudding most effective when done as soon as the buds can be handled without causing damage to the bud retained. This will generally be the crown bud, although experienced growers often select a side bud in preference, if the crown bud seems likely to bloom too early. Other variations are also tried, especially with cultivars subject to producing 'split blooms' but I have no personal experience to offer in this respect.

Exhibitors of Floribunda roses usually remove the crown or central bud in order to obtain a more even truss of flowers; the central bud sometimes produces a flower which is not only larger but also earlier and likely to be over when the other flowers are at their peak.

Differences of opinion are not uncommon in the world of roses; it would be a much less interesting vocation or hobby were it otherwise. It is therefore not surprising that many commercial rose growers do not think irrigation is necessary and it is quite apparent that they succeed very well without watering in any form other than that provided by natural precipitation. One well known firm on the other hand has laid on overhead irrigation on all its rose fields to supplement the somewhat erratic natural supplies which are available in some seasons. Much can be done to conserve moisture by good cultivation supplemented by mulching, especially in medium and heavy soils. In gardens with a low water table, light soil or chalk or gardens in towns, a few weeks of dry hot weather soon have an adverse effect especially on roses growing on walls and some assistance is required. Many gardens in these days have irrigation schemes for their lawns and if combined with a rose garden, this seems ideal provided water is not likely to be cut off when most required, something only too likely to happen in some areas, where human needs must have priority. Much could be written on this subject but I will just end by saying that roses will live without irrigation in most gardens but there are very many where they will be greatly improved by its intelligent use and give, as a result, greater pleasure. Much of the success achieved by the roses in Queen Mary's Garden, Regent's Park, London, is due to regular feeding combined with adequate moisture.

Summer pruning of roses is really covered by dead-heading, the only other form being to cut flowers for home decoration when longer stems are required as a rule. Long stems should not be cut, if possible, from newly planted roses in the first year; once established this rule can be relaxed. In the late autumn tall growths should be cut back to prevent wind rocking which can do considerable harm. Not only are the bushes loosened in the soil, but a sizeable hole can develop which will fill up with water and can become solid ice in severe weather and is detrimental to the plant. Where this has occurred, the roots should be firmed and the hole filled in.

Pruning and Training of Roses

Pruning of roses always arouses interest amongst rosarians or people who grow roses and much has been said on the subject, some wise, some not so, some entertaining perhaps, but generally confusing in what should be quite simple if certain principles are understood. Much has also been written, no doubt this will continue, indeed, I am just going to make my own small contribution, which will, I hope, be understood.

What should be clear is that to get the best results from roses, some pruning is necessary, regular pruning in some instances and that this should be done correctly. There is such a wide difference in habit of roses grown in our gardens, from the tiny miniatures to the huge scramblers, also in size of flowers and form, and this tends to complicate matters, unless the basic principles are understood, which will simplify the technique required.

What is really required is that unproductive growths are got rid of and productive growths are retained and encouraged so as to produce flowers and in some cases hips also. To do this, the plant must be kept healthy, therefore all dead or diseased wood should be removed, preferably when seen, not left until what is considered to be the correct date. Frequently such growths will have to be removed at the base to a point from where a young healthy shoot is growing. It is important that light and air should be able to penetrate to the centre of the plant and this is frequently impeded by crossing shoots which should also be removed, as should any that are damaged or weak, as these are not likely to produce good flowers in any case. As a further aid to keeping an open-centred plant, pruning back to an outward-pointing bud is likely to help, so it is important to ensure that a bud pointing in the right direction is found before cutting back to it.

Most gardeners will be concerned more with pruning of Hybrid Tea roses and Floribundas which produce their flowers on growth of the current year, as do climbers. Ramblers, many shrub and species roses, and old garden roses also, generally flower on growths of the previous year. As pruning at the wrong time may in some instances remove most if not all of the flowering growths, it is important that the operator should know which group a plant belongs to before pruning it.

Before discussing the various groups, however, I would like to deal with the best time, as there are two schools of thought which annually express their views, especially with regard to roses that flower on growths made during the current year, thus covering the most generally popular groups. The first school favours pruning in the dormant period, immediately after leaf fall, usually late November (although this differs in some cultivars) to January, while the plants are ostensibly at rest. The second school favours in general, March and April pruning, varying according to the part of the country, the further north being later, as severe weather lasts longer.

Dormant period pruning has an advantage that work is not so pressing at that period as in the Spring and therefore a little more time can be taken to ensure making a good job. This method is perfectly safe in sheltered gardens, especially in the warmer areas, and where climatic conditions are mild, also near the sea where frost is rarely experienced. Some regard should always be paid to local conditions; where these ensure that extremely low temperatures are not experienced, then dormant-period pruning is rendered tolerably safe.

Personally, I have never been keen on commencing pruning on a fixed date; weather conditions vary from year to year, so that advantage has to be taken if possible when weather is suitable. Thus pruning during severe weather is out, as being likely to injure the plants and very uncomfortable for the pruner. It should be commenced in time to ensure completion before young growths have attained any size, as too much bleeding or loss of sap is not only wasteful of the plant's energy but likely to weaken it also. In practice, I have found it best to commence with shrub roses which generally only entails thinning out some older or worn-out growths, allowing room for and encouraging younger growths which are, of course, more productive. Floribundas come next, the most vigorous first and finishing up with the Hybrid Teas.

Newly planted roses of all types should be pruned early the first spring following; this will help overcome strain on the root-system which will have been upset by moving and the plants not being established. It may well be that some gardeners will consider this early pruning dangerous. I would just remind them that commercial growers 'head back' their recently budded stocks in January and February, if weather is reasonable, without ill effect on their current year's crop.

I do not advocate late planting; sometimes, however, it cannot be avoided and when this is so, it is often easier to prune the bush in the hand before planting, especially if the operator has reached an age when bending to ground level is no longer easy. This initial pruning should be somewhat severe, cutting the growths back to two or three eyes from the base, especially in the case of Hybrid Teas and Floribundas.

Top *A 'maiden' for planting*

Below *The same pruned ready to plant. As well as the stems, the roots have been shortened*

Hybrid Teas

Established Hybrid Teas, whatever type of pruning is adopted, should have all dead, weak or damaged shoots removed, being useless and, moreover, sites for the introduction of disease. Hard pruning, except in the first year after planting, is still used by exhibitors, who generally carry out this technique annually so as to reduce the number of growths and concentrate the efforts of the plant in producing a limited number of flowers of good, possibly exceptional size, combined with good shape. In northern gardens, particularly where exposed to severe climatic conditions, severe pruning is frequently necessary because growths are so severely frosted that only near the base of the plant can sound wood be found, indicated by the colour of pith when cut; if brown, it is unsound, so cut back until it is firm and white. Two or three sound basal eyes, preferably cut back to an outward-pointing one, will provide a good tree, somewhat later in coming into flower than where lighter pruning can be practised.

Light pruning has become more popular and, of course, more flowers are produced as a result; as these are also earlier, this is generally welcomed. It is also more satisfactory with some robust growers, such as 'Peace' and cultivars of that habit, apt to produce 'blind' growths which fail to produce flowers until they break again later. Light pruning may be just removing a third or so of the previous year's growth but after a few years is apt to produce large, leggy bushes with flowers of poor quality. When that stage is reached hard pruning back into old wood, one foot (0·3 m.) or so from the ground becomes necessary and means a belated first crop that year. Severe no doubt, but it works, so long as all growths are cut back.

For ordinary garden purposes where a good show of roses of reasonable quality is required, pruning back five to seven eyes from the base of the previous year's growth, cutting weaker growths back to two eyes, in other words an intermediate system, is probably best. Some cultivars have the excellent habit of breaking naturally from near the base of the plant, a habit which enables the grower to cut away older wood above and thus keep renewing young growths in his plants. This young healthy wood, so long as it is well ripened before winter, is the best for producing good flowers.

Floribundas

Floribunda roses in the main, are grown to produce masses of bloom and plenty of colour in the garden. Generally this type breaks more freely from the base, therefore this trend should be encouraged by removal of older growths at every opportunity and the young growths shortened by a third. Older growths where kept, can be shortened to five or six eyes. These will help to provide a succession of flowers. Floribunda roses like Hybrid Teas, should be pruned severely the first season after planting. Knowledge of individual cultivars is of importance when pruning; differences in habit of growth can thus be sorted out, each being treated to ensure a good performance.

Standards

Pruning of standards, tree-roses, which are generally Hybrid Teas or Floribundas, should follow the same pattern as

Top *A bush rose before pruning*

Centre *The crossing branches are removed*

Below *The same bush pruned to 5–7 eyes*

Left *A standard tree-rose before pruning and* Right *The same standard tree-rose after pruning*

advocated for bushes, although generally it will tend to be fairly severe. Two reasons can be given for this; the standard has to depend on one long stem for its food supply, so this inclines to reduction of vigour and if lightly pruned, a very large head will become subject to wind damage, especially if in an exposed garden. On the whole then, standards should never be left beyond four or five eyes. Weeping standards, when well grown and using a suitable cultivar such as 'Crimson Shower' which has flexible young growths, which when budded on a tall stem become pendulous, can be a striking feature in any garden, especially when in an isolated position. Pruning is generally simply removing at the base old flowering growths after flowering has been completed, provided there are enough young growths to replace them. If not, sufficient old growths should be retained, cutting back lateral growths to a couple of eyes. Sometimes stiffer and less suitable types of roses are used for weeping standards, in which the main branches have to be tied down, generally these require shortening of lateral growth to three or four eyes. If strong growths are available, these should be tied down carefully and used for replacing older wood.

Climbing sports

Several of the climbing roses are climbing sports of the bush Hybrid Tea roses and like their parents flower on growths produced during the current year. Some of these cultivars grow very strongly and if pruned, produce more strong growths rather than a good crop of flowers. Horizontal training will induce lateral flowering growths and these should be shortened back in the spring to a couple of eyes. A number of vigorous young growths are usually produced according to the cultivar, some from near the base, some up in the plant. These should be retained and tied in where there is space, or an old branch may on occasion be removed to provide room. The only other pruning required is the removal of unripened tips of growths or where they extend beyond their allotted space.

Polyantha pompons

Polyantha pompons have been replaced by Floribundas which are much better in form, with a much wider range of colour and give a better performance generally. Pruning as for Floribundas suits them very well, some such as 'Yvonne Rabier' will, by light tipping of the stronger growths, build up into a 3 ft (0·9 m.) shrub in a year or two and become most attractive.

Miniatures

Miniature roses are not really part of the general garden scene as I see it, but require an area or bed to themselves. However they require some pruning and following the general rules, all normal growths can be pruned back to three or four eyes, weakly ones removed or cut back to one eye. Easier still, perhaps, they will break very well if cut back to within a few inches of the plant base. Some cultivars are apt to produce one or two rather strong growths which upset the symmetry of the plant. These should be removed entirely or cut back severely to maintain the low bushy compact habit which is most desirable in this class.

Shrubs

In general the pruning of shrub roses does not present great difficulty and even if a season is missed generally little harm results. The majority will not need any pruning at all in the first season after planting. They should be encouraged to build up growth. These roses should be considered as shrubs in which the size and shape is important. As with other shrubs, each plant should be considered on its merits and requirements and pruned accordingly. I like to be able to walk all round and consider carefully before starting on the pruning of any shrub rose. In general this need not be nearly as rigorous as in the Hybrid Teas and Floribundas and much can be lost by excessive hard pruning down nearly to the ground which can reduce a large shrub to a travesty of its proper appearance.

The majority of shrub roses flower on shoots made the previous season which begin to grow immediately after the flowering period. Therefore the object of pruning should be to encourage such shoots. For this purpose some summer pruning is desirable, cutting the shoots that have flowered down to a strong young growth. This will generally be obvious. A few exhausted and old shoots which may have flowered poorly should at the same time be removed entirely down to ground level. This operation will also help to obviate any build-up of pests and diseases. Roses which are grown for their hips and their flowers such as the *moyesii* group, *R. holodonta*, *R. woodsii fendleri*, *R. virginiana* and some of the *rugosa* group as well as large shrub roses such as 'Scharlachglut' obviously should not be pruned at this time although in the case of the Rugosas some growers will prune off some of the dead flower heads after the first flowering and rely for their hips on the later flowers. The older shrub roses should be treated on the same basis as the more modern shrubs but some of the weaker-growing Centifolias and their Moss sports will probably need little pruning though they and the Gallicas should have mildewed tips removed, cutting 2–3 in. (5·1–7·6 cm.) below signs of infection.

The main pruning will still remain the winter one and this is best combined with tying in and training of the larger shrubs and climbers to their supports. In all except the colder areas this can begin at any time convenient, preferably, when the weather is not icy cold. The starting time will vary from season to season, sometimes after a cold spell which brings on early dormancy and leaf fall, mid-December will not be too early, in other seasons which have been mild in the early part of the winter it is better to wait till January. It is usually well to aim at completing all such pruning by the middle of March, especially in the south.

Strong shoots of vigorous shrubs may be tipped back by about a third and it is often helpful to do this early to avoid wind-rock. Sometimes however, they may be used for horizontal training round the supports and both this and the tip pruning will tend to encourage side breaks and shoots. As with Hybrid Teas and Floribundas all very old and weak wood should be cut out. Often one finds an old woody stem with only a weak shoot at the top and generally it is better to cut this right to the ground with a saw. The longer side shoots should usually be spur-pruned back to within 2 or 3 in. (5·1–7·6 cm.) of the main stem. At any rate they should be thinned out by removing entirely the weaker ones.

Top *A Miniature rose before pruning.
The secateurs (pruning shears) show
the scale*

Below *The same Miniature pruned*

For pruning old Climbers on walls the same technique will apply but before cutting at the base it is generally better to trace the branch back from the top and ascertain that there are not sufficient good shoots on the particular stem to justify keeping it.

Hedges of such roses as the strong *gallica versicolor*, which require to be kept to an even height, once they are well established, may be pruned with shears in winter, taking the branches down to an even 3 ft (0·9 m.) or as desired and no harm will be done. Some of the finest hedges of roses I know are pruned like this. The same applies to hedges of the Scotch and Sweet Briers, only the height is generally considerably taller. The Rugosa roses 'Frau Dagmar Hartopp' and 'Schneezwerg' also respond well to this treatment but I prefer to prune with secateurs or pruning shears the Hybrid Musks such as 'Penelope' which are also sometimes used for loose hedges most effectively. In their case some summer pruning is usually worth while to encourage a good autumn display, although this means losing the hips, which in November can be peculiarly attractive as they change slowly to soft coral pink.

Climbers
The repeat flowering climbers have a somewhat different habit of flowering, they flower on laterals which have been pruned back to two or three eyes in autumn and also from young growths which may be produced from the base or other parts of the plant. Horizontal or spiral training, the latter where grown on pillars or tripods, helps to make production of young growths from the base a reality and avoid leggy specimens. The only pruning required is the removal of old flower heads, except where hips are required, and old or unwanted growths, the latter generally when there is young replacement growth available.

Ramblers
Rambler roses, especially those with *R. wichuraiana* blood in their veins, such as 'Crimson Shower' and the older but well known 'Dorothy Perkins', should be pruned as soon as convenient after the flowering season is over, generally about September. This type usually produces sufficient young growths from the base of the plant to replace the old flowering growths. Where they do not do this sufficiently, the best older growths can be retained, cutting back the laterals to a couple of eyes from the main stem. This method is not, however, practicable, with such cultivars as the well known 'Albertine', 'American Pillar' and 'Albéric Barbier', which only infrequently produce basal growths and these only as a rule when an older branch has been cut back. In these roses, young growths should be retained, cutting out older wood to make room and encourage further new growth. Sometimes climbers and ramblers get out of control as people moving house all too frequently find. In such cases the only solution, other than removal, is to cut back to a couple of feet (0·6 m.) from the base of the rose, retaining the younger growths at that length, and cut out, generally a saw will be required, the very old growths at the base. No flowers will be forthcoming in the first year after this treatment but it will enable training of the ensuing growths to be carried out with flowers to follow in the next year.

Roses can be trained on walls most effectively, especially where there is unrestricted space, as on the boundary wall of a garden. In such a situation the ideal method is to fan train, that is to spread the growths out like the ribs of a fan. Those at the sides can be pulled down almost to the horizontal when they will flower more freely. It is an easy matter after flowering to remove old shoots as required and replace them with younger and more vigorous growths. This is admirably illustrated by 'Maigold', superb when trained on a wall as illustrated here; the same specimen can be seen in flower, **249**, p. 47.

On houses large open spaces are not always available because of windows, and sometimes advantage can be taken of this by planting under the window and training growths up either side. Sufficient space must be available under the window to allow the growths to be pulled down horizontally before taking them up vertically on either side; at least 3 ft (0·9 m.) will be required.

Pegging down, or horizontal training can also be practised on the ground and this is most easily done with ramblers, especially of the *wichuraiana* type in which the old flowering growths are removed when finished and replaced with the young basal growths. In the illustration, the cultivars 'Crimson Shower' and 'Sanders' White' are shown trained in this manner. It is worth noticing that the young growths have been protected from direct contact with the wire pins used to keep them in position. This is a useful method on banks or sometimes under a tree where surface roots do not permit planting close to the stem. Many strong growing roses such as 'Uncle Walter', 'Frau Karl Druschki', 'Hugh Dickson' may also be trained to strong canes or wooden stakes 12–18 in. (30–46 cm.) above ground level, indeed this method has been used frequently for many of the strong growing Hybrid Perpetuals, Hybrid Musks and even some of the Climbers, when planted in large beds. These cultivars are generally too stiff in growth and apt to snap off if pegged into the ground, so this somewhat gentler method is more effective.

Species
The pruning of rose species and their near allies, ramblers or scramblers, can be simply handled by leaving them to nature, especially if planted to grow up and through trees or over hedges. Once established and growing strongly, the weak growths of the plants first years can be removed entirely at the base; after that they can be expected to look after themselves although an odd strong growth can sometimes be tied to a branch to induce it to go in the right direction, usually an exercise only for the young and brave enthusiast. Dead or weak growths can be removed by sawing out at the base and removing piecemeal with the aid of loppers, an exercise demanding considerable patience.

The species which grow as shrubs are not so difficult to handle. They do not get tangled up to the same extent and many of them throw up young growths either from the base or the lower part of the shrub. These young growths are most valuable and should be accommodated by removing an old stem or two after flowering, or if hips are a feature, after these are no longer ornamental. It is usually most convenient to do so in January or February before the main pruning is begun.

Top *The climbing rose 'Maigold' trained against a wall*

Below *'Crimson Shower' and 'Sanders' White Rambler', both* wichuraiana *Ramblers, pegged down to flower on the ground*

Tools

Tools are required for pruning and while no doubt a good pruning knife will give the cleanest cut, few have the skill to use it properly, or even to keep it properly sharpened. A good pair of secateurs or pruning shears is most satisfactory and there is a range available at various prices. Everyone has, I suppose, a personal preference, and mine is the Felco. Where older bushes and shrubs have to be dealt with these may not be powerful enough. This is where a pair of long-handled pruners or loppers are useful. Even these can be stumped by an old shrub rose; when this is so, a narrow-bladed folding saw is ideal. Ordinary pruning saws are generally too wide for gaining access to the centre of the shrub. All pruning should be done at a slight angle and where the current season's growths are being cut, this should be in the direction in which the bud is pointing, $\frac{1}{4}$ in. (0.6 cm.) away and above, of course. It remains a good maxim to buy good tools and to look after them. Clean, sharp tools are always easier to work with.

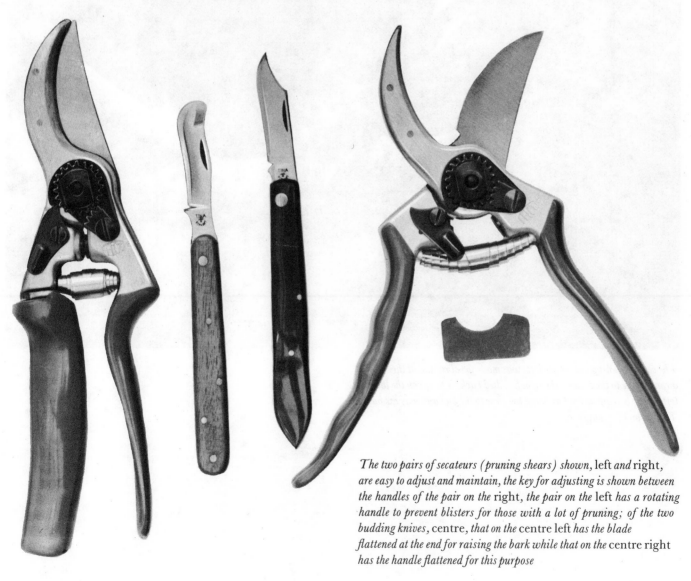

The two pairs of secateurs (pruning shears) shown, left *and* right, *are easy to adjust and maintain, the key for adjusting is shown between the handles of the pair on the* right, *the pair on the* left *has a rotating handle to prevent blisters for those with a lot of pruning; of the two budding knives,* centre, *that on the* centre left *has the blade flattened at the end for raising the bark while that on the* centre right *has the handle flattened for this purpose*

The centre pruning cut, upper left, was made too close and at the
wrong angle to the eye and the stem has died back. The cut on the lower
left shows tearing as well as being too close to the bud and may die back.
The cut on the right is correct

Propagation

Propagation is a fascinating aspect of the rose world to many, therefore something must be written about it. Nature's own method to renew or increase the rose population is by seed, but few plants for our gardens are produced in this way. Some seed firms do offer seeds of several species including *R. multiflora nana*, the so-called 'Fairy Rose'. This if sown under glass in spring will flower within 3 months producing tiny flowers in shades of pink. These will scarcely satisfy the connoisseur but beginners frequently find they have a fascination of their own. It should also be taken into account, I suppose, that many of our roses in gardens today are actually growing on other roses (known as stocks) which have been grown from seed.

In recent years also, indeed I suppose for many years, there has been a great and undying interest in new cultivars of roses produced at considerable expenditure of time and money by breeders which will produce tomorrow's cultivars. An exciting, hopeful, enchanting business, which has to be brought to fruition through seed and the resultant seedlings, one usually for the specialist, although amateurs have also played a notable part.

One of the few horticultural platitudes I know is that roses should if possible be grown on their own roots, that is from cuttings. Commercially it is hardly a viable proposition for various reasons: amount of material required; inequality of crop; time taken to produce good saleable plants and the fact that many cultivars, particularly Hybrid Teas with pithy growth, are just not suitable. Taken all round, the percentage rooted is much lower than that produced by budding. Possible exceptions are some Ramblers and Miniatures, which root readily, but these do not produce better plants than those budded, in the equivalent time.

However, where only a few plants are required, growers can produce several very useful plants which will not produce suckers and on good soils, will give a useful performance. Such roses as 'American Pillar', 'Chaplin's Pink Climber' and 'Dorothy Perkins' are seen in so many gardens, simply because these and allied cultivars, root so easily from cuttings. 'Goldfinch' also, seldom seen in nurseries, but in some areas is found in nearly every garden, as are roses derived from *R. rugosa* or *R. chinensis*. Many Floribundas will produce good plants from cuttings and I have had useful plants from 'Pink Supreme', 'Super Star' and 'Duftwolke' in Hybrid Teas, by using well ripened pencil-thick shoots. Cuttings taken in September and early October, of well ripened wood can be made about 9 in. (22·9 cm.) long and inserted in a small trench based with sharp sand. Treat the cuttings with a hormone rooting powder suitable for hardwood cuttings and remove all leaves except two or three at the top; insert the cuttings up to these leaves and 6 in. (15·2 cm.) apart. Fill in the trench and firm, watering if necessary. A sheltered narrow border is perhaps the best place to make a cutting bed. Allow 1 ft (0·3 m.) between rows.

Although the larger shrub and species climber roses are usually propagated commercially by budding as other roses, the amateur frequently likes to grow some from cuttings and to have a plant on its own roots which will only produce suckers of its own type to make a thicket. The Spinosissimas, *R. foetida* and its derivatives, and *R. virginiana*, will do this freely. Most of the shrub roses, particularly the older ones, the Hybrid Chinas, some Rugosas and many of the Hybrid Perpetuals, will grow easily from cuttings taken in late summer, from well-ripened shoots, in the way already indicated. They are best placed in a cool, north-facing border, rather than in a hot sunny one. If spaced about 6 in. (15·2 cm.) apart, these can then be left in position until the following autumn, when they can be cut back and transplanted into their final position. The Hybrid Musks can readily be propagated in this way. Some growers, however, recommend transplanting into their final position soon after the cuttings have callused over at the base, in which case the cuttings can be plunged in the soil in a bunch initially. This obviates any shock on transplanting, but one must take care to keep the young plants clean around the base, and if good branching from near the base is required, they should be cut back when they have grown to about 18 in. (45·7 cm.). Shrub roses can also be propagated from cuttings of main, over-vigorous shoots, taken during the winter from the prunings, but these are usually slower to root and less certain than those taken in the early autumn. However, it is often successful and may appeal to the economically minded gardener who hates to waste good material. Such plants in their second season can make good Christmas gifts.

Although budding, as it is called, has been for a long time recognized as the commercial method of propagating roses in all parts of the world, including the British Isles, it is also an operation which provides the amateur with considerable satisfaction. It is a fascinating sight to visit a rose nursery in July or early August when rose budding is going on and see this operation in the field. The skill and speed with which these specialists cut out the eyes and insert them in the T-cut which has been made with a razor sharp knife, has to be seen to be believed. Rubber or plastic ties are now used instead of raffia and this has helped to speed up the job so that a team, one budding, the other tying, can bud at least one thousand stocks a day, some operators doing many more.

One of the great advantages of budding is that only one 'eye' is required to produce a plant, a matter of great importance with new or scarce cultivars. It has to be borne in mind that rose cultivars start off as one plant; when this is a new and very distinct rose, any early build up of stock is of considerable significance to the grower.

Bud-wood of the required cultivar should be selected from shoots on which the flowers have just faded and can be tested for maturity by the thorns; if these snap off easily, it is just right. Cut the shoot, 8–12 in. (20·3–30·5 cm.) in length, with several buds or eyes, take off all thorns and cut off the leaves, leaving ½ in. (1·3 cm.) of stalk to use as a handle. Label and stand in water until required.

Being a surgical operation, budding should be done quickly and cleanliness is essential. Soil should be drawn away from the rootstock, down to the roots and the stem should be cleaned with a piece of cloth. Bend the stock over, holding the top growth down by placing one foot on it. Make a cross cut about an inch (2·5 cm.) above the roots, just deep enough to penetrate the soft bark and complete the T-cut from the middle down to the roots. Now reverse your knife and use the end of the handle to gently raise the bark from the top in two flaps. The bark should lift cleanly and will do so more easily if stocks have been watered a few days previously. Now cut an eye from the stick, commencing ½ in. (1·3 cm.) above, drawing the blade downwards and bringing it out again the same distance below. You should now have a shield of bark containing the eye, which you hold by the handle and remove the small piece of wood behind, without damage to the eye. Still holding the shield by the handle, push it down the T-cut as far as it will go under the flaps. Remove the surplus above the cross cut and stretch the rubber or plastic tie over the bud, bringing the wire staple through behind to the other end of the tie. When budding has been completed, the soil can be drawn back again over the roots. The ties generally disintegrate in a few weeks as the stock swells. Some growers still prefer to use raffia, especially for standards. The raffia is generally cut in lengths of 18 in. (45·7 cm.) and kept moist. Bind the shield in with the raffia fairly tightly above and below the bud, leaving it exposed. In three weeks' time, the ties may have become too tight and swelling under the bud apparent. If this is so, cut a couple of raffia strands carefully, just to ease the tie slightly. Sometimes a few buds start growing and even produce a flower before the end of the season, but the majority remain dormant until the following spring. In spring comes the 'heading back', generally in February if weather is favourable, although some growers do it during any of the first three months of the year. This is simply the removal of the brier stock above the inserted bud, leaving a small stump of an inch (2·5 cm.) or so; this is done by hand where numbers are small and by power-operated blades in up-to-date nurseries.

Amateurs often find it worth while to put a 2 ft (0·6 m.)

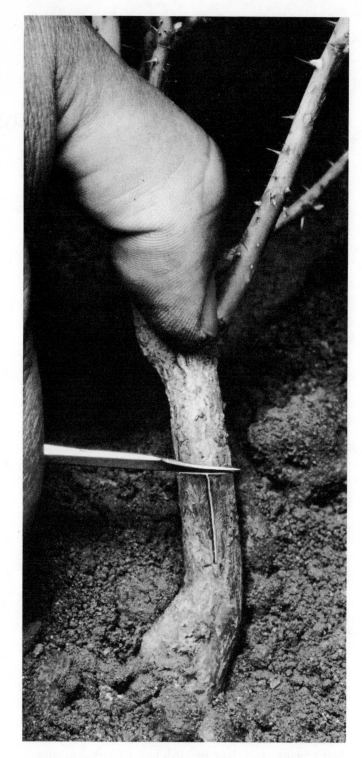

Top *Making a T-cut in the stock*

OPPOSITE PAGE
Top *Cutting a bud from its stem*

Centre *Removing the wood from behind the eye*

Below *The wood removed showing the eye*

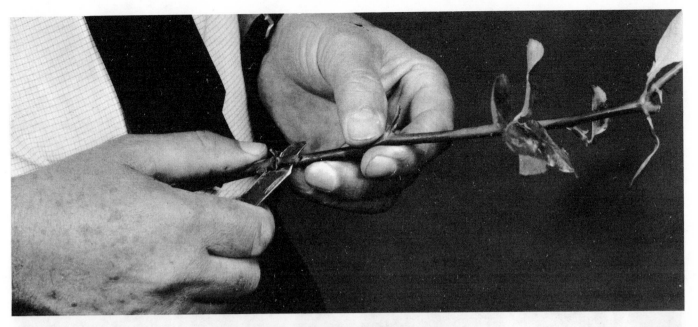

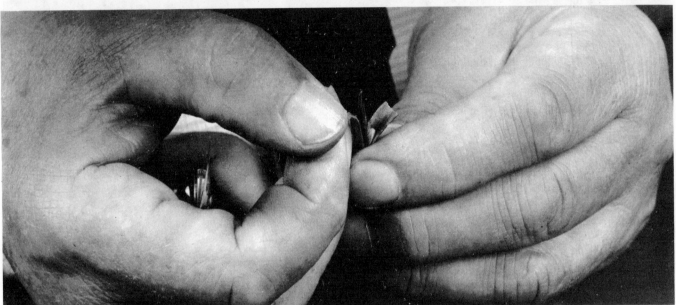

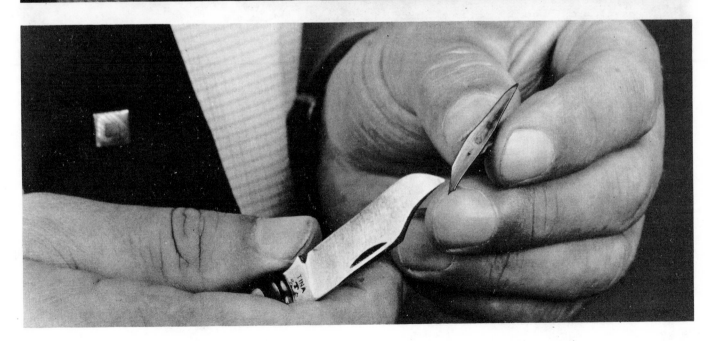

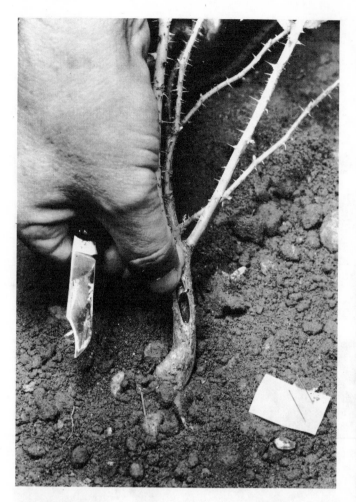

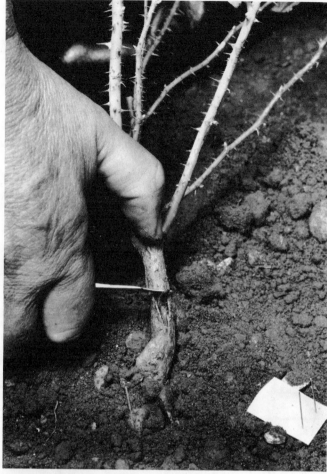

Top left *Inserting the bud into the stock*

Top right *Trimming the top of the slip after the bud has been inserted*

Below *Securing the bud with a rubber tie*

xxxiv

cane to each plant to which the young growth can be tied, in due course, to prevent 'blowing out' in windy weather. Plants on some stocks such as *R. multiflora* are more likely to do this and considerable losses can result. The plant is completely gone and all the labour goes for nothing. This can be overcome to a considerable degree by pinching back the first growth to 4 inches (10·2 cm.), an operation which delays flowering for another couple of weeks. Some exhibitors favour flowers from 'maidens', as these new plants are called, and can vary their date of flowering according to their requirements to some extent. These also are the plants nurserymen offer for sale the following autumn, after the first flowering season when they are transplanted to their permanent quarters.

It will soon be realized that budding roses in quantity is a strenuous form of exercise day after day, not for those who may take it up as a hobby after retirement. Do not despair if 'budding' intrigues you; standards and half standards are much easier to get at and the technique is just the same, although the place where it is carried out differs according to the stock used.

Various stocks are used by rose producers and seedlings are preferable. Seedlings are less likely to transmit viruses and they also develop a deeper and better root system which is not so easily damaged on replanting. *R. canina*, or seedling brier in its wild form, has for a long time been the most popular but selections from it are becoming better known and more widely used as they give more uniform growth. These selections include 'Schmid's Ideal', 'Succes', 'Heinsohn's Record', 'Brogs', 'Pfander', 'Inermis' and 'Pollmers'. *R. eglanteria* has also been used, especially for late budding, but as it is very thorny and difficult to bud, it has lost favour. *R. multiflora* and its form 'Inermis' are now popular with some growers, especially on lighter soils. Roses on this stock make large trees, but are not so successful on alkaline soils. Breaking into growth early, it may not be suitable for very cold areas and should be tried on a small scale before extensive use. *R. coriifolia froebelii* (*laxa*) now finds favour with some growers who claim that it produces better quality blooms, but it requires more soil moisture. It is quite apparent, therefore, that no such thing as an ideal rose stock exists and one should be chosen which suits, as far as possible, the type of soil in which it is to be planted. *R. rugosa* is now little used as a stock for roses in bush form but *R. rugosa hollandica*, regarded by some as a hybrid form of which there are several strains, is grown especially for the production of stems for standard or tree roses.

Budding on *R. rugosa* is done at $3\frac{1}{4}$–$3\frac{1}{2}$ ft (1–1·1 m.) for standards, one foot (0·3 m.) lower for half standards and round about 5 feet (1·5 m.) for weeping standards. In this case the budding is carried out on the main stem which was produced the previous year. Commercially, two buds are inserted on opposite sides of the stem as a general rule. Opinions vary and some growers favour single budding but a second seems a useful insurance against damage or even the demise of the first: indeed my own preference is for three, not only as a safeguard, but to get a better head. *R. canina* 'Pfander' produces useful stems from which I have personally obtained good results. Reputed to give longer life than *R. rugosa*, 'Pfander' is easy to bud and the suckers are easily recognized as the thorns are not so numerous as those of *R. rugosa*. Budding is done into the main stem, two or three buds being inserted. When buds begin to grow in spring, it is good practice, I think, to pinch hard as this produces a nice bushy head and reduces the danger of 'blowing out'. One can tie canes to the main stems and the maiden growths to these, when dealing with small quantities, but if there are several, it is somewhat time consuming. Standards, like bush roses, can be moved to their permanent site the second autumn after budding, or the stems can be planted where they are required and budded *in situ*.

In the U.S.A., the rose named 'Dr Huey', a Climber resulting from a cross between 'Ethel' (a 'Dorothy Perkins' seedling) and 'Gruss an Teplitz' is used frequently as an understock under the name of 'Shafter'. It has to be propagated by vegetative means so it is extremely important that the material used should be virus-free. The famous raiser of Miniature roses, Ralph S. Moore, has also raised a shrub rose 'Pink Clouds' by crossing the Miniature 'Oakington Ruby' with *R. multiflora* which he uses to provide the 10–12 in. (25·4–30·5 cm.) stems required for standard Miniatures, the American Miniature tree roses.

'Odorata' is an understock only suitable for warm climates, not being hardy, and is a Chinese garden form of *R. × odorata*. It is vigorous, sometimes known as 'Indica major' and is used in parts of Australia, the Mediterranean countries and America. The Chinese name is 'Fun Jwan Lo'. *R. × fortuniana*, supposedly a hybrid between *R. banksiae* and *R. laevigata* but bearing considerable resemblance to the Banksian roses, is used as an understock for warm climates such as the Mediterranean countries and Western Australia. 'Gloire des Rosomanes', a China × Bourbon hybrid, is used intensively in California, U.S.A., as an understock under the name of 'Ragged Robin' and has also played a part as an ancestor of the Hybrid Perpetual roses. At least one firm uses a cultivar they name 'sayi' which appears to be a form of *R. acicularis* and is claimed to be exceptionally fibrous rooted. These are some of the stocks used. It is desirable to choose one most suitable for your climate and soil.

Seedling rose stocks are generally available in three sizes, 3–5 mm., 4–6 mm. and 5–8 mm. For those who wish to bud early, the larger size is easier to work. Planting can be done in well prepared ground from December onwards to March when soil conditions are suitable. In nurseries, planting is now generally done by machine in rows 3 ft (0·9 m.) apart to allow for mechanical cultivation, although some growers are trying to reduce this. The plant distances vary somewhat at about $7\frac{1}{2}$–10 in. (19–25 cm.). Amateurs and small growers generally plant by hand and rows 2 ft (0·6 m.) apart are quite satisfactory, making sure roots only are below the ground level. When planting is completed, draw some soil up by hoe to cover the necks. By planting the stocks at a slight angle, budding is made easier.

Spring grafting, or bench grafting, is a specialized form of propagation carried out from January until May under glass, usually used for roses to be grown under glass for the cut flower market. Miniature roses also are now produced by this method and it is also used by breeders to work up stocks of new cultivars quickly.

Pests and Diseases

I suppose a book on roses would not be considered complete were not some reference made to pests and diseases, and much has been written on this aspect of rose growing. More too will be written as constant research goes on, but most of us who grow roses are really most interested in getting something easy to apply and effective, without killing our enthusiasm. Dressing up in rubber suits, goggles and all the paraphernalia of the space age, the equipment required by the professional grower to apply some modern chemicals, is not really calculated to give pleasure to the amateur.

PESTS

Aphides

The most common as well as one of our most prolific pests is the aphis or greenfly, although it appears in various guises, green, amber, reddish or black. Easily seen, these insects cluster on the young tips of growing shoots in large numbers. If not destroyed quickly, they deposit a sticky substance – honeydew on the plants, which attracts ants. Sooty mould also develops on leaves which have a deposit of honeydew. Aphides are easily controlled early in the season by using malathion in a fine spray, repeating within three days to catch up with any missed previously. Nicotine is also effective when weather gets warmer, round about 65°F (18 °C). Systemic insecticides now available are considered much more effective by some and with more lasting effect but not satisfying all as yet. There are natural predators, also; ladybirds, tits and sparrows will help but do not as a rule fully control the pest.

Capsid Bugs

These pests are usually noticed after some damage has been done, despite any sprays that might have been applied for other pests, as their main point of attack is the growing tip. The first noticeable damage is usually a rather tattered appearance of the shoot tip, caused by the ragged holes made by the capsid. This is often followed by stunting and almost complete failure of the shoot to develop further. Owing to the speed with which adult bugs can take off, on being disturbed, a systemic spray should be used. The adults are about $\frac{1}{4}$ in. (0·6 cm.) long, green and shield shaped. The nymphs are similar but slightly smaller.

Caterpillars

Various types attack roses as well as many other plants, so a lookout has to be kept for their depredations. On roses these are the biting and chewing larvae of moths and systemic insecticides should be applied at regular intervals and at the rate advised by the makers.

Frog-hopper

Cuckoo-spit or common garden frog-hopper is easily identified by the frothy sap or spittle-like mess which surrounds it, but never becomes a serious menace to rose growers. It is often seen on weeds and other plants. The small yellow nymph inside the protective spittle can be killed by hand or by a contact spray such as malathion, forcefully applied to penetrate the spittle.

Leaf-rolling sawfly

This has become quite common in some areas, especially in gardens where there are sheltered corners and trees where apparently the fly likes to hover. Frequently the damage is only slight as many of the leaves which are rolled do not contain anything. The fly apparently prospects before laying, rolling each leaf in consequence, although missing out many in the laying process. When noticed, spraying is too late of course, but trichlorphon should deal with any caterpillars which hatch out, and result in fewer flies.

Red Spider

This pest has long been familiar as a pest under glass but has, of recent years, attacked roses growing outside and is probably more difficult to deal with than all those already mentioned, especially as the mites build up a resistance to pesticides so quickly as to become immune to some of them. Thus malathion, which I used to find effective, now appears to be less so, if not altogether useless. Living on the underside of the leaves, red spider mites are not easy to detect, but their effect on the rose leaves becomes apparent by the loss of colour and premature leaf fall, which is bound to have a deleterious effect on the vigour of the plants. It is obvious that steps to control this pest must be taken and it has been suggested that spraying with a tar-oil winter wash will destroy any eggs, followed by two sprayings during summer with petroleum white oil. Systemic insecticides are also of value in gardens. Clearance of all weeds and rubbish in which they can hibernate is a sensible precaution.

Thrips

Sometimes known as thunder flies, these cause some damage to rose blooms in hot dry spells of weather, being especially severe on 'Ophelia' and members of that family. Light coloured roses seem somewhat susceptible, or perhaps the damage shows up more, the edges of the petals becoming discoloured. The malathion and nicotine sprays recommended against aphides should give some control.

DISEASES

Black Spot

This may well be called the 'Clean Air Disease' as in industrial areas it seldom if ever reveals its presence. Even in the pure air of the country, some areas seem to be more severely attacked than others, and it appears to be more virulent in some parts of the south-west. The spots appear on the lower leaves, like a splash of ink with fringed edges, which grow larger and eventually several may fuse together. Later the leaves may become yellow and drop off in severe attacks, the whole plant becoming defoliated prematurely. Sometimes the stems also become infected. At present there is no cure but preventative measures can be taken and good results have been attained by the use of maneb. Used in conjunction with other materials, maneb has also kept rust and mildew under control. The programme is to spray in January with 5 lb. (2·3 Kg.) of Bordeaux Mixture to 25 gallons (113·6 l.) of water, before pruning the roses which had long growths shortened back in late November or December. All leaves and debris are swept up before spraying and the surface of the soil should be well drenched with the spray also to control any fallen spore-bearing material. In March, immediately after the roses have been pruned, they must be sprayed with maneb at 8 oz. (227 g.) to 25 gallons (113·6 l.) of water and so thoroughly that the surface of the soil is also covered. From June onwards spray the roses fortnightly and add 4 oz. (113 g.) dinocap (25% wettable powder) as a mildew preventative, together with a spreading agent.

Powdery Mildew

Probably the most common disease, mildew is easily recognized as it looks something like a sprinkling of flour on the leaves and shoots–especially on young growths in the autumn. In severe attacks, the young growths become twisted and contorted and the mildew is so dense that it looks like a white felt coat on the buds and stems. It is frequently encouraged by soft growth produced by over generous use of nitrogenous fertilizers so that good cultural treatment is called for. Dryness at the root always seems to be an important factor, very noticeable in some cultivars when planted against walls or fences where rain has difficulty in reaching. Some cultivars are more susceptible than others, 'Dorothy Perkins', planted near a wall, being notorious. Fortunately some are resistant and this is mentioned in descriptions. It has been suggested that mildew overwinters on Ramblers, especially if somewhat neglected, and much good, certainly no harm, is done if the tips of laterals and young growths are removed carefully and burnt.

Rust

Rose rust is considered by many as the most serious disease of the rose and is most common in moister and warmer areas. Research work has established that several species of rust exist. Some rose cultivars, such as 'Fashion', are apparently more susceptible. 'Conrad F. Meyer' has also been removed from one well known garden because of its 'addiction'. It is most noticeable when, during summer, the orange coloured spores appear as pustules on the underside of the leaves; later these appear to turn black and the leaves fall prematurely, weakening the plant. Prevention is better than cure has long been an axiom, repeated *ad lib.* for the benefit of gardeners; in addition to the programme I have mentioned for Black Spot, there are proprietary preparations available which should be used. It is now possible to get compatible combinations embracing insecticides, fungicides and foliar feeds which do not damage the plants.

Stem canker

This especially causes trouble on oldish plants, usually started by careless use of a mower or some other implement which has caused damage to the stem. An old shoot with a hole or broken patch with scaly edges, or a split, are the most obvious signs, usually surrounded by a cork callus which in time encircles the stem and eventually weakens it sufficiently to cause death. These cankered stems should be cut away cleanly.

Viruses

These diseases appear to be more serious in the United States and Australia than in Great Britain. The Rose Mosaic virus most often seen, shows up the veins as a pale yellow in strong contrast to the green of the rest of the leaf. Line Pattern Mosaic shows up on some cultivars as pale wavy lines, sometimes in an oak-leaf pattern and has occurred on some U.S.A. cultivars. Several Floribundas have also shown a 'ringspot' infection and I have noticed virus disease in *R. rugosa* stems. If infected stocks are destroyed by the nurseryman, the ordinary rosarian is unlikely to suffer any ill effect to his roses as, so far as is known at present, these diseases mainly spread through vegetative propagation, by budding or grafting using either buds or stocks which are infected. So far as the amateur is concerned, if any plant appears to be deteriorating in health and you are interested and can take it to a laboratory for plant diseases, do so but do not leave it in the garden to infect others. In such cases a good bonfire is the best preventative measure.

Pests and Diseases of Shrubs and Climbers

While no roses can be claimed to be completely disease-free the majority of shrub and climbing roses need very much less attention in these respects than do the Hybrid Teas and some of the Floribundas, while the really strong Rambler covering an old tree or the strong Climber up to the eaves of a house or covering an old shed is obviously out of reach of the amateur's spray lance. Also in this case one relies for effect on the abundance of flower rather than on the perfection of each individual flower. So they must live with their troubles and a certain amount of defoliation from black spot and attack by aphids may result but in general such roses are vigorous enough to withstand this without any harm and to flower again well the next year. This applies also to the majority of the larger shrub roses, 'Nevada', 'Marguerite Hilling', 'Frühlingsgold' and 'Cantabrigiensis'.

The main diseases and pests of shrub roses and Climbers are the same as those of other roses, aphis, leaf-rolling sawfly, caterpillars, black spot, mildew and occasionally rust. The smaller shrub roses and newly planted ones will benefit from sharing the same spray programme as the Hybrid Teas and Floribundas and the same sprays at the same strengths are appropriate. Roses such as the Rugosas and Sweet Briers are very resistant to nearly all the pests and diseases of roses, but unfortunately *Rosa foetida* and some of its derivatives, particularly the 'Austrian Copper' are particularly sensitive to black spot and quickly tend to become almost completely defoliated if they are not sprayed and may infect others. They are so sensitive to this disease that some growers banish them from their gardens; at any rate it is worth while growing them apart from other roses if this is possible. On the other hand their beauty is so striking that they are worth the trouble of spraying.

Some of the older ramblers derived from *R. wichuraiana*, such as the old 'Dorothy Perkins', are very sensitive to mildew particularly when planted on walls and if unsprayed can become almost white with it. Most of these, however, are out of date varieties anywhere and the more modern recurrent climbers such as 'New Dawn' seem to be very resistant to all diseases. So are some of the Ramblers derived from *R. sempervirens* such as 'Félicité et Perpétue', while 'Albéric Barbier', although a *wichuraiana* seedling seems to be very resistant.

Pests and diseases are also related to the pruning programme. A thickly congested unpruned bush with a number of weak young and crossing growths will tend to be more susceptible to black spot and mildew than a more open-pruned bush where light and air can reach all parts. Again good garden hygiene is very helpful in combating pests and diseases, particularly the clearing up of all dead branches and twigs cut out and also the shaking out and then cleaning up of dead leaves at the base on which spores of black spot can overwinter. It is good practice also to spray the ground below the roses in winter or early spring with a strong fungicide or with a solution of Jeyes Fluid.

For shrub roses good cultivation and an open sunny position are undoubtedly the main factors in pest and disease avoidance, but sometimes an extreme attack of caterpillars, leaf-curlers or black spot will require sprays. It is better of course to spray when one notices the first signs of this than to wait until it is severe. Some of the older Centifolias and their Moss sports are weak growers and sensitive to black spot and a regular spraying will benefit them. In wet weather some of the old shrub roses with tightly balled flowers such as 'Cardinal de Richelieu' and 'Souvenir d'Alphonse Lavallée' may tend to rot before they open and there is little that the grower can do about this. It helps, however, to remove all old and spent flowers from the truss, thus letting in more air.

In general, however, shrub, rambler and climbing roses are very resistant and usually give little more trouble from pests and diseases than do other shrubs in the garden. This is one of their great merits.

Plants to Associate with Roses

For those of us who grow roses for pleasure in the garden one of the most enjoyable features is to indulge in our hobby in our own particular way, sometimes slightly tempered to our partner's views to insure more harmony in our domestic bliss. So the question of association of plants with roses, while well received in some quarters, is equally unacceptable in others. 'Let the Queen reign without attendants' writes Mr Harry Wheatcroft. Equally eminent, Mr Graham Thomas considers the growing of Hybrid Teas or Floribundas in beds of segregated colours one of the dullest forms of gardening. So there you have the voices of authority. In my own small way I agree with neither. Some of our modern Hybrid Teas, 'Blessings', 'Duftwolke', 'Mischief', 'Piccadilly', 'Ernest H. Morse' and 'Wendy Cussons', to select but a few, are quite capable, if planted at a reasonable distance and grown well,

of so covering the soil that additional plants are not required during summer months. If considered desirable, space will have to be left for this purpose. Possibly even more so, modern Floribundas in even greater variety 'Lilli Marleen', 'Marlena', 'Pernille Poulsen', 'City of Belfast', 'Escapade', 'City of Leeds' and 'Tip Top' can be relied upon to do the same. 'Marlena' and 'Tip Top' could even be grown under taller roses as ground cover plants.

I am not greatly enamoured with bare soil in rose beds from December to April each season, but even less so in borders where shrub roses in variety and at greater distances apart are grown. So I enjoy the harbingers, a few snowdrops, the common one *Galanthus nivalis*, followed by *Crocus*, not the large Dutch cultivars which I prefer naturalized in grass, but some of the *C. chrysanthus* forms; 'Ladykiller', 'Cream Beauty',

'Snow Bunting' and 'Zwanenburg' are all free-flowering and so beautiful. There are many others which can be selected from any good bulb catalogue but one which should not be missed out is *C. tomasinianus*. This crocus also has some deeper coloured forms but its own pale mauvish-blue is so delightful in early spring and, seeding all over the place as it does in cultivated ground, it makes a delightful carpet and is no trouble at all in and round about shrub roses. A few *Tulipa kaufmanniana*, particularly some of the mixed hybrids which go under various names, will follow on and generally flower very well for two or three seasons before they disappear. The bulbs may be difficult to lift but not impossible. Wonderful on a sunny spring day, it is easy to see, when fully expanded, why the original of this type is known as the Water-lily Tulip.

Another favourite combination of mine is one of the golden daffodils flowering in conjunction with the young crimson shaded foliage of one of the red roses such as 'Uncle Walter', not so entrancing I grant you as the daffodils dancing in the breeze of Wordsworth, but still beautiful in contrast.

In addition to these bulbs which bring hope as well as joy after dull winter days, there is much to be said for a few early flowering plants which will neither interfere nor clash with the roses, especially if their foliage continues to look pleasing during the summer as the paler forms of *Alyssum saxatile* such as 'Citrinum' or 'Silver Queen' and the biscuit yellow 'Dudley Neville'. The latter can only be increased by cuttings, the other forms can be grown from seed. The silvery-grey foliage remains attractive for a long time. *Ajuga* also, particularly forms of *A. reptans* are useful and *Phlox subulata* are excellent mat-forming plants with pale pink, lavender and deeper pink flowers.

In the early days of my career the underplanting of roses with named violas was almost a *sine qua non* in some gardens, the favourite being 'Maggie Mott', an attractive lavender-mauve. In many areas labour and other conditions have made such traditions useless but violas from seed can still provide a good early show and although not a usual procedure, I do not see why pansies of the 'Clear Crystal' strain should not be used, particularly the azure blues. In borders where there is more room and soil conditions are good there are a number of plants which can be grown, care being taken not to allow them to dominate the roses but rather to complement them. Another function is to smother weeds, saving some back breaking work and preventing root damage by too much hoeing. Few plants are better for this than some of the hardy geraniums of which there are many cultivars; *Geranium endressii* in its several forms and *G. macrorrhizum* also in several forms, *album* to my mind being particularly attractive. My own favourite for association with roses is *G.* 'Johnson's Blue' which I sometimes think was specially destined to wrap round the underpins of 'Queen Elizabeth' or perhaps 'Sarah van Fleet'.

Lady's Mantle, *Alchemilla mollis* is now recognized as one of the best ground cover plants with handsome dew capturing leaves. If the greenish-yellow flowers do not appeal, you can cut them off and will not then be invaded by seedlings, although in truth they are easy to get rid of. *Stachys lanata*, the well known Lamb's Ears, is ideal for underplanting some of the hot-coloured roses, the non-flowering form sometimes known as 'Silver Carpet' being best.

Plants with flowers in shades of blue are of particular value in underplanting roses, which do not themselves have this colour represented, consequently a good contrast is provided. Campanulas are ideal in many ways, easy to grow and adaptable, also having an extended flowering season. 'Birch Hybrid', *C. portenschlagiana*, and *C. carpatica* forms, some of which are white, are all worthy of a place.

Rose 'Super Star' I have underplanted with *Hebe pinguifolia* 'Pagei', a hummocky plant with small glaucous grey leaves, an attractive combination. *Santolina chamaecyparissus*, the whitish grey-green Cotton Lavender, is also an excellent foil for these newer colours which are now so popular in roses, but they should be sheared over in March to prevent flowering and to keep the plants more compact in habit. Easily propagated from autumn cuttings in a cold frame, a stock should be maintained, as indeed it should of the *Hebe*, for plants sometimes succumb after a very cold wet winter. This is also true for *Salvia officinalis*, the Common Sage, which is most useful, especially in the soft purplish-grey form 'Purpurascens'. Hostas are recognized as being amongst the best of our ground cover plants but in the main, they are somewhat large except in open spaces amongst largish shrub roses. There is a large number of species and some cultivars from which to select. A favourite of mine is *H. fortunei* 'Albopicta' in which the large leaves are yellow, edged green, becoming green with age.

This is a selection of the plants I would grow to underplant Hybrid Tea and Floribunda roses. Many others could be suggested, but one has to stop somewhere.

Other associations can be made, and *Clematis* most notably are frequently grown in conjunction with climbing roses in particular. It is easier, I think, to keep these attractive plants in garlanding proximity with roses, if cultivars are chosen which can be pruned hard in the spring, taking away the old growths which are apt to become tangled. A selection could be 'Comtesse de Bouchard', pink; 'Jackmanii Superba', deep purple; 'Madame le Coultre', white with yellow stamens; 'Perle d'Azure', light blue; and 'Ville de Lyon', carmine-red. The deciduous *Ceanothus* are also useful to provide the blues which are unavailable in roses, 'Gloire de Versailles', sky blue, and the deeper coloured 'Topaz' are ideal and are easily controlled by spring pruning, when they can be cut in February or March to within a few inches of the old wood.

Some readers will inevitably have their own ideas of other plants which give them pleasure in association with roses, such as *Lilium regale* and I was favourably impressed this year to see a garden with old garden roses carpeted with *Myosotis*, the well known and beautiful blue Forget-me-not, a common plant so easily grown from self sown seedlings, but so effective when seen *en masse*.

Shrub roses, especially the older ones, do not mix well, however, with beds of Hybrid Teas and Floribundas. Their form and scale are quite different and so is the system of pruning. Also their colours are often less strong, more subtle and will be killed particularly by the strong orange-reds of many modern roses. They may well be planted as the predominant shrubs in mixed borders of shrubs and bulbs, with a few ground cover herbaceous plants towards the front, and I like this better than a solid planting with roses only. Their form, when out of flower, has not sufficient variation to make a border of them interesting throughout the year. The word predominant, however, is important. The roses should be the main feature and I think it is possible to intersperse shrub and climbing roses, using the Climbers on pillars or fences towards the back, but many growers tend to keep them separate.

In planning the border, one must, however, remember eventual size, for giants such as 'Nevada', 'Frühlingsgold' and 'Marguerite Hilling' are quite capable of growing 6 ft (1·8 m.) high and as much across in four or five years. This means that there should be at least 6 ft (1·8 m.) between them and the next rose if one of equal dimensions is chosen for the neighbour. Many of the Rugosas and Hybrid Musks will attain an equal size, although they may take a little longer. *Rosa moyesii* and *R.* × *highdownensis* may in time grow even larger than 'Nevada' in spread. On the other hand, few of the Bourbons, Hybrid Perpetuals or Centifolias will be more than 3–4 ft (0·9–1·2 m.) across, even after some years, and so may be planted a little closer, but not too much. It is pleasant and also helpful for pruning and cultivation to be able to go all round the rose without being caught up in its neighbours.

Backgrounds are important also when placing one's shrub roses. White and pale blush flowers show up infinitely more against the dark green background of an evergreen hedge or group of shrubs than against an open mixture of other shrubs and plants. White roses mingle also with silver-leaved plants such as the weeping pear *Pyrus salicifolia pendula*, such an effective tree in any garden. Scarlet and red roses too are offset well by silver-leaved plants and an edging to the bed of the silver-leaved *Stachys lanata*. The finest background of all for roses is an old grey stone wall, or the mellow Cotswold yellowish-grey stone, and I well remember the lovely combination that a group of *R. rubrifolia* made with the silvery *Artemisia arborescens* against such a wall. This is the finest shrub rose for coloured foliage and for giving an unusual note to the border. All colours, however, look well against such a wall.

The formal rose garden is usually not the place for shrub roses whose growth is essentially natural and informal. It is rather the preserve of the Hybrid Tea and Floribunda, but if the garden is on a considerable scale, some shrubs at the back or round the edges away from the entrance may help to give height and variety to a display otherwise of a rather monotonous, uniform height. I find such variation pleasing but not all rose growers will agree. Climbers introduced as pillar roses may also be included effectively.

Grass is an unfailing good background for all roses. Few gardeners today, however, will be willing to face the labour of cutting the edges and weeding numbers of small beds in a lawn, while designers will find them fussy as well as being extremely tiresome to mow around. But large rose beds of shrubs and Climbers can be made with informal curving edges that are easy to mow. If one has a straight edge, paving stones will make a good edge between grass and bed, and when small creeping plants such as pinks are allowed to spread over the labour of constant edging will be saved. While real grey stone undoubtedly looks best, the cheaper stone substitutes do weather and will be acceptable in most cases. One of the most lovely rose borders I know has such a

stone edging about 1½ ft (0·5 m.) wide while it is backed by an old stone wall on which rose climbers grow. About 2 ft (0·6 m.) from the wall is another stone path which is largely hidden from the front by the summer growth but is very useful to stand on when one is tending the wall climbers or the shrub roses towards the back of the border.

Plants to mingle with the roses depend largely on the taste of the grower. In a shrub rose border I planted recently, I have placed at one end a silver-leaved weeping pear and a group of white *Philadelphus* 'Beauclerk', with arching habit and strong scent, to be seen against a background of dark green. Beside them I have placed some of the white Rugosas, 'Blanc Double de Coubert' and 'Schneezwerg', which will gradually merge into the paler blush pinks of the fine *alba* rose 'Great Maiden's Blush' and *R. pomifera* 'Duplex'. These in their turn will merge into the deeper pinks and paler yellows, though including 'Canary Bird'. The other end will include darker reds such as 'Baron Girod de l'Ain' and 'Roger Lambelin' and some of the dusky purples such as 'Cardinal de Richelieu' and 'Tuscany'. These could equally have been put at the other end to contrast with the silver-leaved pear and the white *Philadelphus*.

To make some colour in the later summer and autumn, I suggest planting in the gaps some of the hardier fuchsias of which there is a great variety now. The red and white 'Madame Cornelisen' is always striking. In colder areas they should be cut down in autumn and covered with a small mound of ashes or bracken, or both, but in the warmer parts this is not necessary. Blue *Agapanthus* are also excellent for later flowering and will combine well with white *Veratrum*. The Headbourne Hybrid strain of *Agapanthus* seem to be quite hardy in most regions. They also like sun and flower after most of the shrub roses will be over. Paeonies too are lovely and will flower with the roses or, in the case of the very lovely pale yellow *P. mlokosewitschii*, a little before. Their foliage is decorative for a long season and in the autumn assumes bright red tints. It can be cleared away with the winter pruning of the roses. For bold, low foliage and a contrast of form from the feathery foliage of the roses to large entire bold leaves, a few hostas are good while bergenias will also give some early spring colour in their flowers. 'Ballawley' is still one of the best. There is a great variety of hostas. I like the bold blue-grey *H. glauca* which is often still known as *H. sieboldiana*. Individual leaves of this may be nearly a foot (0·3 m.) across. *Alchemilla mollis* is another invaluable plant for the front of the border and its ochreous yellow flowers are a good foil for some roses, especially a pale pink Musk rose such as 'Penelope'. It spreads quickly also and makes a good ground cover which keeps down most weeds. Silver-leaved plants are important and make good contrast which enhances the colour of the roses. Apart from the *Stachys lanata* mentioned above, of which the nearly flowerless form 'Silver Carpet' should be chosen, the artemisias will combine well. There is a very pretty and very silvery dwarf called *A. schmidtii* which is almost prostrate and has filigree fine foliage, as has the larger *A. arborescens*, but this is mainly a plant for the warmer areas. Some of the helichrysums are excellent also, such as *H. petiolatum* which is tender and needs renewing from cuttings after each winter, and *H. lineatum* which is rather hardier, but both of these do tend to take rather a lot of space. While the border is growing and rather thin, a few of the large biennial statue-like Scotch thistle, *Onopordon*, will also look well but one must be careful of excessive seedlings.

All these plants should, however, be prevented from growing within 2 ft (0·6 m.) or so of the bases of the roses, especially during the period when they are becoming established.

The return from such a border will be cumulative. In the first year one can expect some flower but it is unlikely to make a great display and we want to encourage growth.

As mentioned earlier spring bulbs will create an interest when the roses make no show. Daffodils planted in large drifts of one colour will look well and may be grown under the roses. They are best planted fairly deep about 4–6 in. (10·2–15·2 cm.), so that they will escape a light forking over and weeding. Deep forking at any rate is undesirable among roses and weed control is better accomplished by mulches, while some growers now use chemical weed killers extensively during the dormant period of the roses and even during the summer, taking great care to keep the chemicals off the leaves. The little *Crocus* species such as *C. tomasinianus* for very early spring flowering, sometimes starting in January, and *C. speciosus* for September-flowering, will do no harm to the roses and also seem oblivious to light forking while, in the lighter soils at least, they spread freely by seeding. On chalky soils, especially near the south coast, of England, blue *Anemone blanda* spreads to make a thick carpet in late February or March depending on the season. A few ornamental alliums also look well, such as the purple globes of *A. christophii* (still better known as *A. albo-pilosum*) in front of the large 8 ft (2·4 m.) bushes of the dusky reddish-purple 'Zigeunerknabe'.

The value of roses with fine hips in the garden is great and they have a dual purpose effect, first a fine display of flower and then an early autumn display of bright orange-red, scarlet or terracotta hips. *R. moyesii* and its varieties and hybrids are among the finest, but plenty of space should be allowed for these and they look well on their own in a corner or overhanging a low wall. An old bush of *R.* × *highdownensis*, such as the original one at Highdown, may be 10 ft (3 m.) high and as much across. One should give them a place where the sun will shine through them but a dark green background is not so important. In flower the darker crimson forms of *R. moyesii* and the very dark, almost maroon-red *R.* × *pruhoniciana* only really light up when the sun shines through them and they look superb silhouetted against a blue summer's sky. *R. holodonta* is usually slightly more compact in growth and has even slightly brighter and larger hips. It is a plant which should be much more widely grown. Some of the other shrub roses will also make good hips, if left untrimmed after flowering. The brilliant crimson 'Scharlachglut' has some of the largest and most abundant red hips that I know, hanging in great clusters and lasting into late autumn, while the pink Damask 'St Nicholas' is unusually fine in its round orange-scarlet clusters of hips. We usually prune it by picking these for the home in October and November. Even in early December as I write, the terracotta-pink hips of the climbing 'Mme Grégoire Staechelin' are lovely against a grey wall and are even now only beginning to drop. They are very large and seem to have benefited from the very warm summer

while the vigour of this rose is so great that it can afford to bear such a crop. The round scarlet marbles of *R. virginiana* are splendid among its scarlet foliage and this rose will make a low rounded shrub about 4 ft (1·2 m.) high, lovely when contrasted with the grey foliage of the small shrubby *Phlomis fruticosa* or *Senecio laxifolius*.

The places for Climbers and Ramblers are considerable and many like to extend them to growing up old trees. These are more suitable for Ramblers than Climbers. This is perhaps as well since some of the Ramblers, especially those derived from *R. wichuraiana* such as 'Dorothy Perkins', are very susceptible to intense mildew when grown on a wall or in any place where there is not a good circulation around. Only a large tree or a big wall will be suitable for a really rampant Rambler like the superb 'Kiftsgate' form of *R. filipes* or, on a slightly less rampant scale 'Wedding Day'. The original plant of 'Kiftsgate' has quite submerged its support and is now a vast towering thicket quite impenetrable. One of the finest plants I know has been grown up behind a wall at the end of a large mill pond at Sutton Courtenay in Berkshire and now cascades down as a broad waterfall over the front of the wall. This is the plant shown in our photograph. It would look marvellous growing up and over ancient yews.

Old apple trees, often unpruned for long and useless for fruit growing, are excellent supports for many of these Ramblers such as the less vigorous *R. longicuspis* with its lovely shining foliage and with large clusters of creamy-white flowers, or the slightly pinker-flushed 'Francis E. Lester' or that delightfully named and rarely seen rose 'Rambling Rector'. It is a vigorous Rambler with slightly greyish-green foliage and is covered, usually in late June, with large clusters of white flowers like a *moschata*. Large shrubby semi-climbers such as 'Mme Plantier' may be used with good effect up old apple trees set in grass which is not mown till late June to allow the foliage of the daffodils to ripen. So strong, however, are some of the roses that they may bring down the old trees and it may prove necessary in time to provide some extra support. Such roses become a tangled mass and the only pruning one can do is to cut out from time to time as much as possible of the dead wood and a few of the older stems, possibly right down to the base. 'Albertine' is another rose that looks lovely smothering an old tree, but even so the finest specimens I have seen have been grown against south-facing walls. In warmer parts a few of the *gigantea* hybrids such as 'Sénateur Amic' can be grown up into old trees and look superb during their early summer flowering. One plant I know of the 'Sénateur' grows through a mass of honeysuckle on an old tree and the two combine well, the honeysuckle starting to flower when the rose leaves off. In warmer countries such as the Riviera coast of France and Italy, in the warmer states of the U.S.A. such as California, and also in Australia, these hybrids of *R. gigantea* will grow vast and require substantial supports and are one of the finest features of their gardens. In England they can also be grown against a wall and will soon reach the top, as has the old plant of 'La Belle Portugaise' on the walls of the Royal Horticultural Societys' laboratory.

When Ramblers are planted to grow over old trees, they should be planted well away from the base of the tree, where it is often very dry and may be barren and shaded; 6 ft

(1·8 m.) away is usually not too much. The leading shoots should be trained up into the branches with the aid of a rope or by long bamboo. Once they are established in the branches and have their own grip, this support can be removed.

For large walls the two finest Climbers I know are the yellow 'Mermaid', a very vigorous rose which is in a class all its own, and the pink 'Mme Grégoire Staechelin', although she only has one season of flower. 'Mermaid' has a long recurrent season which may extend well into November. 'Mme Grégoire' looks her best against a grey stone wall or a white one but even a brick one does not kill her beauty entirely. The very dark red 'Guinée' is a rose I would not wish to be without. Less vigorous, it nevertheless can reach 12 ft (3·7 m.) or more on a wall. 'Guinée' may also be grown in a cold or cool greenhouse for early flowers and to provide summer shading. Some of the new recurrent flowering roses are very brilliant against a wall while most will do well as pillar roses. The finest specimen I have seen of the very bright 'Danse du Feu' grew against a grey stone house and was dazzling although not offensive. It had the wall to itself to the exclusion of other roses. Among the newer ones, I particularly like 'Altissimo' with clusters of dark but bright red, large, single flowers; 'Casino' with large yellow flowers of hybrid tea type, produced singly; 'Copenhagen' with large, rich scarlet flowers; 'Don Juan' with scented, deep red large flowers and well shaped buds; and 'Galway Bay' with large deep pink flowers.

Some of the modern roses are half way between pillar roses which will grow up to 6–8 ft (1·8–2·4 m.) and large shrubs and their form is largely a result of the system of pruning adopted. Such are 'Constance Spray', 'Golden Showers' and 'Maigold'. Treated as Climbers they look superb. I anticipate that more of the roses now being raised may fall into this category and the dividing lines of the old classification will become lost.

The older fashioned pergola method of growing Climbers and Ramblers is becoming less popular but it is undoubtedly a good method. It is necessary to have really stout support; the rustic type of unpeeled larch pole rarely stays the course and after some years tends to rot at ground level, though its useful life can be prolonged considerably by steeping it in creosote or other preservative, or even better, setting it in a drainpipe set in the ground in concrete, but one must be careful that water cannot run down inside between the pipe and the pole. A good example of a heavy pergola may be seen at Kew in the Royal Botanic Gardens, while there are delightful examples of the use of ironwork, as arched hoops covering ironwork posts, in the rose garden at La Bagatelle and at the Roserie de L'Haÿ, both on the outskirts of Paris. This is very suitable for the older and more vigorous Ramblers and they look superb towards the end of June, making a semi-formal layout. In both cases, in the beds beside them, other roses are grown on pillars and this seems to suit particularly roses such as 'New Dawn' which stands out by reason of its abundance of flower as do some of the less vigorous Ramblers such as 'Excelsa' and 'Sander's White'. The pillar method is also suitable for the less vigorous recurrent-flowering Climbers. An excellent and most effective example can be seen in the circle of pillar roses surrounding Queen Mary's Garden in Regent's Park, London, where there is one of the finest collections of roses in the world. These pillars are joined by heavy ropes hanging in bold loops; between and along these the roses are trained when they have reached the top of the pillar. This method, technically known as a catenary, has been followed also along the back of the long rose borders in the Royal Horticultural Society's garden at Wisley in Surrey. Probably these arrangements will be too large for the smaller garden but variations on them can easily be made and undoubtedly the pillar method of growing the Climbers will prove most effective. Some gardeners prefer to vary this by having three pillars arranged as a triangle, leaning inwards towards a peak with cross pieces, and training the rose over these, as can be seen in the Savill Garden in Windsor Great Park. Undoubtedly this is suitable both for the larger shrub rose and the only moderately vigorous Climber, but it looks rather bare when the rose is first planted and for the first year or two.

Whichever method one adopts, however, there is no reason why all gardeners should not enjoy the superb abundance of flower and luxuriance of which these roses are capable and which they achieve in fewer years than practically any other flowering shrub.

Acknowledgments

Mr Patrick M. Synge, F.L.S., V.M.H., has been responsible for the descriptions of most of the shrub roses, old and new, the Climbers and Ramblers as well as the species and their near crosses, and gladly acknowledges the help and collaboration of his colleague. Mr S. Millar Gault, M.B.E., F.L.S., V.M.H., has described the remainder as well as the large number of Floribunda and Hybrid Tea roses. In the Introduction Mr Gault has written about the cultivation, pruning and propagation of roses and plants to grow with Hybrid Teas and Floribundas. Mr Synge has added notes concerning the pruning of shrub roses and the pests and diseases of shrubs, Climbers and Ramblers, their placing in the garden and plants to grow with them, as well as a brief History of the Rose. In addition Mr Gault supervised the bulk of the photography. The photographs were taken by Mr Ernest Crowson, F.R.P.S., A.I.I.P.

The Introduction and rose descriptions have been checked, on behalf of The Royal Horticultural Society and The Royal National Rose Society, by Mr E. F. Allen (Introduction, species and first crosses); Mr J. S. Mattock (shrubs and Modern Climbers); Major-General R. F. B. Naylor (Hybrid Teas and Floribundas); Mr G. D. Rowley (species, shrubs and climbers).

The authors and photographer are greatly indebted to Mr L. G. Turner, Secretary of The Royal National Rose Society, St Albans, England, and the Society's staff as well as to the many rosarians and nurserymen who have helped by allowing their roses to be photographed. In particular the authors wish to thank:

Mr C. D. Brickell, B.Sc., Director, The Royal Horticultural Society Garden, Wisley, Surrey;

R. Harkness & Co. Ltd, The Rose Gardens, Hitchin, Hertfordshire;

Major I. K. C. Hobkirk, M.V.O., M.C., Bailiff of the Royal Parks Division and the Superintendent and staff, Regent's Park, London;

Lieutenant-Colonel and Mrs P. Laycock, The Mill House, Sutton Courtenay, Berkshire;

J. Mattock Ltd, The Rose Nurseries, Nuneham Courtenay, Oxford;

The National Trust and Mr Burrows, Hidcote Manor, Gloucestershire;

Major-General R. F. B. Naylor, C.B., C.B.E., D.S.O., M.C., D.H.M., Past President, The Royal National Rose Society, Dancer's Hill House, Barnet, Hertfordshire;

Mr N. Nicholson, the National Trust, and their joint head gardeners Miss P. Schwerdt and Miss Kreutzberger, Sissinghurst Castle, Cranbrook, Kent;

Mr & Mrs Robinson, Hyde Hall, Chelmsford, Essex;

Sir Eric Savill, K.C.V.O., and Mr T. H. Findlay, M.V.O., V.M.H., Savill Gardens, The Great Park, Windsor, Berkshire.

In addition the authors wish to thank Herr Wilhelm Kordes, 2201 Sparrieshoop über Elmshorn, Holstein, Germany, for advice on the roses to be photographed; the British distributors of Felco secateurs (pruning shears) and Tina knives, Messrs Burton McCall & Co., Leicester, are also thanked for supplying goods for the pruning and budding photographs. Mr Synge would like to acknowledge particularly the help he has received from the writings of Mr Graham S. Thomas, without whose pioneer works his task would have been much more laborious.

The Plates

1
R. banksiae banksiae

2
R. banksiae lutea

3
R. banksiae lutescens

4
R. californica
'Plena'

5
R. cooperi

6
R. ×dupontii

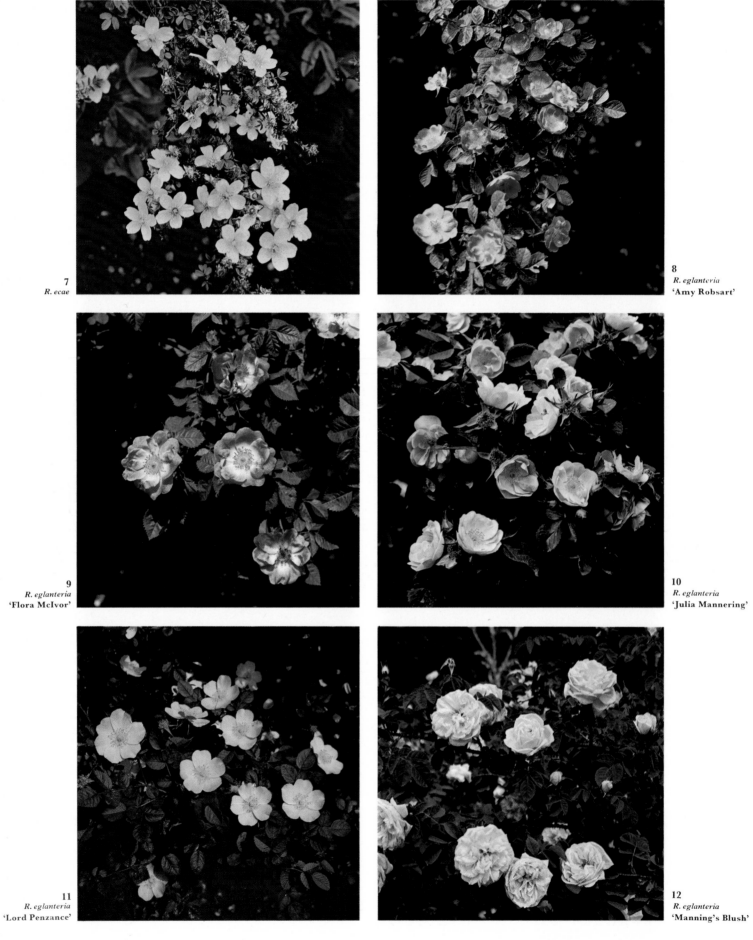

7
R. ecae

8
R. eglanteria
'Amy Robsart'

9
R. eglanteria
'Flora McIvor'

10
R. eglanteria
'Julia Mannering'

11
R. eglanteria
'Lord Penzance'

12
R. eglanteria
'Manning's Blush'

13
R. eglanteria
'Meg Merrilies'

14
R. farreri persetosa

15
R. fedtschenkoana

16
R. foetida bicolor

17
R. forrestiana

18
R. gentiliana

19 *R. filipes* **'Kiftsgate'**

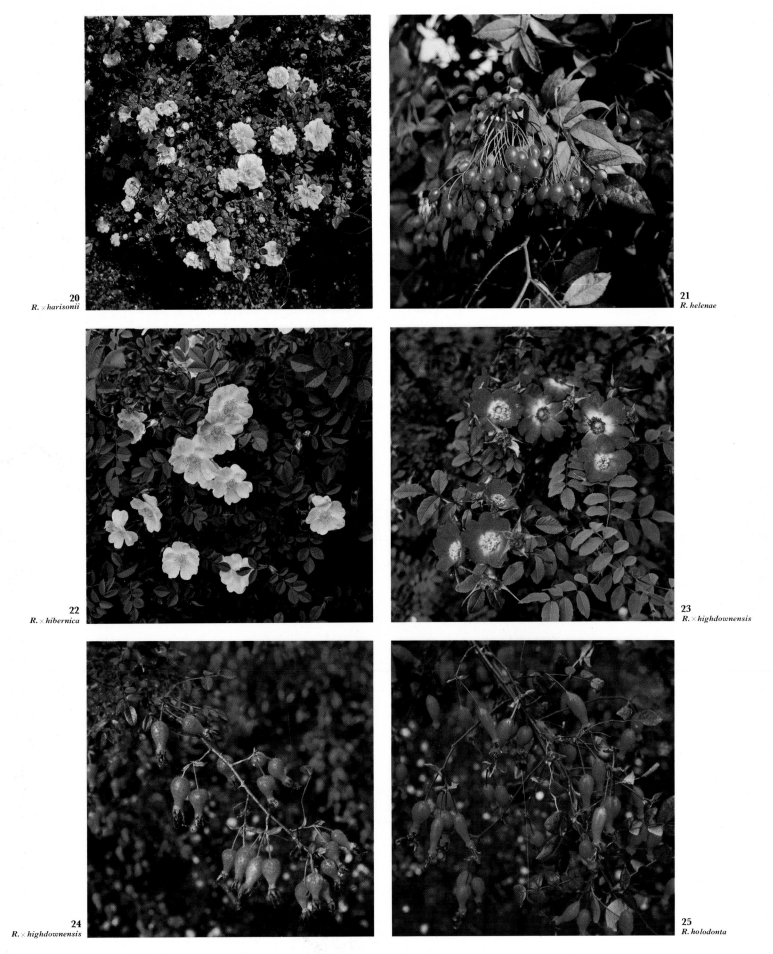

20
R. ×harisonii

21
R. helenae

22
R. ×hibernica

23
R. ×highdownensis

24
R. × highdownensis

25
R. holodonta

38
R. pomifera
'Duplex'

39
R. primula

40
R. × pruhoniciana

41
R. × pteragonis
'Cantabrigiensis'

42
R. × pteragonis
'Earldomensis'

43
R. × pteragonis
'Headleyensis'

44
R. × *pteragonis*
'Headleyensis'

45
R. roxburghii

46
R. roxburghii

47
R. rubrifolia

48
R. rubrifolia

49
R. sericea
'Heather Muir'

50
R. sericea pteracantha

51
R. setipoda

52
R. spinosissima altaica

53
R. spinosissima hispid

54
R. spinosissima
'Double White'

55
R. spinosissima
'Double Yellow'

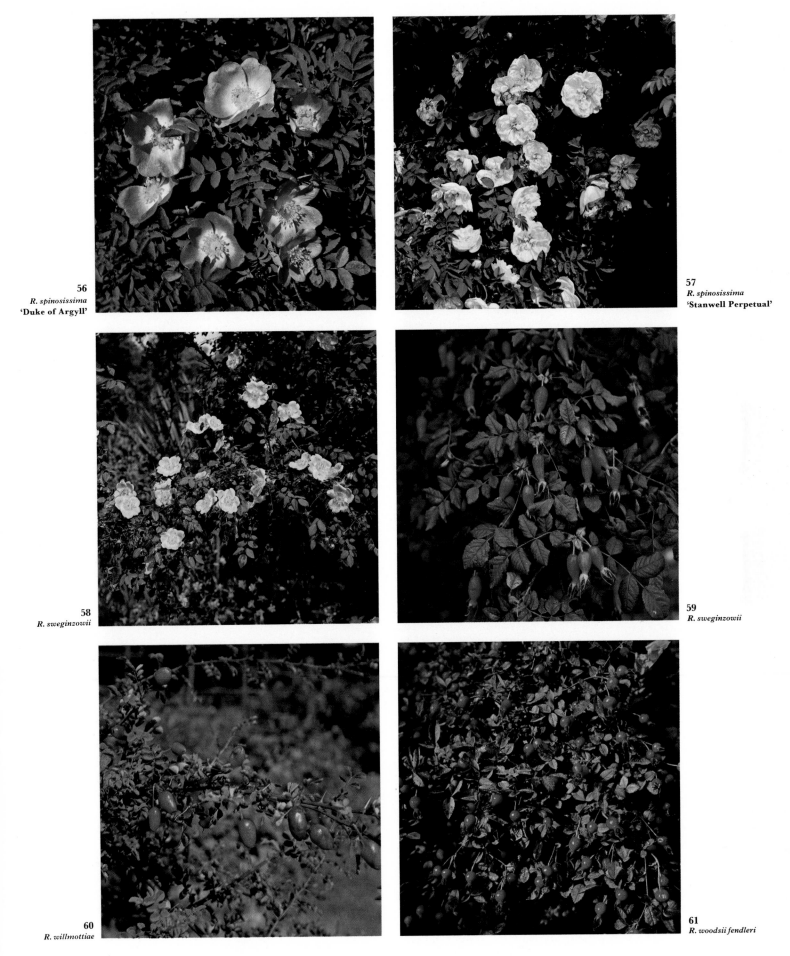

56
R. spinosissima
'Duke of Argyll'

57
R. spinosissima
'Stanwell Perpetual'

58
R. sweginzowii

59
R. sweginzowii

60
R. willmottiae

61
R. woodsii fendleri

62
'Alba Maxima'

63
'Belle Amour'

64
'Céleste'
'Celestial'

65
'Félicité
Parmentier'

66
'Königin von
Dänemark'

67
'Maiden's Blush'

68
'Fantin Latour'

69
'Paul Ricault'

70
'Petite de
Hollande'

71
'Tour de Malakoff'

72
'Gloire des
Mousseux'

73
'Jeanne de
Montfort'

74
'Lanei'

75
'Mousseux du Japon'

76
'William Lobb'

77
'Blush Damask'

78
'Comte de Chambord'

79
'Hebe's Lip'

'Reine Blanche'

'Rubrotincta'

80
'Ispahan'

81
'Jacques Cartier'

82
'Mme Zöetmans'

83
'Cardinal de
Richelieu'

84
'Charles de Mills'

85
'Hippolyte'

86
'Officinalis',
R. gallica officinalis,
R. gallica maxima

87
'Petite
Orléanaise'

88
'Président de Sèze'

89
'Rose du
Maître d'Ecole'

90
'Sissinghurst Castle'
'Rose des Maures'

91
'Tuscany Superb'

92
'Versicolor',
R. gallica versicolor,
'Rosa Mundi'

93
'Bourbon Queen'

'Souvenir de la
Princesse de Lamballe'

94
'Honorine de
Brabant'

95
'Kathleen Harrop'

96
'La Reine Victoria'

97
'Louise Odier'

98
'Mme Isaac
Pereire'

99
'Mme Lauriol
de Barny'

100
'Mme Pierre Oger'

101
'Prince Charles'

102
'Souvenir de
St Anne's'

103
'Variegata
di Bologna'

104
'Zéphirine Drouhin'

105
'Zigeunerknabe'

'Gipsy Boy'

106
'Baron Girod
de l'Ain'

107
'Baroness
Rothschild'

108
'Baronne Prévost'

109
'Empereur du Maroc'

110
'Ferdinand Pichard'

111
'Frau Karl
Druschki'

112
'Mrs John Laing'

113
'Paul Neyron'

114
'Reine des
Violettes'

115
'Roger Lambelin'

116
'Souvenir du
Docteur Jamain'

117
'Vick's Caprice'

118
'Buff Beauty'

119
'Cornelia'

120
'Felicia'

121
'Moonlight'

122
'Penelope'

123
'Prosperity'

124
'Thisbe'

125
'Vanity'

126
'Hermosa'

127
'Viridiflora',
R. chinensis viridiflora

128
'Agnes'

129
'Alba',
R. rugosa alba

130
'Blanc Double
de Coubert'

131
'Conrad F. Meyer'

132
'Frau Dagmar
Hartopp'

133
'Mrs Anthony
Waterer'

134
'Pink Grootendorst'

135
'Roseraie de l'Haÿ'

136
'Rubra',
R. rugosa rubra

137
'Sarah van Fleet'

138
'Scabrosa',
R. rugosa scabrosa

139
'Schneezwerg'

140
'Ballerina'

141
'Berlin'

142
'Bonn'

143
'Canary Bird'

144
'Canary Bird'

145
'Cappa Magna'

146
'Cerise Bouquet'

147
'Chianti'

148
'Chinatown'

' Ville de Chine'

149
'Clair Matin'

150
'Complicata'

151
'Complicata'

152 'Complicata'

153
'Constance Spry'

154
'Coryana',
R.×coryana

155
'Dorothy
Wheatcroft'

156
'Düsterlohe'

157
'Elmshorn'

158
'Erfurt'

28

159
'First Choice'

160
'Fred Loads'

161
'Fritz Nobis'

162
'Frühlingsanfang'

163
'Frühlingsduft'

164
'Frühlingsmorgen'

165 'Frühlingsgold'

166
'Goldbusch'

167
'Golden Chersonese'

168
'Golden Wings'

169
'Hamburg'

170
'Heidelberg'

'Gruss an Heidelberg'

171
'Hunter'

172
'Kassel'

173
'Kathleen Ferrier'

174
'Lady Curzon'

175
'Lady Sonia'

176
'Lafter'

177
'Lavender Lassie'

178
'Marguerite
Hilling'

'Pink Nevada'

179
'Nevada'

180
'Lyric'

181
'Magenta'

'Kordes' Magenta'

182
'Munster'

183
'Nymphenburg'

184
'Oskar Scheerer'

185
'Prestige'

186
'Radway Sunrise'

187
'Scharlachglut'
'Scarlet Fire'

188
'Sparrieshoop'

189
'The Wife of Bath'

190
'The Yeoman'

191
'Wilhelm'
'Skyrocket'

192
'Albéric Barbier'

193
'Albertine'

194
'Allen Chandler'

195
'American Pillar'

196
R. × anemonoides ,
R. sinica 'Anemone'

197
R. × anemonoides
'Ramona'

198
'Blairi No. 2'

199
'Chaplin's Pink
Climber'

200
'Claire Jacquier'

201
'Crimson Shower'

202
'Dawson'

203
'Elegance'

243
'Fugue'

244
'Galway Bay'

245
'Golden Showers'

246
'Handel'

247
'Joseph's Coat'

248
'Leverkusen'

249
'Maigold'

250
'Meg'

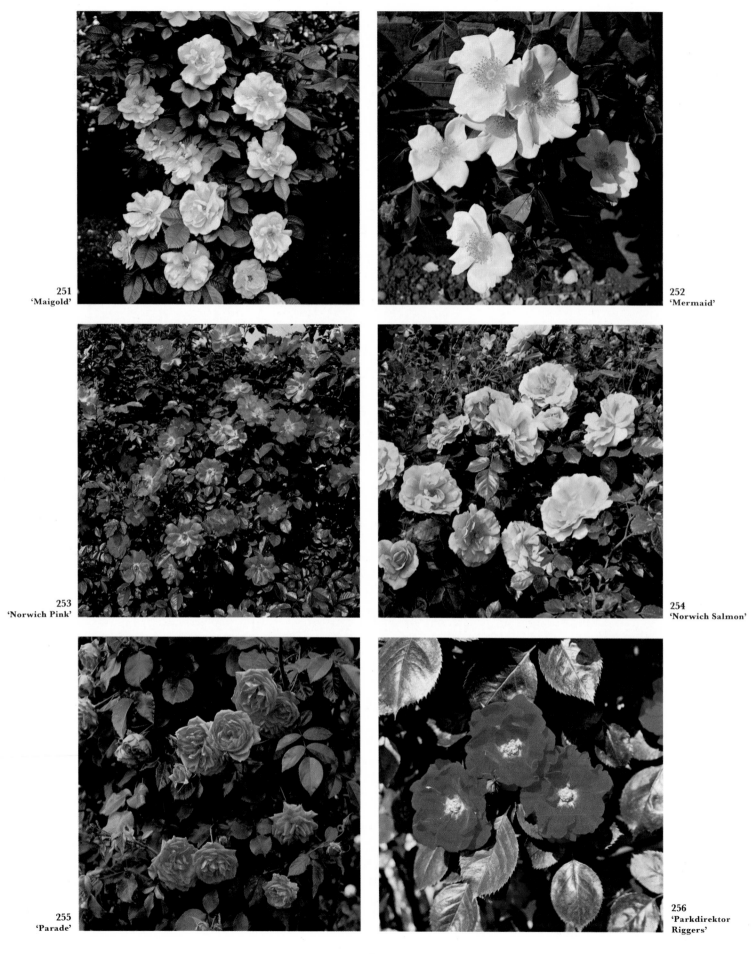

251
'Maigold'

252
'Mermaid'

253
'Norwich Pink'

254
'Norwich Salmon'

255
'Parade'

256
'Parkdirektor
Riggers'

48

257
'Pink Perpétue'

258
'Ritter von
Barmstede'

259
'Santa Catalina'

260
'Soldier Boy'

261
'Swan Lake'

262
'Sweet Sultan'

263
'Climbing Allgold'

264
'Climbing
Cécile Brunner'

265
'Climbing
Lady Hillingdon'

266
'Climbing
Lady Sylvia'

267
'Climbing
Mons. Paul Lédé'

268
'Climbing
Pompon de Paris'

269
'Alec's Red'

270
'Apricot Silk'

271
'Arianna'

272
'Ballet'

273
'Beauté'

274
'Birmingham Post'

51

275
'Bond Street'

276
'Bonsoir'

277
'Brandenberg'

278
'Brasilia'

279
'Buccaneer'

280
'Caramba'

281
'Casanova'

282
'Champs-Elysées'

'K

283
'Chicago Peace'

284
'Christian Dior'

285
'City of Gloucester'

286
'Constanze'

327
'Lady Sylvia'

328
'Lucy Cramphorn'

'Maryse Kriloff'

329
'Mme Louis
Laperrière'

330
'Mainzer Fastnacht'

'Blue Moon'

'Sissi'

331
'Margaret'

332
'Maria Callas'

'Miss All-American
Beauty'

333
'McGredy's Yellow'

334
'Mellow Yellow'

335
'Mischief'

336
'Mister Lincoln'

337
'Mrs Oakley Fisher'

338
'Mojave'

339
'Montezuma'

340
'Mullard Jubilee'

'Electron'

341
'My Choice'

342
'National Trust'

343
'Norman Hartnell'

344
'Northern Lights'

345
'Paris-Match'

346
'Pascali'

347
'Peace'
'Gioia'
'Gloria Dei'
'Mme A. Meilland'

348
'Peer Gynt'

349
'Pharaoh'
'Pharaon'

350
'Piccadilly'

351
'Pink Favorite'

352
'Pink Peace'

353
'Pink Supreme'

354
'Prima Ballerina'
'Première Ballerina'

355
'Princess'

356
'Princess Margaret
of England'

357
'Red Devil'

'Cœur d'Amour'

358
'Red Lion'

359
'Red Queen'

'Liebestraum'

360
'Rose Gaujard'

361
'Royal Highness'

'Königliche Hoheit'

362
'Samourai'

'Scarlet Knight'

363
'Santa Fé'

364
'Sarah Arnot'

365
'Serenade'

366
'Silva'

367
'Summer Holiday'

368
'Super Sun'

369
'Super Star'

'Tropicana'

370
'Sutter's Gold'

69

371
'Tiffany'

372
'Timothy Eaton'

373
'Wendy Cussons'

374
'Whisky Mac'

375
'Wiener Charme'

'Charme de Vienne'

'Charming Vienna'

'Vienna Charm'

376
'Winefred Clark'

377
'Adair Roche'

378
'Allgold'

379
'Ama'

380
'America's
Junior Miss'

381
'Anna Louisa'

382
'Anne Cocker'

383
'Apricot Nectar'

384
'Arabian Nights'

385
'Arakan'

386
'Arthur Bell'

387
'Beatrice'

388
'Blessings'

389
'Busy Lizzie'

390
'Centenaire de
Lourdes'

'Mrs Jones'

391
'Chanelle'

392
'Charles Dickens'

393
'Charleston'

394
'Charlotte
Elizabeth'

395
'Charm of Paris'
'Pariser Charm'

396
'Charming Maid'

397
'Chorus Girl'

398
'City of Belfast'

399
'City of Leeds'

400
'Courvoisier'

401
'Dainty Bess'

402
'Dainty Maid'

403
'Dearest'

404
'Dr Barnardo'

405
'Dream Waltz'

406
'Elysium'

407
'Elizabeth of Glamis'
'Irish Beauty'

408
'Escapade'

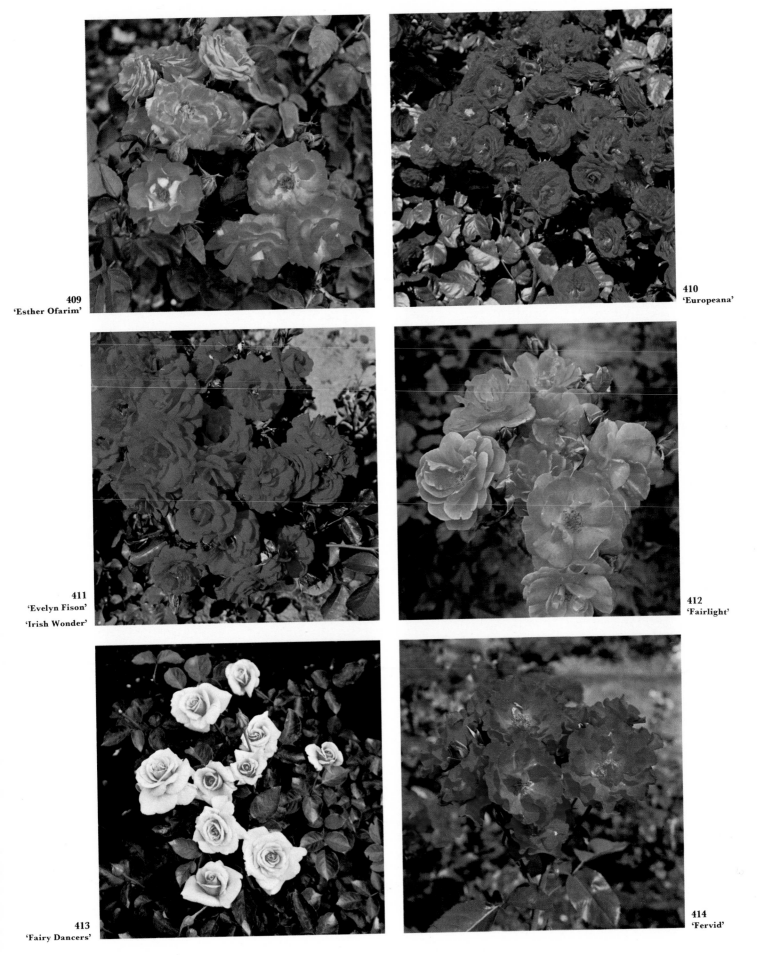

409
'Esther Ofarim'

410
'Europeana'

411
'Evelyn Fison'

'Irish Wonder'

412
'Fairlight'

413
'Fairy Dancers'

414
'Fervid'

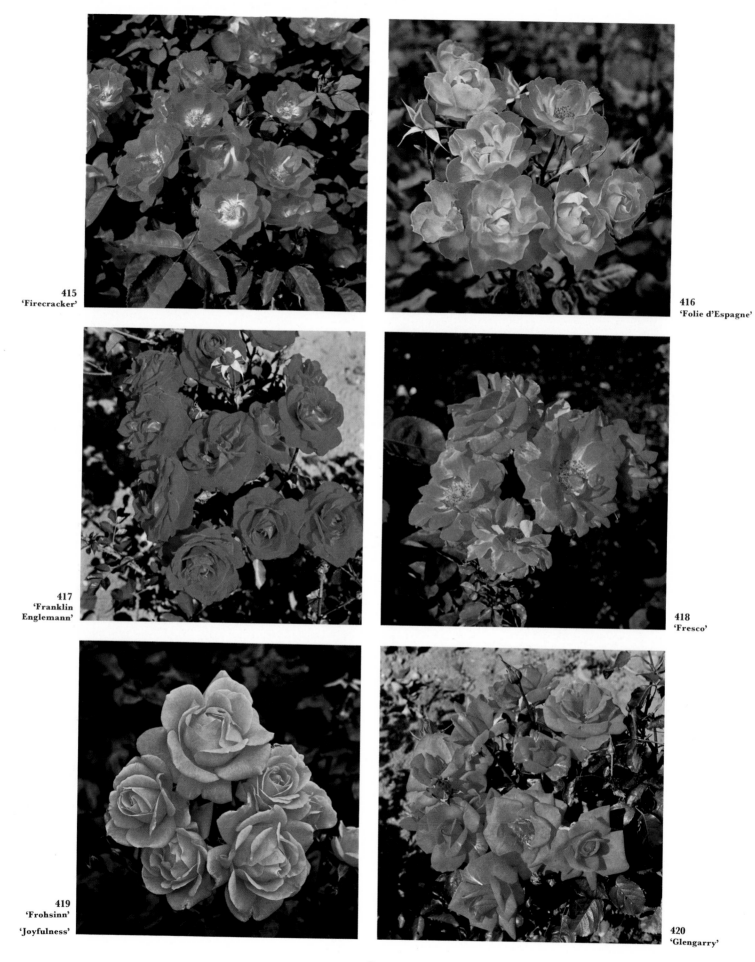

415
'Firecracker'

416
'Folie d'Espagne'

417
'Franklin
Englemann'

418
'Fresco'

419
'Frohsinn'
'Joyfulness'

420
'Glengarry'

®

421
'Golden Slippers'

422
'Goldschatz'
'Golden Treasure'

423
'Gruss an Aachen'

424
'Gustav Frahm'

425
'Happy Event'

426
'Heartbeat'

427
'Highlight'

428
'Horstmann's
Rosenresli'

'Rosenresli'

429
'Ice White'

'Vison Blanc'

430
'Irish Mist'

431
'Ivory Fashion'

432
'Jan Spek'

433
'Joybells'

434
'Jubilant'

435
'Kim'

436
'King Arthur'

437
'Korona'

438
'Lagoon'

439
'Lilac Charm'

440
'Lilli Marleen'

441
'Manx Queen'

'Isle of Man'

442
'Marita'

443
'Marlena'

444
'Masquerade'

445
'Lake Como'

446
'Margo Koster'

447
'Megiddo'

448
'Merlin'

449
'Mevrouw Nathalie
Nypels'

'Natalie Nypels'

450
'Michelle'

451
'Molly McGredy'

452
'Nordia'

453
'Moon Maiden'

454
'News'

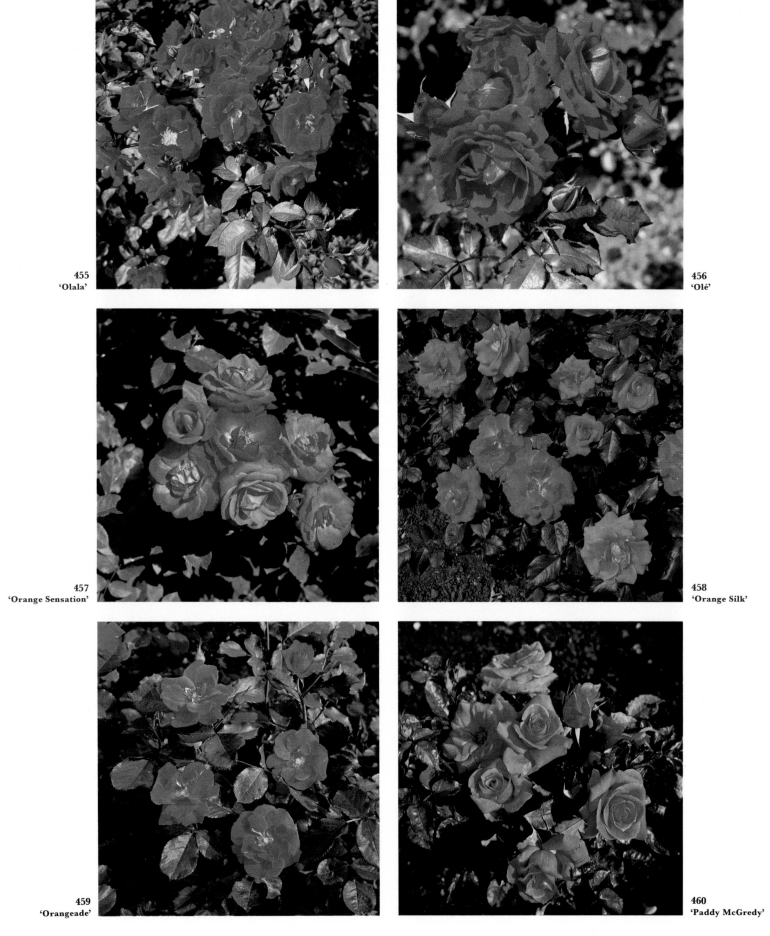

455
'Olala'

456
'Olé'

457
'Orange Sensation'

458
'Orange Silk'

459
'Orangeade'

460
'Paddy McGredy'

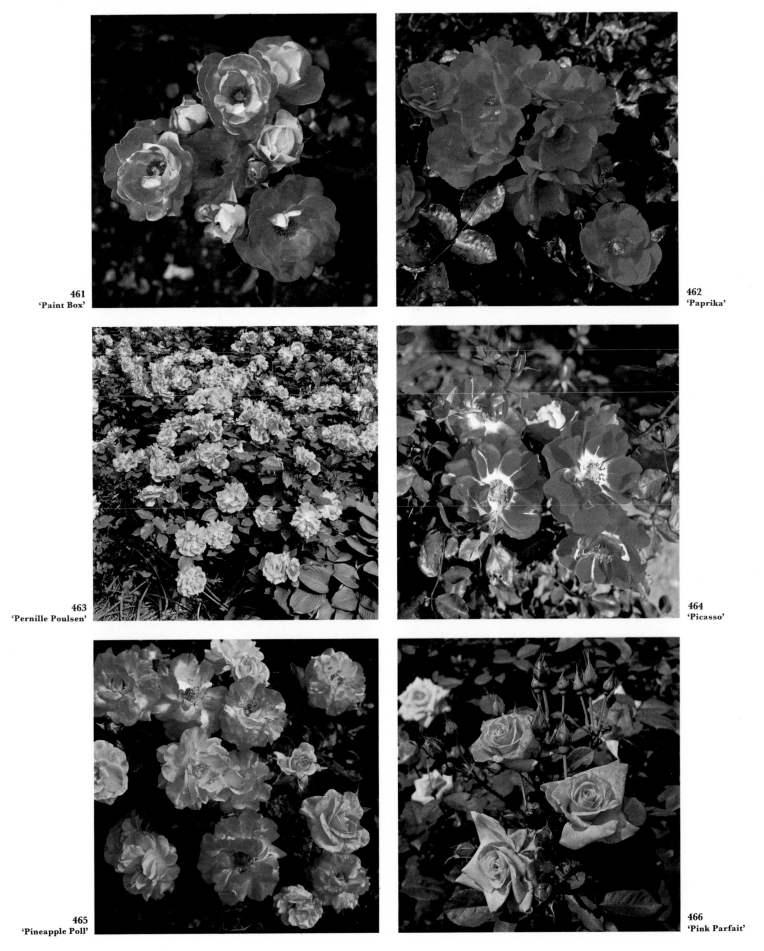

461
'Paint Box'

462
'Paprika'

463
'Pernille Poulsen'

464
'Picasso'

465
'Pineapple Poll'

466
'Pink Parfait'

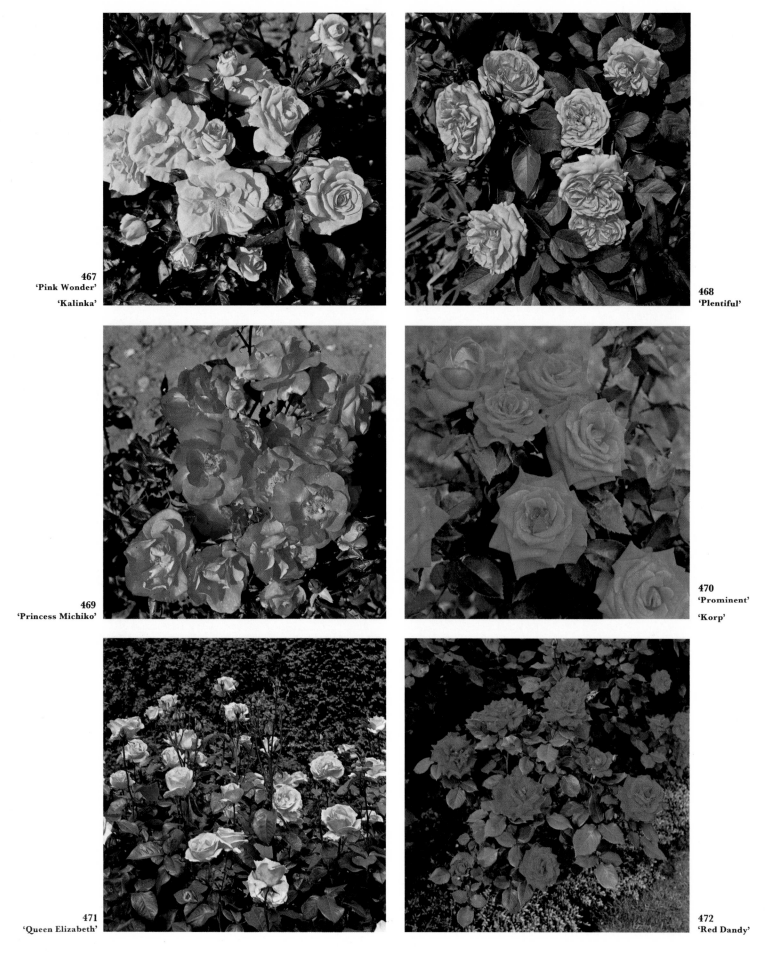

467
'Pink Wonder'
'Kalinka'

468
'Plentiful'

469
'Princess Michiko'

470
'Prominent'
'Korp'

471
'Queen Elizabeth'

472
'Red Dandy'

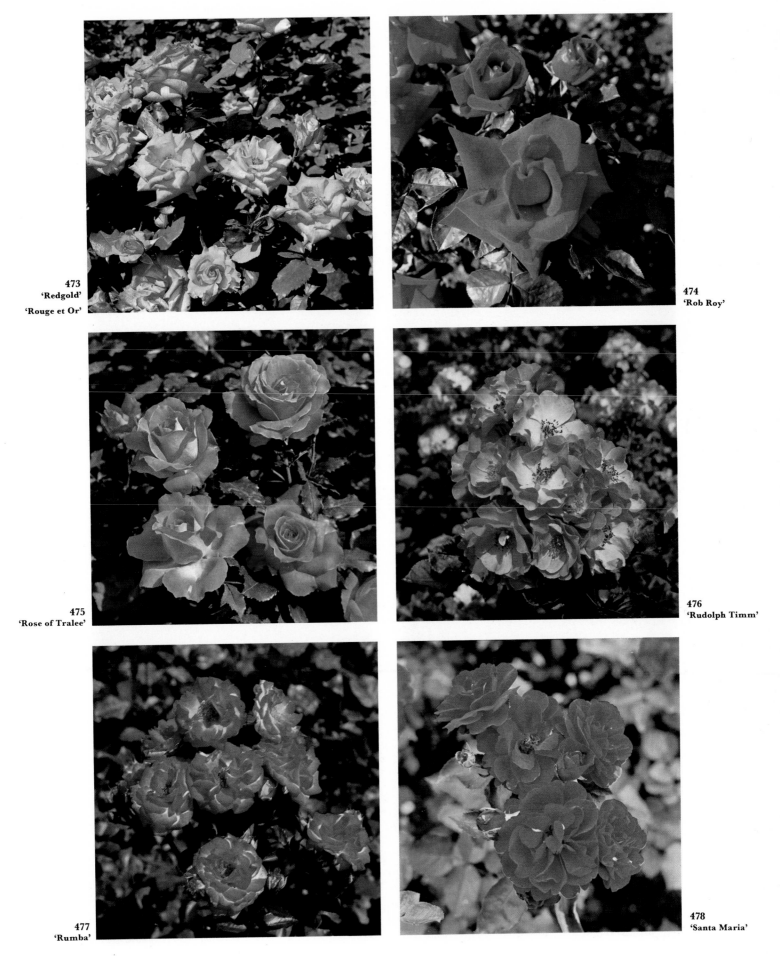

473
'Redgold'
'Rouge et Or'

474
'Rob Roy'

475
'Rose of Tralee'

476
'Rudolph Timm'

477
'Rumba'

478
'Santa Maria'

479
'Scarlet Queen
Elizabeth'

480
'Scented Air'

481 'Schneewittchen', 'Fée des Neiges', 'Iceberg'

489
'Stroller'

490
'Telstar'

491
'The Fairy'

492
'The Optimist'
'Sweet Repose'

493
'Tombola'

494
'Travesti'

495
'Vera Dalton'

496
'Vesper'

497
'Violet Carson'

498
'Yellow Cushion'

499
'Yvonne Rabier'

500
'Zambra'

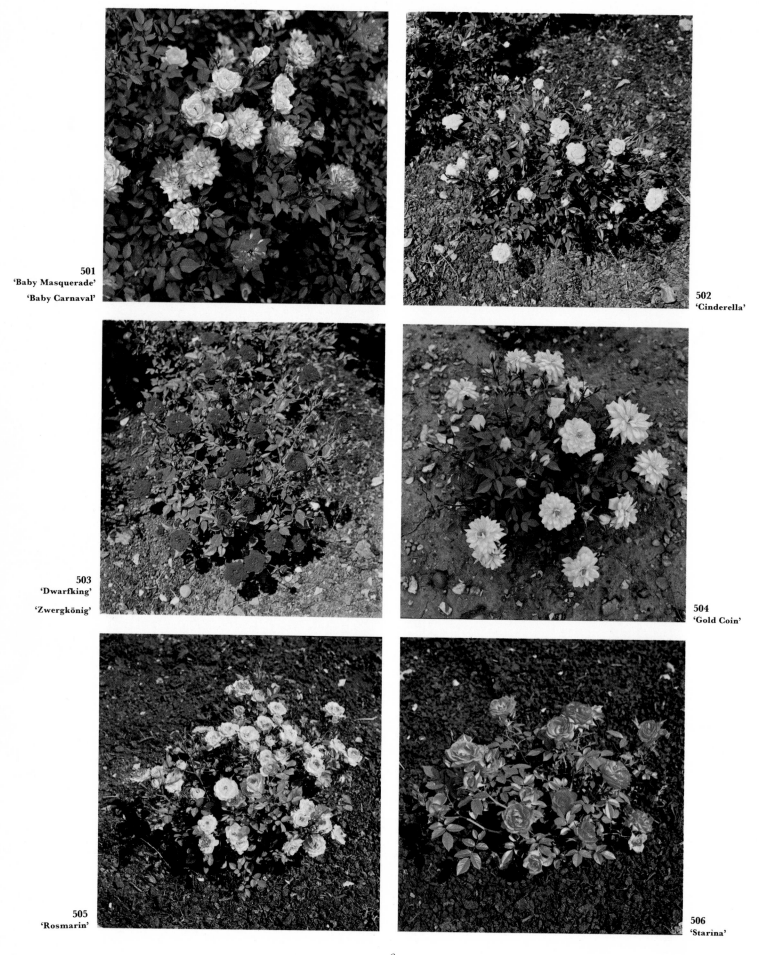

501
'Baby Masquerade'
'Baby Carnaval'

502
'Cinderella'

503
'Dwarfking'
'Zwergkönig'

504
'Gold Coin'

505
'Rosmarin'

506
'Starina'

The Dictionary

Abyssinian Rose see *R.* × *richardii*

'Adair Roche' Fl.
Rosy-pink and silver, 3 ft (0·9 m.) 1968
Raised by S. McGredy IV, N. Ireland.
Parentage: 'Paddy McGredy' × unnamed 'Femina' seedling
An upright, vigorous grower, 3 ft (0·9 m.) high, with medium green glossy foliage. The medium sized flowers are full, borne in trusses and are mid-rosy-pink with a silver reverse. A new cultivar of promise. **377**, p. 71.
T.G.C., R.N.R.S. 1968.

'Adam Messerich' B.
Deep pink, recurrent, 6 ft (1·8 m.) 1920
Raised by P. Lambert, Germany.
Parentage: 'Frau Oberhofgärtner Singer' × ('Louise Odier' seedling × 'Louis Philippe')
Bourbon shrub or pillar rose of medium vigour and with few thorns. Flowers large, semi-double, deep warm pink, slightly cupped on first opening, strongly scented, some think, of raspberry. Mid-June to July but recurrent flowering with a good later summer season.

'Africa Star' Fl.
Rosy-mauve, 1½ ft (0·5 m.) 1965
Raised by O. West, Rhodesia.
A moderate grower, 1½ ft (0·5 m.) high, with dull bronze-green foliage. The full, short petalled flowers are rosy-mauve in colour and

are frequently quartered in appearance. Very slightly scented. Has a long flowering season but requires good cultivation and is subject to black spot.

'Agnes' Rg.
Amber-yellow, recurrent, 8 ft (2·4 m.) 1922
Raised by Dr W. Saunders, Canada.
Parentage: *R. rugosa* × *R. foetida persiana*
Very vigorous tall *rugosa* hybrid up to 8 ft (2·4 m.) with spreading arching branches. Flowers double, pale tawny or amber-yellow, paling nearly to cream at edge, ball-shaped, about 3 in. (7·6 cm.) across with crinkled petals and deeper in colour towards centre. Very floriferous. Scented. Early to mid-June and slightly recurrent. Foliage dark green. Makes a large straggly bush. The flower has very little appearance of *R. rugosa* but the foliage and vigour show signs of this ancestry. **128**, p. 23.
A.M., R.H.S. 1951.

'Alain Blanchard' C.
Purplish-crimson, summer, 4 ft (1·2 m.) 1829
Raised by Vibert, France.
An old shrub rose of medium size, often rather straggly, up to 4ft (1·2 m.). Flowers bright purplish-crimson, semi-double, cupped when first opening. As it matures, the flower becomes mottled with deeper maroon shading, and petals become more purple, sometimes with a mottled effect of lighter crimson. Mid to late June. Not one of the most effective varieties. A much improved cultivar, possibly a sport from the original, is known as 'Alain Blanchard Panachée' in which the flowers are richer in colour and striped with deep purplish-crimson.

'Alain Blanchard Panachée' see under **'Alain Blanchard'**

'Alba', *R. rugosa alba* Rg.
White, recurrent, 5 × 5 ft (1·5 × 1·5 m.)
Vigorous spreading shrub up to 5 ft (1·5 m.) and as much across. Flowers single, large, pure white with a silky texture and pale brown stamens, up to 3½ in. (8·9 cm.) across. Mid to late June and recurrent throughout summer. Foliage light apple-green, rugulose. Probably an albino form of the species. Hips large, bright orange-scarlet maturing to deep tomato-red, broadly flask-shaped. **129**, p. 23.

'Alba Maxima' A.
White, summer, 8 ft (2·4 m.)
The Great Double White or Jacobite Rose. A vigorous shrub up to 8 ft (2·4 m.) and sometimes as much through. Flowers double or semi-double, of medium size, creamy-white, tinged buff, slightly at first, becoming almost pure white, opening flat, scented, free-flowering. Mid to late June and not recurrent. Foliage grey-green. A very old form which has withstood great neglect. Close to 'Great Maidens' Blush' but with less pink and more fully double. *R.* 'Alba Semiplena' is usually regarded as a sport from 'Alba Maxima'. It was obviously much more widely grown in the last century than it is today and was included in some of the old Dutch flower pieces as well as in later paintings. **62**, p. 12.

'Albéric Barbier' R.
Creamy-white, early summer, 25 ft (7·6 m.) 1900
Raised by Barbier, France.
Parentage: *R. wichuraiana* × 'Shirley Hibberd'
Very vigorous rambler. Flowers single or in small clusters, bud creamy-white flushed with buff-yellow towards centre, fully double, opening to an almost white flower with a pale buff-yellow centre, rather formless when mature, 3½ in. (8·9 cm.) across.

Slightly scented. Mid-season, mid to late June with a few scattered flowers later in season. Very floriferous. Foliage dark glossy green, 5 pointed leaflets on the reddish petioles, long lasting, almost ever-green. Still a very desirable rose for its very healthy, rich shining foliage; its great vigorous shoots 10 ft (3 m.) long, and its pleasant combination of cool greenery and pale yellow. Excellent for growing into an old tree or will cover a large pillar. **192**, p. 36.

'Albertine'   R.

Coppery-pink, early summer, 20 ft (6·1 m.) 1921
Raised by Barbier, France.
Parentage: *R. wichuraiana* × 'Mrs Arthur Robert Waddell'
Very vigorous, woody rambler. Flowers in small clusters, warm coppery-pink or salmon-pink, semi-double, nearly double, 4 in. (10·2 cm.) across, bud bright salmon-red, strongly scented, like a small Hybrid Tea when young. Very floriferous. Mid-season, mid to late June but not recurrent. Foliage good, deep green with 5 small leaflets. One of the most vigorous of climbers, giving an abundance of flower in mid-June. It is excellent for covering a wall or fence or growing up into a tree. Will easily cover a wall space 20 ft (6·1 m.) high and 20 ft (6·1 m.) long, with flowers so dense that hardly any green will show. Very prickly. After flowering the woody flowering shoots may be cut out or cut back to young vigorous growth. Don't be afraid to prune vigorously as the rose will repay with a greater vigour. Still deservedly one of the most popular climbing roses. It tends to fade quickly in hot sun but scent carries strongly in the air. Resists bad weather well but susceptible to mildew. **193**, p. 36.

'Alec's Red'   HT.

Cherry-red, 3 ft (0·9 m.) 1970
Raised by J. Cocker & Sons Ltd, Scotland.
Parentage: 'Duftwolke' × 'Dame de Coeur'
A vigorous upright grower, 3 ft (0·9 m.) in height with light to medium green, mat foliage. The large, full flowers are sometimes borne singly on strong stems, or, especially in autumn, in trusses of several together. Cherry-red in colour, very fragrant, the blooms flatten out when fully open and present a colourful spectacle in the garden. This new cultivar has already aroused tremendous interest amongst professional growers, an interest quickly extending to amateurs. Provides a prolific crop of bloom in summer and again in autumn, with some blooms between. One of the best reds at the present time. **269**, p. 51.
C.M., R.N.R.S. 1969; H.E.M.M., R.N.R.S. 1969; P.I.T., R.N.R.S. 1970; G.M., R.N.R.S. 1970.

'Alison Wheatcroft'   Fl.

Deep apricot, 2½ ft (0·8 m.) 1959
Discovered by Wheatcroft Bros Ltd, England.
Parentage: 'Circus' sport
A more robust grower than the parent, 2½ ft (0·8 m.) high, with dark green, bronze-tinted foliage. The flowers are deep apricot, edged and flushed crimson, semi-double, opening quickly so that the centre soon shows. Flowers very freely summer and autumn and resists weather fairly well. A light scent. This cultivar provides a more colourful bed than its parent. May require protection against mildew and black spot.

'Allegro'   HT.

Geranium-red, 4 ft (1·2 m.) 1962
Raised by A. Meilland, France.
Parentage: ('Happiness' × 'Independence') × 'Soraya'
A vigorous, very upright grower, up to 4 ft (1·2 m.) high with glossy, dark green foliage. The bright geranium-red blooms are of medium size, generally borne 3 to 5 per stem, but frequently singly, and are resistant to rain. Little scent. Useful for cutting, but too tall to be effective for bedding.
R.G.M. 1962; H.G.M. 1962; A.M., R.H.S. 1962.

'Allen Chandler'   Cl.

Deep crimson, early summer, 15 × 15 ft (4·6 × 4·6 m.) 1923
Raised by Chandler, England.
Parentage: 'Hugh Dickson' × unnamed seedling
Very vigorous climber. Flowers in small clusters of up to 3, bright deep crimson, velvety, very large, 5½ in. (14 cm.) across, semi-double showing yellow stamens, very floriferous, scented, early to mid-June with a 3-week season, but recurrent through summer after main flush. Foliage good with large leaflets of hybrid tea type. Probably still the finest general purpose deep crimson climber. There is a wonderful specimen on the gatehouse at Sissinghurst Castle, England, where it grows up to 20 ft (6·1 m.) and as much across and is covered with flower each year. It is more vigorous than 'Climbing Etoile de Hollande' though without such strong scent, much larger in flower and deeper in colour than 'Paul's Scarlet Climber' (**219**, p. 40). Orange-red hips in autumn, but these are seldom seen as old roses are cut off. **194**, p. 36.
G.M., R.N.R.S. 1923.

'Allgold'   Fl.

Bright buttercup-yellow, 2½ ft (0·8 m.) 1956
Raised by E. B. LeGrice, England.
Parentage: 'Goldilocks' × 'Ellinor LeGrice'
A moderately vigorous, compact grower, 2½ ft (0·8 m.) high, with glossy, bright green, small, very healthy foliage. The slightly scented flowers are semi-double, bright buttercup-yellow, remarkably stable in colour and rain resistant. Commencing to flower early, this is a profuse bloomer and continues until late in the season. Disease resistant and not yet surpassed as a bedder in this colour. **378**, p. 71.
G.M., R.N.R.S. 1956; A.M., R.H.S. 1956.

Abbreviations and Symbols used in the text

Rose classifications

A.	Alba		HT.	Hybrid Tea
B.	Bourbon		MCl.	Modern, large-flowered climber
C.	Centifolia		Min.	Miniature
Ch.	China		Moss	Centifolia muscosa
Cl.	Climber		MSh.	Modern shrub
D.	Damask		P.	Penzance Sweet Brier
Fl.	Floribunda		R.	Rambler
G.	Gallica		Rg.	Rugosa
HM.	Hybrid Musk		Sp.	Species and first hybrids
HP.	Hybrid Perpetual		Sw.	Sweet Brier

Rose Awards and Societies

A.A.R.S.	All-America Rose Selection
A.G.M.	Award of Garden Merit
A.M.	Award of Merit
A.R.S.	American Rose Society
B.B.G.M.	Baden Baden Gold Medal, Germany
B.G.M.	Bagatelle Gold Medal, Paris
C.C.V.	Clay Challenge Vase for scent
C.M.	Certificate of Merit
D.F.P.	David Fuerstenberg Prize
F.C.C.	First Class Certificate
G.G.M.	Geneva Gold Medal
G.M.	Gold Medal
G.M.C.B.	Gold Medal City of Belfast
G.M.H.G.M.	Gertrude M. Hubbard Gold Medal
G.R.H.	Golden Rose of The Hague
G.T.A.B.	Golden Thorn Award Belfast
H.E.M.M.	The Henry Edland Memorial Medal for the most fragrant rose of the year
H.G.M.	The Hague Gold Medal
L.G.M.	Lyon Gold Medal, France
M.G.M.	Madrid Gold Medal
N.G.M.C.	National Gold Medal Certificate
P.G.M.	Portland Gold Medal, Oregon, U.S.A.
P.I.T.	President's International Trophy
R.B.	Prize for the most fragrant rose, Roeulx, Belgium
R.B.G.M.	Roeulx, Belgium, Gold Medal
R.G.M.	Rome Gold Medal
R.H.S.	The Royal Horticultural Society, London
R.N.R.S.	The Royal National Rose Society, Great Britain*
T.G.C.	Trial Ground Certificate
U.A.B.	The 'Uladh' Award for fragrance, Belfast

National Rose Society awards, before 1965, are included here under R.N.R.S.

The illustration numbers are in **bold type** and the page numbers in light type preceded by p.

'Allgold, Climbing' see **'Climbing Allgold', 236**, p. 50.

'Aloha'   MCl.Sh.
Pink, recurrent, 5–10 ft (1·5–3 m.) 1949
Raised by E. S. Boerner, U.S.A.
Parentage: 'Mercedes Gallart' × 'New Dawn'
Climber or shrub rose of moderate vigour, about 5 or 10 ft (1·5–3 m.), depending on cultivation. Hybrid tea type flowers, double, large, deep pink in centre, fading to blush-pink near outside, centre becoming salmon-terracotta as it ages, scented, free-flowering. Mid to late June and recurrent. One of the best recent introductions possibly owing some of its free-flowering to 'New Dawn' but much larger in flower and deeper in colour. With pruning it can also be grown as a large shrub. **230**, p. 43.

'Altissimo'   MCl.Sh.
Blood-red-crimson, recurrent, 6–8 ft (1·8–2·4 m.) 1966
Raised by Delbard-Chabert, France.
Parentage: 'Ténor' × unrecorded rose
Climber or shrub rose of moderate vigour, 6 to 8 ft (1·8–2·4 m.). Flowers singly or in small clusters, single, very large up to 5 in. (12·7 cm.) across, blood-red shaded crimson, velvety, with large central boss of golden-brown stamens. Free-flowering. Unscented. Mid-June, recurrent flowering till late autumn; does not appear to fade in bright sun. Young shoots purplish-crimson. Foliage mat, deep green with large leaflets. Hips large. A sturdy grower and a very promising addition to the deep red recurrent climbers and a very good colour. **231**, p. 43.
C.M., R.N.R.S. 1965; G.M., Orléans 1969.

'Ama'   Fl.
Light scarlet-crimson, 2½ ft (0·8 m.) 1955
Raised by W. Kordes, Germany.
Parentage: 'Obergärtner Wiebicke' × 'Independence'
A vigorous, compact grower, 2½ ft (0·8 m.) high, with semi-glossy, dark green, abundant foliage. The light scarlet-crimson flowers are semi-double, very freely produced in summer and autumn, in fair sized trusses of about 5 flowers. Weather resistance is good. A good bedding cultivar which is also effective as a standard. **379**, p. 71.

'Ambrosia'   Fl.
Amber, 2½ ft (0·8 m.) 1962
Raised by A. Dickson & Sons Ltd, N. Ireland.
Parentage: seedling × 'Shepherd's Delight'
A moderately vigorous grower, 2½ ft (0·8 m.) high with mat dark foliage. The large single flowers are amber and assume mauve tints with age, an unusual but pleasing colour. Lightly scented. Production of bloom free over a long period in large clusters.

'American Pillar'   R.
Pink, summer, 15 ft (4·6 m.) 1902
Raised by Dr W. Van Fleet, U.S.A.
Parentage: (*R. wichuraiana* × *R. setigera*) × unnamed red Hybrid Perpetual
Very vigorous rambler. Flowers in large clusters, single, bright bluish-pink with white eye, each flower quite large, very floriferous. Unscented. Summer flowering late June to mid-July but not recurrent. Formerly a very popular rose but possibly superseded by the Kordes' recurrent-flowering climber 'Dortmund' (**241**, p. 45) which is a much pleasanter colour. Subject to mildew. Should be pruned hard by cutting out flowering shoots down to ground in late July and tying in new shoots. Suitable for rose arch or pergola. **195**, p. 36.
A.M., R.H.S. 1909.

'America's Junior Miss'   Fl.
Soft coral-pink, 3 ft (0·9 m.) 1964
Raised by E. S. Boerner, U.S.A.
Parentage: 'Seventeen' × 'Demure' seedling
A vigorous, bushy grower, 2½–3 ft (0·8–0·9 m.) high with glossy foliage. The double, medium sized flowers are soft coral-pink, fragrant and freely produced. Good for cut flowers, attractive for decorative purposes. Sometimes improperly known as 'Junior Miss'. **380**, p. 71.

'Amy Robsart' see under *R. eglanteria*, **8**, p. 2.

'Anna Louisa'   Fl.
Blush-pink, 2 ft (0·6 m.) 1967
Raised by G. de Ruiter, Holland.
Parentage: 'Highlight' × 'Valeta'
A low grower of branching habit, about 2 ft (0·6 m.) high with glossy mid-green foliage. Produced in small trusses, the flowers are medium sized, hybrid tea shaped, of a delicate blush-pink shade and have definite charm. Resists wet well but may require protection against black spot. **381**, p. 71.

'Anna Wheatcroft'   Fl.
Light vermilion, 2½ ft (0·8 m.) 1958
Raised by M. Tantau, Germany.
Parentage: 'Cinnabar' seedling × unknown
A fairly robust grower with glossy, dark green foliage, which attains a height of 2½ ft (0·8 m.). The large semi-double flowers are an attractive shade of light vermilion which deepens with age and are enhanced by the golden-yellow stamens. A profuse bloomer, it often produces large heads in the autumn which can be very effective when used for exhibition. Slight scent.
A.M., R.H.S. 1957; T.G.C., R.N.R.S. 1960.

'Anne Cocker'   Fl.
Light vermilion, 3 ft (0·9 m.) 1969
Raised by J. Cocker & Sons Ltd, Scotland.
Parentage: 'Highlight' × 'Königin der Rosen'
An upright vigorous grower, 2½–3 ft (0·8–0·9 m.) high with mid-green glossy foliage. The medium sized flowers are borne in large trusses with fairly long individual stems to each flower, are light vermilion in colour rather late in coming into bloom but free-flowering afterwards. Last well when cut, but have no scent. This cultivar is quite distinctive in appearance and should be useful for exhibitors of Floribunda roses in addition to its garden value. May require protection from mildew in bad areas. **382**, p. 71.
C.M., R.N.R.S. 1969.

'Anne Letts'   HT.
Pale pink, 2½ ft (0·8 m.) 1953
Raised by G. F. Letts & Sons, England.
Parentage: 'Peace' × 'Charles Gregory'
A vigorous, tall branching grower, 2½ ft (0·8 m.) high, very thorny, with large dark green, glossy foliage. The moderately full blooms are pale pink, paler on reverse side, giving a silvery effect, and generally of sufficiently fine form to be good for exhibition when disbudded. Very free-flowering producing two good crops, but very susceptible to damage from rain. Protection against mildew and black spot may be required in some areas. Sweetly scented.
C.M., R.N.R.S. 1953.

'Anne of Geierstein' see under *R. eglanteria*

'Anne Watkins'   HT.
Apricot, 3 ft (o·9 m.) 1963
Raised by Watkins Roses Ltd, England.
Parentage: 'Ena Harkness' × 'Grand'mère Jenny'
A fairly vigorous grower, 3 ft (o·9 m.) high, with a very upright habit but somewhat thin in appearance. Should be planted about 1½ ft (o·5 m.) apart to create a good effect in the garden. Foliage is semi-glossy, dark green and rather small. Blooms are moderately full, shapely apricot with light creamy-pink flushes and flushed red on outside petals. Flowers are freely produced in summer and autumn, with a few between, often singly, sometimes 3 to each stem. Colour retention and weather resistance are very good and there is some scent. Protection against black spot may be required. C.M., R.N.R.S. 1962.

'Anny'   Min.
Shell-pink, 6 in. (15·2 cm.) 1949
Raised by P. Dot, Spain.
Parentage: 'Rouletii' × 'Perla de Montserrat'
A dainty, well proportioned plant, 4–6 in. high (10·2–15·2 cm.), on its own roots. The very small, ½ in. (1·3 cm.) flowers are a delicate shell-pink fading to white. Very attractive.

Apothecary's Rose see **'Officinalis', 86**, p. 16.

Apple Rose see *R. pomifera*, **37**, p. 7.

'Apricot Nectar'   Fl.
Pinkish-apricot, 3 ft (o·9 m.) 1965
Raised by E. S. Boerner, U.S.A.
Parentage: unnamed seedling × 'Spartan'
A vigorous bushy grower, 3 ft (o·9 m.) high with dark green glossy foliage. The double, somewhat cupped flowers are an attractive pinkish-apricot with yellow base and are freely produced over a long season. Suspected of being addicted to virus when first introduced, this charming rose seems to have got rid of this affliction and is well worth a place, especially if pastel colours are appreciated. Pleasant scent. **383**, p. 72.
A.A.R.S. 1966.

'Apricot Silk'   HT.
Apricot, 4 ft (1·2 m.) 1965
Raised by C. Gregory & Son Ltd, England.
Parentage: 'Souvenir de Jacques Verschuren' seedling
A fairly vigorous grower, 4 ft (1·2 m.) high, with glossy, dark green, bronze tinted foliage. The long pointed buds open into attractive apricot flowers which are moderately full, freely produced and stand well when cut. Mildew prone in some gardens. **270**, p. 51.

'Arabian Nights'   Fl.
Salmon-orange, 3 ft (o·9 m.) 1963
Raised by S. McGredy IV, N. Ireland.
Parentage: 'Spartan' × 'Beauté'
A tall vigorous grower, 3 ft (o·9 m.) high, with plentiful, deep green foliage, crimson tinted when young. The large double flowers are produced in clusters, with few but large petals, which open quickly in an attractive salmon-orange and are slightly fragrant. **384**, p. 72.
T.G.C., R.N.R.S. 1964.

'Arakan'   Fl.
Pale rosy-pink, 2 ft (o·6 m.) 1968
Raised by R. Harkness & Co. Ltd, England.
Parentage: 'Pink Parfait' × 'Ivory Fashion'

An upright, neat growing Floribunda, about 2 ft (o·6 m.) high, with well formed double flowers, very pale rosy-pink with a slight scent. Useful for cutting. May require protection against mildew. **385**, p. 72.

'Arianna'   HT.
Carmine-rose, 2½ ft (o·8 m.) 1968
Raised by M. L. Meilland, France.
Parentage: 'Charlotte Armstrong' × ('Peace' × 'Michèle Meilland')
A vigorous, upright grower with dark leathery foliage. The large double flowers are carmine-rose, suffused coral, high centred, freely produced and have a slight scent. **271**, p. 51.
B.G.M. 1965; R.G.M. 1965; H.G.M. 1965.

'Arthur Bell'   Fl.
Bright yellow, 3 ft (o·9 m.) 1965
Raised by S. McGredy IV, N. Ireland.
Parentage: 'Cläre Grammerstorf' × 'Piccadilly'
A vigorous, very upright grower, at least 3 ft (o·9 m.) high with abundant, very glossy, mid-green foliage. The large, semi-double flowers, shapely when young becoming cup shaped when open, are bright yellow paling to cream as they age and produced in clusters of about 5, sometimes more. This cultivar resists wet weather well and is unusually fragrant for a Floribunda. **386**, p. 72.
C.M., R.N.R.S. 1964.

'Assemblage des Beautés', 'Rouge Eblouissante'   G.
Bright purplish-crimson, summer, 4 ft (1·2 m.) *c.* 1790

Abbreviations and Symbols used in the text

Rose classifications

A.	Alba	HT.	Hybrid Tea
B.	Bourbon	MCl.	Modern, large-flowered climber
C.	Centifolia	Min.	Miniature
Ch.	China	Moss	Centifolia muscosa
Cl.	Climber	MSh.	Modern shrub
D.	Damask	P.	Penzance Sweet Brier
Fl.	Floribunda	R.	Rambler
G.	Gallica	Rg.	Rugosa
HM.	Hybrid Musk	Sp.	Species and first hybrids
HP.	Hybrid Perpetual	Sw.	Sweet Brier

Rose Awards and Societies

A.A.R.S.	All-America Rose Selection
A.G.M.	Award of Garden Merit
A.M.	Award of Merit
A.R.S.	American Rose Society
B.B.G.M.	Baden Baden Gold Medal, Germany
B.G.M.	Bagatelle Gold Medal, Paris
C.C.V.	Clay Challenge Vase for scent
C.M.	Certificate of Merit
D.F.P.	David Fuerstenberg Prize
F.C.C.	First Class Certificate
G.G.M.	Geneva Gold Medal
G.M.	Gold Medal
G.M.C.B.	Gold Medal City of Belfast
G.M.H.G.M.	Gertrude M. Hubbard Gold Medal
G.R.H.	Golden Rose of The Hague
G.T.A.B.	Golden Thorn Award Belfast
H.E.M.M.	The Henry Edland Memorial Medal for the most fragrant rose of the year
H.G.M.	The Hague Gold Medal
L.G.M.	Lyon Gold Medal, France
M.G.M.	Madrid Gold Medal
N.G.M.C.	National Gold Medal Certificate
P.G.M.	Portland Gold Medal, Oregon, U.S.A.
P.I.T.	President's International Trophy
R.B.	Prize for the most fragrant rose, Roeulx, Belgium
R.B.G.M.	Roeulx, Belgium, Gold Medal
R.G.M.	Rome Gold Medal
R.H.S.	The Royal Horticultural Society, London
R.N.R.S.	The Royal National Rose Society, Great Britain*
T.G.C.	Trial Ground Certificate
U.A.B.	The 'Uladh' Award for fragrance, Belfast

National Rose Society awards, before 1965, are included here under R.N.R.S.

The illustration numbers are in **bold type** and the page numbers in light type preceded by p.

Shrub rose of medium size and compact habit. Flowers bright pinkish-crimson, flushed with purple, fully double and quartered, but sometimes showing a small button eye in centre, about 3 in. (7·6 cm.) across, in small clusters. Mid to late June. Leaflets large, slightly rugulose, usually 5. A striking Gallica rose but one which does not really live up to its name, and now rarely seen in gardens.

'Atlantis'   Fl.
Light purplish-lilac, 2½ ft (0·8 m.) 1970
Raised by R. Harkness & Co. Ltd, England.
Parentage: 'Orangeade' × 'Lilac Charm'
A fairly vigorous, upright grower, 2½ ft (0·8 m.) high, with very shiny foliage. The single flowers are produced in clusters, an unusual shade of light purplish-lilac, showing yellow stamens. Little scent. This cultivar brings another unusual colour into roses. May require protection against mildew.
R.G.M. 1969.

Attar of Roses see *R. damascena trigintipetala*

Austrian Copper see *R. foetida bicolor,* **16,** p. 3.

'Autumn Sunlight'   MCl.
Bright orange-vermilion, recurrent, 8 ft (2·4 m.) 1965
Raised by C. Gregory & Son Ltd, England.
Parentage: 'Danse du Feu' × 'Climbing Goldilocks'
Vigorous modern climber or pillar rose with flowers of hybrid tea type. Flowers of medium size, double, very bright orange-vermilion, singly or in small clusters, free-flowering, scented; mid to late June and recurrent. Foliage bright green, glossy. A promising new rose for those who like this very strong colour.

'Baby Carnaval' see **'Baby Masquerade', 501,** p. 96.

'Baby Crimson' see **'Perla de Alcanada'**

'Baby Darling'   Min.
Salmon-orange, 12 in. (30·5 cm.) 1964
Raised by R. S. Moore, U.S.A.
Parentage: 'Little Darling' × 'Magic Wand'
A dwarf bushy plant, 8–12 in. (20·3–30·5 cm.) high, with small double flowers in an attractive blend of salmon-orange. Resistant to mildew.

'Baby Gold' see **'Baby Gold Star'**

'Baby Gold Star', 'Estrellita de Oro'   Min.
Cream to deep butter-yellow, 15 in. (38·1 cm.) 1935
Raised by P. Dot, Spain.
Parentage: 'Eduardo Toda' × 'Rouletii'
A medium to large plant depending on whether it is on its own roots or on a stock, up to 15 in. (38·1 cm.). The colour also varies from cream to deep butter-yellow. Slightly fragrant. Name sometimes wrongly abbreviated to 'Baby Gold'.

'Baby Masquerade', 'Baby Carnaval'   Min.
Yellow to dark red, 15 in. (38·1 cm.) 1956
Raised by M. Tantau, Germany.
Parentage: 'Tom Thumb' × 'Masquerade'
A vigorous grower up to 15 in. (38·1 cm.) high, rather coarse for this class, especially when on a stock. Like 'Masquerade', the

flowers are yellow, changing to pink and crimson, darkening as the flowers age. Petals roll back along the edges, presenting a starry appearance. Flowers freely over a long period and has a slight fragrance. One of the most popular cultivars which is also very attractive as a standard on a 12 in. (30·5 cm.) stem. **501,** p. 96.

'Baby Ophelia'   Min.
Pink, 12 in. (30·5 cm.) 1961
Raised by R. S. Moore, U.S.A.
Parentage: *(R. wichuraiana* × 'Floradora') × 'Little Buckaroo'
A bushy grower, 8–10 in. (20·3–25·4 cm.) high, with glossy foliage. The small flowers are slightly cupped, shell-pink suffused apricot and yellow at base. Very free-flowering and fragrant.

'Baccara'   HT.
Vermilion, 3 ft (0·9 m.) 1956
Raised by F. Meilland, France.
Parentage: 'Happiness' × 'Independence'
A vigorous upright grower with glossy dark green foliage, reddish-bronze in early stages of growth, 3 ft (0·9 m.) in height but attaining more under glass where it is generally grown for cut flower markets. The full, well formed flowers are of medium size, vermilion-red with darker shading on outer petals but are devoid of scent. Seldom grown out of doors as it dislikes rain, but very suitable for cutting and, when grown under glass, stands well. A good cropper.

'Ballerina'   MSh.
Pink, recurrent, 4 ft (1·2 m.) 1937
This rose, with some resemblance to a Polyantha, is an attractive vigorous grower up to 4 ft (1·2 m.) in height and therefore suitable for bedding. The small, abundant foliage is semi-glossy and light green, presenting an air of lightness in keeping with the delicate pink single flowers which have a white centre. Produced abundantly in summer in large trusses, with a good autumn performance to follow, they resist weather well and have a slight musk fragrance. Bentall is credited with raising this cultivar although he may have found it on the Reverend J. H. Pemberton's nursery when he took it over, or alternatively, bred it from Hybrid Musks there. Makes a good standard. **140,** p. 25.

'Ballet'   HT.
Deep rose-pink, 2½ ft (0·8 m.) 1958
Raised by R. Kordes, Germany.
Parentage: 'Florex' × 'Karl Herbst'
A vigorous, branching grower of medium height with semi-glossy, light green foliage. The deep rose-pink blooms are full and shapely and bear a strong resemblance to 'Dame Edith Helen' but are almost scentless. A good bedding rose which resists weather well but may require protection from black spot. **272,** p. 51.
A.M., R.H.S. 1962.

'Bambino'   Min.
Rose-pink, 12 in. (30·5 cm.) 1953
Discovered by P. Dot, Spain.
Parentage: 'Perla de Alcanada' sport
A compact grower with perfectly shaped rose-pink blooms. Flowers freely and has a slight scent.

'Bantry Bay'   MCl.
Light rose-pink, recurrent, 9–10 ft (2·7–3 m.) 1967
Raised by S. McGredy IV, N. Ireland.
Parentage: 'New Dawn' × 'Korona'
A vigorous grower, well clothed with medium green, semi-glossy foliage. The fairly large flowers are semi-double light rose-pink,

tinged salmon and borne in profusion in well spaced trusses throughout the season. Suitable for pillar, wall or fence. **232**, p. 43. C.M., R.N.R.S. 1967.

'Baron Girod de l'Ain'   HP.
Dark crimson, recurrent, 5 ft (1·5 m.) 1897
Discovered by Reverchon, France.
Parentage: 'Eugène Fürst' sport
Vigorous Hybrid Perpetual shrub rose, usually not over 5 ft (1·5 m.). Flowers large, double, bright darkish crimson-red with a white edge to petals which are pleasantly crinkled with wavy edge, 3–4 in. (7·6–10·2 cm.) across, cup-shaped on opening. Retains its colour well, maturing to a good purplish-crimson. Strongly scented. Mid to late June and slightly recurrent throughout summer and autumn. Rather similar in flower to 'Roger Lambelin' (**115**, p. 20) but usually makes a more vigorous shrub. One of the finest roses in this group for its colour. Foliage with large broad leaflets. **106**, p. 19.

'Baroness Rothschild'   HP.
Deep pink, recurrent, 6 ft (1·8 m.) 1868
Discovered by Pernet Père, France.
Parentage: 'Souvenir de la Reine d'Angleterre' sport
Vigorous Hybrid Perpetual shrub up to 6 ft (1·8 m.). Flowers large, double, deep pink towards centre, lighter shell-pink on outside, cupped on opening, outer petals recurving. Free-flowering, scented. Like a small double tree paeony but tends to be rather untidy when going over. Mid to late June and slightly recurrent in autumn. Foliage with large leaflets. **107**, p. 19.
F.C.C., R.H.S. 1868, as 'Mme La Baronne de Rothschild'.

'Baronne Edmond de Rothschild'   HT.
Ruby-red, 3½ ft (1·1 m.) 1968
Raised by A. & F. Meilland, France.
Parentage: ('Baccara' × 'Crimson King') × 'Peace'
A vigorous grower, 3½ ft (1·1 m.) high with glossy dark green, leathery foliage. The large double, high centred flowers are unfading ruby-red with silvery-rose reverse and are very fragrant. This cultivar has been wrongly offered in some catalogues as 'Baroness Rothschild', a name already given to a Hybrid Perpetual rose which is still in cultivation and described above.
R.G.M. 1968; L.G.M. 1968.

'Baronne Prévost'   HP.
Purplish-pink, recurrent, 5 ft (1·5 m.) 1842
Raised by Desprez, France.
Hybrid Perpetual shrub of medium vigour and erect growth, usually not over 5 ft (1·5 m.). Flowers large, bright purplish-pink, double, opening flat and quartered like a Damask rose, with a small button eye in centre, about 4 in. (10·2 cm.) across. Free-flowering, scented. Mid to late June and recurrent through summer and early autumn. **108**, p. 19.

'Beatrice'   Fl.
Pink, 2½ ft (0·8 m.) 1968
Raised by S. McGredy IV, N. Ireland.
Parentage: 'Paddy McGredy' × ('Kordes' Perfecta' × 'Montezuma')
A vigorous, upright grower, about 2½ ft (0·8 m.) high. The rose-pink blooms are very freely produced in medium sized, well shaped trusses. One of the most continuous blooming cultivars I know, beginning early and going right through until late September, when the photograph was taken. Slightly fragrant. Useful for public park and garden display. **387**, p. 72.

'Beauté'   HT.
Light orange, 2½ ft (0·8 m.) 1953
Raised by C. Mallerin, France.
Parentage: 'Mme Joseph Perraud' × unnamed seedling
A fairly vigorous, branching grower, just over 2½ ft (0·8 m.) high. Foliage is abundant, dark green and semi-glossy. The long pointed orange buds open into warm, light orange flowers, shapely but rather loose, weather resistant and with a slight fragrance. Free-flowering and a good bedder. **273**, p. 51.
C.M., R.N.R.S. 1954.

'Beauty of Glazenwood' see under **R. × odorata**

'Beauty Secret'   Min.
Crimson-red, 12 in. (30·5 cm.) 1965
Raised by R. S. Moore, U.S.A.
Parentage: 'Little Darling' × 'Magic Wand'
A vigorous, bushy grower, 10–12 in. (25·4–30·5 cm.) high, with glossy foliage. Small double, high centred flowers, crimson-red in colour and very fragrant. A popular cultivar in the U.S.A.

'Bel Ange'   HT.
Rosy-salmon-pink, 3 ft (0·9 m.) 1962
Raised by L. Lens, Belgium.
Parentage: ('Independence' × 'Papillon Rose') × ('Charlotte Armstrong' × 'Floradora')
A strong upright grower with dark green foliage, tinted red. The

---

Abbreviations and Symbols used in the text

Rose classifications

A.	Alba	HT.	Hybrid Tea
B.	Bourbon	MCl.	Modern, large-flowered climber
C.	Centifolia	Min.	Miniature
Ch.	China	Moss	Centifolia muscosa
Cl.	Climber	MSh.	Modern shrub
D.	Damask	P.	Penzance Sweet Brier
Fl.	Floribunda	R.	Rambler
G.	Gallica	Rg.	Rugosa
HM.	Hybrid Musk	Sp.	Species and first hybrids
HP.	Hybrid Perpetual	Sw.	Sweet Brier

Rose Awards and Societies

A.A.R.S.	All-America Rose Selection
A.G.M.	Award of Garden Merit
A.M.	Award of Merit
A.R.S.	American Rose Society
B.B.G.M.	Baden Baden Gold Medal, Germany
B.G.M.	Bagatelle Gold Medal, Paris
C.C.V.	Clay Challenge Vase for scent
C.M.	Certificate of Merit
D.F.P.	David Fuerstenberg Prize
F.C.C.	First Class Certificate
G.G.M.	Geneva Gold Medal
G.M.	Gold Medal
G.M.C.B.	Gold Medal City of Belfast
G.M.H.G.M.	Gertrude M. Hubbard Gold Medal
G.R.H.	Golden Rose of The Hague
G.T.A.B.	Golden Thorn Award Belfast
H.E.M.M.	The Henry Edland Memorial Medal for the most fragrant rose of the year
H.G.M.	The Hague Gold Medal
L.G.M.	Lyon Gold Medal, France
M.G.M.	Madrid Gold Medal
N.G.M.C.	National Gold Medal Certificate
P.G.M.	Portland Gold Medal, Oregon, U.S.A.
P.I.T.	President's International Trophy
R.B.	Prize for the most fragrant rose, Roeulx, Belgium
R.B.G.M.	Roeulx, Belgium, Gold Medal
R.G.M.	Rome Gold Medal
R.H.S.	The Royal Horticultural Society, London
R.N.R.S.	The Royal National Rose Society, Great Britain*
T.G.C.	Trial Ground Certificate
U.A.B.	The 'Uladh' Award for fragrance, Belfast

National Rose Society awards, before 1965, are included here under R.N.R.S.

The illustration numbers are in **bold type** and the page numbers in light type preceded by p.

large double flowers are well formed, rosy-salmon-pink with a deeper pink reverse and are produced freely. Scented. A good garden rose which has sometimes been catalogued as 'Belle Epoque', a different cultivar.

'Belle Amour' A.
Pale salmon-pink, summer, 6 ft (1·8 m.)
Parentage: probably *R.* × *alba* × *R.* × *damascena* but origin unknown.
Found at and introduced from a convent in Germany. Vigorous shrub up to 6 ft (1·8 m.). Flowers semi-double, cupped on first opening, pale salmon-pink, strongly scented, with slight acrid spicy scent, which has been compared to myrrh. Flowers in clusters. Mid to late June. Foliage dark grey-green. **63**, p. 12.

'Belle Blonde' HT.
Golden-yellow, 2 ft (0·6 m.) 1955
Raised by F. Meilland, France.
Parentage: 'Peace' × 'Lorraine'
A fairly vigorous, upright grower of medium height with glossy dark green foliage. The full, medium sized flowers are bright golden-yellow, freely produced and fragrant. In black spot areas, some protection may be required.

'Belle de Crécy' G.
Deep pinkish-purple, summer, 5 ft (1·5 m.) before 1848?
Introduced by Roeser, France.
Gallica rose of loose, rather straggly growth and medium vigour up to 5 ft (1·5 m.). Flowers pink in bud, opening deep pinkish-purple, maturing rather untidily to violet-mauve; small to medium size, mid-June. Flowers of rather similar colour to 'Cardinal de Richelieu' but not such a good flower. Scented. Poor in a very dry season but perhaps better with more moisture; other authors have been more enthusiastic. Raised probably early in the nineteenth century. Nearly thornless.

'Belle des Jardins' see *R.* × *centifolia* **'Variegata'**

'Belle of Portugal' see **'Belle Portugaise'**

'Belle Poitevine' Rg.
Pale purplish-pink, 5 × 5 ft (1·5 × 1·5 m.) 1894
Raised by G. Bruant, France.
A vigorous Rugosa hybrid up to 5 ft (1·5 m.) and as much across, making a large bush, and also suitable for an informal hedge. Flowers large, semi-double, pale purplish-pink, deeper in bud, opening flat. Scent slight. Early to mid-June and recurrent. Foliage of rugosa type, bright green. Hips large, orange-red. Rarely grown but a good variety. Appears to be identical with 'Souvenir de Christophe Cochet'.

'Belle Portugaise', 'Belle of Portugal' Cl.
Pale pink, early summer, 16 ft (4·9 m.) 1903
Raised by H. Cayeux, Portugal.
Parentage: *R. gigantea* × 'Reine Marie Henriette'
Very vigorous Climber up to 16 ft (4·9 m.) or more but in cool climates requires to be planted on a warm wall. There is a famous old plant against the laboratory wall near the entrance to R.H.S. Garden, Wisley, England, reaching right to eaves. Flowers double, large, rather drooping, with long pointed buds, pale salmon-pink with outwardly rolled petals, opening to rather a loose flower. Strongly scented. Early to mid-June with abundant flowering but not recurrent. Foliage grey-green with pointed leaflets. These *gigantea* hybrids are magnificent and very vigorous climbers for warmer gardens as on French and Italian Rivieras and in California.
A.M., R.H.S. 1959.

'Bengali' Fl.
Orange and gold, 2 ft (0·6 m.) 1966
Raised by W. Kordes, Germany.
Parentage: 'Dacapo' × seedling
A bushy compact grower with medium sized flowers in an unusual shade of orange on a gold background. Delicately fragrant and flowering continuously during the summer. A promising bedder.

'Berlin' MSh.
Orange-scarlet, recurrent, 5 ft (1·5 m.) 1949
Raised by W. Kordes, Germany.
Parentage: 'Eva' × 'Peace'
A vigorous, upright shrub about 5 ft (1·5 m.) high with dark leathery foliage and large red thorns. The fine, single, orange-scarlet flowers 3½ in. (8·9 cm.) across, are enhanced by yellow stamens and produced in great clusters, intermittently over a long season. One of a large group raised by W. Kordes about 1949 with rather similar garden characters. Sometimes described as Hybrid Musk but more of a vigorous Floribunda type. Lightly scented. **141**, p. 25.

'Bettina' HT.
Orange, 2½ ft (0·8 m.) 1953
Raised by F. Meilland, France.
Parentage: 'Peace' × ('Mme Joseph Perraud' × 'Demain')
A vigorous grower of medium height with dark green, bronze tinted, glossy foliage. The orange blooms have a golden base and are heavily veined in deeper hues of red and bronze. Free-flowering, with some fragrance. Protection from black spot may be required. T.G.C., R.N.R.S. 1953.

'Betty Uprichard' HT.
Light salmon-pink, 3 ft (0·9 m.) 1922
Raised by A. Dickson & Sons Ltd, N. Ireland.
A cultivar well known to older rosarians, still fairly vigorous, growing to over 3 ft (0·9 m.), with light green, semi-glossy foliage. Semi-double flowers of light salmon-pink with coppery-carmine reverse, which are freely produced and sweetly scented. Protection from mildew is sometimes necessary for this distinctive rose. A.M., R.H.S. 1921.

'Birmingham Post' HT.
Pale pink, 3 ft (0·9 m.) 1969
Raised by Watkins Roses Ltd, England.
Parentage: 'Queen Elizabeth' × 'Wendy Cussons'
A vigorous upright grower, over 3 ft (0·9 m.) in height. The large, full blooms are pale pink with deeper reverse, of good shape and a slight scent. Foliage is luxuriant, leathery and medium green. The blooms last well and this should be a useful cultivar for the exhibitor. **274**, p. 51.
T.G.C., R.N.R.S. 1968.

'Bischofsstadt Paderborn' MSh.
Brilliant scarlet, summer, 4 ft (1·2 m.) 1964
Raised by R. Kordes, Germany.
A very vigorous grower, about 4 ft (1·2 m.) high, with immense trusses of single, saucer-shaped, brilliant scarlet flowers which are produced continuously throughout the summer.

'Bit o' Sunshine' Min.
Clear yellow, 18 in. (45·7 cm.) 1956
Raised by R. S. Moore, U.S.A.

Parentage: 'Copper Glow' × 'Zee'
A rather tall grower for this class, up to 18 in. (45·7 cm.) high. The semi-double flowers are also large, clear yellow, sometimes flushed red in cool weather. Fragrant.

'Black Boy' MSh.
Purplish-crimson, early summer, 6 ft (1·8 m.) 1958
Raised by W. Kordes, Germany.
Parentage: 'World's Fair' × 'Nuits de Young'
Modern shrub rose up to 6 ft (1·8 m.). Buds mossy. Flowers double, purplish-crimson, large but rather open and loose. Scented. Mid to late June and not noticeably recurrent. Raised by W. Kordes in 1958 in an attempt to combine the charm of an old rose with the recurrent flowering of a deep crimson Floribunda, but rarely grown now.

'Blairi No. 2' Cl.B.
Pale pink, early summer, 15 ft (4·6 m.) 1845
Raised by Blair, England.
Parentage: *R. chinensis* × 'Tuscany'
Bourbon climbing rose, vigorous up to 15 ft (4·6 m.). Flowers double, large pale blush-pink with deeper pink centre and deeper veining. Mid-June, and only slightly recurrent. A rose that is rarely seen today but which is still worth growing. There is a good specimen on the courtyard wall near the entrance to Hidcote garden, Gloucestershire, England. Shoots mahogany coloured. It is reported to resent strong winter pruning and old shoots which have flowered should be thinned out after flowering. **198**, p. 37.

'Blanc Double de Coubert' Rg.
White, recurrent, 5 × 5 ft (1·5 × 1·5 m.) 1892
Raised by Cochet-Cochet, France.
Parentage: possibly *R. rugosa* × 'Sombreuil'
Large spreading shrub up to 5 × 5 ft (1·5 × 1·5 m.). Flowers large, pure snowy-white, semi-double, beautifully formed with slightly pleated petals like silk, up to 4½ in. (11·4 cm.) across. Very fragrant. One of the most beautiful of the white roses, early June, recurrent throughout season. Forms a loose shrub, not quite so vigorous as *(rugosa)* 'Alba', but there are specimens 10 ft (3 m.) high and as much through. Hips not so frequent as in 'Alba' but when formed of equal size and shape, bright orange-scarlet. **130**, p. 23.
A.M., R.H.S. 1895; A.G.M., R.H.S.

'Blanche Moreau' Moss Sh.
White, summer, 5 ft (1·5 m.) 1880
Raised by Moreau-Robert, France.
Parentage: 'Comtesse de Murinais' × 'Quatre Saisons Blanc'
Shrub of medium vigour up to 5 ft (1·5 m.), very prickly with dark stems. Flowers of medium size, a good white with green button centre, double, about 3 in. (7·6 m.) across, scented, in small clusters. Bud well mossed, sticky, slightly fragrant and with brownish tinge in moss. Mid to late June but slightly recurrent with a few autumn flowers. One of the most beautiful and also one of the best growers among the Moss roses, the green and brown moss offsetting well the white of the flowers. A *centifolia* in type, it has been compared to a small camellia.

'Blessings' HT.
Soft coral-pink, 3 ft (0·9 m.) 1967
Raised by C. Gregory & Son Ltd, England.
Parentage: 'Queen Elizabeth' × unnamed seedling
A vigorous, bushy, branching grower up to 3 ft (0·9 m.) high, with rather dull foliage. The large flowers are full, borne several together, soft coral-pink in colour and slightly fragrant. Originally classed as a Floribunda, and illustrated here with the Floribundas, this rose has now been reclassified Hybrid Tea. A cultivar which has already proved to be an exceptionally good and attractive bedder. **388**, p. 72.
B.B.G.M.; C.M., R.N.R.S. 1968.

'Bloomfield Abundance' Ch.
Pale pink, recurrent, 6 ft (1·8 m.) 1920
Raised by G. C. Thomas, U.S.A.
Parentage: possibly 'Sylvia' (Rambler) × 'Dorothy Page-Roberts' (Hybrid Tea) *or* 'Cécile Brunner' sport
Shrub of medium vigour up to 6 ft (1·8 m.), close in appearance of flowers and with its neat small leaflets to 'Cécile Brunner'. Flowers small with narrow pointed buds, pale pink, shaped like a miniature Hybrid Tea rose. Free-flowering in large clusters from mid-June onwards. Distinguished from 'Cécile Brunner' by its habit of making vigorous long branching shoots with large clusters of flowers in late summer, and also by the very long calyx lobes, twice the length of the bud, which reflex downwards as the flower opens. 'Climbing Bloomfield Abundance' see under 'Climbing Cécile Brunner' (**264**, p. 50).
A.M., R.H.S. 1953.

'Bloomfield Abundance, Climbing' see under 'Climbing Cécile Brunner', 264, p. 50.

'Blue Boy' MSh.
Lilac-pink, early summer, 4½ ft (1·4 m.) 1958
Raised by W. Kordes, Germany.
Parentage: 'Louis Gimard' × 'Independence'
Modern shrub rose up to 4½ ft (1·4 m.) but not very vigorous and misnamed for colour. Flowers double, large, of hybrid tea form, lilac-pink flushed deep purplish-maroon with some violet tones, variable in colour as it matures and fades, fragrant. Not recurrent. Raised from an old Moss rose and a Floribunda.

Abbreviations and Symbols used in the text

Rose classifications

A.	Alba	HT.	Hybrid Tea
B.	Bourbon	MCl.	Modern, large-flowered climber
C.	Centifolia	Min.	Miniature
Ch.	China	Moss	Centifolia muscosa
Cl.	Climber	MSh.	Modern shrub
D.	Damask	P.	Penzance Sweet Brier
Fl.	Floribunda	R.	Rambler
G.	Gallica	Rg.	Rugosa
HM.	Hybrid Musk	Sp.	Species and first hybrids
HP.	Hybrid Perpetual	Sw.	Sweet Brier

Rose Awards and Societies

A.A.R.S.	All-America Rose Selection
A.G.M.	Award of Garden Merit
A.M.	Award of Merit
A.R.S.	American Rose Society
B.B.G.M.	Baden Baden Gold Medal, Germany
B.G.M.	Bagatelle Gold Medal, Paris
C.C.V.	Clay Challenge Vase for scent
C.M.	Certificate of Merit
D.F.P.	David Fuerstenberg Prize
F.C.C.	First Class Certificate
G.G.M.	Geneva Gold Medal
G.M.	Gold Medal
G.M.C.B.	Gold Medal City of Belfast
G.M.H.G.M.	Gertrude M. Hubbard Gold Medal
G.R.H.	Golden Rose of The Hague
G.T.A.B.	Golden Thorn Award Belfast
H.E.M.M.	The Henry Edland Memorial Medal for the most fragrant rose of the year
H.G.M.	The Hague Gold Medal
L.G.M.	Lyon Gold Medal, France
M.G.M.	Madrid Gold Medal
N.G.M.C.	National Gold Medal Certificate
P.G.M.	Portland Gold Medal, Oregon, U.S.A.
P.I.T.	President's International Trophy
R.B.	Prize for the most fragrant rose, Roeulx, Belgium
R.B.G.M.	Roeulx, Belgium, Gold Medal
R.G.M.	Rome Gold Medal
R.H.S.	The Royal Horticultural Society, London
R.N.R.S.	The Royal National Rose Society, Great Britain*
T.G.C.	Trial Ground Certificate
U.A.B.	The 'Uladh' Award for fragrance, Belfast

*National Rose Society awards, before 1965, are included here under R.N.R.S.

The illustration numbers are in **bold type** and the page numbers in light type preceded by p.

'Blue Moon' see **'Mainzer Fastnacht', 330**, p. 62.

'Blush China' see under *R. chinensis*

'Blush Damask'   D.
Pale lilac-pink, early summer, 4 ft (1·2 m.)
A Damask shrub of medium vigour, making a dense twiggy bush up
to 4 ft (1·2 m.). Flowers rather small but often abundant, double,
pale lilac-pink, darker in centre, quartered. Scented. Sometimes
nodding since stems are inclined to be weak. Mid-June. Foliage
dark green. A beautiful rose which is recommended for its free-
flowering habit, but its flowering season is rather short. Sometimes
known as 'Blush Gallica'. It has been suggested from its dense
twiggy habit that it might be a hybrid with a Scots Brier (*spinosissima*)
as it does not fit very easily into either the Damask or the Gallica
group. **77**, p. 14.

'Blush Gallica' see under **'Blush Damask'**, **77**, p. 14.

'Blush Rambler'   R.
Pale pink, summer, 15 ft (4·6 m.) 1903
Raised by B. R. Cant, England.
Parentage: 'Crimson Rambler' × 'The Garland'
Vigorous rambler up to 15 ft (4·6 m.), suitable for pillar or pergola
or for growing up into an old tree. Flowers in large clusters, semi-
double, rather small, up to 1½ in. (3·8 cm.) across, cupped, blush-
pink, deeper on opening with gold stamens, scented, free-flowering,
late June to early July but not recurrent. Foliage light green. Has
inherited strong *R. multiflora* characteristics from its parents. Not
so useful now that we have several recurrent climbers but still a
pretty rose where there is space. It is well grown in the Roserie de
L'Haÿ outside Paris.
A.M., R.H.S. 1903.

'Bond Street'   HT.
Deep salmon-pink, 3 ft (0·9 m.) 1965
Raised by S. McGredy IV, N. Ireland.
Parentage: 'Radar' × 'Queen Elizabeth'
A tall, upright vigorous grower, 3 ft (0·9 m.) high, with medium
green, semi-glossy foliage. The large, double flowers are deep
salmon-pink, deepening towards the edges of the petals. Fragrant
and free flowering. **275**, p. 52.
C.M., R.N.R.S. 1965.

'Bonn'   MSh.
Orange-scarlet, recurrent, 5 ft (1·5 m.) 1950
Raised by W. Kordes, Germany.
Parentage: 'Hamburg' × 'Independence'
An upright bushy grower, 5 ft (1·5 m.) high, with glossy foliage. The
semi-double flowers are produced in fairly large trusses of a dull
orange-scarlet colour which fades with a purplish tinge, typical of its
male parent. Sweet scent. If dead-headed, flowers over a long
season. If not dead-headed, produces a good crop of hips, which
colour to deep red late in the season. **142**, p. 25.
C.M., R.N.R.S. 1950; A.M., R.H.S. 1962.

'Bonsoir'   HT.
Peach, 3 ft (0·9 m.) 1968
Raised by A. Dickson & Sons Ltd, N. Ireland.
A vigorous upright grower to 3 ft (0·9 m.) with large, dark green,
glossy foliage. The very full blooms are shapely, freely produced,
peach-pink in colour with deeper shadings and are fragrant. This
rose does not like very wet weather but has already attracted
attention and is considered promising. **276**, p. 52.
C.M., R.N.R.S. 1966.

'Border Coral'   Fl.
Coral-salmon, 2 ft (0·6 m.) 1957
Raised by G. de Ruiter, Holland.
Parentage: 'Signal Red' × 'Fashion'
A vigorous, spreading grower, about 2 ft (0·6 m.) high, with glossy,
dark green foliage. The medium sized flowers are semi-double,
produced in clusters very freely, and are coral-salmon suffused with
yellow at the base. Slightly fragrant, this cultivar is at its best in
autumn. May require protection against black spot.
C.M., R.N.R.S. 1957.

'Boule de Neige'   B.
Creamy-white, summer, 5 ft (1·5 m.) 1867
Raised by F. Lacharme, France.
Parentage: 'Blanche Lafitte' × 'Sappho'
A vigorous Bourbon shrub up to 5 ft (1·5 m.), usually rather erect in
growth. Flowers double, creamy-white, usually with a little deep
pink towards edge of petals, rounded like a small white ball, about
2½ in. (6·4 cm.) across, pink in the bud. Scented. Borne in small
clusters. Mid-June but recurrent throughout summer. Foliage
rather dark green. One of the best roses in this group.

'Bourbon Queen', 'Souvenir de la Princesse de Lamballe'   B.
Purplish-pink, summer, 10 ft (3 m.) 1835
A rather loose growing but vigorous Bourbon shrub or pillar rose
up to 10 ft (3 m.). Usually pruned to grow as a lower shrub or
sometimes a hedge. Flowers semi-double, pink with purplish tint
towards centre, paler towards outer edges, good pink in bud,
cupped slightly on opening, about 3 in. (7·6 cm.) across. A little
deeper in colour than 'Fantin Latour', but not so floriferous.
Mid-June and only slightly recurrent. Foliage slightly glaucous.
Raised in 1835, the name being taken from the Isle de Réunion,
then known as the Isle de Bourbon, where the first Bourbon rose
occurred. **93**, p. 17.

'Brandenburg'   HT.
Deep salmon, 3 ft (0·9 m.) 1965
Raised by R. Kordes, Germany.
Parentage: ('Spartan' × 'Prima Ballerina') × 'Karl Herbst'
A tall vigorous grower with broad, leathery, medium green foliage,
red when young. The large shapely blooms are deep salmon,
shading to deep salmon-red and are freely produced. Suitable for
exhibition, the flowers have little scent but open freely, even in wet
weather and are useful for cutting. **277**, p. 52.

'Brasilia'   HT.
Light scarlet, 3 ft (0·9 m.) 1968
Raised by S. McGredy IV, N. Ireland.
Parentage: 'Kordes' Perfecta' × 'Piccadilly'
A tall, vigorous, upright grower, to at least 3 ft (0·9 m.), with
abundant, semi-glossy, medium green foliage, crimson in the early
stages. Flowers are shapely on opening, moderately full becoming
loose, light scarlet with a reverse of pale gold. Requires fairly close
planting, when it makes a most effective bed which stands up to
bad weather. **278**, p. 52.
T.G.C., R.N.R.S. 1967.

Briers, Scotch see *R. spinosissima* varieties, **52-55**, p. 10; **56, 57**,
p. 11.

Briers, Sweet see *R. eglanteria* varieties, **8-12**, p. 2; **13**, p. 3.

'Brilliant' see **'Detroiter'**

'Buccaneer'   HT.
Yellow, 4 ft (1·2 m.) 1952
Raised by H. C. Swim, U.S.A.
Parentage: 'Golden Rapture' × ('Max Krause' × 'Capt. Thomas')
A vigorous, very tall and upright grower reaching 4 ft (1·2 m.) or
more with healthy, slightly glossy, medium green foliage. The
medium sized flowers which develop from urn shaped buds are
buttercup-yellow and seldom fade. A profuse bloomer which
resists rain well, this cultivar is too tall except for very large beds or
the back of a border. **279**, p. 52.
T.G.C., R.N.R.S. 1955; G.G.M. 1952.

'Buff Beauty'   HM.
Apricot to buff-yellow, recurrent, 6 × 6 ft (1·8 × 1·8 m.) 1939
Raiser probably Rev. J. H. Pemberton, England.
Parentage: unknown × 'William Allen Richardson'
Vigorous Hybrid Musk shrub rose up to 6 ft (1·8 m.) and as much
across with spreading arching habit. Flowers in large clusters, semi-
double or double, of medium size, opening deep apricot-yellow and
paling at edge as flower matures, very fragrant, and floriferous. Late
June to mid-July and recurrent through summer, often with its best
flowering in early autumn and often lasting in flower till mid-
November. One of the most beautiful of this group with lovely
melting tones of apricot and yellow in its flowers. Foliage dark
green, glossy, bronze-tinted when young. **118**, p. 21.
A.G.M., R.H.S.

Burnet Rose see *R. spinosissima*

Burr Rose see *R. roxburghii*, **45, 46**, p. 9.

'Busy Lizzie'   Fl.
Pastel pink, 2½ ft (0·8 m.) 1971
Raised by R. Harkness & Co. Ltd, England.
Parentage: ('Pink Parfait' × 'Masquerade') × 'Dearest'
A compact bushy grower, 2½ ft (0·8 m.) high, with medium green,
semi-glossy foliage. The moderately, full flowers are borne several
together in good trusses and are a soft pastel pink colour. A useful
cultivar for bedding, being very free-flowering. **389**, p. 73.
T.G.C., R.N.R.S. 1969.

Cabbage Rose see *R. × centifolia*

'Camaieux'   G.
Pale pink striped purplish-crimson, summer, 4 ft (1·2 m.) 1830
Raised by Vibert, France.
A Gallica rose of only medium vigour, up to 4 ft (1·2 m.) with
arching growth. Flowers semi-double, rather loose, pale pink,
liberally splashed and streaked with strong purplish-crimson.
maturing and fading to a violet-grey, of medium size. Fragrant.
Late June. One of the most distinctive of the old striped roses.
Foliage grey-green.

'Cameo, Climbing' see **'Pink Cameo'**

'Canary Bird'   MSh.
Bright yellow, late spring, 7 ft × 7 ft (2·1 × 2·1 m.)
Vigorous modern shrub rose up to 7 ft (2·1 m.) under good con-
ditions. Formerly considered a wild form of *R. xanthina* under name
R. xanthina spontanea but now more often regarded as a hybrid from
R. xanthina with another unknown parent, possibly *R. hugonis*.
Forms a large shrub with upright shoots though arching over in
upper part. Stems rich chocolate-brown and not very prickly.

Flowers single, very bright canary-yellow, each about 2 in. (5·1 cm.)
across, very numerous in long sprays along branches. Very early
flowering in May to early June, usually one of the earliest to flower
but not recurrent. Foliage grey-green, delicate with small leaflets.
Hips dark maroon, not very large. A very valuable garden plant,
brighter in colour than *R. pteragonis* 'Cantabrigiensis' (**41**, p. 8) but
usually not so vigorous and may die back in hot or poor soils, but
when well grown quite spectacular. Can be used for a rose hedge
effectively or grown as a standard in which form it is a most striking
shrub. **143, 144**, p. 25.

'Cantabrigiensis' see *R. × pteragonis* **'Cantabrigiensis'**,
41, p. 8.

'Canterbury'   MSh.
Terracotta-pink, recurrent, 4 ft (1·2 m.) 1968
Raised by D. Austin Ltd, England.
Parentage: ('Monique' × 'Constance Spry') × unnamed seedling
Shrub rose of medium vigour up to 4 ft (1·2 m.) with bushy open,
spreading growth. Flowers semi-double, large, up to 5 in. (12·7 cm.)
across, in clusters, good terracotta-pink, deeper in centre, bud full
and deeper pink, opening to show large golden centre. Mid to late
June and recurrent. Scent strong, spicy. A beautiful rose.

'Capitaine John Ingram'   Moss Sh.
Purplish-crimson, summer, 5 ft (1·5 m.) 1854
Raised by M. Laffay, France.
Vigorous shrub up to 5 ft (1·5 m.). Flowers double, rather globular,

---

Abbreviations and Symbols used in the text

Rose classifications

A.	Alba	HT.	Hybrid Tea
B.	Bourbon	MCl.	Modern, large-flowered climber
C.	Centifolia	Min.	Miniature
Ch.	China	Moss	Centifolia muscosa
Cl.	Climber	MSh.	Modern shrub
D.	Damask	P.	Penzance Sweet Brier
Fl.	Floribunda	R.	Rambler
G.	Gallica	Rg.	Rugosa
HM.	Hybrid Musk	Sp.	Species and first hybrids
HP.	Hybrid Perpetual	Sw.	Sweet Brier

Rose Awards and Societies

A.A.R.S.	All-America Rose Selection
A.G.M.	Award of Garden Merit
A.M.	Award of Merit
A.R.S.	American Rose Society
B.B.G.M.	Baden Baden Gold Medal, Germany
B.G.M.	Bagatelle Gold Medal, Paris
C.C.V.	Clay Challenge Vase for scent
C.M.	Certificate of Merit
D.F.P.	David Fuerstenberg Prize
F.C.C.	First Class Certificate
G.G.M.	Geneva Gold Medal
G.M.	Gold Medal
G.M.C.B.	Gold Medal City of Belfast
G.M.H.G.M.	Gertrude M. Hubbard Gold Medal
G.R.H.	Golden Rose of The Hague
G.T.A.B.	Golden Thorn Award Belfast
H.E.M.M.	The Henry Edland Memorial Medal for the most fragrant rose of the year
H.G.M.	The Hague Gold Medal
L.G.M.	Lyon Gold Medal, France
M.G.M.	Madrid Gold Medal
N.G.M.C.	National Gold Medal Certificate
P.G.M.	Portland Gold Medal, Oregon, U.S.A.
P.I.T.	President's International Trophy
R.B.	Prize for the most fragrant rose, Roeulx, Belgium
R.B.G.M.	Roeulx, Belgium, Gold Medal
R.G.M.	Rome Gold Medal
R.H.S.	The Royal Horticultural Society, London
R.N.R.S.	The Royal National Rose Society, Great Britain*
T.G.C.	Trial Ground Certificate
U.A.B.	The 'Uladh' Award for fragrance, Belfast

National Rose Society awards, before 1965, are included here under R.N.R.S.

The illustration numbers are in **bold type** and the page numbers
in light type preceded by p.

of medium size, dark crimson-purple maturing to deep purple with some variation of lighter tones and button centre. Bud with large mossy calyx of tawny green or dark red. A useful rose for its dark colour and usually retaining a better shape as the flower matures than does 'Nuits de Young'. Mid to late June. Not recurrent.

'Cappa Magna' MSh.
Crimson-red, recurrent, 5 ft (1·5 m.) 1965
Raised by Delbard-Chabert, France.
Parentage: 'Ténor' seedling
An upright, vigorous grower to about 5 ft (1·5 m.) with large dark green, glossy foliage. The semi-double, velvety crimson-red flowers are cupped, with wavy petals and are produced in very large trusses, too large sometimes for the stems to hold upright. Increasing age may decrease this tendency but it appears to be a useful addition to shrub roses. Unfortunately unscented. **145**, p. 25.
T.G.C., R.N.R.S. 1967.

'Caramba' HT.
Red and silver, 3 ft (0·9 m.) 1967
Raised by M. Tantau, Germany.
A vigorous, bushy grower, just above 3 ft (0·9 m.) in height, with abundant semi-glossy, dark green foliage, red in the early stages of growth. Very full flowers of medium size, red with silver reverse, a most striking bicolor. Although scentless, this appears to be a cultivar of considerable promise for bedding or display. **280**, p. 52.
T.G.C., R.N.R.S. 1967.

'Cardinal de Richelieu' G.
Dark violet-purple, summer, 5 ft (1·5 m.) c. 1840
Raised by M. Laffay, France.
Gallica. Shrub rose of medium vigour up to 5 ft (1·5 m.) with few thorns. Buds notably round in small clusters, flowers dome-shaped at first, always rather rounded, opening dark velvety-purple, lighter at base of petals, fading to Parma violet when flower tends to fall apart rather untidily; about 3 in. (7·6 cm.) across; its petals are overlaid with a dark-grey bloom giving a sumptuous effect unlike that of any other rose. Its colour is, however, much more violet than are a cardinal's robes. Fragrant. Foliage dark green. This rose needs to be well pruned after flowering and to be grown and fed generously. In hot dry sandy soils it can be miserable and not worth growing. **83**, p. 15.

'Carla' HT.
Soft pink, 3 ft (0·9 m.) 1963
Raised by G. de Ruiter, Holland.
Parentage: 'Queen Elizabeth' × 'The Optimist'
A vigorous upright grower, 3 ft (0·9 m.) high, with dark foliage. The medium sized, double flowers are soft pink, shaded salmon and are produced freely on long stems. One of the best roses for cutting.

'Carolin' see **'Coralín'**

'Carolyn' see **'Coralín'**

'Casanova' HT.
Yellow, 4 ft (1·2 m.) 1964
Raised by S. McGredy IV, N. Ireland.
Parentage: 'Queen Elizabeth' × 'Kordes' Perfecta'
A vigorous, tall, upright grower, with glossy dark green foliage. The full, fragrant straw yellow blooms fade to buff and are freely produced, with the best display in the autumn. Its height makes it suitable only for very large beds or for borders. **281**, p. 53.
T.G.C., R.N.R.S. 1964.

'Casino' MCl.
Deep yellow, recurrent, 12 ft (3·7 m.) 1963
Raised by S. McGredy IV, N. Ireland.
Parentage: 'Coral Dawn' × 'Buccaneer'
A vigorous climber up to 12 ft (3·7 m.) high with large, glossy dark green foliage. The flowers are shapely, hybrid tea type when young, deep yellow becoming soft yellow when fully open. Repeats quite well and has some scent. Gives best results if not too exposed during winter. Suitable for walls or pillars.
G.M., R.N.R.S. 1963; A.M., R.H.S. 1964.

'Cécile Brunner', 'Mignon', 'Mme Cécile Brunner', Ch.
'The Sweetheart Rose'
Pale pink, recurrent, 4 ft (1·2 m.) 1881
Raised by Veuve Ducher, France.
Parentage: possibly *R. multiflora* × 'Mme de Tartas'
Shrub rose of medium vigour, usually not over 4 ft (1·2 m.), often rather less, distinguished by small neat foliage and numerous miniature blooms of perfect form. Flowers scented, thimble-like in size, pale blush-pink, slightly deeper in centre, buds long-pointed. Mid-June and recurrent throughout summer. Its pruning should be limited to the cutting out of weak growth with occasional removal of older branches, but it should not be pruned too hard. A valuable rose for its neat appearance and for cutting; it is surpassed for garden display by its climbing form.

'Cécile Brunner, Climbing' see **'Climbing Cécile Brunner'**, **264**, p. 50.

'Celebration' Fl.
Salmon-pink, 2½ ft (0·8 m.) 1961
Raised by A. Dickson & Sons Ltd, N. Ireland.
Parentage: 'Dickson's Flame' × 'Circus'
A fairly vigorous, bushy grower, 2½ ft (0·8 m.) high, with medium green, healthy foliage. The medium sized flowers are semi-double, slightly cupped, salmon-pink with a lighter reverse, fading a little, especially in hot weather. Free-flowering. Slight fragrance. Resists wet weather very well.
C.M., R.N.R.S. 1962.

'Céleste', 'Celestial' A.
Clear pink, summer, 6 × 6 ft (1·8 × 1·8 m.)
Vigorous shrub up to 6 ft (1·8 m.) and as much through. Bud narrow and pointed, opening to a clear and quite bright pink semi-double rose, cup-shaped and later saucer-shaped, showing golden stamens with a few petaloids in centre, 3½ in. (8·9 cm.) across. Mid-season up to late June. Sweetly scented. In clusters of 2–3. Foliage slightly glaucous green, 5–7 leaflets, rather rounded. One of the finest old roses I know for foliage and my favourite of all the old roses for its delicacy and clearness of pink colouring unsurpassed for the beautiful combination of flower and foliage. Prune out some of the older and weaker flowering wood after it has flowered and again in winter. It tends to make strong shoots from the old wood and may be cut back to these. Origin unknown, but painted by Redouté as *R. damascena* 'Aurora', by Alfred Parsons in *The Genus Rosa* as *R. alba rubicunda* and by Andrews as *R. erubescens*. Mr G. Thomas suggests that it may be of Dutch origin towards the end of the eighteenth century. **64**, p. 12.
A.M., R.H.S. 1948.

'Celestial' see **'Céleste'**, **64**, p. 12.

'Célina' Moss Sh.
Purplish-crimson, summer, 4 ft (1·2 m.) 1855
Raised by M. Hardy, France.
Shrub of only medium vigour. Flower purplish-crimson, semi-

double, of medium size. Mid-late June, not recurrent. Mr G. Thomas observes that it gets mildew very badly and he does not think it a worthy variety. It is not very common in cultivation, perhaps for this reason. Raised in 1855 it should not be confused with the Damask rose 'Celsiana'.

'Celsiana'   D.
Pink, summer, 5 ft (1·5 m.) before 1750
A Damask rose of vigorous growth up to 5 ft (1·5 m.). Flowers in clusters, large, semi-double, bright dog rose pink, fading to a blush-pink, with prominent golden centre, opening wide, about 4 in. (10·2 cm.) across. Scented. Foliage greyish-green, also scented. A beautiful old rose raised prior to 1750 and figured by Redouté.

'Centenaire de Lourdes', 'Mrs Jones'   Fl.
Soft rose, 6 ft (1·8 m.) 1958
Raised by Delbard-Chabert, France.
Parentage: ('Frau Karl Druschki' × seedling) × unnamed seedlings
A vigorous, open, bushy grower, 6 ft (1·8 m.) high, with clusters of large, semi-double, soft rose flowers that have waved petals. Scented. Although classified as a Floribunda, this attractive rose is much better placed amongst shrub roses where its tall, somewhat lax growths will be much more at home. Continues flowering right into late October if weather permits. **390**, p. 73.

'Cerise Bouquet'   MSh.
Cerise-crimson, early summer, 9 × 6 ft (2·7 × 1·8 m.) 1958
Raised by W. Kordes, Germany.
Parentage: *R. multibracteata* × 'Crimson Glory'
Vigorous modern shrub rose with graceful arching growth up to 9 ft (2·7 m.) high and 6 ft (1·8 m.) across. Flowers semi-double, of medium size, usually in clusters on long sprays, cerise-crimson, opening flat to show stamens. Mid-June to mid-July but not usually recurrent. Foliage delicate, grey-green. Now established as a very popular shrub rose, distinct in its growth. **146**, p. 26.
A.M., R.H.S. 1958.

'Champs-Elysées'   HT.
Deep crimson, 2½ ft (0·8 m.) 1957
Raised by F. Meilland, France.
Parentage: 'Monique' × 'Happiness'
A fairly vigorous, branching grower of medium height with mid-green, rather small mat foliage. The full, somewhat cupped flowers are deep velvety crimson, without any tendency to fade and are particularly good in autumn. There is little scent but because of its habit, freedom of flowering and bushy growth, this is a very useful bedding rose. The flowers also last well when cut. **282**, p. 53.
M.G.M. 1957.

'Chanelle'   Fl.
Buff, peach, pink and cream, 2½ ft (0·8 m.) 1959
Raised by S. McGredy IV, N. Ireland.
Parentage: 'Ma Perkins' × ('Fashion' × 'Mrs William Sprott')
A vigorous grower, 2½ ft (0·8 m.) high, with glossy, dark foliage. The flowers are shapely in the early stages, opening flat in a suffusion of buff, peach, pink and cream shades. This is a very useful healthy cultivar, which resists wet well and flowers abundantly well into the autumn. Some fragrance. **391**, p. 73.
C.M., R.N.R.S. 1958; M.G.M. 1959.

'Chanson d'Eté' see **'Summer Song'**

'Chapeau de Napoléon' see *R.* × *centifolia* **'Cristata'**

'Chaplin's Pink Climber'   Cl.R.
Bright pink, summer, 15 ft (4·6 m.) 1928
Raised by Chaplin Bros Ltd, England.
Parentage: 'Paul's Scarlet Climber' × 'American Pillar'
A very vigorous grower, at least 10 ft (3 m.) high, with glossy dark green foliage. The large, semi-double flowers are bright pink with golden stamens in medium sized clusters, very freely produced but with no recurrent bloom. I find the colour somewhat garish, nevertheless this has for many years been a very popular cultivar, frequently seen in gardens, on fences particularly. **199**, p. 37.
G.M., R.N.R.S. 1928.

'Chaplin's Pink Companion'   MCl.
Silvery-salmon-pink, summer, 12 ft (3·7 m.) 1961
Raised by H. J. Chaplin, England.
Parentage: 'Chaplin's Pink Climber' × 'Opera'
A vigorous grower, up to 12 ft (3·7 m.) high with glossy foliage. The medium sized flowers are produced with exceptional freedom in clusters over quite a long period but with no recurrence of bloom: they are silvery-salmon-pink in colour, an attractive shade and possessing some fragrance. More suitable for screens or pergolas in the open, than on a wall where mildew may become troublesome. **234**, p. 43.
C.M., R.N.R.S. 1961; A.M., R.H.S. 1961.

'Charles de Mills'   G.
Crimson-maroon, summer, 5 ft (1·5 m.)
Shrub rose, strong growing up to 5 ft (1·5 m.). Flowers large, up to 4½

Abbreviations and Symbols used in the text

Rose classifications

A.	Alba	HT.	Hybrid Tea
B.	Bourbon	MCl.	Modern, large-flowered climber
C.	Centifolia	Min.	Miniature
Ch.	China	Moss	Centifolia muscosa
Cl.	Climber	MSh.	Modern shrub
D.	Damask	P.	Penzance Sweet Brier
Fl.	Floribunda	R.	Rambler
G.	Gallica	Rg.	Rugosa
HM.	Hybrid Musk	Sp.	Species and first hybrids
HP.	Hybrid Perpetual	Sw.	Sweet Brier

Rose Awards and Societies

A.A.R.S.	All-America Rose Selection
A.G.M.	Award of Garden Merit
A.M.	Award of Merit
A.R.S.	American Rose Society
B.B.G.M.	Baden Baden Gold Medal, Germany
B.G.M.	Bagatelle Gold Medal, Paris
C.C.V.	Clay Challenge Vase for scent
C.M.	Certificate of Merit
D.F.P.	David Fuerstenberg Prize
F.C.C.	First Class Certificate
G.G.M.	Geneva Gold Medal
G.M.	Gold Medal
G.M.C.B.	Gold Medal City of Belfast
G.M.H.G.M.	Gertrude M. Hubbard Gold Medal
G.R.H.	Golden Rose of The Hague
G.T.A.B.	Golden Thorn Award Belfast
H.E.M.M.	The Henry Edland Memorial Medal for the most fragrant rose of the year
H.G.M.	The Hague Gold Medal
L.G.M.	Lyon Gold Medal, France
M.G.M.	Madrid Gold Medal
N.G.M.C.	National Gold Medal Certificate
P.G.M.	Portland Gold Medal, Oregon, U.S.A.
P.I.T.	President's International Trophy
R.B.	Prize for the most fragrant rose, Roeulx, Belgium
R.B.G.M.	Roeulx, Belgium, Gold Medal
R.G.M.	Rome Gold Medal
R.H.S.	The Royal Horticultural Society, London
R.N.R.S.	The Royal National Rose Society, Great Britain*
T.G.C.	Trial Ground Certificate
U.A.B.	The 'Uladh' Award for fragrance, Belfast

National Rose Society awards, before 1965, are included here under R.N.R.S.

The illustration numbers are in **bold type** and the page numbers in light type preceded by p.

in. (11·4 cm.) across, crimson-maroon, fully double and well quartered with an intricate and intriguing pattern of slightly crinkled petals. Fragrant. On maturing, flowers show some dark purple tints. Mid to late June. One of the finest flowers in the Gallica group and recommended for general garden purposes. One flower also makes a wonderful buttonhole which is also certain to be admired. Sometimes known as 'Bizarre Triomphant'. **84**, p. 15.

'Charles Dickens'   Fl.
Salmon, 2½ ft (0·8 m.) 1970
Raised by S. McGredy IV, N. Ireland.
Parentage: 'Paddy McGredy' × 'Elizabeth of Glamis'
An upright, vigorous grower, 2½ ft (0·8 m.) high, with semi-glossy dark green foliage. Borne in trusses, the moderately full flowers are salmon, with a deeper reverse and are freely produced over a long period. Faint scent. Has a good bedding habit. **392**, p. 73.
T.G.C., R.N.R.S. 1970.

'Charleston'   Fl.
Yellow, 3 ft (0·9 m.) 1963
Raised by A. Meilland, France.
Parentage: 'Masquerade' × ('Radar' × 'Caprice')
A grower of moderate vigour, between 2½ and 3 ft (0·8–0·9 m.) in height, with dark green, glossy foliage. The large, semi-double flowers are yellow, flushed with crimson, eventually becoming crimson, a striking contrast in the early stages. Slightly fragrant. This free-flowering cultivar can only be recommended for areas where black spot and mildew do not present problems. **393**, p. 73.

'Charlotte Elizabeth'   Fl.
Deep rose-pink, 3 ft (0·9 m.) 1965
Raised by A. Norman, England.
Parentage: 'Sheila Elizabeth' × 'Queen Elizabeth'
A vigorous, upright grower, some 3 ft (0·9 m.) high, with abundant, mid-green, glossy foliage. The blooms are large, semi-double, well formed in the early stages, deep rose-pink, produced in small trusses, flowering freely in summer and again in autumn. Weather resistance is good and there is some scent. **394**, p. 73.
C.M., R.N.R.S. 1965.

'Charm of Paris', 'Pariser Charme'   HT
Clear salmon-pink, 2½ ft (0·8 m.) 1965
Raised by M. Tantau, Germany.
Parentage: 'Prima Ballerina' × 'Montezuma'
A vigorous, spreading grower, 2½ ft (0·8 m.) high, with abundant deep green, semi-glossy foliage. The flowers are double, well formed, clear salmon-pink and sweetly fragrant. Classified at first as a Floribunda and illustrated as this, is now regarded as a Hybrid Tea. A very healthy cultivar, good for bedding but does not like wet weather. **395**, p. 74.
C.M., R.N.R.S. 1965; H.E.M.M., R.N.R.S. 1966.

'Charme de Vienne' see **'Wiener Charme', 375**, p. 70.

'Charming Maid'   Fl.
Coppery-pink, 3 ft (0·9 m.) 1953
Raised by E. B. LeGrice, England.
Parentage: 'Dainty Maid' × 'Mrs Sam McGredy'
A tall, vigorous grower, 3 ft (0·9 m.) high, with dark glossy foliage. The lovely single flowers are large with slightly waved petals, in small, well spaced clusters, coppery-pink in colour with golden base. Pleasant light scent. Takes time to get established but is an attractive bedding rose with some flowerless gaps between crops. **396**, p. 74
G.M., R.N.R.S. 1953.

'Charming Vienna' see **'Wiener Charme', 375**, p. 70.

'Chaucer'   MSh.
Blush-pink, recurrent, 3–4 ft (0·9–1·2 m.) 1970
Raised by D. Austin, England.
Modern shrub rose of fair vigour. Flowers double, a warm blush-pink, paler outside, cupped on first opening, maturing paler, 3½ in. (8·9 cm.) across, in large clusters. Scent strong, slightly acrid and reminiscent of myrrh. Mid-June to early July and then recurrent. Slightly more vigorous than others in the raiser's series.

'Cherryade'   MCl.Sh.
Deep pink, recurrent, 6 ft (1·8 m.) 1961
Raised by G. de Ruiter, Holland.
Parentage: 'New Dawn' × 'Red Wonder'
Sometimes described as a semi-climber or large shrub growing up to 6 ft (1·8 m.). Vigorous. Flowers large, 4 in. (10·2 cm.) across, double and of good form, deep pink to cherry-red, scented, free-flowering. Mid-June and recurrent.

Cherokee Rose see **_R. laevigata_**

Chestnut Rose see **_R. roxburghii_, 45, 46**, p. 9.

'Chianti'   MSh.
Deep purple-maroon, summer, 5 ft (1·5 m.) 1967
Raised by D. Austin, England.
Parentage: 'Cardinal de Richelieu' × 'Dusky Maiden'
A vigorous, free-blooming shrub, 5 ft (1·5 m.) high. The semi-double flowers are produced in small clusters of deep purplish-maroon. Slightly scented, has only one display but the rich colour and the form of the flowers will appeal to those who like old garden roses. **147**, p. 26.

'Chicago Peace'   HT.
Yellow and pink, 4 ft (1·2 m.) 1962
Discovered by S. C. Johnston, U.S.A.
Parentage: 'Peace' sport
A vigorous, tall, branching grower, similar to its parent in habit, 4 ft (1·2 m.) high, with large glossy dark green foliage. The large, very full blooms have an orange and yellow base, overlaid with deep pink which lightens with age, and are freely produced. Fragrance is slight but an outstanding cultivar when at its best and useful for exhibition. Occasional blooms show partial reversion to 'Peace'. **283**, p. 53.
P.G.M. 1961.

China Rose see **_R. chinensis_**

'Chinatown', 'Ville de Chine'   MSh.
Deep yellow, recurrent, 5 ft+ (1·5 m.) 1963
Raised by N. D. Poulsen, Denmark.
Parentage: 'Columbine' × 'Cläre Grammerstorf'
Sometimes classed as a Floribunda, this is really a shrub of 5 ft (1·5 m.) and over in height, a vigorous bushy, rather stiff grower with dark, glossy foliage. The large, double flowers are deep yellow, sometimes edged pink, and are very fragrant. Useful for a large bed especially if pegged down. **148**, p. 26.
G.M., R.N.R.S. 1963; A.M., R.H.S. 1965.

Chinquapin Rose see **_R. roxburghii_, 45, 46**, p. 9.

'Chorus Girl' Fl.
Deep vermilion, 2 ft (0·6 m.) 1971
Raised by H. Robinson, England.
Parentage: 'Highlight' × seedling
A bushy, compact grower, just over 2 ft (0·6 m.) high. Moderately full flowers of a deepish vermilion-red and borne in trusses are very freely produced over a long season. Medium, mat, mid-green foliage. **397**, p. 74.
C.M., R.N.R.S. 1970.

'Christian Dior' HT.
Scarlet, 4 ft (1·2 m.) 1959
Raised by F. Meilland, France.
Parentage: ('Independence' × 'Happiness') × ('Peace' × 'Happiness')
A vigorous, tall upright grower with semi-glossy, medium green foliage, red in early stages. Blooms are large, well formed, full, velvety scarlet with paler reverse and little if any scent. Flowers freely and although rather tall for bedding, it is a useful exhibition rose if it can be kept free of mildew. **284**, p. 53.
G.G.M. 1958; A.M., R.H.S. 1958; A.A.R.S. 1962.

'Chrysler Imperial' HT.
Deep crimson, 3 ft (0·9 m.) 1952
Raised by Dr W. E. Lammerts, U.S.A.
Parentage: 'Charlotte Armstrong' × 'Mirandy'
A moderately vigorous grower of upright habit and a height of about 3 ft (0·9 m.). The foliage, which is semi-glossy and dark green, may require protection from mildew and rust in some areas. The vivid, deep crimson blooms are very full and fragrant but are apt to 'blue' as they age.
P.G.M. 1951; A.A.R.S. 1953.

'Cinderella' Min.
Shell pink, 10 in. (25·4 cm.) 1953
Raised by J. de Vink, Holland.
Parentage: 'Cécile Brunner' × 'Tom Thumb'
An upright, thornless grower, up to 10 in. (25·4 cm.), with small, shell pink flowers shading off to white, very shapely but which do not like strong sun. Rated highly in the U.S.A. as a disease and weather resistant cultivar. **502**, p. 96.

'Cineraire' Min.
Rich red, 6 in. (15·2 cm.)
Discovered by E. Murrell, England.
A small plant, 4–6 in. (10·2–15·2 cm.) high, with cupped, rich red flowers which have a white centre. They last well but have no fragrance.

'Circus' Fl.
Yellow with pink, salmon and scarlet, 2 ft (0·6 m.) 1956
Raised by H. C. Swim, U.S.A.
Parentage: 'Fandango' × 'Pinocchio'
A fairly vigorous grower, 2 ft (0·6 m.) in height, with semi-glossy, dark green foliage. The medium sized, double flowers are shapely when young, produced in large clusters, basically yellow suffused pink, salmon and scarlet, always pleasing even when old. Resists wet reasonably well and has a light scent. A good bedding rose.
G.G.M. 1955; G.M., R.N.R.S. 1955; A.A.R.S. 1956.

'City of Belfast' Fl.
Vermilion-scarlet, 2½ ft (0·8 m.) 1968
Raised by S. McGredy IV, N. Ireland.
Parentage: 'Evelyn Fison' × ('Circus' × 'Korona')
A free, bushy grower, 2½ ft (0·8 m.) high, with glossy, medium green foliage, reddish in the early stages of growth. The flowers are very freely produced in large trusses of bright velvety vermilion-scarlet, with slightly frilled petal edges. This cultivar has already proved to be a good bedder with a long season of flower. Disease and weather resistant. Good for small gardens. **398**, p. 74.
P.I.T., R.N.R.S. 1967; G.M., R.N.R.S. 1967; A.M., R.H.S. 1968.

'City of Gloucester' HT.
Saffron-yellow, 3 ft (0·9 m.) 1970
Raised by J. Sanday Ltd, England.
Parentage: 'Gavotte' × 'Buccaneer'
A tall, upright grower, 3 ft (0·9 m.) high, with mat mid-green foliage. The fairly large flowers are full, shapely, saffron-yellow with gold shadings, borne singly and several together. This new cultivar has possibilities as an exhibition bloom. **285**, p. 53.
T.G.C., R.N.R.S. 1970.

'City of Hereford' HT.
Rose-pink, 3 ft (0·9 m.) 1967
Raised by E. B. LeGrice, England.
Parentage: 'Wellworth' × 'Spartan'
A branching grower around 3 ft (0·9 m.) high with light green mat foliage. The large flowers are full, somewhat globular in appearance, medium rose-pink with deeper pink reverse, giving an overall appearance of deep pink and with a strong fragrance. Generally produced singly early in the season, in trusses later. May require protection against mildew.
U.A.B. 1969.

Abbreviations and Symbols used in the text

Rose classifications

A.	Alba	HT.	Hybrid Tea
B.	Bourbon	MCl.	Modern, large-flowered climber
C.	Centifolia	Min.	Miniature
Ch.	China	Moss	Centifolia muscosa
Cl.	Climber	MSh.	Modern shrub
D.	Damask	P.	Penzance Sweet Brier
Fl.	Floribunda	R.	Rambler
G.	Gallica	Rg.	Rugosa
HM.	Hybrid Musk	Sp.	Species and first hybrids
HP.	Hybrid Perpetual	Sw.	Sweet Brier

Rose Awards and Societies

A.A.R.S.	All-America Rose Selection
A.G.M.	Award of Garden Merit
A.M.	Award of Merit
A.R.S.	American Rose Society
B.B.G.M.	Baden Baden Gold Medal, Germany
B.G.M.	Bagatelle Gold Medal, Paris
C.C.V.	Clay Challenge Vase for scent
C.M.	Certificate of Merit
D.F.P.	David Fuerstenberg Prize
F.C.C.	First Class Certificate
G.G.M.	Geneva Gold Medal
G.M.	Gold Medal
G.M.C.B.	Gold Medal City of Belfast
G.M.H.G.M.	Gertrude M. Hubbard Gold Medal
G.R.H.	Golden Rose of The Hague
G.T.A.B.	Golden Thorn Award Belfast
H.E.M.M.	The Henry Edland Memorial Medal for the most fragrant rose of the year
H.G.M.	The Hague Gold Medal
L.G.M.	Lyon Gold Medal, France
M.G.M.	Madrid Gold Medal
N.G.M.C.	National Gold Medal Certificate
P.G.M.	Portland Gold Medal, Oregon, U.S.A.
P.I.T.	President's International Trophy
R.B.	Prize for the most fragrant rose, Roeulx, Belgium
R.B.G.M.	Roeulx, Belgium, Gold Medal
R.G.M.	Rome Gold Medal
R.H.S.	The Royal Horticultural Society, London
R.N.R.S.	The Royal National Rose Society, Great Britain*
T.G.C.	Trial Ground Certificate
U.A.B.	The 'Uladh' Award for fragrance, Belfast

National Rose Society awards, before 1965, are included here under R.N.R.S.

The illustration numbers are in **bold type** and the page numbers in light type preceded by p.

'City of Leeds'   Fl.
Rich salmon, 3 ft (0·9 m.) 1966
Raised by S. McGredy IV, N. Ireland.
Parentage: 'Evelyn Fison' × ('Spartan' × 'Red Favorite')
A vigorous upright grower, 2½ ft to 3 ft (0·8–0·9 m.) high, with
semi-glossy dark green foliage. The moderately full flowers are
very shapely in the early stages, opening out later, and are a rich
salmon colour. They are very freely produced over a long season
and this is one of the best bedding cultivars at the present time
although the flowers spot in very wet weather. **399**, p. 74.
G.M., R.N.R.S. 1965.

'City of York', 'Direktor Benschop'   MCl.R.
Creamy-white, 12 ft (3·7 m.) 1945
Raised by M. Tantau, Germany.
Parentage: 'Prof. Gnau' × 'Dorothy Perkins'
A vigorous rambler with double flowers of moderate size, yellow
in centre, becoming creamy-white on outside. Very free-flowering.
Scented. Late June to early July but not usually recurrent. Foliage
luxuriant, deep glossy green. Although only rarely grown, the
flowers are larger than those of 'Albéric Barbier' (**192**, p. 36)
although otherwise somewhat resembling it and it is not quite such a
rampant grower, but it has some characteristics of a *wichuraiana*
rambler. **235**, p. 43.
N.G.M.C., A.R.S. 1950.

'Clair Matin'   MSh.Cl.
Pastel pink, recurrent, 7 or 12 ft (2·1 or 3·7 m.) 1960
Raised by M. L. Meilland, France.
Parentage: 'Fashion' × (('Independence' × 'Orange Triumph')
× 'Phyllis Bide')
This attractive rose can be grown as a climber when it may attain a
height of 12 ft (3·7 m.) or as a shrub 7 ft (2·1 m.) tall. Vigorous,
branching well, with dark leathery foliage providing an attractive
setting for the pastel pink, medium sized flowers. Slightly fragrant.
One of the prettiest of modern roses more often grown as a climber
than a shrub. **149**, p. 26.
B.G.M. 1960.

'Claire Jacquier'   Cl.
Pale creamy-yellow, recurrent, 20 ft (6·1 m.) 1888
Raised by A. Bernaix, France.
Parentage: possibly *R. multiflora* × early Tea rose hybrid
Vigorous Noisette climber up to 20 ft (6·1 m.) or more. Flowers
semi-double in clusters of about 5, pale cream with stronger buff
apricot-yellow centre, scented, slightly untidy in flower. Free-
flowering. Mid to late June, recurrent. Foliage luxuriant, dark
shining green with pointed leaflets. A once popular climber with
buds of lovely shape and dainty flowers and still useful where a
vigorous rose in this colour is wanted. **200**, p. 37.
A.M., R.H.S. 1889.

'Climbing Allgold'   Cl.Fl.sport
Bright golden-yellow, recurrent, 8 ft (2·4 m.) 1961
Discovered by Gandy Roses Ltd, England.
Parentage: 'Allgold' sport
Climber or pillar roses, up to 8 ft (2·4 m.) with flowers similar to its
parent Floribunda (**378**, p. 71). Flowers semi-double, very bright
and unfading-yellow, in clusters, each flower about 3 in. (7·6 cm.)
across. Mid-June and recurrent. Slightly scented. It should only
be pruned very lightly until well established. **263**, p. 50.

'Climbing Bloomfield Abundance' see under **'Climbing
Cécile Brunner'**, **264**, p. 50.

'Climbing Cameo' see **'Pink Cameo'**

'Climbing Cécile Brunner'   Cl.Ch.sport
Shell-pink, recurrent, 20 ft (6·1 m.) 1894
Discovered by F. P. Hosp, U.S.A.
Parentage: 'Cécile Brunner' sport
Vigorous climber for wall up to 20 ft (6·1 m.) and as much across.
Much more free-flowering than its parent 'Cécile Brunner' and
with slightly larger flowers and foliage. Flowers quite small in
sprays with long pointed buds of delicate form, double, pale
blush-pink, slightly deeper in centre, 1–1½ in. (2·5–3·8 cm.)
across, like a miniature Hybrid Tea rose. Scented. A mature plant
may be covered with hundreds of flowers. A more valuable garden
plant than the shrub rose. Mid to late June for main flowering but
somewhat recurrent. The rose known as 'Climbing Bloomfield
Abundance' is really 'Climbing Cécile Brunner' and not a climbing
sport of 'Bloomfield Abundance'. **264**, p. 50.

'Climbing Ena Harkness'   Cl.HT.sport
Deep crimson, recurrent, 8 ft (2·4 m.) 1954
Discovered by R. Murrell and by Gurteen & Ritson Ltd, England.
Parentage: 'Ena Harkness' sport
Climber or pillar rose of medium vigour with flowers similar to
parent (**301**, p. 57). Flowers freely in summer but with few flowers
later. The weakness of the flower stalks and resultant hanging of the
flowers, deprecated in the bush form, is acceptable in the climber,
bringing them more into view.

'Climbing Etoile de Hollande'   Cl.HT.sport
Deep crimson, recurrent, 6 ft (1·8 m.) 1931
Discovered by M. Leenders, Holland.
Parentage: 'Etoile de Hollande' sport
Climber or pillar rose of medium vigour. Flowers large, hybrid tea,
double or semi-double, deep velvety crimson, very strongly
scented, buds pointed, free-flowering. Mid-June and recurrent
throughout summer. The climbing sport seems more vigorous now
than its parent and when well grown against a grey stone or white
wall, it is one of our most lovely and strongly scented climbers. It
does well in warm countries such as southern France and Italy but
not in very cold and exposed situations.

'Climbing Fashion'   Cl.Fl.sport
Apricot-salmon, 8 ft (2·4 m.) 1951
Discovered by E. S. Boerner, U.S.A.
Parentage: 'Fashion' sport
Climber or pillar rose of moderate vigour from a parent once very
popular for although it introduced a lovely shade of salmon shaded
orange into the rose world for the first time, it became susceptible to
black spot and rust. Another climbing sport from 'Fashion' was
introduced by J. Mattock, England, in 1955, which is probably
better than the American one. This climbing rose, the only one in
this colour, is still available but may, in some areas, require protection against disease.

'Climbing Iceberg', 'Climbing Schneewittchen'   Cl.Fl.sport
White, recurrent, 8–10 ft (2·4–3 m.) 1968
Discovered by B. R. Cant, England.
Parentage: 'Schneewittchen' sport
A comparatively new and still little tried climbing sport from one
of the most widely grown and deservedly popular Floribunda roses
'Schneewittchen' (**481**, p. 91). Claimed as recurrent flowering
throughout summer. Lightly scented. During the last few years
several climbing sports of this most popular Floribunda, all of which
have similar blooms to their parent, have been discovered. Unfortunately they seem to differ in their freedom of flowering and
ability to repeat. At this stage, therefore, care should be taken when
ordering this cultivar to ensure that it comes from a stock which is
proven to be free-flowering and recurrent.
T.G.C., R.N.R.S. 1969.

'Climbing Lady Hillingdon'   Cl.HT.sport
Apricot-yellow, recurrent, 15 ft (4·6 m.) 1917
Discovered by E. J. Hicks, England.
Parentage: 'Lady Hillingdon', sport
Vigorous climber or pillar rose with large, double flowers of creamy-yellow with buff yellow-apricot centre. Strongly scented and rather drooping so that one may look up into the hanging flowers. Foliage and shoots when young purplish-tinted, later dark green, glossy. It grows best on a warm wall. Free-flowering. Mid-June and recurrent. Much more vigorous than the original Hybrid Tea which is now rarely cultivated and has dropped out of most catalogues. **265**, p. 50.

'Climbing Lady Sylvia'   Cl.HT.sport
Blush-pink, recurrent, 12 ft (3·7 m.) 1933
Discovered by W. Stevens Ltd, England.
Parentage: 'Lady Sylvia' sport
Vigorous climber or pillar rose with large, double flowers, blush-pink, deeper in the centre and with a yellow base to the petals. Strongly scented. Mid-June and recurrent. Should not be pruned heavily as this will result in much growth which may not flower. Horizontal training of young growths will counteract excessive growth and result in more flowers. The parent of this rose, 'Lady Sylvia' (**327**, p. 62), was itself a sport from the famous Hybrid Tea 'Mme Butterfly'. **266**, p. 50.

'Climbing Mme Caroline Testout'   Cl.HT.sport
Rose-pink, recurrent, 8 ft (2·4 m.) 1901
Discovered by Chauvry, France.
Parentage: 'Mme Caroline Testout' sport
Climbing or pillar rose, sport of a very famous old rose which is now hardly grown but still survives in this climbing form. Not very vigorous, rarely over 8 ft (2·4 m.). Flowers bright satin-rose, with darker centre, edged with soft carmine pink. They are very full and globular, a bit 'blowsy' by present day standards but still of sentimental value to many rosarians.

'Climbing Mme Edouard Herriot'   Cl.HT.sport
Coral-red, recurrent, 8 ft (2·4 m.) 1921
Discovered by Ketten Bros., Luxembourg.
Parentage: 'Mme Edouard Herriot' sport
Fairly vigorous climber or pillar rose, still grown and much stronger than its parent, 'Mme Edouard Herriot', the 'Daily Mail Rose' of 1913, which, although once very popular, is not grown widely now. Flowers semi-double, open, rather untidy, coral-red shaded with yellow and bright rosy-scarlet, a striking blend, scented. Foliage bronzy and glossy but sensitive to black spot.

'Climbing Masquerade'   Cl.Fl.sport
Red, pink and yellow, recurrent, 8 ft (2·4 m.) 1958
Discovered by C. J. Dillan, England.
Parentage: 'Masquerade' sport.
Climber or pillar rose of vigorous growth and similar in flower to its parent (**444**, p. 82), giving a heavy first crop but little repeat. Hips should be removed to try and correct this tendency.

'Climbing McGredy's Yellow'   Cl.HT.sport
Yellow, recurrent, 8 ft (2·4 m.) 1937
Discovered by Western Rose Co., U.S.A.
Parentage: 'McGredy's Yellow' sport
Climber or pillar rose of good vigour, free-flowering. Flowers similar to its Hybrid Tea parent (**333**, p. 63).

'Climbing Mrs Herbert Stevens'   Cl.HT.sport
White, 8 ft (2·4 m.) 1923

Discovered by J. Pernet-Ducher, France.
Parentage: 'Mrs Herbert Stevens' sport
Climber or pillar rose of moderate vigour and rather loose straggling growth up to 8 ft (2·4 m.). Flowers double, large, white with creamy-green towards centre, buds long and pointed, scented. Mid to late June, slightly recurrent. Sometimes grown under glass for cutting. Foliage rather sensitive to mildew and black spot. Its parent Hybrid Tea has now almost completely disappeared from catalogues but the climbing sport is still occasionally seen in old gardens and is a beautiful and graceful rose.

'Climbing Mrs Sam McGredy'   Cl.HT.sport
Deep coppery-salmon-red, recurrent, 8 ft (2·4 m.) 1937
Discovered by T. A. H. Buisman & Son, Holland, also sported at Somerset Rose Co., U.S.A. in 1940.
Parentage: 'Mrs Sam McGredy' sport
Climber or pillar rose of good vigour, free-flowering. Flowers large, semi-double or double, coppery-salmon-red, fading to coppery-pink, a striking blend. Sensitive to black spot.

'Climbing Mons. Paul Lédé'   Cl.HT.sport
Blush-pink, 15 ft (4·6 m.) 1913
Discovered by S. Low & Co., England.
Parentage: 'Mons. Paul Lédé' sport
Vigorous climber or pillar rose up to 15 ft (4·6 m.). Flowers large, double or semi-double, pale blush-pink with deeper pink centre, strongly scented; mid to late June with main flowering and then somewhat recurrent. A worthwhile rose but now rarely grown. **267**, p. 50.

Abbreviations and Symbols used in the text

Rose classifications

A.	Alba	HT.	Hybrid Tea
B.	Bourbon	MCl.	Modern, large-flowered climber
C.	Centifolia	Min.	Miniature
Ch.	China	Moss	Centifolia muscosa
Cl.	Climber	MSh.	Modern shrub
D.	Damask	P.	Penzance Sweet Brier
Fl.	Floribunda	R.	Rambler
G.	Gallica	Rg.	Rugosa
HM.	Hybrid Musk	Sp.	Species and first hybrids
HP.	Hybrid Perpetual	Sw.	Sweet Brier

Rose Awards and Societies

A.A.R.S.	All-America Rose Selection
A.G.M.	Award of Garden Merit
A.M.	Award of Merit
A.R.S.	American Rose Society
B.B.G.M.	Baden Baden Gold Medal, Germany
B.G.M.	Bagatelle Gold Medal, Paris
C.C.V.	Clay Challenge Vase for scent
C.M.	Certificate of Merit
D.F.P.	David Fuerstenberg Prize
F.C.C.	First Class Certificate
G.G.M.	Geneva Gold Medal
G.M.	Gold Medal
G.M.C.B.	Gold Medal City of Belfast
G.M.H.G.M.	Gertrude M. Hubbard Gold Medal
G.R.H.	Golden Rose of The Hague
G.T.A.B.	Golden Thorn Award Belfast
H.E.M.M.	The Henry Edland Memorial Medal for the most fragrant rose of the year
H.G.M.	The Hague Gold Medal
L.G.M.	Lyon Gold Medal, France
M.G.M.	Madrid Gold Medal
N.G.M.C.	National Gold Medal Certificate
P.G.M.	Portland Gold Medal, Oregon, U.S.A.
P.I.T.	President's International Trophy
R.B.	Prize for the most fragrant rose, Roeulx, Belgium
R.B.G.M.	Roeulx, Belgium, Gold Medal
R.G.M.	Rome Gold Medal
R.H.S.	The Royal Horticultural Society, London
R.N.R.S.	The Royal National Rose Society, Great Britain*
T.G.C.	Trial Ground Certificate
U.A.B.	The 'Uladh' Award for fragrance, Belfast

*National Rose Society awards, before 1965, are included here under R.N.R.S.

The illustration numbers are in **bold type** and the page numbers in light type preceded by p.

'Climbing Pompon de Paris' Cl.Min.sport
Rose pink, 6 ft (1·8 m.)
Parentage: 'Pompon de Paris' sport
Sometimes known as 'Climbing Rouletii'. The leaves match those
of the miniature bush form but this rose will grow up to 6 ft (1·8 m.)
high. Makes a wonderful display in June with its small rose pink
double flowers and has a few intermittent flowers later. The plant
illustrated was photographed by the Alpine House at the R.H.S.
Garden, Wisley, Surrey, and is growing on its own roots. **268**, p. 50.

'Climbing Shot Silk' Cl.HT.sport
Orange-salmon, flushed carmine, yellow at base, recurrent, 10 ft
(3 m.) 1931
Discovered by C. Knight, Australia.
Parentage: 'Shot Silk' sport
Vigorous climber or pillar rose, now much more often seen than its
parent. The flowers, an attractive salmon-pink shaded yellow, soon
open and are nicely scented. Borne profusely, especially in autumn.
Does not mind wet weather and has handsome glossy foliage. Still
worth growing.

'Climbing Super Star', 'Climbing Tropicana' Cl.HT.sport
Very bright light vermilion, recurrent, 8 ft (2·4 m.) 1965
Discovered by Blaby Rose Gardens, England, and in Europe and
U.S.A. in same year.
Parentage: 'Super Star' sport
Climber or pillar rose, apparently of good vigour and promising.
As a sport of a most brilliant and widely grown rose (**369**, p. 69), it is
likely to become popular.

'Climbing Tropicana' see **'Climbing Super Star'**

'Cocktail' MCl.Sh.
Bright crimson and white, recurrent, 6 ft (1·8 m.) 1957
Raised by F. Meilland, France.
Parentage: ('Independence' × 'Orange Triumph') × 'Phyllis
Bide'
Modern climber for warm walls, pillar or large shrub rose. Flowers
single, bright crimson with large creamy-white or blush-pink
centre round large boss of bright yellow stamens, of medium size,
2–2½ in. (5·1–6·4 cm.) across, singly or in large clusters. Free-
flowering and slightly scented. A striking, rather brash rose, giving
almost a bicolor effect. In a warm sheltered position against a wall
it generally grows well but in a colder position it is inclined to die
back in winter; in warmer parts it is usually a very striking rose. **236**,
p. 44.
A.M., R.H.S. 1958.

'Cœur d'Amour' see **'Red Devil', 357**, p. 67.

'Colibri' Min.
Vivid orange-yellow, 8–10 in. (20·3–25·4 cm.) 1958
Raised by F. Meilland, France.
Parentage: 'Goldilocks' × 'Perla de Montserrat'
A plant of moderate growth, very bushy with glossy foliage. The
small double flowers are vivid orange-yellow, edged coral and
produced in clusters. Slight fragrance. Flowers freely and lasts well.
G.R.H. 1962.

'Colour Wonder' see **'Königin der Rosen', 323**, p. 61.

'Commandant Beaurepaire', 'Panachée d'Angers' B.
Deep purplish-crimson, summer, 5 ft (1·5 m.) 1874

Raised by Moreau-Robert, France.
Bourbon. Vigorous shrub up to 5 ft (1·5 m.), often forming a thick
bush. Flowers large, double, deep purplish-crimson, flecked and
streaked with white or lighter pink irregularly, about 3½ in.
(8·9 cm.) across, slight scent. Rather variable in colour. Borne in
clusters. Mid-June to July, but only very slightly recurrent. Free-
flowering. Foliage dark green, of hybrid tea type. One of the old
striped roses.

'Common Moss Rose' see **R. × centifolia 'Muscosa'**

'Complicata' MSh.Cl.
Bright pink, white centre, early summer, 8 × 8 ft (2·4 × 2·4 m.)
Shrub or pillar rose of tremendous vigour, up to 8 × 8 ft (2·4 ×
2·4 m.) or even more if grown up into an old tree. Origin unknown
and not recorded in any of the old rose books. Arching growth, up to
5 ft (1·5 m.). Flowers large, bright clear pink with white centre,
single with fine boss of golden stamens in centre, up to 5 in.
(12·7 cm.) across, at first saucer-shaped, then opening flat. Mid-
June. Very floriferous, like a much enlarged dog rose of slightly
deeper colour and blooming along the length of its branches.
Foliage and thorns both abundant. This is one of the finest garden
roses, where space is available, and is good on light sandy soils. It
is very effective where trained as a pillar round three supports but is
equally good as a vast sprawling mass. Its clear pink flowers and
very vigorous growth make it fit awkwardly into the Gallica group
of dusky purples and crimsons where it is sometimes placed. Roots
easily from cuttings. **150, 151**, p. 26; **152**, p. 27.
A.G.M., R.H.S. 1968.

'Comte de Chambord' D.
Pink, recurrent, 4 ft (1·2 m.) about 1860
Raised by Moreau-Robert, France.
Parentage: 'Baronne Prévost' × 'Portlandica'
One of the Portland Damask roses and a shrub rose of reasonable
vigour, growing up to 4 ft (1·2 m.). Flowers bright, warm pink,
paler at edges, large, opening rather flat and quartered, outside
petals rolled backwards, strongly scented. Mid-June and recurrent
flowering. Foliage strong green with pointed leaflets. It is surprising
that this beautiful rose is so rarely seen. Probably raised about 1860.
78, p. 14.

'Comtesse du Cayla' Ch.
Coppery-pink, recurrent. 3½ ft (1·1 m.) 1902
Raised by P. Guillot, France.
A China hybrid shrub of rather weak and open slender growth,
usually not over 3½ ft (1·1 m.). Flowers single, of medium size,
opening bright coppery-pink or coral-pink and maturing to
salmon-pink, scented. A bush in flower is like a coat of many colours
or one covered with chameleons, so great is the change in colour as
the flower matures. In this it resembles 'Mutabilis'. Late June,
recurrent. Young foliage is purplish-bronze. Foliage delicate, like
that of a small Hybrid Tea. The flower has an open slightly wind-
swept irregular appearance, like a wild flower, with considerable
charm and beauty Prune lightly, especially young plants.

'Conrad F. Meyer' Rg.
Pale pink, recurrent, 10 ft (3 m.) 1899
Raised by Dr F. Muller, Germany.
Parentage: ('Gloire de Dijon' × 'Duc de Rohan') × R. rugosa
'Germanica'
A very vigorous Rugosa hybrid up to 10 ft (3 m.) with long arching
growths. Stems strong and requiring little support and best grown
towards back of border as otherwise appearance may be rather
gaunt. Flowers large, semi-double, almost double, silvery-pink,

when mature showing large yellow centre, about 4½ in. (11·4 cm.) across. Scented. Mid-June and recurrent in September. Similar is 'Nova Zembla', a white flowered sport of 'Conrad F. Meyer'. Subject to black spot and rust in some areas. **131**, p. 23.

'Constance Spry'   MSh.Cl.
Bright rose, early summer, 8 ft (2·4 m.) 1961
Raised by D. Austin, England.
Parentage: 'Belle Isis' × 'Dainty Maid'
Very vigorous shrub or pillar rose, up to 8 ft (2·4 m.). Flowers large, deep glowing pink in the centre, paler outside, double, 4 in. (10·2 cm.) across, in clusters of 3–4 or singly. Colour close to 'Mme Grégoire Staechelin'. A well formed, full and deep flower of lovely colouring, scent strong but slightly acrid. Not recurrent. Foliage good, deep green, with 3 large leaflets. Growth very vigorous and tending to make long shoots up to 6 ft (1·8 m.) which need support. Can be used effectively against a grey wall or tied into a pillar, but can also be pruned more so as to keep it as a large shrub rose. It is quickly becoming popular as a very beautiful rose, worthily named after a great rose lover who did much to increase our appreciation of the older roses with her writings and flower arrangements. **153**, p. 28.
A.M., R.H.S. 1965.

Cooper's Burmese Rose see *R. cooperi*, **5**, p. 1.

'Copenhagen'   MCl.
Scarlet, recurrent, 10 ft (3 m.) 1964
Raised by N. D. Poulsen, Denmark.
Parentage: seedling × 'Ena Harkness'
A vigorous grower with medium green glossy foliage which has coppery shadings. The large double flowers are full and shapely, rich scarlet in colour and fragrant. Flowers recurrently in small trusses, suitable for walls or tall pillars. Apt to become a bit leggy. **237**, p. 45.
C.M., R.N.R.S. 1963.

'Copper Pot'   Fl.
Copper-orange, 3 ft (0·9 m.) 1968
Raised by A. Dickson & Sons Ltd, N. Ireland.
Parentage: seedling × 'Spek's Yellow'
A tall vigorous grower, upwards of 3 ft (0·9 m.) high, with glossy bronzy foliage. The medium sized flowers are copper-orange with a deeper reverse, produced in trusses and at their best in autumn. Slightly scented. A spectacular cultivar which catches the eye. T.G.C., R.N.R.S. 1968.

'Coral Dawn'   MCl.
Deep coral-pink, recurrent, 10 ft (3 m.) 1952
Raised by E. S. Boerner, U.S.A.
Parentage: ('New Dawn' seedling × unnamed yellow) × unnamed Polyantha
A rose of moderate vigour, climbing up to 10 ft (3 m.) with flowers of hybrid tea type. Flowers double, large, up to 5 in. (12·7 cm.) across, singly or in small clusters, deep coral-pink fading to pale pink at edge of petals, scented, free-flowering. Mid-June and recurrent throughout the summer. **238**, p. 45.

'Coral Star'   HT.
Coral pink, 2½ ft (0·8 m.) 1967
Raised by H. Robinson, England.
Parentage: 'Super Star' × 'Stella'
A fairly vigorous grower, 2½ ft (0·8 m.) high, with mid-green, glossy foliage. The full, shapely flowers are an attractive soft coral pink, with salmon shadings. They are scented and appear to be healthy and weather resistant. **287**, p. 54.

'Coralín', 'Carolin', 'Carolyn', 'Karolyn'   Min.
Turkey red, 18 in. (45·7 cm.) 1955
Raised by M. Dot, Spain.
Parentage: 'Méphisto' × 'Perla de Alcanada'
A compact branching plant, somewhat tall for miniature class, up to 18 in. (45·7 cm.) high, double flowers, turkey red with an orange sheen, producing a coral effect. They last well but have little fragrance.

'Cornelia'   HM.
Apricot-pink, recurrent, 6 ft (1·8 m.) 1925
Raised by Rev. J. H. Pemberton, England.
Vigorous Hybrid Musk shrub rose up to 6 ft (1·8 m.) making a thick bush. Flowers semi-double, in large clusters, rather small, coral or apricot-pink in bud and on first opening, later paler apricot-pink, with a subtle carrying scent and very floriferous. June to mid-July and recurrent throughout summer, usually with good autumn flowering in which often the largest clusters and best coloured flowers are produced. One of the most valuable of this group, makes a good hedging shrub. **119**, p. 21.

'Corona de Oro' see **'Gold Crown'**, **309**, p. 58.

'Coryana', *R. × coryana*   MSh.
Rose-pink, summer, 8 ft (2·4 m.) 1926
Raised by Dr C. C. Hurst, England.
Parentage: *R. roxburghii* seedling
Vigorous shrub rose up to 8 ft (2·4 m.). Open pollinated seedling of

---

Abbreviations and Symbols used in the text

Rose classifications

A.	Alba	HT.	Hybrid Tea
B.	Bourbon	MCl.	Modern, large-flowered climber
C.	Centifolia	Min.	Miniature
Ch.	China	Moss	Centifolia muscosa
Cl.	Climber	MSh.	Modern shrub
D.	Damask	P.	Penzance Sweet Brier
Fl.	Floribunda	R.	Rambler
G.	Gallica	Rg.	Rugosa
HM.	Hybrid Musk	Sp.	Species and first hybrids
HP.	Hybrid Perpetual	Sw.	Sweet Brier

Rose Awards and Societies

A.A.R.S.	All-America Rose Selection
A.G.M.	Award of Garden Merit
A.M.	Award of Merit
A.R.S.	American Rose Society
B.B.G.M.	Baden Baden Gold Medal, Germany
B.G.M.	Bagatelle Gold Medal, Paris
C.C.V.	Clay Challenge Vase for scent
C.M.	Certificate of Merit
D.F.P.	David Fuerstenberg Prize
F.C.C.	First Class Certificate
G.G.M.	Geneva Gold Medal
G.M.	Gold Medal
G.M.C.B.	Gold Medal City of Belfast
G.M.H.G.M.	Gertrude M. Hubbard Gold Medal
G.R.H.	Golden Rose of The Hague
G.T.A.B.	Golden Thorn Award Belfast
H.E.M.M.	The Henry Edland Memorial Medal for the most fragrant rose of the year
H.G.M.	The Hague Gold Medal
L.G.M.	Lyon Gold Medal, France
M.G.M.	Madrid Gold Medal
N.G.M.C.	National Gold Medal Certificate
P.G.M.	Portland Gold Medal, Oregon, U.S.A.
P.I.T.	President's International Trophy
R.B.	Prize for the most fragrant rose, Roeulx, Belgium
R.B.G.M.	Roeulx, Belgium, Gold Medal
R.G.M.	Rome Gold Medal
R.H.S.	The Royal Horticultural Society, London
R.N.R.S.	The Royal National Rose Society, Great Britain*
T.G.C.	Trial Ground Certificate
U.A.B.	The 'Uladh' Award for fragrance, Belfast

National Rose Society awards, before 1965, are included here under R.N.R.S.

The illustration numbers are in **bold type** and the page numbers in light type preceded by p.

R. roxburghii but generally considered to be a hybrid with *R. macrophylla*. Flowers single, rose-pink with a slight bluish tinge, of medium size, opening flat with large boss of yellow stamens. Free-flowering, not scented. From mid-June for some weeks but not recurrent. Foliage usually abundant and growth tends to be rather horizontal. Raised by Dr C. C. Hurst in 1926 during his experiments in rose genetics at Cambridge from seed sent from Kew but rarely grown and little inprovement over *R. roxburghii*. **154**, p. 28.

'Cottage Maid' see *R. × centifolia* **'Variegata'**

'Coupe d'Hébé'   B.
Deep pink, summer, 7 ft (2·1 m.) 1840
Raised by M. Laffay, France.
A vigorous shrub up to 7 ft (2·1 m.) or more, usually with rather loose growth. Flowers medium in size, double, in clusters, deep pink inside, but almost white on outside, fragrant. Late June to mid-July, but not recurrent. The flower heads tend to hang downwards and stalks are weak.

'Couronne d'Or' see **'Gold Crown', 309**, p. 58.

'Courvoisier'   Fl.
Ochre, 2½ ft (0·8 m.) 1969
Raised by S. McGredy IV, N. Ireland.
Parentage: 'Elizabeth of Glamis' × 'Casanova'
A medium upright, bushy grower, 2½ ft (0·8 m.) high, with medium green, glossy foliage. The large full flowers are sometimes borne singly or several together and are a warm shade of ochre yellow. Fragrant. **400**, p. 74.

'Cramoisi Picoté'   G.
Crimson, summer, 4 ft (1·2 m.) 1834
Raised by J. P. Vibert, France.
Gallica rose of medium size with erect growth. Flowers rather small, fully double and globular, crimson, becoming paler as they mature but retaining edge of crimson to petals. Foliage rather small. Rarely seen now in gardens.

'Crested Moss Rose' see *R. × centifolia* **'Cristata'**

'Cricri'   Min.
Salmon, 12 in. (30·5 cm.) 1958
Raised by F. Meilland, France.
Parentage: ('Alain' × 'Independence') × 'Perla de Alcanada'
A dwarf, very bushy grower, 12 in. (30·5 cm.) high, with well formed, very double flowers, salmon shaded coral.

'Crimson China' see under *R. chinensis*

'Crimson Glory'   HT.
Crimson, 2 ft (0·6 m.) 1935
Raised by W. Kordes, Germany.
Parentage: 'Cathrine Kordes' seedling × 'W. E. Chaplin'
A low growing cultivar of spreading habit with semi-glossy, medium green foliage liable to get mildew. The deep velvety crimson flowers are still cherished by some for their rich fragrance although they turn rusty with age. Has been superseded by many of its offspring as it has been much used for breeding new roses. Should not be severely pruned.
G.M., R.N.R.S. 1936.

'Crimson Moss'   Moss Sh.
Dark maroon-purple, summer, 5 ft (1·5 m.)
Moss rose of *centifolia* type. Fairly vigorous shrub up to 5 ft (1·5 m.). Closely resembles the Pink Moss rose but the flowers are much deeper in colour, being dark maroon-purple with some crimson towards centre. Bud very mossy but the rose tends not to open properly. Mid-late June, not recurrent. It is rarely listed now in catalogues.

'Crimson Shower'   Cl.R.
Crimson, recurrent, 8 ft (2·4 m.) 1951
Raised by A. Norman, England.
Parentage: 'Excelsa' seedling
A vigorous grower, up to 8 ft (2·4 m.), with light green glossy foliage. The small, rosette type flowers are freely produced, later than most, in large trusses over a period, crimson in colour. Makes a fine weeping standard as shown in the photograph. **201**, p. 37.

'Criterion'   HT.
Cerise, 3½ ft (1·1 m.) 1966
Raised by G. de Ruiter, Holland.
Parentage: ('Independence' × 'Signal Red') × 'Peace'
A vigorous branching grower, 3½ ft (1·1 m.) high with dark green glossy foliage. The large flowers are well formed and full, opening quickly, and are rich, unfading cerise in colour. Free and continuous flowering, especially in autumn. Protection against black spot may be required. **288**, p. 54.

'Cuisse de Nymphe' see under **'Maidens' Blush', 67**, p. 12.

'Cuisse de Nymphe Emue' see under **'Maidens' Blush', 67**, p. 12.

'Cupid'   Cl.
Light pink, early summer, 15 × 15 ft (4·6 × 4·6 m.) 1915
Raised by B. R. Cant, England.
Very vigorous climber up to 15 ft (4·6 m.) and covering large wall or growing up an old tree. Flowers very large, up to 5 in. (12·7 cm.), single with slightly waved petals, bright flesh-pink tinted with deeper apricot or peach. Mid to late June and not recurrent. Scented. Hips large, orange-red and persistent, sometimes in clusters. A rose which is not often grown now but which is effective where there is space.

'Curiosity'   HT.
Scarlet and gold, 2 ft (0·6 m.) 1971
Introduced by J. Cocker & Sons Ltd, Scotland.
Parentage: 'Cleopatra' sport
A moderate compact grower, in which the normal dark green glossy foliage has become splashed with cream and white variegation, contrasting with the ruby red of the young foliage. The medium sized flowers are well-formed, scarlet with gold reverse, and have some scent. Floral arrangers will find this well named cultivar an added attraction for some of their compositions and it will certainly bring more variety into classes where rose foliage only is allowed. **289**, p. 54.

'Daily Sketch'   Fl.
Pink and silver, 3 ft (0·9 m.) 1960
Raised by S. McGredy IV, N. Ireland.
Parentage: 'Ma Perkins' × 'Grand Gala'
A vigorous grower with very stiff, upright growths, to 3 ft (0·9 m.) in height with glossy, bronze tinted foliage. The double flowers are well formed in the early stages, when they are pink and silver: the pink

deepens to red and increases as the flowers age. Free flowering and fragrant, this is a good cultivar for a difficult position near trees. G.M., R.N.R.S. 1960.

'Dainty Bess'   HT.
Soft rose-pink, 2½ ft (0·8 m.) 1925
Raised by W. E. B. Archer, England.
Parentage: 'Ophelia' × 'K. of K.'
An old but still fairly vigorous cultivar, normally growing 2½ ft (0·8 m.) high, with somewhat sparse, mid green, semi-glossy foliage. The single flowers are soft rose-pink with very distinct dark stamens and a fresh scent. Free flowering, this cultivar has an old world charm and is still to be seen occasionally in gardens. Despite both its parents being classified as hybrid teas this rose has many of the characteristics associated with the floribundas and is included in that section of illustrations. **401**, p. 75.

'Dainty Maid'   Fl.
Silvery-pink and carmine, 3 ft (0·9 m.) 1938
Raised by E. B. LeGrice, England.
Parentage: 'D.T. Poulsen' × unknown
A vigorous, upright grower, 3 ft (0·9 m.) high, with abundant semi-glossy, dark green foliage. The single open flowers are silvery-pink with carmine-pink reverse and attractive stamens. Resists weather reasonably well and has a slight scent. Still a good garden cultivar. **402**, p. 75.
P.G.M. 1941.

'Daisy Hill' see under **'Macrantha'**

Damask Rose see *R.* × *damascena*

'Dame Prudence'   MSh.
Pale blush-pink, recurrent, 3 ft (0·9 m.) 1969
Raised by D. Austin, England.
Parentage: 'Ivory Fashion' × ('Constance Spry' × 'Ma Perkins')
Shrub rose of rather dwarf growth up to 3 ft (0·9 m.). Flowers double, pale blush-pink in centre, pearly and almost white outside, 3½–4 in. (8·9–10·2 cm.) across. Scented. Mid-June and then recurrent. Foliage delicate of hybrid tea type but smaller. A beautiful rose of very delicate colouring, lovely in its bud.

'Danny Boy'   MCl.
Orange-red, recurrent, 6–8 ft (1·8–2·4 m.) 1968
Raised by S. McGredy IV, N. Ireland.
Parentage: 'Uncle Walter' × 'Milord'
A free growing cultivar with large dark green foliage. The large, well formed flowers are an unusual shade of deep orange-red and have a slight scent.

'Danse des Sylphes'   MCl.
Bright crimson, recurrent, 10 ft (3 m.) 1957
Raised by C. Mallerin, France.
Parentage: 'Danse du Feu' × ('Peace' × 'Independence')
Vigorous climber. Flowers semi-double, of medium size and rounded, in large clusters, bright crimson, with slightly less orange-scarlet in the crimson than does its parent 'Danse du Feu', otherwise it can occupy a similar position in the garden. Free-flowering. Mid-June with main flowering but somewhat recurrent. **239**, p. 45.

'Danse du Feu', 'Spectacular'   MCl.
Bright scarlet-crimson, recurrent, 10 ft (3 m.) 1953
Raised by C. Mallerin, France.

Parentage: 'Paul's Scarlet Climber' × *R. multiflora* seedling
A vigorous climber with bright glossy green foliage, bronze-tinted when young. Flowers semi-double, rather globular, singly or in clusters up to 3 in. (7·6 cm.) across, very bright scarlet-crimson, slightly scented. Free-flowering. Mid-June with spectacular main flowering but slightly recurrent throughout summer. One of the most popular bright red climbers which rarely fails to make a striking effect. **240**, p. 45.
C.M., R.N.R.S. 1954.

'Dawson', 'The Dawson Rose'   R.
Deep pink, summer, 15 ft (4·6 m.) 1888
Raised by J. Dawson, U.S.A.
Parentage: *R. multiflora* × 'Général Jacqueminot'
Vigorous rambler but chiefly now of historical interest as being the first *multiflora* hybrid raised in the United States. Flowers in large clusters, double or semi-double, rather small, deep cerise-pink, free-flowering. Late June to mid-July but not very recurrent. Now superseded by ramblers with better colour and more recurrent flowering climbers. **202**, p. 37.

'De Meaux', *R.* × *centifolia pomponia*   C.
Deep pink, early summer, 3 ft (0·9 m.)
Dwarf shrub, rarely over 3 ft (0·9 m.), rather dense twiggy growth and foliage smaller than in a typical *centifolia* and lighter green. Buds rounded opening flat, clear rather sugary pink, much smaller than in *centifolia*, often only 1 in. (2·5 cm.) across, scented. Early to mid-June, sometimes starting in May, not recurrent. Known to Redouté as *Rosa pomponia* and the flowers do resemble a miniature

---

Abbreviations and Symbols used in the text

Rose classifications

A.	Alba	HT.	Hybrid Tea
B.	Bourbon	MCl.	Modern, large-flowered climber
C.	Centifolia	Min.	Miniature
Ch.	China	Moss	Centifolia muscosa
Cl.	Climber	MSh.	Modern shrub
D.	Damask	P.	Penzance Sweet Brier
Fl.	Floribunda	R.	Rambler
G.	Gallica	Rg.	Rugosa
HM.	Hybrid Musk	Sp.	Species and first hybrids
HP.	Hybrid Perpetual	Sw.	Sweet Brier

Rose Awards and Societies

A.A.R.S.	All-America Rose Selection
A.G.M.	Award of Garden Merit
A.M.	Award of Merit
A.R.S.	American Rose Society
B.B.G.M.	Baden Baden Gold Medal, Germany
B.G.M.	Bagatelle Gold Medal, Paris
C.C.V.	Clay Challenge Vase for scent
C.M.	Certificate of Merit
D.F.P.	David Fuerstenberg Prize
F.C.C.	First Class Certificate
G.G.M.	Geneva Gold Medal
G.M.	Gold Medal
G.M.C.B.	Gold Medal City of Belfast
G.M.H.G.M.	Gertrude M. Hubbard Gold Medal
G.R.H.	Golden Rose of The Hague
G.T.A.B.	Golden Thorn Award Belfast
H.E.M.M.	The Henry Edland Memorial Medal for the most fragrant rose of the year
H.G.M.	The Hague Gold Medal
L.G.M.	Lyon Gold Medal, France
M.G.M.	Madrid Gold Medal
N.G.M.C.	National Gold Medal Certificate
P.G.M.	Portland Gold Medal, Oregon, U.S.A.
P.I.T.	President's International Trophy
R.B.	Prize for the most fragrant rose, Roeulx, Belgium
R.B.G.M.	Roeulx, Belgium, Gold Medal
R.G.M.	Rome Gold Medal
R.H.S.	The Royal Horticultural Society, London
R.N.R.S.	The Royal National Rose Society, Great Britain*
T.G.C.	Trial Ground Certificate
U.A.B.	The 'Uladh' Award for fragrance, Belfast

*National Rose Society awards, before 1965, are included here under R.N.R.S.

The illustration numbers are in **bold type** and the page numbers in light type preceded by p.

pompon. An old rose, thought to have arisen in the seventeenth century, it is well worth growing for its delicacy of flower. Origin not known, but sometimes attributed to Sweet in 1789.

'Dearest' Fl.
Salmon-pink, 2½ ft (0·8 m.) 1960
Raised by A. Dickson & Sons Ltd, N. Ireland.
Parentage: seedling × 'Spartan'
A vigorous bushy grower, 2½ ft (0·8 m.) high, with glossy, dark green foliage. The double flowers are shapely in the bud stage, opening flat, a warm salmon-pink which lightens slightly with age. Produced freely in large trusses, they have a very pleasant scent. Somewhat unhappy in wet weather but a good bedding cultivar in normal weather. **403**, p. 75.
A.M., R.H.S. 1960; G.M., R.N.R.S. 1961; F.C.C., R.H.S. 1962.

'Detroiter', 'Brilliant', 'Schlösser's Brilliant' HT.
Scarlet, 2 ft (0·6 m.) 1952
Raised by R. Kordes, Germany.
Parentage: 'Poinsettia' × 'Crimson Glory'
A fairly vigorous, upright grower to about 2 ft (0·6 m.). The semi-glossy, dark green foliage is somewhat sparse. The full, high centred flowers are rich scarlet and freely produced but have little scent. Protection from mildew may be required in some areas. An exhibitor's rose.
G.M., R.N.R.S. 1952.

'Devotion' Fl.
Blush-pink, 3½ ft (1·1 m.) 1971
Raised by R. Harkness & Co. Ltd, England.
Parentage: 'Orange Sensation' × 'Peace'
A tall, bushy grower, 3½ ft (1·1 m.) high, with mid-green, semi-glossy foliage. The blush-pink, hybrid tea type flowers are shaded deeper pink and have some fragrance. May require protection against mildew.
T.G.C., R.N.R.S. 1968.

'Dickson's Flame' Fl.
Scarlet-flame, 2 ft (0·6 m.) 1958
Raised by A. Dickson & Sons Ltd, N. Ireland.
Parentage: 'Independence' seedling × 'Nymph'
A fairly vigorous grower, 2 ft (0·6 m.) high, with small glossy leaves. The large, semi-double flowers are scarlet-flame in colour, non-fading but inclined to hang down.
G.M., R.N.R.S. 1958.

'Dimples' Fl.
Creamy-white, 2½ ft (0·8 m.) 1967
Raised by E. B. LeGrice, England.
A medium grower up to 2½ ft (0·8 m.) high, with glossy foliage. The full flowers are creamy-white with attractive golden centre. Freely produced in well spaced trusses. May require protection against black spot and mildew.

'Diorama' HT.
Apricot yellow, 3 ft (0·9 m.) 1965
Raised by G. de Ruiter, Holland.
Parentage: 'Peace' × 'Beauté'
A vigorous branching grower, 3 ft (0·9 m.) high, with large medium green semi-glossy foliage. The apricot yellow blooms open quickly and are flushed pink when young but retain their colour well, and are sweet scented. This cultivar is especially good in autumn, resisting wet weather well and is proving popular. A good bedding rose which may require protection against black spot. **290**, p. 54.
T.G.C., R.N.R.S. 1965.

'Direktor Benschop' see 'City of York', **235**, p. 43.

'Dr A. J. Verhage', 'Golden Wave' HT.
Golden-yellow, 2 ft (0·6 m.) 1960
Raised by G. Verbeek & Zn, Holland.
Parentage: 'Tawny Gold' × ('Baccara' × seedling)
A 2 ft (0·6 m.) high cultivar of medium vigour with small dark green, glossy foliage and moderately sized flowers. These are golden-yellow, reasonably full and shapely and quite fragrant. Not a success generally outside, requiring very sheltered conditions but a lovely rose when grown under glass where it has proved a good forcer. **291**, p. 54.

'Dr Barnardo' Fl.
Deep crimson, 3 ft (0·9 m.) 1969
Raised by R. Harkness & Co. Ltd, England.
Parentage: 'Vera Dalton' × 'Red Dandy'
A strong grower, 2½–3 ft (0·8–0·9 m.) high with ample glossy, medium green foliage. The flowers are freely produced in trusses, deep crimson in colour, nicely formed in bud and have a slight scent. **404**, p. 75.
T.G.C., R.N.R.S. 1968.

'Dr W. Van Fleet' Cl.R.
Pale pink, early summer, 20 ft (6·1 m.) 1910
Raised by Dr W. Van Fleet, U.S.A.
Parentage: (R. wichuraiana × 'Safrano') × 'Souvenir du Président Carnot'
Vigorous climber or rambler up to 20 ft (6·1 m.). Flowers double of medium size, pale cameo-pink fading almost to white, scented. Very free-flowering. This rose blooms mostly on old wood and so should be pruned with moderation. Mid to late June but not recurrent and for this reason now largely superseded by 'New Dawn' (**216**, p. 40) its recurrent flowering sport.

Dog Rose see *R. canina*

'Dometil Beccard' see *R. × centifolia* 'Variegata'

'Don Juan' MCl.
Dark red, recurrent, 8 ft (2·4 m.) 1958
Raised by M. Malandrone, Italy.
Parentage: 'New Dawn' seedling × 'New Yorker'
A very promising new climber with dark green, leathery foliage. Moderate vigour. Flowers large up to 5 in. (12·7 cm.) across, double, well formed, velvety dark crimson, strongly scented. Mid-June and recurrent.

'Doreen' HT.
Orange-yellow, 2 ft (0·6 m.) 1950
Raised by H. Robinson. England.
Parentage: 'Lydia' × 'McGredy's Sunset'
A reasonably vigorous cultivar of medium height with dark green, glossy bronze tinted foliage. The moderately full blooms are orange-yellow with orange and scarlet shadings; they are freely produced, especially in autumn. Resists wet weather very well but may require protection from black spot which does not attack it so readily in standard form. A unique colour. **292**, p. 54.
T.G.C., R.N.R.S. 1951.

'Dorothy Peach' HT.
Yellow, 2½ ft (0·8 m.) 1958
Raised by H. Robinson, England.
Parentage: 'Lydia' × 'Peace'

A vigorous bushy grower, 2½ ft (0·8 m.) in height with abundant medium green, semi-glossy foliage. The blooms are soft yellow with pink tinges on outer petals and these colours last well. Resistance to weather is reasonable; very free flowering and, owing to its habit, suitable for small gardens. Excellent as a standard and useful for exhibition when well grown. Has a sweet scent but may require protection from black spot. **293**, p. 55.
G.M., R.N.R.S. 1959.

'Dorothy Perkins'   R.
Bright pink, early summer, 10 ft (3 m.) 1901
Raised by Jackson & Perkins, U.S.A.
Parentage: *R. wichuraiana* × 'Mme Gabriel Luizet'
Vigorous and for long a most popular rambler but now largely superseded. Flowers in large clusters, double or semi-double, rather small, bright shocking-pink with bluish tones, abundant in flowers. Late June to mid-July but not recurrent. Foliage bright green on long straggling growths. Very subject to mildew and so not suitable for walls but still grown to cover pergolas and for screens.
A.M., R.H.S. 1902.

'Dorothy Wheatcroft'   MSh.
Bright orient-red, recurrent, 6 ft (1·8 m.) 1961
Raised by M. Tantau, Germany.
A vigorous, upright grower which does not spread much, from 5–6 ft (1·5–1·8 m.) in height, with large, glossy bright green leaves. The semi-double flowers have scalloped edges, and are produced in huge trusses, particularly in autumn, bright orient-red which fades with a pinkish tinge. Weather resistance is good and there is a slight fragrance. Sometimes regarded as a Floribunda. **155**, p. 28.
G.M., R.N.R.S. 1961; A.M., R.H.S. 1960.

'Dortmund'   MCl.
Crimson-red and white, recurrent, 8–10 ft (2·4–3 m.) 1955
Raised by W. Kordes, Germany.
Parentage: seedling × *R. kordesii*
A vigorous climber with dark green glossy foliage, which is in my experience always healthy. The large, single flowers are crimson-red with a white eye around the boss of buff-yellow stamens, and are freely produced in large clusters. A recurrent bloomer if dead-headed, otherwise a large crop of hips absorbs the plant's energy and reduces late flowering. A good pillar rose, indeed one of the best of the *kordesii* roses which may also be grown as a large shrub. **241**, p. 45.

'Double White' see *R. spinosissima* **'Double White', 54**, p. 10.

'Double Yellow' see *R. spinosissima* **'Double Yellow', 55**, p. 10.

'Dream Waltz'   Fl.
Deep red, 3½ ft (1·1 m.) 1969
Raised by M. Tantau, Germany.
A free growing, upright cultivar, about 3½ ft (1·1 m.) high, with glossy foliage. The large double flowers are deep, unfading red with a velvety bloom on the petals which increases their attraction. No scent. Appears to be a continuous flowering cultivar. **405**, p. 75.

'Dreamland' see **'Traumland'**

'Du Maître d'Ecole' see **'Rose du Maître d'Ecole'**

'Duc de Guiche'   G.
Purplish-crimson, summer, 5 ft (1·5 m.) before 1829
Raised by Prévost, France.
A Gallica rose of medium vigour up to 5 ft (1·5 m.). Flowers bright purplish-crimson, fully double, rather globular but slightly quartered when mature and showing a small green eye; veined with purple. Mid to late June. Not a very distinguished rose in a hot season. Raiser and date of raising uncertain.

'Duchesse de Montebello'   G.
Pale pink, summer, 5 ft (1·5 m.) before 1829
Raised by M. Laffay, France.
A rose of medium vigour, but rather loose growth and needing strong support, up to 5 ft (1·5 m.). Flowers fully double, globular, pale blush to shell-pink, of medium size. Fragrant. Mid to late June. Flowers grow in long sprays and are beautiful for cutting. Foliage greyish-green. A shrub which needs to be grown generously to give a good effect, but it is one of considerable charm which I have enjoyed for many years. Usually placed as a Gallica but nearer to an Alba in habit.

'Duchesse d'Istrie' see under **'William Lobb', 76**, p. 14.

'Duet'   HT.
Crimson, 2½ ft (0·8 m.) 1960
Raised by H. C. Swim, U.S.A.
Parentage: 'Fandango' × 'Roundelay'
A vigorous, well branched grower, 2½ ft (0·8 m.) high, with leathery

---

Abbreviations and Symbols used in the text

Rose classifications

A.	Alba	HT.	Hybrid Tea
B.	Bourbon	MCl.	Modern, large-flowered climber
C.	Centifolia	Min.	Miniature
Ch.	China	Moss	Centifolia muscosa
Cl.	Climber	MSh.	Modern shrub
D.	Damask	P.	Penzance Sweet Brier
Fl.	Floribunda	R.	Rambler
G.	Gallica	Rg.	Rugosa
HM.	Hybrid Musk	Sp.	Species and first hybrids
HP.	Hybrid Perpetual	Sw.	Sweet Brier

Rose Awards and Societies

A.A.R.S.	All-America Rose Selection
A.G.M.	Award of Garden Merit
A.M.	Award of Merit
A.R.S.	American Rose Society
B.B.G.M.	Baden Baden Gold Medal, Germany
B.G.M.	Bagatelle Gold Medal, Paris
C.C.V.	Clay Challenge Vase for scent
C.M.	Certificate of Merit
D.F.P.	David Fuerstenberg Prize
F.C.C.	First Class Certificate
G.G.M.	Geneva Gold Medal
G.M.	Gold Medal
G.M.C.B.	Gold Medal City of Belfast
G.M.H.G.M.	Gertrude M. Hubbard Gold Medal
G.R.H.	Golden Rose of The Hague
G.T.A.B.	Golden Thorn Award Belfast
H.E.M.M.	The Henry Edland Memorial Medal for the most fragrant rose of the year
H.G.M.	The Hague Gold Medal
L.G.M.	Lyon Gold Medal, France
M.G.M.	Madrid Gold Medal
N.G.M.C.	National Gold Medal Certificate
P.G.M.	Portland Gold Medal, Oregon, U.S.A.
P.I.T.	President's International Trophy
R.B.	Prize for the most fragrant rose, Roeulx, Belgium
R.B.G.M.	Roeulx, Belgium, Gold Medal
R.G.M.	Rome Gold Medal
R.H.S.	The Royal Horticultural Society, London
R.N.R.S.	The Royal National Rose Society, Great Britain*
T.G.C.	Trial Ground Certificate
U.A.B.	The 'Uladh' Award for fragrance, Belfast

National Rose Society awards, before 1965, are included here under R.N.R.S.

The illustration numbers are in **bold type** and the page numbers in light type preceded by p.

foliage. The moderate sized blooms are full, well formed in early stages, crimson in colour with a lighter reverse, slightly fragrant. **295**, p. 56.

'Duftwolke', 'Fragrant Cloud', 'Nuage Parfumé' HT.
Geranium-red, 2½–3½ ft (0·8–1·1 m.) 1964
Raised by M. Tantau, Germany
Parentage: seedling × 'Prima Ballerina'
An outstanding cultivar which has rapidly become one of the most popular roses throughout the world. Its vigorous upright growth has abundant, glossy, dark green foliage, generally resistant to disease but may require protection from black spot in some areas. The large full blooms are shapely enough for exhibition and are produced freely, especially in summer and autumn, with intermittent blooms between. The geranium-red blooms fade to purplish-red in hot weather and require regular dead-heading to retain their effect in the garden. Colour is improved in autumn and retained better at that season; the scent at all times is delicious. The weather resistance of the blooms is reasonably good; these are usually produced 4 or 5 on a stem. Very useful also in half or full standard form. **296**, p. 56.
G.M., R.N.R.S. 1963; P.I.T., R.N.R.S. 1964; A.M., R.H.S. 1964; F.C.C., R.H.S. 1968.

'Duke of Argyll' see *R. spinosissima* **'Duke of Argyll'**, **56**, p. 11.

'Duke of Windsor', 'Herzog von Windsor' HT.
Orange-vermilion, 2½ ft (0·8 m.) 1968
Raised by M. Tantau, Germany.
Parentage: 'Prima Ballerina' × unnamed seedling
The parentage above is officially given by the R.N.R.S. but Harry Wheatcroft quotes the raiser as attributing it to 'Spartan' × 'Montezuma'. An upright bushy grower, 2½ ft (0·8 m.) high, with abundant dark green, semi-glossy foliage and very suitable for bedding. The flowers are of medium size, well formed when young but opening out quickly to a loose formation. Borne several together, the deep orange-vermilion blooms change to a more salmon shade with age but continue to be pleasing except in very wet weather. They are very fragrant. In some areas protection against mildew is required. **294**, p. 55.
H.E.M.M. 1968; C.M., R.N.R.S. 1968; A.M., R.H.S. 1968.

'Duplex' see *R. pomifera* **'Duplex'**, **38**, p. 8.

'Düsterlohe' MSh.Cl.
Rose-pink, early summer, 4–5 ft (1·2–1·5 m.) 1931
Raised by W. Kordes, Germany.
Parentage: ('Venusta Pendula' × 'Daisy Hill') × 'Miss C. E. van Rossem'
Modern large shrub of loose, rather sprawling growth of up to 4–5 ft (1·2–1·5 m.) but another form of this rose grows to 7 ft (2·1 m.) and may be allowed to sprawl into old trees. Flowers semi-double, usually in small clusters, of medium size, rather globular on first opening, deep rose-pink, becoming slightly purplish-pink as flower matures, white in centre, about 3½ in. (8·9 cm.) across, not scented. Mid to late June, not recurrent, but free-flowering. Foliage neat, dark green growth very thorny. Hips persistent, large, light orange. Parentage has sometimes erroneously been given as *R. gallica* × *R. canina*. **156**, p. 28.

'Dwarfking', 'Zwergkönig' Min.
Deep red, 12 in. (30·5 cm.) 1957
Raised by W. Kordes, Germany.
Parentage: 'World's Fair' × 'Tom Thumb'
A compact grower up to 12 in. (30·5 cm.) high with glossy foliage.

The small double flowers are cupped, becoming flat, rich deep red in colour which is retained well. **503**, p. 96.

'Earldomensis' see *R.* × *pteragonis* **'Earldomensis'**, **42**, p. 8.

'Easlea's Golden Rambler' Cl.
Yellow, early summer, 12 ft (3·7 m.) 1932
Raised by W. Easlea & Sons Ltd, England.
A beautiful rose, almost unique among climbers in colour, scent and its fine shiny foliage. Vigorous and suitable for pillar or pergola, but not a rambler in the usual sense. Flowers large, semi-double, of hybrid tea type, buds bright yellow with occasional red flecks, opening to deep creamy-yellow and showing good boss of golden stamens, 4½ in. (11·4 cm.) across. Strongly scented; borne singly or in small clusters. Free-flowering in June but non-recurrent. Foliage good, dark olive-green, shiny, 3–5 broadly ovate leaflets of unusual shape. Cut flowering shoots back about August-September to the young shoots which will have developed.
G.M., R.N.R.S. 1932; A.M., R.H.S. 1932.

'Easter Morning' Min.
Ivory white, 12 in. (30·5 cm.) 1960
Raised by R. S. Moore, U.S.A.
Parentage: 'Golden Glow' × 'Zee'
A vigorous plant, up to 12 inches (30·5 cm.) high, with glossy foliage. The double flowers, somewhat large for a miniature, are an exquisite ivory white, not so free as some but highly regarded in the U.S.A. Slightly scented. Weather and mildew resistant.

'Eden Rose' HT.
Deep pink, 3½ ft (1·1 m.) 1950
Raised by F. Meilland, France.
Parentage: 'Peace' × 'Signora'
A very tall, vigorous grower with large leathery, glossy, medium green foliage with bronze tints when young. The deep pink blooms have a silvery pink reverse, are large, full, scented, somewhat globular and at times of sufficiently good form for exhibition. Colour retention is good and this cultivar flowers more freely if not severely pruned. Protection against mildew is advisable. **297**, p. 56.
G.M., R.N.R.S. 1950; A.M., R.H.S. 1950.

'Eiffel Tower' HT.
Pink, 3 ft (0·9 m.) 1963
Raised by D. L. Armstrong and H. C. Swim, U.S.A.
Parentage: 'First Love' × unnamed seedling
A tall, vigorous grower with large, light green, semi-glossy foliage. The very long pointed buds open out into full, well shaped blooms of medium pink with long strong stems, ideal for cutting. Free flowering and fragrant.
G.G.M. 1963; R.G.M. 1963.

'Eleanor' Min.
Deep coral pink, 12 in. (30·5 cm.) 1960
Raised by R. S. Moore, U.S.A.
Parentage: (*R. wichuraiana* × 'Floradora') × (seedling × 'Zee')
An upright bushy grower, to 12 in. (30·5 cm.) high with glossy foliage. The freely produced flowers are small, double, deep coral pink with a white base, a lovely colour. An established favourite.

'Electron' see **'Mullard Jubilee'**, **340**, p. 64.

'Elegance' Cl.
Pale yellow, recurrent, 15 ft (4·6 m.) 1937
Raised by Dr & Mrs W. D. Brownell, U.S.A.

Parentage: 'Glenn Dale' × ('Mary Wallace' × 'Miss Lolita Armour')
Vigorous climber of hybrid tea type, up to 15 ft (4·6 m.). Flowers large, double, clear pale yellow, slightly deeper in centre, fading to pale cream at outer edges, scented, free-flowering. A magnificent sight in mid to late June, slightly recurrent and resisting bad weather well. Foliage luxuriant, dark, glossy. **203**, p. 37.

'Elida' HT.
Deep vermilion, 3 ft (0·9 m.) 1966
Raised by M. Tantau, Germany.
A vigorous, upright grower, about 3 ft (0·9 m.) high, with dark green, semi-glossy foliage, red in early stages of growth. The medium sized flowers are full and shapely, deep vermilion tinted burnt orange, bringing a splash of brilliant colour into the garden. Good in autumn. **298**, p. 56.

'Elizabeth Harkness' HT.
Cream buff, 2½ ft (0·8 m.) 1969
Raised by R. Harkness & Co. Ltd, England.
Parentage: 'Red Dandy' × 'Piccadilly'
A bushy grower of medium height and mid green, semi-glossy foliage. The large blooms are creamy buff, tinged pink and amber with a tendency to deepen in autumn. Commencing to bloom early and well throughout the summer this variety's excellent form of flower should make it useful for exhibition as well as for the garden. Sweetly scented. Usually a healthy grower. **299**, p. 56.
C.M., R.N.R.S. 1969.

'Elizabeth of Glamis', 'Irish Beauty' Fl.
Salmon-pink, 3 ft (0·9 m.) 1964
Raised by S. McGredy IV, N. Ireland.
Parentage: 'Spartan' × 'Highlight'
A moderately vigorous grower, 2½–3 ft (0·8–0·9 m.) high, with semi-glossy, mid-green foliage. The large and sweetly fragrant flowers are double, well formed when young, eventually opening flat, salmon-pink with apricot suffusions, fading slightly with age, but always beautiful. Weather resistance is reasonably good and it repeats well. This cultivar seems to be selective in its requirements and when happy it is a joy in the garden. Sometimes it sulks, particularly in cold, exposed situations. **407**, p. 76.
P.I.T., R.N.R.S. 1963; G.M., R.N.R.S. 1963; C.C.V., R.N.R.S. 1963; A.M., R.H.S. 1964; F.C.C., R.H.S. 1968.

'Elmshorn' MSh.Cl.
Cherry-red, recurrent, 6 ft (1·8 m.) 1951
Raised by W. Kordes, Germany.
Parentage: 'Hamburg' × 'Verdun'
Modern and vigorous shrub rose up to 6 ft (1·8 m.) and suitable as a low climber. Flowers double, bright cherry-red, small medium in size about 1½ in. (3·8 cm.) across, but in large clusters, not scented. Free-flowering. Mid to late June, then recurrent, usually with good late autumn flowering. Usually a vigorous rose for the back of the border with less orange in the red flowers than in 'Bonn' (**142**, p. 25) or 'Berlin' (**141**, p. 25). **157**, p. 28.

'Elysium' Fl.
Light salmon pink, 3 ft (0·9 m.) 1961
Raised by R. Kordes, Germany.
A vigorous tall grower, 3 ft (0·9 m.) high, but bushy, with glossy, mid-green foliage. The large full flowers are well formed in the early stages, slightly cupped when open, light salmon pink and freely produced; they have a pleasant light scent. Not at its best in rainy weather. **406**, p. 75.
C.M., R.N.R.S. 1961; A.M., R.H.S. 1963.

'Embassy' HT.
Pale gold, 3 ft (0·9 m.) 1969
Raised by J. Sanday Ltd, England.
Parentage: 'Gavotte' × ('Magenta' × 'Spek's Yellow')
A fairly vigorous, upright grower with dark green, glossy foliage and 2½–3 ft (0·8–0·9 m.) high. The large full flowers are pale gold with apricot and carmine veining, beautifully formed and suitable for exhibition. Slightly fragrant. **300**, p. 56.

'Emily Gray' Cl.
Buff-yellow, early summer, 12 ft (3·7 m.) 1918
Raised by Dr A. H. Williams, England.
Parentage: 'Jersey Beauty' × 'Comtesse du Cayla'
Vigorous climber up to 12 ft (3·7 m.) with fine glossy foliage, dark bronze-tinted when young. Flowers of medium size in clusters, semi-double, deep golden-buff to yellow showing strong boss of yellow stamens. Mid to late June but not recurrent. Scented. Best planted in a warm place and reported in the United States as not reliably hardy north of Maryland.
G.M., R.N.R.S. 1916.

'Empereur du Maroc' HP.
Deep crimson, recurrent, 4 ft (1·2 m.) 1858
Raised by Guinoisseau, France.
Parentage: 'Géant des Batailles' seedling
A not very vigorous Hybrid Perpetual and seldom over 4 ft (1·2 m.). Flowers double, deep crimson-red shaded maroon but without purplish tinge, of medium size, slightly quartered, sometimes with a white streak in the petal, opening flat. Strongly scented. Mid to late June, slightly recurrent. **109**, p. 19.

Abbreviations and Symbols used in the text

Rose classifications

A.	Alba	HT.	Hybrid Tea
B.	Bourbon	MCl.	Modern, large-flowered climber
C.	Centifolia	Min.	Miniature
Ch.	China	Moss	Centifolia muscosa
Cl.	Climber	MSh.	Modern shrub
D.	Damask	P.	Penzance Sweet Brier
Fl.	Floribunda	R.	Rambler
G.	Gallica	Rg.	Rugosa
HM.	Hybrid Musk	Sp.	Species and first hybrids
HP.	Hybrid Perpetual	Sw.	Sweet Brier

Rose Awards and Societies

A.A.R.S.	All-America Rose Selection
A.G.M.	Award of Garden Merit
A.M.	Award of Merit
A.R.S.	American Rose Society
B.B.G.M.	Baden Baden Gold Medal, Germany
B.G.M.	Bagatelle Gold Medal, Paris
C.C.V.	Clay Challenge Vase for scent
C.M.	Certificate of Merit
D.F.P.	David Fuerstenberg Prize
F.C.C.	First Class Certificate
G.G.M.	Geneva Gold Medal
G.M.	Gold Medal
G.M.C.B.	Gold Medal City of Belfast
G.M.H.G.M.	Gertrude M. Hubbard Gold Medal
G.R.H.	Golden Rose of The Hague
G.T.A.B.	Golden Thorn Award Belfast
H.E.M.M.	The Henry Edland Memorial Medal for the most fragrant rose of the year
H.G.M.	The Hague Gold Medal
L.G.M.	Lyon Gold Medal, France
M.G.M.	Madrid Gold Medal
N.G.M.C.	National Gold Medal Certificate
P.G.M.	Portland Gold Medal, Oregon, U.S.A.
P.I.T.	President's International Trophy
R.B.	Prize for the most fragrant rose, Roeulx, Belgium
R.B.G.M.	Roeulx, Belgium, Gold Medal
R.G.M.	Rome Gold Medal
R.H.S.	The Royal Horticultural Society, London
R.N.R.S.	The Royal National Rose Society, Great Britain*
T.G.C.	Trial Ground Certificate
U.A.B.	The 'Uladh' Award for fragrance, Belfast

*National Rose Society awards, before 1965, are included here under R.N.R.S.

The illustration numbers are in **bold type** and the page numbers in light type preceded by p.

'Empress Josephine' see **'Francofurtana'**

'Ena Harkness'   HT.
Crimson-scarlet, 2½ ft (0·8 m.) 1946
Raised by A. Norman, England.
Parentage: 'Crimson Glory' × 'Southport'
A vigorous branching grower, 2½ ft (0·8 m.) high with semi-glossy, medium green foliage. The bright crimson-scarlet blooms are well formed and of superb texture but inclined to droop if not well grown, especially in hot weather. Very free flowering, generally at its best in autumn, this cultivar has long been popular as the best in this colour. Weather resistance is good and as a rule, the blooms are fragrant, although a strain exists which seems lacking in this respect. Popular as a standard. **301**, p. 57.
G.M., R.N.R.S. 1945; A.M., R.H.S. 1946; P.G.M. 1955.

'Ena Harkness, Climbing' see **'Climbing Ena Harkness'**

'Eos' see **R. (**moyesii × **'Magnifica') 'Eos', 31**, p. 6.

'Erfurt'   MSh.
Rose-pink, recurrent, 5 ft (1·5 m.) 1939
Raised by W. Kordes, Germany.
Parentage: 'Eva' × 'Reveil Dijonnais'
Modern shrub rose, vigorous up to 5 ft (1·5 m.) with long arching growth, flushed with red when young. Flowers semi-double, large, deep rose-pink with prominent white or yellowish-white base to petals and boss of deep gold stamens, becoming slightly blue-tinged as flower matures, scented. Mid to late June and recurrent, very floriferous. This is still one of the most valuable shrub roses in its colour. Sometimes described as a Hybrid Musk. **158**, p. 28.

'Ernest H. Morse'   HT.
Red, 3 ft (0·9 m.) 1964
Raised by W. Kordes, Germany.
A vigorous, tall, upright grower with abundant, semi-glossy, dark green foliage. The flowers are a rich turkey-red colour and are usually well formed, but open quickly to show loose centre. Free flowering, resisting wet weather well and sweetly scented, this cultivar has quickly attained popularity as a good garden rose and is occasionally useful for exhibition. **302**, p. 57.
G.M., R.N.R.S. 1965; A.M., R.H.S. 1968.

'Eroica' see **'Erotika'**

'Erotika', 'Eroica'   HT.
Dark red, 2½ ft (0·8 m.) 1968
Raised by M. Tantau, Germany.
A very vigorous upright grower with dark glossy foliage. The large, double, well formed flowers are velvety dark red and have some fragrance. Flowers freely in summer and again in autumn.

'Escapade'   Fl.
Rosy-magenta, 2½–3 ft (0·8–0·9 m.) 1967
Raised by R. Harkness & Co. Ltd, England.
Parentage: 'Pink Parfait' × 'Baby Faurax'
A vigorous, very bushy grower with abundant, glossy light green foliage which is generally healthy. The large semi-double flowers open out to show the stamens, and are a light rosy-magenta with a white centre. Non-fading. Very productive and seldom out of flower, this cultivar makes a very useful bedder. Resists weather reasonably well and has a pleasant musky scent. **408**, p. 76.
C.M., R.N.R.S. 1967; B.B.G.M. 1969; G.T.A.B. 1969.

'Esther Ofarim'   Fl.
Vermilion and yellow, 1½ ft (0·5 m.) 1970
Raised by R. Kordes, Germany.
A moderate grower, dwarf, bushy and compact with mid-green, semi-glossy foliage. The vermilion-scarlet flowers have a white reverse flushed with vermilion, the whole effect being translucent vermilion and yellow. Hybrid tea shaped flowers in early stages, opening out later; produced freely over a long season, several together and in trusses. May require watching for black spot. **409**, p. 77.
T.G.C., R.N.R.S. 1970

'Estrellita de Oro' see **'Baby Gold Star'**

'Etendard', 'New Dawn Rouge', 'Red New Dawn'   Cl.
Deep red, recurrent, 12 ft (3·7 m.) 1956
Raised by M. Robichon, France.
Parentage: 'New Dawn' × unnamed seedling
Vigorous climber or pillar rose, up to 12 ft (3·7 m.). Flowers in large clusters, semi-double, deep carmine-red, quite large, scented. Free-flowering from mid-June and recurrent. Foliage dark green, glossy. **204**, p. 38.

'Etoile de Hollande, Climbing' see **'Climbing Etoile de Hollande'**

'Etude'   MCl.
Deep rose-pink, recurrent, 6–8 ft (1·8–2·4 m.) 1965
Raised by C. Gregory & Son Ltd, England.
Parentage: 'Danse du Feu' × 'New Dawn'
A vigorous grower, restrained in height with light green glossy foliage. The medium sized semi-double flowers are deep-rose-pink, touched with salmon and have some fragrance. Freely recurring bloom over a long period makes this a very useful rose for pillars or fences. **242**, p. 45.
C.M., R.N.R.S. 1964; A.M., R.H.S. 1967.

'Eugène Fürst'   HP.
Bright carmine, recurrent, 5 ft (1·5 m.) 1875
Raised by Soupert & Notting, Luxembourg.
Parentage: 'Baron de Bonstetten' hybrid
Vigorous Hybrid Perpetual shrub, but usually not over 5 ft (1·5 m.). Flowers large, double, cupped on opening, bright carmine with darker flush. Not nearly as dark as 'Baron Girod de l'Ain' (**106**, p. 19) which sported from it but a rather similar flower and a valuable garden plant although more rarely seen than the 'Baron'. Scented.

'Europeana'   Fl.
Deep crimson, 2½ ft (0·8 m.) 1963
Raised by G. de Ruiter, Holland.
Parentage: 'Ruth Leuwerik' × 'Rosemary Rose'
A vigorous branching grower, 2–2½ ft (0·6–0·8 m.) high with very glossy, bronze-green foliage, coppery when young. The flowers are a striking deep crimson, rosette shaped and produced in large, heavy trusses which may require support in heavy rain, or close planting to prevent contact with the soil. Protection against mildew is required in some areas. **410**, p. 77.
H.G.M. 1962; C.M., R.N.R.S. 1963; A.M., R.H.S. 1965; A.A.R.S. 1968.

'Eve Allen'   HT.
Cherry red and old gold, 3 ft (0·9 m.) 1964
Raised by E. M. Allen, England.
Parentage: 'Karl Herbst' × 'Gay Crusader'

A branching grower, upwards of 3 ft (0·9 m.) in height, with semi-glossy, medium green foliage. The moderately full flowers are cherry red with old gold reverse, forming a bright pleasing bicolor. The flowers open quickly and are scented. Protection against black spot may be required. **303**, p. 57.
T.G.C., R.N.R.S. 1964.

'Evelyn Fison', 'Irish Wonder'   Fl.
Vivid red, 2½ ft (0·8 m.) 1961
Raised by S. McGredy IV, N. Ireland.
Parentage: 'Moulin Rouge' × 'Korona'
A vigorous branching grower, 2½ ft (0·8 m.) high, with small, medium green foliage. The large double vivid red flowers with scarlet are freely produced throughout the season and slightly fragrant. One of the best and brightest bedding roses with good weather resistance. **411**, p. 77.
G.M., R.N.R.S. 1963; A.M., R.H.S. 1964.

'Excelsa', 'Red Dorothy Perkins'   R.
Crimson, summer, 10 ft (3 m.) 1909
Raised by M. H. Walsh, U.S.A.
Vigorous hybrid *wichuraiana* rambler up to 10 ft (3 m.). Flowers in large clusters, small, double, globular and dainty, bright crimson with white centre. Late June to mid-July but not recurrent, very free-flowering. Foliage light green, glossy. One of the finest of the *wichuraiana* but now rarely seen and perhaps surpassed by 'Crimson Shower' for its larger flowers and longer period of flowering. 'Excelsa' is lovely when grown as a weeping standard and looks very well in the Bagatelle Rose Garden, Paris.
G.M.H.G.M., A.R.S. 1914; A.M., R.H.S. 1916.

'Fairlight'   Fl.
Coppery-salmon to flame, 2 ft (0·6 m.) 1964
Raised by H. Robinson, England.
Parentage: 'Joybells' × seedling
A compact, bushy grower, 2 ft (0·6 m.) with coppery-bronze foliage, turning to dark green as it matures. The full blooms are well formed in early stages, borne in medium sized trusses, coppery-salmon to flame, shaded yellow at base and very freely produced. Slightly fragrant. A useful cultivar which may require protection against mildew. **412**, p. 77.
T.G.C., R.N.R.S. 1964; C.M., R.N.R.S. 1965.

'Fairy Dancers'   Fl.
Blush-pink, 2 ft (0·6 m.) 1969
Raised by J. Cocker & Sons Ltd, Scotland.
Parentage: 'Wendy Cussons' × 'Diamond Jubilee'
A low growing cultivar, 2 ft (0·6 m.) high, with small flowers of hybrid tea formation with a charm of their own. Borne in small sprays, the flowers are blush-pink with shades of apricot, delightful as cut flowers for decorative purposes. Slightly fragrant. **413**, p. 77.

'Fantin Latour'   C.
Pale pink, summer, 5 ft (1·5 m.)
Vigorous and free-flowering shrub rose. Flowers double in clusters of 2–5, pale blush pink, slightly deeper to shell pink in centre, fully-petalled, slightly cup-shaped and deeper in colour when first opening, later opening flat and become paler. Delicately scented. One of the most delicate in colour and beautiful of all the shrub roses. Flowers 3½ in. (8·9 cm.) across. Mid-late June. Non-recurrent. Foliage good green. 3–5 large leaflets. Stem not very prickly. Rightly one of the favourite shrub roses, close to many of those of the old Dutch painters and also those of Fantin Latour, the French painter. A good grower but fading in bright sun. Origin and date of raising unknown. One of the very few old roses to have been awarded both A.M. and A.G.M. of R.H.S. **68**, p. 13.
A.M., R.H.S. 1959; A.G.M., R.H.S. 1968.

Farrer's Threepenny-bit Rose see under *R. farreri*

'Fashion, Climbing' see **'Climbing Fashion'**

'Fée des Neiges' see **'Schneewittchen'**, **481**, p. 91.

'Felicia'   HM.
Apricot-pink, recurrent, 5 × 9 ft (1·5 × 2·7 m.) 1928
Raised by Rev. J. H. Pemberton, England.
Parentage: 'Trier' × 'Ophelia'
A vigorous Hybrid Musk shrub rose of slightly lower and more spreading compact growth than most of the others of the group, usually about 5 ft (1·5 m.) high and up to 9 ft (2·7 m.) across. Flowers apricot-pink in bud, blending on opening to silvery-pink, in clusters, very free-flowering, slightly larger in flower than 'Cornelia' (**119**, p. 21) but otherwise close in colour. Late June to mid-July and recurrent. A valuable plant for its almost continuous flowering, makes a good hedge. **120**, p. 21.
A.G.M., R.H.S.

'Félicité et Perpétue'   R.
White, summer, 20 ft (6·1 m.) 1827
Raised by A. A. Jacques, France.
Parentage: *R. sempervirens* hybrid, but details unrecorded
Very vigorous rambler up to 20 ft (6·1 m.), derived from *R. sempervirens*. Flowers in large clusters, rather small, 1½ in. (3·8 cm.) across, globular, double, creamy-white to white, flesh-tinted on

---

Abbreviations and Symbols used in the text

Rose classifications

A.	Alba	HT.	Hybrid Tea
B.	Bourbon	MCl.	Modern, large-flowered climber
C.	Centifolia	Min.	Miniature
Ch.	China	Moss	Centifolia muscosa
Cl.	Climber	MSh.	Modern shrub
D.	Damask	P.	Penzance Sweet Brier
Fl.	Floribunda	R.	Rambler
G.	Gallica	Rg.	Rugosa
HM.	Hybrid Musk	Sp.	Species and first hybrids
HP.	Hybrid Perpetual	Sw.	Sweet Brier

Rose Awards and Societies

A.A.R.S.	All-America Rose Selection
A.G.M.	Award of Garden Merit
A.M.	Award of Merit
A.R.S.	American Rose Society
B.B.G.M.	Baden Baden Gold Medal, Germany
B.G.M.	Bagatelle Gold Medal, Paris
C.C.V.	Clay Challenge Vase for scent
C.M.	Certificate of Merit
D.F.P.	David Fuerstenberg Prize
F.C.C.	First Class Certificate
G.G.M.	Geneva Gold Medal
G.M.	Gold Medal
G.M.C.B.	Gold Medal City of Belfast
G.M.H.G.M.	Gertrude M. Hubbard Gold Medal
G.R.H.	Golden Rose of The Hague
G.T.A.B.	Golden Thorn Award Belfast
H.E.M.M.	The Henry Edland Memorial Medal for the most fragrant rose of the year
H.G.M.	The Hague Gold Medal
L.G.M.	Lyon Gold Medal, France
M.G.M.	Madrid Gold Medal
N.G.M.C.	National Gold Medal Certificate
P.G.M.	Portland Gold Medal, Oregon, U.S.A.
P.I.T.	President's International Trophy
R.B.	Prize for the most fragrant rose, Roeulx, Belgium
R.B.G.M.	Roeulx, Belgium, Gold Medal
R.G.M.	Rome Gold Medal
R.H.S.	The Royal Horticultural Society, London
R.N.R.S.	The Royal National Rose Society, Great Britain*
T.G.C.	Trial Ground Certificate
U.A.B.	The 'Uladh' Award for fragrance, Belfast

National Rose Society awards, before 1965, are included here under R.N.R.S.

The illustration numbers are in **bold type** and the page numbers in light type preceded by p.

first opening. Scented, very floriferous, late flowering early to mid-July. Foliage light green, rather dainty, glossy, almost evergreen. This is one of the most charming of the older climbing roses with its masses of neat button-like flowers. It will grow vigorously up into an old tree, making long shoots each year. Prune lightly only, cutting out dead and very old wood and shortening back flowering shoots. Named after the two daughters of A. A. Jacques who had named them in honour of the two girls killed in an arena near Carthage and who were later canonized as the saints, St Felicitas and St Perpetua. Jacques was a gardener to Louis Philippe, Duc d'Orléans, before he became King of France. This rose is said to be so vigorous in New Zealand that it covers whole cottages. **205**, p. 38.

'Félicité Parmentier'   A.
White or pale salmon-pink, summer, 4 ft (1·2 m.) 1836
Shrub rose of medium vigour up to 4 ft (1·2 m.). Flowers white with pale salmon-pink centre, double, rather globular, of medium size, 2½ in. (6·4 cm.) across, tending to fade to a creamy tinge particularly near edges, scented. Mid-late June, not recurrent but free-flowering. Buds creamy-yellow. Foliage less grey than in other Alba roses. **65**, p. 12.

'Femina'   HT.
Coppery-salmon-pink, 3 ft (0·9 m.) 1963
Raised by J. Gaujard, France.
Parentage: 'Fernand Arles' × 'Mignonne'
A vigorous upright grower of medium height, up to 3 ft (0·9 m.), with semi-glossy bronze tinted foliage and medium-sized coppery-salmon-pink blooms. The flowers are freely produced, open quickly and resist wet weather. Protection from black spot is required in some areas.

'Ferdinand Pichard'   HP.
Pink streaked crimson, recurrent, 5 ft (1·5 m.) 1921
Raised by R. Tanne, France.
Hybrid Perpetual shrub of medium vigour and rather spreading habit, but not often over 5 ft (1·5 m.). Flowers of medium size, semi-double, opening pink, fading to pale blush-pink, almost white, heavily streaked and splashed irregularly with crimson, deepening as the flower ages. Scented. Free-flowering. Mid to late June and recurrent through summer and autumn. A fine bushy rose, valuable for its recurrent flowering. Foliage rather light green. **110**, p. 20.

'Fervid'   Fl.
Scarlet, 3½ ft (1·1 m.) 1960
Raised by E. B. LeGrice, England.
Parentage: 'Pimpernel' × 'Korona'
A tall upright grower, 3½ ft (1·1 m.) or more in height, with plentiful mid-green foliage. The vivid scarlet flowers are almost single, cupped and slightly waved and produced freely in medium trusses; they retain their colour well and are slightly fragrant. This cultivar thrives on light soils. **414**, p. 77.
T.G.C., R.N.R.S. 1961; G.R.H. 1969.

'Fête des Mères' see **'Mothersday'**

'Firecracker'   Fl.
Bright carmine, 2½ ft + (0·8 m.) 1956
Raised by E. S. Boerner, U.S.A.
Parentage: 'Pinocchio' seedling × 'Numa Fay' seedling
A fairly compact, bushy grower, just over 2½ ft (0·8 m.) high with semi-glossy, light green foliage. The semi-double flowers are an attractive bright carmine shading to a yellow base. Freely produced and at their best in cool weather. **415**, p. 78.
C.M., R.N.R.S. 1955.

'First Choice'   MSh.
Bright scarlet, recurrent, 5 ft (1·5 m.) 1958
Raised by H. Morse & Sons, England.
Parentage: 'Masquerade' × 'Sultane'
Modern shrub rose of medium vigour up to 5 ft and rather spreading in growth. Flowers single, large, up to 5 in. (12·7 cm.) across, bright scarlet-crimson with yellow base to petals, which turns to white as the flowers age, and prominent yellow stamens, in clusters. Slightly scented. Mid to late June and recurrent. It tends to deepen from bright colour in hot sun. **159**, p. 29.

'First Love', 'Premier Amour'   HT.
Pink, 3 ft (0·9 m.) 1951
Raised by H. C. Swim, U.S.A.
Parentage: 'Charlotte Armstrong' × 'Show Girl'
A tall, somewhat spindly grower which requires close planting to be effective, with light green, somewhat pointed, semi-glossy foliage. The blooms are variable in colour, from pale to rose pink with deeper shadings, are freely produced and have a slight fragrance. An excellent cultivar for cutting, being very pretty, particularly in the bud stage, the buds being unusually long and pointed with wiry stems. **304**, p. 57.
C.M., R.N.R.S. 1952.

'F. J. Grootendorst'   Rg.
Bright crimson, recurrent, 8 ft (2·4 m.) 1918
Raised by De Goey, Holland.
Parentage: *R. rugosa* 'Rubra' × 'Mme Norbert Levavasseur'
Vigorous Rugosa hybrid rose up to 8 ft (2·4 m.) making large bush, prickly with rugosa type foliage but with smaller leaflets. Flowers small, bright crimson-red with a slight blue-magenta tinge, double and with petals fringed, rather ball-like, about 1½ in. (3·8 cm.) across, but borne in large clusters. Although both vigorous and floriferous, I do not find either its colour or its shape very pleasing and it is quite scentless. The flowers always seem too small for the size of bush. Two sports from it have been named – 'Grootendorst Supreme' and 'Pink Grootendorst' (**134**, p. 24). They vary only in colour, being fairly similar in form and size of flower and are not so vigorous.

'Flaming Peace' see **'Kronenbourg'**, **325**, p. 61.

'Flora McIvor' see under *R. eglanteria*, **9**, p. 2.

'Flower Girl' see **'Sea Pearl'**, **484**, p. 92.

'Folie d'Espagne'   Fl.
Yellow and orange, 3½ ft (1·1 m.) 1965
Raised by O. Soenderhousen, Denmark.
Parentage: unnamed seedlings of raiser.
A strong, sturdy, free grower, 3½ ft (1·1 m.) high, with dark green glossy foliage. The flat, double flowers are yellow and orange, with scarlet edges to petals. Continuous flowering and slightly fragrant. **416**, p. 78.
T.G.C., R.N.R.S. 1965.

'For You' see **'Para Ti'**

'Fortune's Double Yellow' see under *R.* × *odorata*

'Fragrant Cloud' see **'Duftwolke'**, **296**, p. 56.

'Francis E. Lester'   R.
White, early summer, 15 ft (4·6 m.) 1946
Raised by Lester Rose Gardens, U.S.A.
Parentage: seedling from the Hybrid Musk 'Kathleen'
Vigorous rambler up to 15 ft (4·6 m.). Flowers single, in large
clusters, creamy-white to white, slightly pink in bud, giving an
effect of pale apple blossom on first opening. Strongly scented and
flowering in late June to early July but only slightly recurrent.
Foliage luxuriant, bright glossy green. A lovely sight when grown
into and over an old tree. The small, oval, orange-red hips make a
beautiful contribution in October and November. **206**, p. 38.

'Francofurtana'   G.
Purplish-rose, summer, 4 ft (1·2 m.) 16th century
Parentage reputedly: *R. cinnamomea* × *R. gallica*.
The Frankfurt Rose, sometimes also known as 'Souvenir de
l'Impératrice Josephine' or just 'Empress Josephine'. A Gallica rose
of only moderate vigour up to 4 ft (1·2 m.). Flowers semi-double,
deep purplish-rose, veined with a deeper colour with wavy petals,
rather loose. Scent slight. Mid to late June. Distinguished by large
hips, shaped like a top. Foliage grey-green; branches with few
thorns. This is a very old rose whose nomenclature has been much
confused. It has also been known as *R. turbinata,* under which name it
was featured by Redouté.

'François Juranville'   R.
Salmon-pink, recurrent, 25 ft (7·6 m.) 1906
Raised by Barbier, France.
Parentage: *R. wichuraiana* × 'Mme Laurette Messimy', a China
rose.
Very vigorous rambler up to 25 ft (7·6 m.) with rather weeping
habit. Flowers double, quite large, opening flat, salmon-coral pink,
deeper in centre, singly or in small clusters, petals slightly quilled,
strongly scented. Colour varies in depth with season and moisture
in soil being paler under dry conditions. Mid-June to early July,
slightly recurrent; suitable for growing over a large pergola or up
into an old tree and with 'Albéric Barbier' (**192**, p. 36) one of the
finest of the older ramblers. Stems dusky purplish-red. Foliage
luxuriant, glossy green, bronzy when young. **207**, p. 38.

'Franklin Englemann'   Fl.
Bright scarlet, 2½ ft (0·8 m.) 1970
Raised by A. Dickson & Sons Ltd, N. Ireland.
Parentage: 'Heidelberg' × ('Detroiter' × seedling)
A fairly tall, somewhat open grower, 2½ ft (0·8 m.) high, with large,
well shaped flowers, hybrid tea type, bright scarlet and very freely
produced. **417**, p. 78.

'Frau Dagmar Hartopp', 'Fru Dagmar Hastrup',   Rg.
  R. rugosa rosea
Pale pink, recurrent, 3–4 ft (0·9–1·2 m.) 1914
Parentage: *R. rugosa* seedling
Spreading shrub usually more compact in growth than other
rugosa roses. Flowers single, clear shell-pink with golden stamens,
cup-shaped, opening saucer-shaped, up to 3½ in. (8·9 cm.) across.
Mid-June, throughout season. Hips bright tomato-red, large and
globular, often borne with flowers and nearly the finest among
roses. Foliage typical *rugosa,* fresh apple-green. Good dwarf
hedges about 3 ft (0·9 m.) tall have been made of this rose and prove
very satisfactory, flowering over a long period and standing winter
clipping to an even height. **132**, p. 23.
A.G.M., R.H.S. 1958; A.M., R.H.S. 1958.

'Frau Karl Druschki', 'Reines des Neiges', 'Snow   HP.HT.
  Queen', 'White American Beauty'
White, recurrent, 6 ft (1·8 m.) 1901
Raised by P. Lambert, Germany.

Parentage: 'Merveille de Lyon' × 'Mme Caroline Testout'
Technically a Hybrid Tea by ancestry. Vigorous shrub making a
large woody 6 ft (1·8 m.) bush if only very lightly pruned. Flowers
large, double, pure white, slightly flushed pale lemon-green at base,
buds sometimes with slight pink flush, of hybrid tea type. Unfortunately not scented, but very floriferous with flowers in large
clusters. Recurrent flowering. One of the great roses, it has remained popular since its raising in 1901. It is still one of the best
and most weather resistant white roses. It makes long growths
which can be pegged down to produce a thicket but should not be
pruned hard back like a Hybrid Tea rose. It needs only light tip
pruning and should be allowed to become a large, woody bush,
occasionally cutting out completely very old woody stems. It can
suffer badly from mildew and needs spraying against this. When
weakly grown it also suffers from black spot. **111**, p. 20.
A.M., R.H.S. 1902.

'Fred Gibson'   HT.
Amber-yellow, 3 ft (0·9 m.) 1968
Raised by J. Sanday Ltd, England.
Parentage: 'Gavotte' × 'Buccaneer'
A tall vigorous grower, to over 3 ft (0·9 m.), with dark green,
semi-glossy foliage, reddish in the early stages of growth. The large,
beautifully formed blooms are amber-yellow to apricot, often borne
singly, sometimes in small clusters later in the season. Colour ap-
pears to be deeper in some areas. This is a very promising cultivar
for the exhibitor and is already becoming popular for this purpose.
Slight fragrance. **305**, p. 57.
T.G.C., R.N.R.S. 1968.

Abbreviations and Symbols used in the text

Rose classifications

A.	Alba	HT.	Hybrid Tea
B.	Bourbon	MCl.	Modern, large-flowered climber
C.	Centifolia	Min.	Miniature
Ch.	China	Moss	Centifolia muscosa
Cl.	Climber	MSh.	Modern shrub
D.	Damask	P.	Penzance Sweet Brier
Fl.	Floribunda	R.	Rambler
G.	Gallica	Rg.	Rugosa
HM.	Hybrid Musk	Sp.	Species and first hybrids
HP.	Hybrid Perpetual	Sw.	Sweet Brier

Rose Awards and Societies

A.A.R.S.	All-America Rose Selection
A.G.M.	Award of Garden Merit
A.M.	Award of Merit
A.R.S.	American Rose Society
B.B.G.M.	Baden Baden Gold Medal, Germany
B.G.M.	Bagatelle Gold Medal, Paris
C.C.V.	Clay Challenge Vase for scent
C.M.	Certificate of Merit
D.F.P.	David Fuerstenberg Prize
F.C.C.	First Class Certificate
G.G.M.	Geneva Gold Medal
G.M.	Gold Medal
G.M.C.B.	Gold Medal City of Belfast
G.M.H.G.M.	Gertrude M. Hubbard Gold Medal
G.R.H.	Golden Rose of The Hague
G.T.A.B.	Golden Thorn Award Belfast
H.E.M.M.	The Henry Edland Memorial Medal for the most fragrant rose of the year
H.G.M.	The Hague Gold Medal
L.G.M.	Lyon Gold Medal, France
M.G.M.	Madrid Gold Medal
N.G.M.C.	National Gold Medal Certificate
P.G.M.	Portland Gold Medal, Oregon, U.S.A.
P.I.T.	President's International Trophy
R.B.	Prize for the most fragrant rose, Roeulx, Belgium
R.B.G.M.	Roeulx, Belgium, Gold Medal
R.G.M.	Rome Gold Medal
R.H.S.	The Royal Horticultural Society, London
R.N.R.S.	The Royal National Rose Society, Great Britain*
T.G.C.	Trial Ground Certificate
U.A.B.	The 'Uladh' Award for fragrance, Belfast

National Rose Society awards, before 1965, are included here under R.N.R.S.

The illustration numbers are in **bold type** and the page numbers
in light type preceded by p.

'Fred Loads' MSh.
Light vermilion, recurrent, 7 ft (2·1 m.) 1967
Raised by R. A. Holmes, England.
Parentage: 'Orange Sensation' × 'Dorothy Wheatcroft'
A vigorous modern shrub rose with upright growth to 7 ft (2·1 m.)
or more if lightly pruned, of floribunda type. Flowers single to
semi-double, light vermilion or orange-pink, large up to 4 in.
(10·2 cm.) across, in large clusters, scented. Free-flowering, recurrent. Quickly established in popularity for its free-flowering,
bright colour and vigour. Good for back of rose bed. **160**, p. 29.
G.M., R.N.R.S. 1967; A.M., R.H.S. 1967.

'Frensham' Fl.
Deep crimson, 4 ft (1·2 m.) 1946
Raised by A. Norman, England.
Parentage: seedling × 'Crimson Glory'
A vigorous, branching grower up to 4 ft (1·2 m.) high, with an
abundance of glossy green foliage. The semi-double, deep crimson
flowers are produced freely over a long season and are weather
resistant. This cultivar was, for many years. the most popular
floribunda for large beds and hedges and was extensively planted.
It is no longer in the first flight due to the tendency to mildew which
it has now developed in many gardens.
G.M., R.N.R.S. 1943; G.M., A.R.S. 1955.

'Fresco' Fl.
Orange-vermilion and yellow, 2½ ft (0·8 m.) 1968
Raised by G. de Ruiter, Holland.
Parentage: 'Metropole' × 'Orange Sensation'
A vigorous, bushy grower, 2½ ft (0·8 m.) high, well furnished with
dark green, glossy foliage, tinted bronze when young. The blooms are
nicely shaped when young and full, opening to orange-vermilion
with a golden-yellow reverse, a very gay combination. Flowers are
produced singly and in trusses with quick succession. They do not
mind rain. May have to be safeguarded against black spot. **418**,
p. 78.

'Fritz Nobis' MSh.
Pale salmon-pink, early summer, 5 ft (1·5 m.) 1940
Raised by W. Kordes, Germany.
Parentage: 'Joanna Hill' × R. eglanteria 'Magnifica'
Modern shrub rose of medium vigour, up to 5 ft (1·5 m.). Flowers
semi-double, pale salmon-pink, of medium size, opening flat with
some quartering like an old rose, free-flowering. Scented. Mid-
June to early July, but not recurrent. Of hybrid spinosissima type.
One of the most beautiful of summer flowering roses of modern
raising. Hips rounded, dark red, persistent. **161**, p. 29.
A.M., R.H.S. 1959.

'Frohsinn', 'Joyfulness' Fl.
Light salmon, 3 ft (0·9 m.) 1961
Raised by M. Tantau, Germany.
Parentage: 'Horstmann's Jubiläumsrose' × 'Circus'
A tall, vigorous bushy grower, 3 ft (0·9 m.) high, with glossy bronze
tinted foliage. The large, semi-double flowers develop from long
pointed buds, hybrid tea shape in early stages, light salmon-
pink, fading slightly with age. Lightly scented. May require
protection against black spot. **419**, p. 78.
C.M., R.N.R.S. 1963.

'Frosty' Min.
Greenish white, 12 in. (30·5 cm.) 1953
Raised by R. S. Moore, U.S.A.
Parentage: (R. wichuraiana × unnamed seedling) × self

A compact spreading grower, up to 12 in. (30·5 cm.) high, with
glossy foliage. The very small, double flowers are greenish white
with an attractive button eye. Scented.

'Fru Dagmar Hastrup' see **'Frau Dagmar Hartopp', 132**, p. 23.

'Frühlingsanfang' MSh.
Ivory, early summer, 9 × 9 ft (2·7 × 2·7 m.) 1950
Raised by W. Kordes, Germany.
Parentage: 'Joanna Hill' × R. spinosissima altaica
A handsome shrub of luxuriant growth, when well established
reaching 8–9 ft (2·4–2·7 m.) in height and across. The large single
flowers are deliciously fragrant, freely borne along arching branches, ivory-white in colour. Maroon-red hips are produced in
autumn, frequently accompanied by autumn colouring of the
leathery leaves. **162**, p. 29.
A.M., R.H.S. 1964.

'Frühlingsduft' MSh.
Cream-lemon, early summer, 8 × 8 ft (2·4 × 2·4 m.) 1949
Raised by W. Kordes, Germany.
Parentage: 'Joanna Hill' × R. spinosissima altaica
A vigorous shrub with tall arching branches 7–8 ft (2·1–2·4 m.)
high. In this cultivar the blooms have leaned much more towards
'Joanna Hill', being double, almost of hybrid tea form, creamy-
lemon in colour, flushed with apricot-pink towards the centre and
very fragrant. **163**, p. 29.
A.M., R.H.S. 1953.

'Frühlingsgold' MSh.
Yellow, mainly spring, 7 × 7 ft (2·1 × 2·1 m.) 1937
Raised by W. Kordes, Germany.
Parentage: 'Joanna Hill' × 'R. spinosissima hispida
One of the finest shrubs which can be grown in any garden of
sufficient size to contain it and show off its beauty. The vigorous
growths arch outwards, almost as wide as high, generally about 7 ft
(2·1 m.) but in Queen Mary's Garden, Regent's Park, London, at
least 12 ft (3·7 m.). The creamy-yellow flowers, up to 5 in. (12·7 cm.)
across with rich yellow stamens, festoon the branches along their
length, fading to creamy-white in hot sunshine; a wonderful sight.
Occasionally a late flurry of blooms is produced. The heavy
fragrance carries for some distance and fortunately this shrub grows
well on most soils. Leaves are slightly grey-green with 5 leaflets.
Appears disease-free. Sometimes called 'Spring Gold'. Considered
by many the finest of Herr Kordes' Frühlings series. **165**, p. 30.
A.M., R.H.S. 1950; F.C.C., R.H.S. 1955; A.G.M., R.H.S. 1965.

'Frühlingsmorgen' MSh.
Pink, mainly spring, 6 × 5 ft (1·8 × 1·5 m.) 1942
Raised by W. Kordes, Germany.
Parentage: ('E. G. Hill' × 'Cathrine Kordes') × R. spinosissima
altaica
A fairly vigorous shrub on good soils, with ample mat grey-green
foliage. Most beautiful single flowers, up to 4½ in. (11·4 cm.)
across, clear rose-pink with yellow centre and purplish-maroon
stamens which add to its attraction. Flowers freely in spring with
occasional flowers in late summer on a 6 ft (1·8 m.) high shrub.
Sometimes called 'Spring Morning'. **164**, p. 29.
A.M., R.H.S. 1951

'Fugue' MCl.Sh.
Bright crimson-red, recurrent, 10 ft (3 m.) 1958
Raised by M. L. Meilland, France.
Parentage: 'Alain' × 'Guinée'

Vigorous climber or may be grown as a large shrub. Flowers semi-double of medium size, in clusters, bright crimson-red. Slightly scented. Free-flowering. Mid-June and somewhat recurrent. Foliage luxuriant, glossy. **243**, p. 46.
M.G.M. 1958.

'Gail Borden' HT.
Deep rose, 2½ ft (0·8 m.) 1956
Raised by W. Kordes, Germany.
Parentage: 'Mev. H. A. Verschuren' × 'Viktoria Adelheid'
A vigorous, tall, branching grower, upwards of 2½ feet high, with large very glossy handsome dark green foliage. The large full blooms are sometimes somewhat globular but are frequently sufficiently well formed for exhibition purposes. The deep rose pink flowers have yellow shadings and are creamy yellow on the reverse, fading slightly as they age, profusely borne in summer and again in autumn where there is a tendency to throw up large basal growths with several large blooms which are particularly effective at that time. **306**, p. 57.
G.M., R.N.R.S. 1957.

'Galway Bay' MCl.
Salmon-pink, recurrent, 8–10 ft (2·4–3 m.) 1966
Raised by S. McGredy IV, N. Ireland.
Parentage: 'Heidelberg' × 'Queen Elizabeth'
A vigorous cultivar with medium green foliage. The large semi-double flowers are freely produced in small clusters over a long period and are salmon-pink, deepening towards the edges. Ideal for pillars, having plenty of basal growth. **244**, p. 46.

'Garnette' Fl.
Dull crimson, 2 ft (0·6 m.) 1951
Raised by M. Tantau, Germany.
Parentage: ('Rosenelfe' × 'Eva') × 'Heros'
A short bushy grower with dark foliage and somewhat dull crimson flowers when grown outside. Much more suited to cultivation under glass where, if disbudded, it is very suitable for cut flowers with longer lasting qualities than other types of roses.

'Garvey' HT.
Pink, 2½ ft (0·8 m.) 1960
Raised by S. McGredy IV, N. Ireland.
Parentage: 'McGredy's Yellow' × 'Karl Herbst'
A tall vigorous upright grower with large glossy, medium green foliage which is very thorny. The full, globular flowers are soft peach-pink deepening to rosy salmon. They are freely produced and resistant to rain. **307**, p. 58.
C.M., R.N.R.S. 1961; A.M., R.H.S. 1961.

'Gavotte' HT.
Rose pink and silver, 3 ft (0·9 m.) 1963
Raised by J. Sanday Ltd, England.
Parentage: 'Ethel Sanday' × 'Lady Sylvia'
A vigorous spreading grower of medium height with semi-glossy, dark green foliage. The large, very full flowers are rose pink with a silvery reverse, fragrant and freely produced. Formation is of exhibition standard but needs a good deal of disbudding and is not at its best in wet weather; nevertheless it is a popular exhibition cultivar. **308**, p. 58.
C.M., R.N.R.S. 1962; A.M., R.H.S. 1965.

'Gay Gordons' HT.
Flame red and deep yellow, 2 ft (0·6 m.) 1969
Raised by J. Cocker & Sons Ltd, Scotland.
Parentage: 'Belle Blonde' × 'Karl Herbst'

A bushy grower of under average height which has dark glossy foliage and is very free flowering. The medium sized flowers are flame red and deep yellow, a brilliant bicolor which looks bright and attractive. There is not much scent and protection from black spot may be required.

'Geisha', 'Pink Elizabeth Arden' Fl.
Clear pink, 2½ ft (0·8 m.) 1964
Raised by M. Tantau, Germany.
A bushy grower, 2½ ft (0·8 m.) high, with leathery, dark green foliage. The large, semi-double flowers are an attractive shade of pure clear pink and are freely produced in large clusters. A very good bedding cultivar with some scent. Weather resistant.

'Général Kléber' Moss Sh.
Deep pink, summer, 5 ft (1·5 m.) 1856
Raised by M. Robert, France.
Vigorous shrub up to 5 ft (1·5 m.), making a thickset bush. Flowers large, double, a good pink, opening flat to show a small button eye, scented, quartered with wavy petals around centre, up to 5 in. (12·7 cm.) across. Bud mossy. Mid-late June but not recurrent. A very fine rose which should be more widely grown, both for its size of flower and the clearness of its colour which has been compared to 'Céleste' – high praise indeed.

'Georg Arends' HT.
Rose-pink, recurrent, 6 ft (1·8 m.) 1910
Raised by W. Hinner, Germany.

<table>
<tr><td colspan="2" align="center">**Abbreviations and Symbols used in the text**</td></tr>
<tr><td colspan="2" align="center">**Rose classifications**</td></tr>
<tr><td>A. Alba</td><td>HT. Hybrid Tea</td></tr>
<tr><td>B. Bourbon</td><td>MCl. Modern, large-flowered climber</td></tr>
<tr><td>C. Centifolia</td><td>Min. Miniature</td></tr>
<tr><td>Ch. China</td><td>Moss Centifolia muscosa</td></tr>
<tr><td>Cl. Climber</td><td>MSh. Modern shrub</td></tr>
<tr><td>D. Damask</td><td>P. Penzance Sweet Brier</td></tr>
<tr><td>Fl. Floribunda</td><td>R. Rambler</td></tr>
<tr><td>G. Gallica</td><td>Rg. Rugosa</td></tr>
<tr><td>HM. Hybrid Musk</td><td>Sp. Species and first hybrids</td></tr>
<tr><td>HP. Hybrid Perpetual</td><td>Sw. Sweet Brier</td></tr>
</table>

Rose Awards and Societies

A.A.R.S. All-America Rose Selection
A.G.M. Award of Garden Merit
A.M. Award of Merit
A.R.S. American Rose Society
B.B.G.M. Baden Baden Gold Medal, Germany
B.G.M. Bagatelle Gold Medal, Paris
C.C.V. Clay Challenge Vase for scent
C.M. Certificate of Merit
D.F.P. David Fuerstenberg Prize
F.C.C. First Class Certificate
G.G.M. Geneva Gold Medal
G.M. Gold Medal
G.M.C.B. Gold Medal City of Belfast
G.M.H.G.M. Gertrude M. Hubbard Gold Medal
G.R.H. Golden Rose of The Hague
G.T.A.B. Golden Thorn Award Belfast
H.E.M.M. The Henry Edland Memorial Medal
        for the most fragrant rose of the year
H.G.M. The Hague Gold Medal
L.G.M. Lyon Gold Medal, France
M.G.M. Madrid Gold Medal
N.G.M.C. National Gold Medal Certificate
P.G.M. Portland Gold Medal, Oregon, U.S.A.
P.I.T. President's International Trophy
R.B. Prize for the most fragrant rose, Roeulx, Belgium
R.B.G.M. Roeulx, Belgium, Gold Medal
R.G.M. Rome Gold Medal
R.H.S. The Royal Horticultural Society, London
R.N.R.S. The Royal National Rose Society, Great Britain*
T.G.C. Trial Ground Certificate
U.A.B. The 'Uladh' Award for fragrance, Belfast

National Rose Society awards, before 1965, are included here under R.N.R.S.

The illustration numbers are in **bold type** and the page numbers in light type preceded by p.

Parentage: 'Frau Karl Druschki' × 'La France'
A tall and vigorous Hybrid Tea shrub up to 6 ft (1·8 m.). Flowers large, clear rose-pink, described as being like a strawberry ice, fully double like a Hybrid Tea bloom with recurved outer petals, scented. Mid to late June and recurrent. Should be grown and pruned like 'Frau Karl Druschki' (**111**, p. 20) but presumably deriving its colour and scent from 'La France'. Although once considered by some authorities the most beautiful pink rose ever raised, it is unfortunately not by any means common in cultivation.

'Geranium' see *R. moyesii* **'Geranium', 32, 33**, p. 7.

'Germania' see under **'Gloire de Ducher'**

'Ginger Rogers'   HT.
Salmon, 3½ ft (1·1 m.) 1969
Raised by S. McGredy IV, N. Ireland.
Parentage: 'Super Star' × 'Miss Ireland'
A vigorous, upright grower with medium green coppery foliage. The moderately full blooms are salmon and have a slight fragrance. The good long stems render this a suitable cultivar for cutting. T.G.C., R.N.R.S. 1968.

'Gioia' see **'Peace', 347**, p. 65.

'Gipsy Boy' see **'Zigeunerknabe', 105**, p. 19.

'Glengarry'   Fl.
Brilliant vermilion, 3 ft (0·9 m.) 1969
Raised by J. Cocker & Sons Ltd, Scotland.
Parentage: 'Evelyn Fison' × 'Wendy Cussons'
A promising new cultivar of vigorous growth, about 3 ft (0·9 m.) high, with semi-glossy, mid-green foliage. The large flowers are full, of good form when young, sometimes borne singly and sometimes several together. They are a brilliant vermilion colour and have a slight scent. Growth is healthy. **420**, p. 78.
C.M., R.N.R.S. 1968.

'Gloire de Dijon'   Cl.
Buff-orange, recurrent, 10 ft (3 m.) 1853
Raised by Jacotot, France.
Parentage: 'Desprez'? × 'Souvenir de la Malmaison'
Climber of moderate vigour up to 10 ft (3 m.) with flowers of hybrid tea type. Flowers double, about 4 in. (10·2 cm.) across, buff-orange in centre fading to pale creamy-yellow on outer petals opening rather flat and irregularly quartered, sometimes tinted with apricot-pink, free-flowering, strongly scented. Early June and recurrent throughout season. One of the great old roses which is still worth growing. In some stocks there seems to have been a slight loss of vigour. Best grown against a wall but can be treated as a pillar rose in warm areas; older plants tend to be leggy at base, but this can be obscured with other planting. **208**, p. 38.

'Gloire de Ducher'   HP.
Bright purplish-crimson, recurrent, 7 ft (2·1 m.) 1865
Raised by Ducher, France.
Tall Hybrid Perpetual shrub or pillar rose up to 7 ft (2·1 m.). Flowers large, double, bright purplish-crimson, shaded maroon, showing small button eye when mature. Scented, petals of velvety texture. Mid to late June and recurrent, usually with good autumn blooming. Makes long shoots which may be either tied to pillar or pegged down. Sometimes known also as 'Germania', a synonym shared with a Hybrid Tea rose.

'Gloire de Guilan'   D.
Pink, early summer, 4 ft (1·2 m.)
Introduced 1949
This Damask is of a rather loose, sprawling habit up to 4 ft (1·2 m.). Flowers rich clear pink, semi-double, cupped on opening, heavily scented. Mid-June. Foliage apple-green. Introduced in 1949 by Miss Nancy Lindsay from the Caspian area of Persia, under number NL 1001, where it was grown for scent and for making rose water.

'Gloire des Mousseux'   Moss Sh.
Deep pink, summer, 4 ft (1·2 m.) 1852
Raised by M. Laffay, France.
Shrub of medium vigour. Flowers large, double, deep pink towards centre fading to a pale blush pink towards edges, slightly quartered, borne in small clusters; buds mossy but not as distinct as in some varieties, the calyx reflexing to leave bud clear. Mid to late June, not recurrent. Foliage tends to be rather light green. **72**, p. 13.

'Gloria Dei' see **'Peace', 347**, p. 65.

'Gold Coin'   Min.
Yellow, 10 in. (25·4 cm.) 1967
Raised by R. S. Moore, U.S.A.
Parentage: 'Golden Glow' × 'Magic Wand'
A bushy compact grower, 8–10 in. (20·3–25·4 cm.) high, with plentiful light green foliage. The small double flowers are full, canary yellow in colour and produced over a long season. This appears to be one of the best yellow miniatures. **504**, p. 96.
T.G.C., R.N.R.S. 1970.

'Gold Crown', 'Corona de Oro', 'Couronne d'Or'   HT.
'Goldkrone'
Deep yellow, 4 ft (1·2 m.) 1960
Raised by R. Kordes, Germany.
Parentage: 'Peace' × 'Spek's Yellow'
A vigorous upright, very tall cultivar with large, leathery, semi-glossy dark green, bronze tinted leaves. The full, deep yellow blooms have pink tinges on the outer petals but hold the colour well. Some early growths are apt to be blind but generally it flowers profusely, particularly in autumn. Formation can be good enough to supply blooms suitable for exhibition although they sometimes develop with split centres. Weather resistance is reasonably good and there is some scent. Owing to its height, this cultivar is only suitable for large beds or borders. **309**, p. 58.
C.M., R.N.R.S. 1960.

'Goldbusch'   MSh.
Ochre-yellow, recurrent, 5 ft (1·5 m.) 1954
Raised by W. Kordes, Germany.
Parentage: 'Golden Glow' × *R. eglanteria* hybrid
Modern shrub rose of spreading habit but up to 5 ft (1·5 m.). Flowers double, or semi-double, deep ochre-yellow in centre, paler on outside, large, buds coral pink. Well scented. Mid to late June but recurrent. Foliage rather yellowish-green when young. A useful addition to the large shrub roses in this colour. **166**, p. 31.
A.M., R.H.S. 1965.

'Golden Chersonese'   MSh.
Yellow, spring, 6–7 ft (1·8–2·1 m.) 1963
Raised by E. F. Allen, England.
Parentage: *R. ecae* × 'Canary Bird'
A bushy upright-growing shrub with plentiful small mat medium

green foliage, 6–7 ft (1·8–2·1 m.) in height; the original plant is now 8 ft (2·4 m.) high, its ultimate. This is a most attractive cultivar which has inherited much of the qualities of its parents and is hardier than *R. ecae*. Smaller in flower than 'Canary Bird', the single flowers are more intense yellow in colour, freely borne along the flowering growths in May and delightfully scented. A welcome addition to spring flowering shrubs and readily propagated from soft-wood cuttings under glass. **167**, p. 31.
A.M., R.H.S. 1966; T.G.C., R.N.R.S. 1969; C.M., R.N.R.S. 1970.

'Golden Melody' see **'Irene Churruca', 317**, p. 60.

'Golden Prince' see **'Kabuki'**

'Golden Scepter' see **'Spek's Yellow'**

'Golden Showers'   MCl.Sh.
Golden-yellow, recurrent, 6–10 ft (1·8–3 m.) 1956
Raised by Dr W. E. Lammerts, U.S.A.
Parentage: 'Charlotte Armstrong' × 'Capt. Thomas'
A strong upright grower, which in a sheltered position as in Queen Mary's Garden, Regent's Park, London, will attain 12 ft (3·7 m.) in height; in colder areas it will reach 6 ft (1·8 m.) and remain as a shrub. The large double flowers open out flat from pointed buds, deep golden-yellow becoming cream as they get older, and have a pleasing fragrance. Very free-flowering over a long season. One of the most recurrent roses with good weather resistance. **245**, p. 46.
A.A.R.S. 1957; P.G.M. 1957; A.M., R.H.S. 1962.

'Golden Slippers'   Fl.
Orange-flame and pale gold, 2 ft (0·6 m.) 1961
Raised by G. J. Von Abrams, U.S.A.
Parentage: 'Goldilocks' × unnamed seedling
A low bushy grower of fair vigour, about 2 ft (0·6 m.) high, with bronze tinted, glossy green foliage. The fairly large, semi-double flowers are produced in clusters, orange-flame with pale gold reverse and golden-yellow centre, a most attractive combination particularly in autumn. Free flowering. This cultivar seems to have been overlooked but is most useful for small beds or in small gardens if given good cultivation. **421**, p. 78.
P.G.M. 1960; A.A.R.S. 1962.

'Golden Times'   HT.
Golden-yellow, 3 ft (0·9 m.) 1972
Raised by J. Cocker & Sons Ltd, Scotland.
Parentage: 'Duftwolke' × 'Golden Splendour'
A tall, upright grower, 3 ft (0·9 m.) high, possibly more when well established, with mat, mid-green foliage. Attractive buds, tinged red, opening into large, very full flowers which are golden-yellow, borne singly and several together. Nicely scented. A promising new cultivar. **310**, p. 58.
T.G.C., R.N.R.S. 1970.

'Golden Treasure' see **'Goldschatz', 422**, p. 79.

'Golden Wave' see **'Dr A. J. Verhage', 291**, p. 54.

'Golden Wings'   MSh.
Primrose-yellow, recurrent, 6 × 6 ft (1·8 × 1·8 m.) 1956
Raised by R. Shepherd, U.S.A.
Parentage: 'Sœur Thérèse' × (*R. spinosissima altaica* × 'Ormiston Roy')
Modern, vigorous shrub rose up to 6 × 6 ft (1·8 × 1·8 m.). Flowers

very large, single or semi-double, light primrose-yellow, deeper towards base of petals, fading to creamy-white as flower matures in centre and large boss of buff-yellow stamens, red at base of filaments, 4½ in. (11·4 cm.) across, lightly scented. Continually in flower from mid-June. Foliage deep yellowish-green with 5–7 leaflets. Very beautiful flower and one of the most valuable among the large yellow shrub roses. Produces good orange-red hips in autumn. Loose growing, and should be pruned in winter by cutting out older branches and shortening others by about a third. Although it has *spinosissima* blood, it has a large flower like 'Frühlingsgold' but deeper in colour and generally a better shape. **168**, p. 31.
A.M., R.H.S. 1965; N.G.M.C., A.R.S. 1958.

'Goldfinch'   R.Sh.
Buff-apricot, early summer, 10 ft (3 m.) 1907
Raised by George Paul, England.
Parentage: 'Hélène' × unknown rose
A vigorous rambler with *R. multiflora* characteristics, and suitable for covering pillars or pergolas up to 10 ft (3 m.) or grown as a 6–7 ft (1·8–2·1 m.) shrub. Flowers in clusters, small, button-like with long pointed buds, buff-apricot in bud and first opening, then fading almost to white, especially in hot weather, semi-double. Free-flowering, strongly scented, late June to early July, not recurrent. An old climber that has a distinct charm in the soft colour of its opening flowers and its neat buds. Easily raised from hard-wood cuttings. **209**, p. 38.
A.M., R.H.S. 1907.

'Goldgleam'   Fl.
Deep yellow, 2½ ft (0·8 m.) 1966
Raised by E. B. LeGrice, England.
Parentage: 'Gleaming' × 'Allgold'
A cultivar of moderate vigour, 2½ ft (0·8 m.) high, with small glossy dark green foliage. The large, semi-double blooms are deep yellow, not quite as deep as 'Allgold', but colour is retained well and there is a slight fragrance. Requires very good cultivation.
T.G.C., R.N.R.S. 1965.

'Goldkrone' see **'Gold Crown', 309**, p. 58.

'Goldmarie'   Fl.
Golden-yellow, 3 ft (0·9 m.) 1958
Raised by R. Kordes, Germany.
Parentage: 'Masquerade' × 'Golden Main'
A vigorous, branching grower, 2½–3 ft (0·8–0·9 m.) high with dark bronze tinted, glossy foliage. The large, frilled flowers are produced in clusters, golden-yellow splashed with crimson on buds and young flowers. Fragrant. A cultivar rather spoiled by dull pink flushing as the flowers age. Protection against mildew is sometimes required and die-back may be a nuisance in bad winters.
A.M., R.H.S. 1958.

'Goldschatz', 'Golden Treasure'   Fl.
Deep golden-yellow, 2½ ft (0·8 m.) 1964
Raised by M. Tantau, Germany.
An upright, open grower, 2½ ft (0·8 m.) high, with glossy dark green foliage. The moderately full, medium sized flowers are hybrid tea type when young, deep golden-yellow which is well retained, but flowers are thin when open. A promising cultivar which requires close planting to be effective. **422**, p. 79.

'Grace Abounding'   Fl.
Creamy-white, 2½ ft (0·8 m.) 1968
Raised by R. Harkness & Co. Ltd, England.
Parentage: 'Pink Parfait' × 'Circus'
A bushy uniform grower, about 2½ ft (0·8 m.) high with glossy, light green foliage. The creamy-white, semi-double flowers are borne in large, somewhat crowded trusses and have a slight musky scent. Very free flowering. This would appear to be a useful cultivar as a foil to other colours.
T.G.C., R.N.R.S. 1970.

'Granadina', 'Grenadine'   Min.
Bright red, 15 in. (38·1 cm.) 1956
Raised by P. Dot, Spain.
Parentage: 'Granate' × 'Coralín'
An upright open plant, up to 15 in. (38·1 cm.) high with dark foliage. The small double flowers are bright red with a scarlet glow and are freely produced. May require protection from black spot.

'Grand'mère Jenny'   HT.
Cream, 3 ft (0·9 m.) 1950
Raised by F. Meilland, France.
Parentage: 'Peace' × ('Julien Potin' × 'Sensation')
A vigorous upright grower, 3 ft (0·9 m.) high with handsome, glossy, medium green foliage. Blooms yellowish cream, outer petals edged and flushed pink, fading slightly with age. Free flowering in summer and autumn, resists weather well and there is a little fragrance. Sometimes regarded as a refined 'Peace' (**347**, p. 65) and more suitable for small gardens being less vigorous. **313**, p. 59.
A.M., R.H.S. 1949; G.M., R.N.R.S. 1950; R.G.M. 1955.

'Grandpa Dickson', 'Irish Gold'   HT.
Yellow, 3 ft (0·9 m.) 1966
Raised by A. Dickson & Sons Ltd, N. Ireland.
Parentage: ('Kordes' Perfecta' × 'Governador Braga da Cruz') × 'Piccadilly'
A vigorous, upright grower with abundant glossy dark green foliage. The blooms are large, very full, generally very shapely and suitable for exhibition. Opens yellow becoming creamy-yellow with a slight tinge of green, edged with pink as the blooms age. Flowers freely in summer and autumn, large trusses of flowers on main growths. Resists wet weather well, also diseases, and has a light fragrance. A good cultivar for garden decoration, especially amongst strong colours. Owing to its upright habit, should be planted closely, not over 18 in. (0·5 m.) apart. Normally it will attain 3 ft (0·9 m.) in height. Appears to be successful in Australia. **314**, p. 59.
G.M., R.N.R.S. 1965; P.I.T., R.N.R.S. 1965; A.M., R.H.S. 1968; G.M.C.B.; G.M. and President's Trophy, R.N.R.S. Australia; H.G.M. 1966; G.R.H. 1966.

'Great Double White Rose' see **'Alba Maxima', 62**, p. 12.

'Great Maidens' Blush' see under **'Maidens' Blush', 67**, p. 12.

'Grenadine' see **'Granadina'**

'Grootendorst Supreme'   Rg.
Crimson, recurrent, 4–5 ft (1·2–1·5 m.) 1936
Introduced by F. J. Grootendorst & Sons, Holland.
Parentage: 'F. J. Grootendorst' sport
The flowers are a darker crimson-red than in the parent and so a bit more pleasant and less harsh in the garden. It does not always have the parent's vigour and the foliage tends to become a yellow-green.

'Gruss an Aachen'   Fl.
Pearly-pink, 2½ ft (0·8 m.) 1909
Raised by P. Geduidig, Germany.
Parentage: 'Frau Karl Druschki' × 'Franz Deegen'
A dwarf grower, 2–2½ ft (0·6–0·8 m.) high, with rich green foliage. The large double flowers are pearly-pink, fading to creamy-white and have a slight fragrance. A favourite with lovers of old garden roses, cast in a different mould from present day cultivars. **423**, p. 79.

'Gruss an Heidelburg' see **'Heidelburg', 170**, p. 31.

'Guinée'   Cl.
Dark crimson, recurrent, 15 ft (4·6 m.) 1938
Raised by C. Mallerin, France.
Parentage: 'Souvenir de Claudius Denoyel' × 'Ami Quinard'
Fairly vigorous climber up to 15 ft (4·6 m.). Unique for its lovely dark velvety crimson-maroon flowers which show up superlatively well against a grey stone or a white wall. Flowers medium to large in size, up to 4½ in. (11·4 cm.) across, pointed in bud, fully double but when mature showing golden stamens in centre, very deep crimson with waved petals, opening rather flat, rich and sumptuous with highlights like finest velvet; in shadow it appears shaded black, but with sunlight on it a good deep crimson. Scented. Early to mid-season, slightly recurrent but with main flowering in early to mid-June for 3–4 weeks. Foliage good with 5 leaflets but sensitive to mildew.

'Guinevere'   HT.
Light rose pink, 2½ ft (0·8 m.) 1967
Raised by R. Harkness & Co. Ltd, England.

Parentage: 'Red Dandy' × 'Peace'
A fairly vigorous, branching grower, 2½ ft (0·8 m.) in height, with abundant mat, light green foliage, very suitable for bedding. The medium sized blooms are light rose pink, fading slightly with age, symmetrical and rather rounded, resisting wet weather well and very free flowering. **311**, p. 58.
T.G.C., R.N.R.S. 1966.

'Gustav Frahm'   Fl.
Crimson-scarlet, 5 ft (1·5 m.) 1959
Raised by W. Kordes, Germany.
Parentage: 'Fanal' × 'Ama'
A very vigorous, upright grower, up to 5 ft (1·5 m.) high, with light green glossy foliage. The medium sized flowers open flat and are a glowing crimson-scarlet deepening towards the petal edges. They are produced in large trusses, somewhat later than most Floribundas. This is a fine cultivar for a large bed. Has little scent. **424**, p. 79.
T.G.C., R.N.R.S. 1958; A.M. R.H.S. 1961.

'Hamburg'   MSh.
Crimson-red, recurrent, 6 ft (1·8 m.) 1935
Raised by W. Kordes, Germany.
Parentage: 'Eva' × 'Daily Mail Scented'
Modern shrub rose of floribunda type and often classified under that group. Tends to make an erect, rather thin bush, height depending on pruning, of medium vigour up to 6 ft (1·8 m.). Flowers semi-double, very bright crimson-red of intense and clear colour, with small centre of buff-yellow stamens, medium to large, in clusters. Mid to late June, recurrent, slightly scented. One of the best for colour in this range. **169**, p. 31.

'Hamburger Phönix'   MCl.
Dark crimson, recurrent, 9 ft (2·7 m.) 1954
Raised by W. Kordes, Germany.
Parentage: R. kordesii × seedling
Kordesii climber or pillar rose of moderate vigour up to 9 ft (2·7 m.). Flowers semi-double, of medium size, in clusters, dark crimson, slight scent. Mid-June and recurrent. Free-flowering. Foliage deep green, glossy, disease resistant. Hips large, orange-red. One of the best of the deep red pillar roses for its unfading colour, freedom of flower and healthy foliage.

'Handel'   MCl.
Cream and pink, recurrent, 8–10 ft (2·4–3 m.) 1965
Raised by S. McGredy IV, N. Ireland.
Parentage: 'Columbine' × 'Heidelberg'
Vigorous in growth, this cultivar is well furnished with dark green glossy foliage which has coppery shades. The moderately full flowers are shapely in bud, opening up cream, flushed and heavily edged deep pink, an unusual but attractive combination. Slightly scented. Recurring freely, this fine climber may require protection against mildew but not against weather. **246**, p. 46.
T.G.C., R.N.R.S. 1965.

'Hansestadt Lübeck', 'Lübeck'   MSh.
Orange-scarlet, recurrent, 5 ft (1·5 m.) 1960
Raised by R. Kordes, Germany.
Modern shrub rose of good vigour up to 5 ft (1·5 m.). Floribunda type. Flowers double, bright orange-scarlet, up to 3½ in. (8·9 cm.) across, in clusters, slightly scented, free-flowering. Mid to late June, recurrent. Foliage dark green.
C.M., R.N.R.S. 1962.

'Happy Event'   Fl.
Light chrome-yellow, 3½ ft (1·1 m.) 1964

Raised by A. Dickson & Sons Ltd, N. Ireland.
Parentage: ('Karl Herbst' × 'Masquerade') × 'Rose Gaujard'
A fairly vigorous, upright grower, 3½ ft (1·1 m.) high with plentiful glossy, dark green foliage. The large, semi-double flowers are borne in clusters, light chrome yellow in colour with the inside of the petals flushed cherry red, fading with age to carmine. **425**, p. 79.
T.G.C., R.N.R.S. 1965.

'Harison's Yellow' see R. × *harisonii*, **20**, p. 5.

'Headleyensis' see R. × *pteragonis* **'Headleyensis'**, **43**, p. 8; **44**, p. 9.

'Heartbeat'   Fl.
Salmon-orange, 3 ft (0·9 m.) 1970
Raised by A. Dickson & Sons Ltd, N. Ireland.
Parentage: 'Castanet' × ('Cornelia' × seedling)
An open grower, 3 ft (0·9 m.) high, with small-leaved, semi-glossy foliage and deep salmon-orange flowers which are unaffected by bad weather. **425**, p. 78.

'Heather Muir' see R. *sericea* **'Heather Muir'**, **49**, p. 9.

'Hebe's Lip', 'Reine Blanche', 'Rubrotincta'   D.
Creamy-white, summer, 4 ft (1·2 m.) 1912
Shrub rose of medium vigour up to 4 ft (1·2 m.). Growth erect and

---

Abbreviations and Symbols used in the text

Rose classifications

A.	Alba	HT.	Hybrid Tea
B.	Bourbon	MCl.	Modern, large-flowered climber
C.	Centifolia	Min.	Miniature
Ch.	China	Moss	Centifolia muscosa
Cl.	Climber	MSh.	Modern shrub
D.	Damask	P.	Penzance Sweet Brier
Fl.	Floribunda	R.	Rambler
G.	Gallica	Rg.	Rugosa
HM.	Hybrid Musk	Sp.	Species and first hybrids
HP.	Hybrid Perpetual	Sw.	Sweet Brier

Rose Awards and Societies

A.A.R.S.	All-America Rose Selection
A.G.M.	Award of Garden Merit
A.M.	Award of Merit
A.R.S.	American Rose Society
B.B.G.M.	Baden Baden Gold Medal, Germany
B.G.M.	Bagatelle Gold Medal, Paris
C.C.V.	Clay Challenge Vase for scent
C.M.	Certificate of Merit
D.F.P.	David Fuerstenberg Prize
F.C.C.	First Class Certificate
G.G.M.	Geneva Gold Medal
G.M.	Gold Medal
G.M.C.B.	Gold Medal City of Belfast
G.M.H.G.M.	Gertrude M. Hubbard Gold Medal
G.R.H.	Golden Rose of The Hague
G.T.A.B.	Golden Thorn Award Belfast
H.E.M.M.	The Henry Edland Memorial Medal for the most fragrant rose of the year
H.G.M.	The Hague Gold Medal
L.G.M.	Lyon Gold Medal, France
M.G.M.	Madrid Gold Medal
N.G.M.C.	National Gold Medal Certificate
P.G.M.	Portland Gold Medal, Oregon, U.S.A.
P.I.T.	President's International Trophy
R.B.	Prize for the most fragrant rose, Roeulx, Belgium
R.B.G.M.	Roeulx, Belgium, Gold Medal
R.G.M.	Rome Gold Medal
R.H.S.	The Royal Horticultural Society, London
R.N.R.S.	The Royal National Rose Society, Great Britain*
T.G.C.	Trial Ground Certificate
U.A.B.	The 'Uladh' Award for fragrance, Belfast

*National Rose Society awards, before 1965, are included here under R.N.R.S.

The illustration numbers are in **bold type** and the page numbers in light type preceded by p.

twiggy as well as prickly. Flowers creamy-white, semi-double, sometimes edged with carmine but more often one or two petals only have slight flush of colour near edge as in our photograph. About 3 in. (7·6 cm.) across. Scented. Mid to late June. Free-flowering. Not one of the most spectacular of the older roses but has a pleasant and charming flower, usually growing easily. Often known as 'Rubrotincta' from the crimson marking. An old rose, not a typical Damask and origin unknown, it may have been a cross between *R. damascena* and *R. alba* or *R. gallica*. **79**, p. 14.

'Heidelberg', 'Gruss an Heidelberg' MSh.Cl.
Bright crimson-red, recurrent, 7 ft (2·1 m.) 1958
Raised by R. Kordes, Germany.
Parentage: 'Sparrieshoop' × 'World's Fair'
Modern shrub or pillar rose of great vigour up to 7 ft (2·1 m.). Flowers semi-double, bright crimson-red with small centre of brownish stamens, a little lighter on reverse, medium to large, in large clusters, with more petals than in 'Hamburg', of not quite so deep a red, but a more vigorous grower. Mid to late June, recurrent, very good in autumn and free-flowering. Foliage deep green, glossy. May require protection against black spot. **170**, p. 31.
C.M., R.N.R.S. 1958; A.M., R.H.S. 1961.

'Helen Traubel' HT.
Light apricot-pink, 3 ft (0·9 m.) 1951
Raised by H. C. Swim, U.S.A.
Parentage: 'Charlotte Armstrong' × 'Glowing Sunset'
A vigorous tall grower, up to 3 ft (0·9 m.) in height, which never seems to have attained the popularity it merits. Foliage is abundant semi-glossy, coppery-green when young becoming dark green. Flowers are of attractive form when young, opening wide later, light apricot-pink, flushed yellow at base of petals, fading slightly. Very free-flowering both summer and autumn, resists weather reasonably well and is very fragrant. The flowers are somewhat variable in colour and sometimes droop, perhaps the reason it has not caught on, nevertheless an attractive rose. **312**, p. 58.
R.G.M. 1951; A.A.R.S. 1952; T.G.C., R.N.R.S. 1952.

'Henri Fouquier' G.
Purplish-pink, summer, 3½ ft (1·1 m.) *c*. 1811
Gallica shrub rose, not very vigorous, up to 3½ ft (1·1 m.), but floriferous. Flowers large, purplish-pink lighter at edges, rather floppy and fading to lilac pink, quartered. Mid to late June.

'Henri Martin' Moss Sh.
Bright purplish-crimson, summer, 6 ft (1·8 m.) 1863
Raised by M. Laffay, France.
Vigorous shrub up to 6 ft (1·8 m.) but usually less. Flowers of medium size, rich and bright, purplish-crimson, double; bud long and very mossy. Flowers in clusters. Mid to late June, not recurrent. Free-flowering. Scented. Stem very prickly. One of the best growers in this section and distinctive for its bright purplish-crimson colour, for which it is sometimes given the name 'Red Moss'.

'Hermosa' Ch.
Lilac-pink, recurrent, 3 ft (0·9 m.) 1840
Raised by Marcheseau.
A China rose of rather dwarf habit and medium vigour, usually not over 3 ft (0·9 m.), close to the Monthly rose, the Old Blush China. Flowers semi-double, rather small, lilac-pink with petals rolled at edges, rather globular, scented. Mid-June and recurrent. 'Hermosa' will make quite a good dwarf hedge of about 3 ft (0·9 m.). **126**, p. 22.

'Herzog von Windsor' see **'Duke of Windsor'**, **294**, p. 55.

'Heure Mauve' HT.
Lilac, 2 ft (0·6 m.) 1962
Raised by C. Mallerin, France.
Parentage: 'Simone' × 'Prelude'
A reasonably vigorous and bushy grower, 2 ft (0·6 m.) in height with semi-glossy medium green foliage. The moderately full blooms are lilac tinted mauve and have a slight fragrance. Shapely in the early stages, they are resistant to wet weather. A useful bedder where the colour is appreciated.
T.G.C., R.N.R.S. 1962.

'Highdownensis' see **R.** × ***highdownensis***, **23, 24**, p. 5.

'Highlight' Fl.
Orange-scarlet, 2½ ft (0·8 m.) 1957
Raised by H. Robinson, England.
Parentage: seedling × 'Independence'
A fairly vigorous, upright grower, 2½ ft (0·8 m.) high, with semi-glossy leaves. The medium sized, double flowers are produced in large clusters, intense orange-scarlet when young but tend to dull off purple-blue with age. Scented. **427**, p. 80.
G.M., R.N.R.S. 1957; A.M., R.H.S. 1957.

Himalayan Musk Rose see **R. moschata nepalensis**

'Hippolyte' G.
Dark purplish-crimson, summer, 5 ft (1·5 m.)
Shrub rose of good vigour, up to 5 ft (1·5 m.). Flowers double, dark purplish-crimson fading to violet, rather rounded, of medium size. Mid to late June. Leaflets rather small for a Gallica. **85**, p. 15.

Holy Rose see **R.** × ***richardii***

'Honey Favorite' HT.
Yellow pink, 2½ ft (0·8 m.) 1962
Discovered by G. J. Von Abrams, U.S.A.
Parentage: 'Pink Favorite' sport
A vigorous healthy grower, 2½ ft (0·8 m.) high with handsome, very glossy light green foliage. The large flowers are pale yellowish-pink with a yellow base, of good formation and are very freely produced. Light honey scent. This is a useful exhibition cultivar, not yet as popular as its parent although it has the same good qualities. Ideal for bedding, flowering a little later than the general run of roses. Sometimes an odd flower shows signs of partial or full reversion to the parent. **315**, p. 60.

'Honorine de Brabant' B.
Pale pink, streaked purplish-crimson, recurrent, 6 ft (1·8 m.)
An old Bourbon rose of the last century. Vigorous, up to 6 ft (1·8 m.) and usually thick and bushy with large leaves. Flowers large, double, pale pink, splashed irregularly with purplish-crimson, opening cupped then becoming quartered, 3½–4 in. (8·9–10·2 cm.) across. Lighter in colour than 'Commandant Beaurepaire' and less conspicuously striped than 'Variegata di Bologna'. Scented. Mid to late June. **94**, p. 17.

'Horstmann's Rosenresli', 'Rosenresli' Fl.
Pure white, 2½ ft (0·8 m.) 1955
Raised by W. Kordes, Germany.
Parentage: 'Rudolph Timm' × 'Lavender Pinocchio'
A short bushy grower, 2½ ft (0·8 m.) high, with heavy, deep green foliage. The large double flowers are pure white, produced in clusters and have some fragrance. Very free flowering, this very hardy rose is almost unknown in the British Isles but visitors to London may see it in Queen Mary's Garden, Regent's Park. Makes a good standard. **428**, p. 80.

'Hugh Dickson' HP.

Bright crimson, recurrent, 10 ft (3 m.) 1905
Raised by H. Dickson Ltd, N. Ireland.
Parentage: 'Lord Bacon' × 'Gruss an Teplitz'
Vigorous Hybrid Perpetual shrub or pillar rose up to 10 ft (3 m.) with long shoots flowering at tips unless pegged down. Flowers large, double, bright crimson, rich in colour, in clusters, of hybrid tea shape, scented. Recurrent. Still grown and formerly much used as a parent in breeding crimson scented roses. Old flowering shoots may be cut right out in autumn.

Hulthemia persica, *Rosa persica*, *R. berberifolia*, Sp.
Rose of Persia

Bright yellow, summer, 2½ ft (0·8 m.) c. 1790
Countries of origin: Iran, Afghanistan, U.S.S.R.
The wild Persian rose of the edges of the deserts, a very beautiful plant but intolerant of wet cold and difficult to maintain in cultivation. Small shrub with silvery grey, simple foliage, about 2½ ft (0·8 m.) high in its native area where it grows in great quantity, spiny and twiggy. When dry in summer much of it breaks away and blows across the desert to be picked up and used for kindling. Flowers deep golden-yellow, the brightest yellow of any rose, with prominent bright red blotch at base of each petal and dark eye, single 1½ in. (3·8 cm.) across. May to July. Hips small, bristly. Best grown in very warm and well-drained position. Difficult to propagate except from seed, also difficult to move and should be planted direct out of the seed pan. It should be tried more in warmer countries than Britain.

× Hulthemosa hardii, *Rosa × hardii* Sh.

Bright yellow, early summer, 4 ft (1·2 m.) 1838
Introduced by Hardy, Belgium.
Parentage: *Hulthemia persica* × *R. clinophylla*
A very lovely bigeneric hybrid with the characteristic flowers of *Hulthemia persica* but larger. Unfortunately it is a weak straggly grower, somewhat tender and very susceptible to mildew, but there have been records of its successful cultivation outside against a wall in warmer parts of Britain such as at Berkeley Castle in Gloucestershire and of which Capt. Berkeley wrote that it had reached 10 ft (3 m.) on the wall of the Castle and he had grown it for 40 years. He preferred a plant on its own roots to one budded. Flowers deep sulphur yellow with bright red blotch at base of each petal, 2½ in. (6·4 cm.) across. Late May to end of June, but it tends to be a sparse flowerer. Leaves irregularly divided into 3 to 7 small leaflets. This lovely plant has so far proved to be sterile and no one has succeeded in breeding from it but with more modern techniques for chromosome doubling it is hoped it may prove possible in the future.

'Hume's Blush Tea-scented China' see under *R. × odorata*

'Humpty-Dumpty' Min.

Bright pink, 6 in. (15·2 cm.) 1952
Raised by J. de Vink, Holland.
Parentage: (*R. multiflora nana* × 'Mrs Pierre S. du Pont' F₂) × 'Tom Thumb'
A small grower, 4–6 in. (10·2–15·2 cm.) high, with very double flowers of bright pink deepening towards the centre, which last well. Slightly fragrant.

'Hunter' MSh.

Scarlet-crimson, recurrent, 6 ft (1·8 m.) 1961
Raised by J. Mattock Ltd, England.
Parentage: *R. rugosa* 'Rubra' × 'Independence'
A vigorous Rugosa hybrid shrub up to 6 ft (1·8 m.). Flowers double, bright scarlet-crimson in clusters. Mid-June and re-

current in autumn. No scent. Foliage nearer that of a Hybrid Tea. A useful garden plant which also makes a conspicuous hedge. **171**, p. 31.

'Ice White', 'Vison Blanc' Fl.

White, 2½ ft (0·8 m.) 1966
Raised by S. McGredy IV, N. Ireland.
Parentage: 'Mme Léon Cuny' × ('Orange Sweetheart' × 'Cinnabar')
A vigorous branching grower 2½–3 ft (0·8–0·9 m.) high with glossy dark green foliage. The semi-double flowers are shapely in the early stages, produced in large clusters, white, slightly creamy towards the centre of the open flowers. Very free-flowering. Stiffer in habit than 'Schneewittchen' (**481**, p. 91). **429**, p. 80.

'Iceberg' see **'Schneewittchen'**, **481**, p. 91.

'Iceberg, Climbing' see **'Climbing Iceberg'**

'Ideal Home' see **'Idylle'**, **316**, p. 60.

'Idylle', 'Ideal Home' HT.

Carmine pink, 2½ ft (0·8 m.) 1960
Raised by Ets J. Laperrière, France.
Parentage: 'Monte Carlo' × 'Tonnerre'
A vigorous grower, just above 2½ ft (0·8 m.) in height with large

---

Abbreviations and Symbols used in the text

Rose classifications

A.	Alba		HT.	Hybrid Tea
B.	Bourbon		MCl.	Modern, large-flowered climber
C.	Centifolia		Min.	Miniature
Ch.	China		Moss	Centifolia muscosa
Cl.	Climber		MSh.	Modern shrub
D.	Damask		P.	Penzance Sweet Brier
Fl.	Floribunda		R.	Rambler
G.	Gallica		Rg.	Rugosa
HM.	Hybrid Musk		Sp.	Species and first hybrids
HP.	Hybrid Perpetual		Sw.	Sweet Brier

Rose Awards and Societies

A.A.R.S.	All-America Rose Selection
A.G.M.	Award of Garden Merit
A.M.	Award of Merit
A.R.S.	American Rose Society
B.B.G.M.	Baden Baden Gold Medal, Germany
B.G.M.	Bagatelle Gold Medal, Paris
C.C.V.	Clay Challenge Vase for scent
C.M.	Certificate of Merit
D.F.P.	David Fuerstenberg Prize
F.C.C.	First Class Certificate
G.G.M.	Geneva Gold Medal
G.M.	Gold Medal
G.M.C.B.	Gold Medal City of Belfast
G.M.H.G.M.	Gertrude M. Hubbard Gold Medal
G.R.H.	Golden Rose of The Hague
G.T.A.B.	Golden Thorn Award Belfast
H.E.M.M.	The Henry Edland Memorial Medal for the most fragrant rose of the year
H.G.M.	The Hague Gold Medal
L.G.M.	Lyon Gold Medal, France
M.G.M.	Madrid Gold Medal
N.G.M.C.	National Gold Medal Certificate
P.G.M.	Portland Gold Medal, Oregon, U.S.A.
P.I.T.	President's International Trophy
R.B.	Prize for the most fragrant rose, Roeulx, Belgium
R.B.G.M.	Roeulx, Belgium, Gold Medal
R.G.M.	Rome Gold Medal
R.H.S.	The Royal Horticultural Society, London
R.N.R.S.	The Royal National Rose Society, Great Britain*
T.G.C.	Trial Ground Certificate
U.A.B.	The 'Uladh' Award for fragrance, Belfast

National Rose Society awards, before 1965, are included here under R.N.R.S.

The illustration numbers are in **bold type** and the page numbers in light type preceded by p.

semi-glossy, dark green foliage, red when young. The full, globular flowers are of medium size, freely produced, often in clusters, carmine pink with an ivory white base, the colour deepening as the flowers age. **316**, p. 60.
C.M., R.N.R.S. 1959; A.M., R.H.S. 1961.

'Incarnata' see under **'Maidens' Blush', 67**, p. 12.

'Innisfree'   Fl.
Orange and yellow, 3 ft (0·9 m.) 1964
Raised by A. Dickson & Sons Ltd, N. Ireland.
Parentage: ('Karl Herbst' × 'Masquerade') × 'Circus'
A vigorous, upright grower, 3 ft (0·9 m.) high, with rather small, light green glossy foliage. The rosette shaped flowers are of medium size, orange and yellow changing to pink and have a slight fragrance.
T.G.C., R.N.R.S. 1964.

'Invitation'   HT.
Rich salmon, 2½ ft (0·8 m.) 1961
Raised by Swim and Weeks, U.S.A.
Parentage: 'Charlotte Armstrong' × 'Signora'
A vigorous branching grower of medium height with glossy medium green foliage. The rich salmon pink blooms have a yellow base and scarlet veining, are shapely, develop quickly and are very fragrant. A good cultivar in the autumn. A healthy rose with few thorns.

'Irene Churruca', 'Golden Melody'   HT.
Buff, 2½ ft (0·8 m.) 1934
Raised by La Florida, Spain.
Parentage: 'Mme Butterfly' × ('Lady Hillingdon' × 'Souvenir de Claudius Pernet')
A vigorous, spreading grower of 2½ ft (0·8 m.) in height, with semi-glossy dark green, bronze tinted foliage. The light buff blooms fade to cream towards the edges, are full, well formed and very fragrant. Free flowering, this cultivar resists rain fairly well but has to be watched for mildew. **317**, p. 60.

'Irene of Denmark', 'Irene von Dänemark'   Fl.
White, 1½ ft (0·5 m.) 1948
Raised by S. Poulsen, Denmark.
Parentage: 'Orléans Rose' × ('Mme Plantier' × 'Edina')
Still reasonably vigorous, about 18 inches (0·5 m.) high, with dark foliage. The fairly large double flowers are cupped, tinted pink in bud but pure white when open, scented and freely produced. Still useful where a compact white cultivar is required.

'Irene von Dänemark' see **'Irene of Denmark'**

'Iris Squire'   Fl.
Soft-rose, 3 ft (0·9 m.) 1966
Raised by Bees Ltd, England.
Parentage: unnamed seedling × 'Queen Elizabeth'
A tall, vigorous grower, 3 ft (0·9 m.) high, with dull foliage. The large flowers are of hybrid tea shape and produced freely over a long season.

'Irish Beauty' see **'Elizabeth of Glamis', 407**, p. 76.

'Irish Gold' see **'Grandpa Dickson', 314**, p. 59.

'Irish Mist'   Fl.
Orange-salmon, 2½ ft (0·8 m.) 1966
Raised by S. McGredy IV, N. Ireland.
Parentage: 'Orangeade' × 'Mischief'
A medium branching grower, 2½ ft (0·8 m.) high with small, semi-glossy dark green foliage. The moderately full flowers are shapely, hybrid tea type, orange-salmon with serrated edges and have a slight fragrance. One of the best bedders to date in this colour range, very free-flowering over a long season, lasting well into autumn. **430**, p. 80.
C.M., R.N.R.S. 1967.

Irish Rose see **R. × hibernica, 22**, p. 5.

'Irish Wonder' see **'Evelyn Fison', 411**, p. 77.

'Isabel de Ortiz'   HT.
Deep pink and silver, 3 ft (0·9 m.) 1962
Raised by R. Kordes, Germany.
Parentage: 'Peace' × 'Kordes' Perfecta'
A vigorous, tall, upright grower with abundant dark green, glossy foliage. The large, very full blooms have great depth and good form, making this a popular cultivar with exhibitors. Best in good weather, the flowers are deep pink with a silvery reverse and are fragrant. **318**, p. 60.
M.G.M. 1961; G.M., R.N.R.S. 1962.

'Isle of Man' see **'Manx Queen', 441**, p. 82.

'Ispahan'   D.
Blush-pink, summer, 8 ft (2·4 m.) before 1832
A vigorous Damask rose with upright growth, to 8 ft (2·4 m.). Flowers clear pink, double, in clusters, fading to a good blush-pink, well quartered, 3½ in. (8·9 cm.) across. Very free-flowering. Mid to late June. Foliage blue-grey with large leaflets. A very desirable and beautiful rose which is one of the best growers in this group and also has a long flowering season. **80**, p. 15.

'Ivory Fashion'   Fl.
Ivory-white, 3 ft (0·9 m.) 1958
Raised by E. S. Boerner, U.S.A.
Parentage: 'Sonata' × 'Fashion'
A moderately vigorous grower, 3 ft (0·9 m.) high with mat green foliage. The large semi-double flowers are of good form when young, opening flat, attractive ivory-white, sometimes shaded buff and produced in large trusses. Slightly scented. This cultivar is best in good weather. **431**, p. 80.

Jacobite Rose see **'Alba Maxima', 62**, p. 12.

'Jacques Cartier'   D.
Pink, summer, 4 ft (1·2 m.) 1868
Raised by Moreau-Robert, France.
A rose of the Portland Damask group, of moderate vigour and erect, up to 4 ft (1·2 m.). Flowers large, opening rich pink, fading to paler pink, almost white at edge, fragrant; double but maturing to a rather untidy flower and in this respect not so good as 'Comte de Chambord'. Mid to late June. **81**, p. 15.

'Jan Spek'   Fl.
Yellow, 2 ft (0·6 m.) 1966
Raised by S. McGredy IV, N. Ireland.
Parentage: 'Cläre Grammerstorf' × 'Faust'

A short vigorous grower, 2 ft (0·6 m.) high, with glossy dark green foliage. The fully double rosette shaped flowers open bright yellow, becoming creamy yellow. Freely produced in trusses over a long season. Where it is happy, a very suitable cultivar for small beds and borders, especially in small gardens. **432**, p. 80. G.T.A.B. 1968; G.R.H. 1970.

'Japonica' see **'Mousseux de Japon'**, **75**, p. 14.

'Jeanie Williams' Min.
Orange-red and yellow, 12 in. (30·5 cm.) 1965
Raised by R. S. Moore, U.S.A.
Parentage: 'Little Darling' × 'Magic Wand'
A vigorous bushy grower, 8–12 in. (20·3–30·5 cm.) high, with small double flowers, orange-red with a yellow reverse. Slightly fragrant.

'Jeanne de Montfort' Moss Sh.
Pink, slightly recurrent, 6 ft (1·8 m.) 1851
Raised by M. Robert, France.
One of the most vigorous moss shrubs. Flower a good warm pink on opening, semi-double, fading to blush pink and almost to white, of medium size, free-flowering, in large clusters. Scented. Bud rather globular with long calyx lobes, well mossed with a brownish tone. Mid to late June, very slightly recurrent with a few autumn flowers. **73**, p. 13.

'John Waterer' HT.
Deep rose-red, 2½ ft (0·8 m.) 1970
Raised by S. McGredy IV, N. Ireland.
Parentage: ('Karl Herbst' × 'Ethel Sanday') × 'Hannah'
A tall, erect grower with dark green mat foliage. The large blooms are full, deep rose-red, sometimes borne singly, at other times several together. They are scented but the colour tends to become dull with age. **319**, p. 60.
C.M., R.N.R.S. 1969.

'Josephine Bruce'
Scarlet, 2½ ft (0·8 m.) 1949
Raised by Bees Ltd, England.
Parentage: 'Crimson Glory' × 'Madge Whipp'
The records give the above mentioned parents although, apparently, it is possible that 'Jane Thornton' was the pollen parent. A vigorous spreading grower, 2½ ft (0·8 m.) in height, with ample, semi-glossy, dark green foliage. The medium sized blooms are well formed and freely produced, and are a glowing velvety scarlet, overlaid with deep maroon shades, really exquisite when at their best and deeply fragrant. Apt to get mildew particularly on young growth in autumn. To correct the sprawling habit, pruning to inward growing eyes is desirable. Very useful as a standard. **320**, p. 60.
T.G.C., R.N.R.S. 1953.

'Josephine Wheatcroft' see **'Rosina'**

'Joseph's Coat' MCl.Sh.
Yellow and red, recurrent, 6–10 ft (1·8–3 m.) 1964
Raised by Armstrong and Swim, U.S.A.
Parentage: 'Buccaneer' × 'Circus'
Officially classified as a climber, this vigorous grower is well furnished with dark green semi-glossy foliage. The semi-double flowers produced in large and medium trusses, are bright yellow, flushed with orange and cherry-red, especially at the edges of the petals; freely produced over a long period, especially in autumn. Slightly fragrant. Trained on a wall, will attain 10 ft (3 m.) but is equally happy in the open where it can be grown as a shrub or, if

pruned hard, will be very effective in a large bed. **247**, p. 46.
T.G.C., R.N.R.S. 1963; B.G.M. 1964.

'Jove' Fl.
Brilliant scarlet, 2 ft (0·6 m.) 1968
Raised by R. Harkness & Co. Ltd. England.
Parentage: 'Vera Dalton' × 'Paprika'
A short, bushy grower, about 2 ft (0·6 m.) high, with abundant glossy dark green foliage. The semi-double, waved flowers are brilliant scarlet, darkening with age, lasting well. Flowers freely during summer and autumn and resists weather well. Little scent but a striking cultivar for small beds. Requires good cultivation.

'Joybells' Fl.
Rich salmon-pink, 2½ ft (0·8 m.) 1961
Raised by H. Robinson, England.
Parentage: unnamed seedling × 'Fashion'
A strong branching grower, about 2½ ft (0·8 m.) high, with very thorny growths and glossy, medium green leaves. The large, full, camellia shaped flowers are produced in large trusses of rich salmon-pink, which softens in shade in warm weather. Always attractive with an old fashioned air about them. **433**, p. 81.

'Joyfulness' see **'Frohsinn'**, **419**, p. 78.

'Jubilant' Fl.
Peach-pink, 3 ft (0·9 m.) 1967
Raised by A. Dickson & Sons Ltd, N. Ireland.

Abbreviations and Symbols used in the text

Rose classifications

A.	Alba	HT.	Hybrid Tea
B.	Bourbon	MCl.	Modern, large-flowered climber
C.	Centifolia	Min.	Miniature
Ch.	China	Moss	Centifolia muscosa
Cl.	Climber	MSh.	Modern shrub
D.	Damask	P.	Penzance Sweet Brier
Fl.	Floribunda	R.	Rambler
G.	Gallica	Rg.	Rugosa
HM.	Hybrid Musk	Sp.	Species and first hybrids
HP.	Hybrid Perpetual	Sw.	Sweet Brier

Rose Awards and Societies

A.A.R.S.	All-America Rose Selection
A.G.M.	Award of Garden Merit
A.M.	Award of Merit
A.R.S.	American Rose Society
B.B.G.M.	Baden Baden Gold Medal, Germany
B.G.M.	Bagatelle Gold Medal, Paris
C.C.V.	Clay Challenge Vase for scent
C.M.	Certificate of Merit
D.F.P.	David Fuerstenberg Prize
F.C.C.	First Class Certificate
G.G.M.	Geneva Gold Medal
G.M.	Gold Medal
G.M.C.B.	Gold Medal City of Belfast
G.M.H.G.M.	Gertrude M. Hubbard Gold Medal
G.R.H.	Golden Rose of The Hague
G.T.A.B.	Golden Thorn Award Belfast
H.E.M.M.	The Henry Edland Memorial Medal for the most fragrant róse of the year
H.G.M.	The Hague Gold Medal
L.G.M.	Lyon Gold Medal, France
M.G.M.	Madrid Gold Medal
N.G.M.C.	National Gold Medal Certificate
P.G.M.	Portland Gold Medal, Oregon, U.S.A.
P.I.T.	President's International Trophy
R.B.	Prize for the most fragrant rose, Roeulx, Belgium
R.B.G.M.	Roeulx, Belgium, Gold Medal
R.G.M.	Rome Gold Medal
R.H.S.	The Royal Horticultural Society, London
R.N.R.S.	The Royal National Rose Society, Great Britain*
T.G.C.	Trial Ground Certificate
U.A.B.	The 'Uladh' Award for fragrance, Belfast

*National Rose Society awards, before 1965, are included here under R.N.R.S.

The illustration numbers are in **bold type** and the page numbers in light type preceded by p.

Parentage: 'Dearest' × 'Circus'

A moderate grower up to 3 ft (0·9 m.) high, with plentiful bronzy-green foliage. The semi-double flowers open flat, are salmon-pink in the bud, opening to peach-pink, paling towards edges. Freely produced. A good bedder in cool weather but looks a bit tired in very hot weather. Some fragrance. **434**, p. 81.
C.M., R.N.R.S. 1965.

'Julia Mannering' see under **R. eglanteria, 10**, p. 2.

'June Park'   HT.
Deep rose pink, 2 ft (0·6 m.) 1958
Raised by B. Park, England.
Parentage: 'Peace' × 'Crimson Glory'
A fairly vigorous spreading grower, to 2 ft (0·6 m.), with semi-glossy dark green foliage. The blooms are full, of good shape, deep rose pink in colour and very fragrant. Pruning to inward pointing eyes will help correct the somewhat sprawling habit. Useful for exhibition when at its best. **321**, p. 61.
G.M., R.N.R.S. 1959; C.C.V., R.N.R.S. 1959.

'June Time'   Min.
Light pink, 12 in. (30·5 cm.) 1963
Raised by R. S. Moore, U.S.A.
Parentage: (R. wichuraiana × 'Floradora') × (('Etoile Luisante' seedling × 'Red Ripples') × 'Zee')
A bushy compact plant, 9–12 in. (22·9–30·5 cm.) high, with glossy foliage. The small double flowers are light pink with a deeper pink reverse, giving a very pretty effect. Very free.

'Junior Miss' see **'America's Junior Miss', 380**, p. 71.

'Kabuki', 'Golden Prince'   HT.
Deep golden-yellow, 3 ft (0·9 m.) 1968
Raised by M. L. Meilland, France.
Parentage: ('Monte Carlo' × 'Bettina') × ('Peace' × 'Soraya')
A vigorous, upright grower, 2½–3 ft (0·8–0·9 m.) high, with bronzy, glossy foliage. The large double flowers are high centred, deep golden-yellow in colour, which does not fade, and are freely produced. Fragrant.

'Kalinka' see **'Pink Wonder', 467**, p. 88.

'Karl Herbst'   HT.
Deep red, 3 ft (0·9 m.) 1950
Raised by W. Kordes, Germany.
Parentage: 'Peace' × 'Independence'
A vigorous, tall, branching grower, 3 ft (0·9 m.) high with glossy, dark green foliage, tinted red when young. The blooms are deep red with lighter reverse, generally well formed and very full but not very fragrant. Very free flowering, it is only at its best in good weather, when it can be up to exhibition standard. Much used by breeders and sometimes known by them as 'the old bull'.
G.M., R.N.R.S. 1950.

'Karolyn' see **'Coralin'**

'Kassel'   MSh.Cl.
Bright scarlet-red, recurrent, 6 ft (1·8 m.) 1958
Raised by R. Kordes, Germany.

Parentage: 'Hamburg' × 'Scarlet Else'
Modern shrub or pillar rose, vigorous, up to 6 ft (1·8 m.). Flowers semi-double, bright cherry-scarlet-red, medium to large, in clusters of floribunda type, scented. Mid to late June, recurrent. One of the best in his series of large crimson shrub roses and very free-flowering. **172**, p. 32.
C.M., R.N.R.S. 1957; A.M., R.H.S. 1964.

'Kathleen Ferrier'   MSh.
Salmon-pink, recurrent, 5 ft (1·5 m.) 1952
Raised by G.A.H. Buisman, Holland.
Parentage: 'Gartenstolz' × 'Shot Silk'
Modern shrub rose of medium vigour, up to 5 ft (1·5 m.). Flowers semi-double, large, deep salmon-pink, paler towards centre, but deeper in colour on outside of petals, in small clusters, strongly scented. Mid to late June, recurrent and good in the autumn. Rather a spreading shrub with pleasant dark bronzy young stems and making vigorous shoots in late summer. **173**, p. 32.
A.M., R.H.S. 1963.

'Kathleen Harrop'   B.
Shell-pink, recurrent, 8 ft (2·4 m.) 1919
Discovered by A. Dickson & Sons Ltd, N. Ireland.
Parentage: 'Zephyrine Drouhin' sport
A Bourbon shrub or pillar rose up to 8 ft (2·4 m.), vigorous. Not so vigorous as her parent, otherwise similar in growth. Flowers light shell-pink, deeper in centre, fading almost to white at edge, darker on outside, double, up to 4 in. (10·2 cm.) across, scented. Mid to late June, recurrent. Foliage light green with 3–5 large pointed leaflets. **95**, p. 17.

'Kazanlik' see **R. damascena trigintipetula**

'Kiftsgate' see under **R. filipes, 19**, p. 4.

'Kim'   Fl.
Canary-yellow, 1½ ft (0·5 m.) 1972
Raised by R. Harkness & Co. Ltd, England.
Parentage: ('Orange Sensation' × 'Allgold') × 'Elizabeth of Glamis'
A dwarf compact grower 1½ ft (0·5 m.) high, bushy habit with small, matt, light to medium green foliage. The full flowers are freely borne in trusses, canary-yellow with a blush of vermilion as they age in the autumn. Ideal for small gardens. **435**, p. 81.
C.M., R.N.R.S. 1970.

'King Arthur'   Fl.
Deep salmon, 3½ ft (1·1 m.) 1967
Raised by R. Harkness & Co. Ltd, England.
Parentage: 'Pink Parfait' × 'Highlight'
A vigorous upright grower of spreading growth up to 3½ ft (1·1 m.). Foliage abundant, mat, medium green with a purple tinge when young. The deep salmon-pink blooms are produced in small trusses and mottle slightly with age. Weather resistance is good and scent is slight. An abundant cropper which repeats quickly, altogether a good garden plant. **436**, p. 81.
C.M., R.N.R.S. 1966.

'King's Ransom'   HT.
Rich yellow, 3 ft (0·9 m.) 1961
Raised by D. Morey, U.S.A.
Parentage: 'Golden Masterpiece' × 'Lydia'
A vigorous grower, upright, spreading sufficiently to make a handsome plant. Very glossy, abundant, dark green foliage which makes an attractive foil for the rich yellow flowers. These are of

medium size, good formation, have a slight scent and reasonable resistance to wet weather. Flowering profusely in summer and autumn, with some between, this is one of the best garden roses in this colour at the present time. Apt to suffer from severe frost, it requires severe pruning to remove frost damaged wood but breaks well. Sometimes a few of these early growths are blind but if lightly pruned, they will soon break and flower. Sometimes gets slight attacks of mildew, in mildew prone areas. **322**, p. 61.
A.A.R.S. 1962.

'Königin der Rosen', 'Colour Wonder', 'Queen of Roses',   HT.
  'Reine des Roses'
Orange salmon, 2 ft (0·6 m.) 1964
Raised by R. Kordes, Germany.
Parentage: 'Kordes' Perfecta' × 'Super Star'
A vigorous grower of short stature with rather small, glossy, dark green foliage. The very full, short petalled flowers are orange salmon in colour with a pale yellow reverse, a new colour break. Quite distinctive in appearance, this cultivar is free flowering and slightly fragrant. **323**, p. 61.

'Königin von Dänemark', 'Queen of Denmark'   A.
Rose-pink, summer, 6 ft (1·8 m.) 1816
Raised by J. Booth, England.
Parentage: 'Maidens' Blush' seedling
Alba shrub of medium vigour, rather loose growing but sometimes up to 6 ft (1·8 m.). Flowers double, vivid carmine-pink, maturing to a soft rose-pink, well quartered on opening with slightly incurved petals and showing small button centre, of medium size, well scented. Mid to late June but not recurrent. Foliage dark green with a bluish tinge. This is one of the finest of this group and makes a good specimen bush. It was raised by John Booth as a seedling of 'Maidens' Blush' and first flowered in 1816, but was not named till 1826. The date 1898 sometimes given, appears to be incorrect. **66**, p. 12.

'Königliche Hoheit' see **'Royal Highness', 361**, p. 67.

'Konrad Adenauer'   HT.
Crimson, 2 ft (0·6 m.) 1954
Raised by M. Tantau, Germany.
Parentage: 'Crimson Glory' × 'Hans Verschuren'
A vigorous branching grower, 2 ft (0·6 m.) in height, with semi-glossy light green foliage. The full, somewhat globular flowers are crimson and are sometimes up to exhibition size. Very fragrant. Precautions against mildew are sometimes necessary.
C.M., R.N.R.S. 1954; A.M., R.H.S. 1954.

'Kordes' Magenta' see **'Magenta', 181**, p. 34.

'Kordes' Perfecta'   HT.
Reddish-pink on cream, 3 ft (0·9 m.) 1957
Raised by W. Kordes, Germany.
Parentage: 'Spek's Yellow' × 'Karl Herbst'
An erect, tall grower, up to 3 ft (0·9 m.) high, with glossy, very dark green foliage, sometimes tinted purple. The large, very full flowers have a high centre, are well formed and much favoured for exhibition. Colour is somewhat variable; early blooms are heavily flushed reddish-pink on a light cream background and sometimes look a bit rough in the early stages. Colour is more stable in the autumn when the flowers become creamy-yellow, flushed pink. Flowers are sometimes borne in large trusses, the heavier blooms inclined to be pendulous and break off in rough weather. Resists bad weather reasonably well but at its best in fine, the flowers

lasting well when cut. The name is usually abbreviated to 'Perfecta'. **324**, p. 61.
A.M., R.H.S. 1957; G.M. and P.I.T., R.N.R.S. 1957; P.G.M. 1958.

'Korona'   Fl.
Orange-scarlet, 3½ ft (1·1 m.) 1955
Raised by W. Kordes, Germany.
A vigorous, upright grower, up to 3½ ft (1·1 m.) where it is happy, with dark glossy foliage. The medium sized, semi-double flowers are clear orange-scarlet, fading slightly in hot weather and are produced in large trusses. Weather resistant and slightly fragrant. This has proved a temperamental cultivar, exceptionally good in some areas, a comparative failure in others. Sometimes has purplish markings on leaves and stems and may require protection against black spot. **437**, p. 81.
G.M., R.N.R.S. 1954.

'Korp' see **'Prominent', 470**, p. 88.

'Kronenbourg', 'Flaming Peace'   HT.
Scarlet crimson and gold, 4 ft (1·2 m.) 1965
Discovered by S. McGredy IV, N. Ireland.
Parentage: 'Peace' sport
A very vigorous cultivar, 4 ft (1·2 m.) high, similar to its parent in most respects except the colour of the blooms, which are scarlet crimson with old gold reverse. As the bloom ages, the crimson deepens and becomes purple, when it loses its appeal to many rose

---

Abbreviations and Symbols used in the text

Rose classifications

A.	Alba	HT.	Hybrid Tea
B.	Bourbon	MCl.	Modern, large-flowered climber
C.	Centifolia	Min.	Miniature
Ch.	China	Moss	Centifolia muscosa
Cl.	Climber	MSh.	Modern shrub
D.	Damask	P.	Penzance Sweet Brier
Fl.	Floribunda	R.	Rambler
G.	Gallica	Rg.	Rugosa
HM.	Hybrid Musk	Sp.	Species and first hybrids
HP.	Hybrid Perpetual	Sw.	Sweet Brier

Rose Awards and Societies

A.A.R.S.	All-America Rose Selection
A.G.M.	Award of Garden Merit
A.M.	Award of Merit
A.R.S.	American Rose Society
B.B.G.M.	Baden Baden Gold Medal, Germany
B.G.M.	Bagatelle Gold Medal, Paris
C.C.V.	Clay Challenge Vase for scent
C.M.	Certificate of Merit
D.F.P.	David Fuerstenberg Prize
F.C.C.	First Class Certificate
G.G.M.	Geneva Gold Medal
G.M.	Gold Medal
G.M.C.B.	Gold Medal City of Belfast
G.M.H.G.M.	Gertrude M. Hubbard Gold Medal
G.R.H.	Golden Rose of The Hague
G.T.A.B.	Golden Thorn Award Belfast
H.E.M.M.	The Henry Edland Memorial Medal for the most fragrant rose of the year
H.G.M.	The Hague Gold Medal
L.G.M.	Lyon Gold Medal, France
M.G.M.	Madrid Gold Medal
N.G.M.C.	National Gold Medal Certificate
P.G.M.	Portland Gold Medal, Oregon, U.S.A.
P.I.T.	President's International Trophy
R.B.	Prize for the most fragrant rose, Roeulx, Belgium
R.B.G.M.	Roeulx, Belgium, Gold Medal
R.G.M.	Rome Gold Medal
R.H.S.	The Royal Horticultural Society, London
R.N.R.S.	The Royal National Rose Society, Great Britain*
T.G.C.	Trial Ground Certificate
U.A.B.	The 'Uladh' Award for fragrance, Belfast

National Rose Society awards, before 1965, are included here under R.N.R.S.

The illustration numbers are in **bold type** and the page numbers in light type preceded by p.

lovers. Fading flowers should be removed quickly in order to retain the bright effect of the younger blooms. **325**, p. 61.

'La Belle Villageoise' see *R. × centifolia* **'Variegata'**

'La Follette' Cl.
Rose-pink, 20 ft (6·1 m.) 1910
Raised by Busby, Lord Brougham's gardener at Cannes, France.
Parentage: *R. gigantea* × unrecorded rose
Very vigorous but half hardy climber, only suitable for a warm position, preferably against a wall. Also grown as a cold greenhouse plant where, as in warmer countries, it may become enormous. Flowers double, large with long pointed bud, a good rose-pink with some cream and coppery-salmon on outside, also sometimes a little carmine. Scented. Free-flowering. Early to mid-June but not recurrent. A very lovely rose comparable to 'Sénateur Amic', where it can be grown. On the French and Italian Rivieras it flowers early and is grown up into trees.
A.M., R.H.S. 1948.

'La France' HT.
Pale pink, recurrent, 4 ft (1·2 m.) 1867
Raised by Guillot Fils, France.
Parentage: possibly 'Mme Victor Verdier' × Tea rose 'Mme Bravy' *or* 'Mme Falcot' seedling
Shrub of medium vigour, not often over 4 ft (1·2 m.). Flowers pale pink semi-double, large, shaped like a Hybrid Tea rose. Considered to be one of the first Hybrid Tea roses. Flowers in clusters, scented, 4 in. (10·2 cm.) across. A rose of historical interest, still grown well at 'La Bagatelle', Paris.

'La Mortola' see under *R. moschata nepalensis*, **29**, p. 6.

'La Reine Victoria' B.
Pale lilac-pink, recurrent, 6 ft (1·8 m.) 1872
Raised by J. Schwartz, France.
A Bourbon shrub of medium vigour, usually with rather narrow and erect growth. Flowers pale lilac-pink, darkest on outside, semi-double to almost double, of medium size, up to 3½ in. (8·9 cm.) across, cupped and retaining this form when mature, petals overlapping like those of a small waterlily, scented. Mid to late June but recurrent. **96**, p. 17.

'La Royale' see under **'Maidens' Blush'**, **67**, p. 12.

'La Rubanée' see *R. × centifolia* **'Variegata'**

'La Séduisante' see under **'Maidens' Blush'**, **67**, p. 12.

'La Virginale' see under **'Maidens' Blush'**, **67**, p. 12.

'Lady Curzon' MSh.Cl.
Pale pink, early summer, 8 × 8 ft (2·4 × 2·4 m.) 1901
Raised by C. Turner, England.
Parentage: 'Macrantha' × *R. rugosa* 'Rubra'
Modern hybrid Rugosa shrub rose of great vigour, sometimes used as a climber into old trees. At Sissinghurst Castle, England, it is 8 × 8 ft (2·4 × 2·4 m.), a large prickly mound but with good foliage. Flowers single, large, up to 4 in. (10·2 cm.) across, pale pink, paler and almost white near centre, with good boss of yellow stamens. Scented. Mid to late June, not recurrent. Valuable in the semi-wild garden where there is plenty of space. **174**, p. 32.

'Lady Godiva' R.
Blush-pink, summer, 10 ft (3 m.) 1907
Discovered by G. Paul, England.
Parentage: 'Dorothy Perkins' sport
A climber with much *R. wichuraiana* blood apparent but of moderate vigour. Flowers in clusters, small, about 1 in. (2·5 cm.) across, very dainty, blush-pink fading almost to white on outside, double or semi-double. Late June to mid-July but not recurrent. Lovely in late June at the rose garden of Bagatelle, outside Paris. My note actually recorded 'enchanting, very pretty'. Much pleasanter than her parent and also claimed to be more resistant to mildew. This rose is the parent of the dwarf sport 'The Fairy' (**491**, p. 94).
A.M., R.H.S. 1908.

'Lady Hillingdon, Climbing' see **'Climbing Lady Hillingdon'**, **265**, p. 50.

'Lady Penzance' see under *R. eglanteria*

'Lady Seton' HT.
Deep rose-pink, 2½ ft (0·8 m.) 1966
Raised by S. McGredy IV, N. Ireland.
Parentage: 'Ma Perkins' × 'Mischief'
A vigorous, fairly tall, branching grower, 2½ ft (0·8 m.), well furnished with semi-glossy, medium green foliage. The full medium sized blooms are deep rose-pink, suffused with salmon, and although they open quickly in warm weather, they last well. Very free flowering, particularly in the autumn, this cultivar is scented and is useful for cutting. **326**, p. 61.
C.M., R.N.R.S. 1964; C.C.V., R.N.R.S. 1964.

'Lady Sonia' MSh.
Deep yellow, recurrent, 6 ft (1·8 m.) 1961
Raised by J. Mattock Ltd, England.
Parentage: 'Grandmaster' × 'Doreen'
Vigorous shrub rose up to 6 ft (1·8 m.) with good bushy growth. Flowers of hybrid tea type, large, semi-double, up to 4 in. (10·2 cm.) across, deep yellow, flushed orange-red in bud, scented. Free-flowering. Mid to late June, recurrent. Foliage dark green, glossy. **175**, p. 32.
A.M., R.H.S. 1960; C.M., R.N.R.S. 1961.

'Lady Sylvia' HT.
Pink, 3 ft (0·9 m.) 1926
Discovered by W. Stevens Ltd, England.
Parentage: 'Mme Butterfly' sport
A vigorous, upright grower which will grow into a sizeable shrub if lightly pruned, with mat, medium green foliage. The light pink blooms have a yellow base, fading slightly with age and are perfectly shaped but are too small for exhibition. Remarkably free flowering particularly in autumn. Full of fragrance, this cultivar and its relations are still great favourites in the garden and especially for cutting for decorative work. Still grown in quantity under glass for the cut flower market, being a good forcer and cropper. Thrips are apt to damage the early blooms in the garden. **327**, p. 62.

'Lady Sylvia, Climbing' see **'Climbing Lady Sylvia'**, **266**, p. 50.

'Lady Waterlow' Cl.
Pink, 12 ft (3·7 m.) 1903
Raised by G. Nabonnand, France.
Parentage: 'La France de '89' × 'Mme Marie Lavallé'
Climber with flowers of hybrid tea type, up to 12 ft (3·7 m.).

Flowers large semi-double to double, a good clear pink with a slightly carmine edge. Scented. Mid to late June, recurrent. Suitable for pillar or pergola or for growing against a wall. An old rose that is still worth growing. **210**, p. 39.

'Lafter'   MSh.
Salmon-rose, recurrent, 5 ft (1·5 m.) 1948
Raised by H. C. Brownell, U.S.A.
Parentage: ('V for Victory' × ('Gen. Jacqueminot' × 'Dr W. Van Fleet')) × 'Pink Princess'
Modern shrub rose of medium vigour, up to 5 ft (1·5 m.). Flowers semi-double, large, in quite large clusters, of floribunda type, deep salmon-rose, darker at base and with large yellow centre fading to salmon-pink, pale apricot on underside, giving almost a bicolor effect. Scented. Mid to late June, recurrent. **176**, p. 32.

'Lagoon'   Fl.
Silvery-lilac, 2½ ft (0·8 m.) 1971–72
Raised by R. Harkness & Co. Ltd, England.
Parentage: 'Lilac Charm' × 'Sterling Silver'
A tall spreading grower, 2½ ft (0·8 m.) high with coppery dark green foliage. The semi-double flowers are silvery-lilac, borne in large trusses. Flowers freely over a long period. **438**, p. 81.
T.G.C., R.N.R.S. 1969.

'Lake Como'   Fl.
Lavender-lilac, 2 ft (0·6 m.) 1968
Raised by R. Harkness & Co. Ltd, England.
Parentage: 'Lilac Charm' × 'Sterling Silver'
A bushy compact grower, about 2 ft (0·6 m.) high, which grows freely. The semi-double flowers form open rosettes of wavy edged petals and are an attractive soft lavender-lilac. They are very freely produced. Sweetly scented. A new cultivar which requires some protection against mildew and is at its best in good weather. **445**, p. 83.

'Lancastrian'   HT.
Crimson scarlet, 2½ ft (0·8 m.) 1965
Raised by C. Gregory & Son Ltd, England.
A vigorous upright grower, 2½ ft (0·8 m.) in height, with glossy, medium green, crimson tinted foliage. The large double flowers are rich velvety crimson scarlet and are very fragrant. A free flowering cultivar, particularly good in autumn but may require protection against mildew.

'Lanei', 'Lane's Moss'   Moss Sh.
Mauvish-crimson, slightly recurrent, 5 ft (1·5 m.) 1845
Raised by M. Laffay, France.
Vigorous shrub rose up to 5 ft (1·5 m.) with rather lax growth and flowers of moss type, but not so heavily mossed as other moss roses. Flowers large, double, deep rosy crimson with mauve overtones fading to deep mauvish-pink, quartered, scented. Mid to late June but slightly recurrent, an unusual character in the Moss rose section. **74**, p. 14.

'Lane's Moss' see **'Lanei'**, **74**, p. 14.

'Lavender Lace'   Min.
Lavender, 10–12 in. (25·4–30·5 cm.) 1968
Raised by R. S. Moore, U.S.A.
Parentage: 'Ellen Poulsen' × 'Debbie'
A compact bushy grower, 10–12 in. (25·4–30·5 cm.) high, with small, light green glossy foliage. The small double flowers are borne in trusses, high centred at first, open afterwards, lavender coloured and fragrant. Very free flowering over a long season.
T.G.C., R.N.R.S. 1970.

'Lavender Lassie'   MSh.
Pinkish-lavender, recurrent, 5–10 ft (1·5–3 m.) 1959
Raised by R. Kordes, Germany.
Modern shrub rose, sometimes described as a Hybrid Musk, of medium vigour up to 5 ft (1·5 m.). Floribunda type. Flowers pink, shaded lavender or pale lavender-purple, semi-double to double with flowers in large clusters, of medium size, about 3 in. (7·6 cm.) across, but full, many-petalled and rather globose, strongly scented, not quite so deep a colour as 'Magenta' and valuable for its colour which is rare among modern shrub roses. Recorded from U.S.A. as 10 ft (3 m.) high and flowering repeatedly. **177**, p. 32.
T.G.C., R.N.R.S. 1959.

'Lawrence Johnston'   Cl.
Bright yellow, recurrent, 20 ft (6·1 m.) 1923
Raised by J. Pernet-Ducher, France.
Parentage: 'Mme Eugène Verdier' × *R. foetida persiana*
One of the great climbers, vigorous and may also be grown as a 10 ft (3 m.) shrub. Flowers semi-double, bright clear yellow, slightly deeper than its sister seedling 'La Rêve', of medium size, rather loose as flower matures. Free-flowering and strongly scented. Early to late June, with a few flowers later. Foliage luxuriant, glossy. The raiser was not interested in it and the only plant was bought by Major Lawrence Johnston of Hidcote Manor, England. It still grows well at Hidcote and was first named as 'Hidcote Yellow'. **211**, p. 39.
A.M., R.H.S. 1948.

Le Petit Rosier à cent feuilles see **'Petite de Hollande'**, **70**, p. 13.

Abbreviations and Symbols used in the text

Rose classifications

A.	Alba	HT.	Hybrid Tea
B.	Bourbon	MCl.	Modern, large-flowered climber
C.	Centifolia	Min.	Miniature
Ch.	China	Moss	Centifolia muscosa
Cl.	Climber	MSh.	Modern shrub
D.	Damask	P.	Penzance Sweet Brier
Fl.	Floribunda	R.	Rambler
G.	Gallica	Rg.	Rugosa
HM.	Hybrid Musk	Sp.	Species and first hybrids
HP.	Hybrid Perpetual	Sw.	Sweet Brier

Rose Awards and Societies

A.A.R.S.	All-America Rose Selection
A.G.M.	Award of Garden Merit
A.M.	Award of Merit
A.R.S.	American Rose Society
B.B.G.M.	Baden Baden Gold Medal, Germany
B.G.M.	Bagatelle Gold Medal, Paris
C.C.V.	Clay Challenge Vase for scent
C.M.	Certificate of Merit
D.F.P.	David Fuerstenberg Prize
F.C.C.	First Class Certificate
G.G.M.	Geneva Gold Medal
G.M.	Gold Medal
G.M.C.B.	Gold Medal City of Belfast
G.M.H.G.M.	Gertrude M. Hubbard Gold Medal
G.R.H.	Golden Rose of The Hague
G.T.A.B.	Golden Thorn Award Belfast
H.E.M.M.	The Henry Edland Memorial Medal for the most fragrant rose of the year
H.G.M.	The Hague Gold Medal
L.G.M.	Lyon Gold Medal, France
M.G.M.	Madrid Gold Medal
N.G.M.C.	National Gold Medal Certificate
P.G.M.	Portland Gold Medal, Oregon, U.S.A.
P.I.T.	President's International Trophy
R.B.	Prize for the most fragrant rose, Roeulx, Belgium
R.B.G.M.	Roeulx, Belgium, Gold Medal
R.G.M.	Rome Gold Medal
R.H.S.	The Royal Horticultural Society, London
R.N.R.S.	The Royal National Rose Society, Great Britain*
T.G.C.	Trial Ground Certificate
U.A.B.	The 'Uladh' Award for fragrance, Belfast

National Rose Society awards, before 1965, are included here under R.N.R.S.

The illustration numbers are in **bold type** and the page numbers in light type preceded by p.

'Leverkusen'   MCl.
Creamy-yellow, recurrent, 10 ft (3 m.) 1954
Raised by W. Kordes, Germany.
Parentage: *R. kordesii* × 'Golden Glow'
Kordesii climber or pillar rose of moderate vigour up to 10 ft
(3 m.). Flowers semi-double, pale creamy-yellow, deeper yellow in
centre, of medium size, in clusters, free-flowering, scented. Mid to
late June with main flowering and slightly recurrent. Foliage deep
glossy green with rather small leaflets. A valuable rose for its freedom of flower and good pale yellow colour. **248**, p. 46.

'Liebestraum' see **'Red Queen', 359**, p. 67.

'Lilac Charm'   Fl.
Lilac, 2 ft (0·6 m.) 1961
Raised by E. B. LeGrice, England.
Parentage: bred from *R. californica* seedlings
A short, bushy grower, 2 ft (0·6 m.) high, with mat dark green
foliage. The single lilac flowers have golden anthers on red filaments
which enhance the beauty of the flowers. Liable to fade in full sun
during hot weather but very freely produced. Lightly scented.
Useful for floral decoration, especially if cut in the bud and opened
in water. Protection from black spot may be required. The parentage quoted is that given by the raiser. **439**, p. 82.
G.M., R.N.R.S. 1961.

'Lilli Marleen'   Fl.
Scarlet-red, 2½ ft (0·8 m.) 1959
Raised by R. Kordes, Germany.
Parentage: ('Our Princess' × 'Rudolf Timm') × 'Ama'
A vigorous, branching grower of dense compact habit which makes
it ideal for bedding purposes. The foliage is abundant, medium
green with bronze tints and semi-glossy. The blooms are scarlet-red
with deeper shadings, very profuse, resistant to weather, borne in
large clusters which stand up well on stiff stems. There is only a
slight fragrance and protection against mildew is sometimes required; nevertheless this is one of the most reliable and effective
roses for garden decoration. **440**, p. 82.
C.M., R.N.R.S. 1959; A.M., R.H.S. 1959; G.R.H. 1966.

'Little Buckaroo'   Min.
Bright scarlet, 18 in. (45·7 cm.) 1956
Raised by R. S. Moore, U.S.A.
Parentage: (*R. wichuraiana* × 'Floradora') × ('Oakington Ruby' ×
'Floradora')
A sprawling plant, up to 18 in. (45·7 cm.) high, with bronzy glossy
foliage. The small double open flowers are bright scarlet with a
white centre and a mass of yellow stamens. Slightly fragrant and
resistant to mildew.
Certificate of International Trials, The Hague 1965.

'Little Flirt'   Min.
Orange-red and gold, 12 in. (30·5 cm.) 1961
Raised by R. S. Moore, U.S.A.
Parentage: (*R. wichuraiana* × 'Floradora') × ('Golden Glow' ×
'Zee')
A vigorous bushy grower, 10–12 in. (25·4–30·5 cm.) high with
light green foliage. The small flowers are double, orange-red with
gold base and reverse, an attractive combination which has in
addition some fragrance.

'Little Princess' see **'Pixie'**

'Little Showoff'   Cl.Min.
Buff-yellow, 6 ft (1·8 m.)
Raised by R. S. Moore, U.S.A.

Parentage: 'Golden Glow' × 'Zee'
An upright, well branched grower, up to 6 ft (1·8 m.) high with
small, semi-double flowers, buff-yellow, sometimes with reddish
tints. Free-flowering.

'Little Sunset'   Min.
Salmon-pink, 15 in. (38·1 cm.) 1967
Raised by W. Kordes, Germany.
Parentage: seedling × 'Tom Thumb'
A free growing plant, 12–15 in. (30·5–38·1 cm.) high with small
light green foliage. The small double flowers are salmon-pink with
a yellow base and are freely produced.

'Lively Lady'   Fl.
Bright vermilion, 3 ft (0·9 m.) 1969
Raised by J. Cocker & Sons Ltd, Scotland.
Parentage: 'Elizabeth of Glamis' × 'Super Star'
An upright vigorous grower, 2½–3 ft (0·8–0·9 m.) high with small,
semi-glossy, medium green foliage. The flowers are large, full, bright
vermilion in colour, borne in trusses and freely produced over a
long season. A healthy plant with a pleasing but not strong fragrance.
T.G.C., R.N.R.S. 1969.

'Lollipop'   Min.
Cherry-red, 9 in. (22·9 cm.) 1959
Raised by R. S. Moore, U.S.A.
Parentage: (*R. wichuraiana* × 'Floradora') × 'Little Buckaroo'
A bushy grower, 9 in. (22·9 cm.) high, with glossy foliage. The small
double flowers are bright cherry-red and are slightly fragrant.

'Lord Penzance' see under *R. eglanteria*, **11**, p. 2.

'Lorna Doone'   Fl.
Crimson-scarlet, 2½ ft (0·8 m.) 1972
Raised by R. Harkness & Co. Ltd, England.
Parentage: 'Red Dandy' × 'Lilli Marleen'
A vigorous, bushy grower, 2½ ft (0·8 m.) high, with semi-glossy dark
green foliage. The full flowers are crimson-scarlet in colour, borne
in trusses and freely produced.

'Louise Odier'   B.
Soft pink, recurrent, 6 ft (1·8 m.) 1851
Raised by M. Margottin, France.
A superb and vigorous Bourbon shrub up to 6 ft (1·8 m.). Flowers
soft, warm pink, sometimes shaded with lilac-pink, double, a round
flower sometimes described as camellia-shaped, scented. Mid to
late June but recurrent throughout the summer. **97**, p. 17.

'Lübeck' see **'Hansestadt Lübeck'**

'Lucky Charm'   Fl.
Golden-yellow, 3 ft (0·9 m.) 1961
Raised by H. Robinson, England.
A tall branching grower, 3 ft (0·9 m.) high, with glossy, bronze
tinted foliage. The large flowers are globular in form, moderately
full, golden-yellow with flushes of red. Fragrant and healthy.

'Lucy Cramphorn', 'Maryse Kriloff'   HT.
Geranium-red, 2½ ft (0·8 m.) 1960
Raised by M. Kriloff, France.
Parentage: 'Peace' × 'Baccara'
A vigorous tall branching grower, 2½ ft (0·8 m.) with abundant,
glossy, dark green foliage which has a coppery tinge. The full, well

formed blooms are vivid geranium-red, going darker with age and are freely produced in summer and autumn. Weather resistance is fairly good. The footstalks of the blooms are somewhat brittle but this is a good reliable cultivar for garden display. **328**, p. 62. C.M., R.N.R.S. 1960.

'Lydia' HT.
Golden-yellow, 2 ft (0·6 m.) 1949
Raised by H. Robinson, England.
Parentage: 'Phyllis Gold' × seedling
A low growing cultivar of moderate vigour and branching growth with glossy, dark green, holly-like foliage. The full bright golden-yellow blooms are of medium size, freely produced and resist weather well. Protection from black spot may be required.

'Lyric' MSh.
Deep pink, recurrent, 5 ft (1·5 m.) 1950
Raised by G. de Ruiter, Holland.
Parentage: 'Sangerhausen' × unknown seedling
Modern shrub rose of medium vigour up to 5 ft (1·5 m.). Floribunda type. Flowers semi-double to double, deep apple-pink, paler at base, of medium size, slightly scented. Mid to late June, recurrent. **170**, p. 34.

'Macrantha' Sh.
Pale pink, summer, 5 ft (1·5 m.)
Large shrub with spreading arching growth so that it is often wider across than high, making a dense bush. Flowers pale pink fading almost to white, single or semi-double, up to 3 in. (7·6 cm.) across, in small clusters, free-flowering. Mid-June to early July but not recurrent. Foliage fine with up to 7 leaflets. Hips round, about ¾ in. (1·9 cm.) across, bright red and persistent till late autumn. A useful rose, especially for covering old stumps or low mounds or fences. Best form is 'Daisy Hill' which is slightly more semi-double with extra petals. The large-flowered plant known as 'Macrantha' today is not the same as *R. macrantha*, said to have been a hybrid of *R. canina* × *R. gallica*, which is believed to have originated in France in the early eighteenth century.

'Mme A. Meilland' see 'Peace', **347**, p. 65.

'Mme Alfred Carrière' Cl.
White, recurrent, 20 ft (6·1 m.) 1879
Raised by J. Schwartz, France.
Very vigorous climber, often classed as a Noisette, with flowers of hybrid tea type. Flowers large, double, opening very pale bluish-pink, quickly fading to snow-white. Strongly scented, abundant flowering. Mid to late June, recurrent. One of the great old roses which always make a fine display and does not seem to have lost any of its vigour, as is shown by the famous and much photographed plant covering a cottage wall at Sissinghurst Castle. Probably best planted against a wall and carefully pruned and trained; it can also be grown on a large pergola or over an old tree, and has been known to succeed on a north wall. Foliage luxuriant, rather light green. **212**, p. 39.

'Mme Butterfly' HT.
Pale pink, 3 ft (0·9 m.) 1918
Discovered by E. G. Hill Co. Inc., U.S.A.
Parentage: 'Ophelia' sport
In spite of its age, still a fairly vigorous, upright grower, 2½–3 ft (0·8–0·9 m.) high with mat, medium green, small foliage. The medium sized blooms are pale pink, shading to yellow at the base and paling off a little as they age; deeper in colour than the parent. The full, shapely flowers are very fragrant, on stiff, almost thornless stems, ideal for decorative purposes and used to be grown under

glass for this purpose. Very productive, requiring a good deal of disbudding, this cultivar is frequently found in gardens in shrub like form and continues to be a considerable favourite of many. Early blooms are apt to be disfigured by thrips in hot dry weather.

'Mme Caroline Testout' HT.
Bright rose-pink, 2–2½ ft (0·6–0·8 m.) 1890
Raised by J. Pernet-Ducher, France.
Parentage: 'Mme de Tartas' × 'Lady Mary Fitzwilliam'
An old Hybrid Tea rose which still retains a reasonably good constitution, with ample mat, medium green foliage. The bright rose-pink blooms retain their colour well, are full and globular, somewhat 'blowsy' by present day standards and are freely produced. Still one of the best as a standard and well worth growing in its climbing form. This famous cultivar has been grown in the same bed at the Royal Botanic Gardens, Kew, for over half a century, reputedly on its own roots, and has only recently been removed. A.M., R.H.S. 1892.

'Mme Caroline Testout, Climbing' see 'Climbing Mme Caroline Testout'

'Mme Cécile Brunner' see 'Cécile Brunner'

'Mme Edouard Herriot, Climbing' see 'Climbing Mme Edouard Herriot'

'Mme Grégoire Staechelin', 'Spanish Beauty' Cl.
Pink, early summer, 15 ft (4·6 m.) 1927

Raised by P. Dot, Spain.
Parentage: 'Frau Karl Druschki' × 'Château de Clos Vougeot'
Very vigorous and free-flowering climber, up to 15 ft (4·6 m.) and as much across. The scented flowers are large, up to 5½ in. (14 cm.) across, semi-double, a real clear pink, slightly deeper on the outside, opening to show central stamens, petals paler towards the base with creamy-yellow flush, bud well-shaped, pointed, rather deeper pink. The clusters of heavy blooms tend to hang slightly downwards which is attractive since the rose very quickly grows up above one. The flowers are sumptuous, even voluptuous, billowing in masses along the branches and gives us one of the most conspicuous and rewarding sights of the rose season, wonderful against a grey stone or a white wall. Early flowering usually first week in June for about three weeks. Foliage luxuriant and a good green with 5 leaflets. Although best against a large wall, quickly growing up to 20 ft (6·1 m.), it may be grown as a pergola or pillar rose. In order to keep it well-furnished in the lower part it needs careful pruning from its first planting, cutting some of the vigorous shoots hard back nearly to the base after flowering or in winter, and when older removing occasionally one or two of the old woody stems right to the base. If left unpruned it tends to make tall woody stems up to 10 ft (3 m.) with flowering branches only at top. Hips large and abundant but only colouring late in October, apricot, flushed pink. **213**, p. 39.
A.M., R.H.S. 1969.

'Mme Hardy'   D.
Creamy-white, summer, 6 ft (1·8 m.) 1832
Raised by M. Hardy, France.
A Damask rose of good vigour up to 6 ft (1·8 m.). Flowers in clusters, of medium size, cupped on first opening, double; opening slightly creamy-white or palest pink, then becoming pure white with built up centre of incurving petals and a small bright green button eye. Scented, with a suggestion of lemon. Mid to late June. Foliage clear green. One of the finest of the old white roses and usually a great favourite, by some even regarded as 'the most beautiful white rose in existence'. Sometimes known as *R. × centifolia alba*.

'Mme Isaac Pereire'   B.
Deep pink, recurrent, 10 ft (3 m.) 1881
Raised by Garçon, France.
A very vigorous Bourbon shrub or pillar rose, up to 10 ft (3 m.), making very stout thorny shoots of up to 6 ft (1·8 m.) in a season. Sometimes grown pegged down over an area, but weeding below can be very painful. Flowers very large, double and very full, showing quartering when mature, deep pink or rose madder, sometimes with slight purplish tinge, up to 5 in. (12·7 cm.) across, strongly scented. Mid to late June and recurrent, flowers in clusters. Frequently the best flowers are obtained from autumn-flowering in September. A luscious, sumptuous, almost blowsy beauty which can be very effective in the garden. **98**, p. 18.

'Mme Lauriol de Barny'   B.
Pale purplish-pink, early summer, 6 ft (1·8 m.) 1868
Raised by Trouillard, France.
Bourbon rose. Vigorous shrub up to 6 ft (1·8 m.) usually making a large bush. Flowers large, double, silvery or pale purplish-pink and quartered when open, strongly scented. Flowers heavy in large clusters of up to 10 and tending to droop. Early to mid-June. Only very slightly recurrent. One of the finest of the Bourbon group. **99**, p. 18.

'Mme Louis Laperrière'   HT.
Deep crimson, 2½ ft (0·8 m.) 1951
Raised by Ets J. Laperrière, France.
Parentage: 'Crimson Glory' × seedling
A moderately vigorous grower of medium height with small, semi-glossy mid-green foliage, purplish-red when young. The medium sized blooms are very freely produced, early, and are full, well

formed and rich deep crimson in colour. Very fragrant, the flowers keep their colour well. A very good bedding rose. **329**, p. 62.
B.G.M. 1950; C.M., R.N.R.S. 1952.

'Mme Neige' see **'Youki San'**

'Mme Pierre Oger'   B.
Silvery-pink, recurrent, 5 ft (1·5 m.) 1878
Discovered by A. Oger, France.
Parentage: 'La Reine Victoria' sport
A Bourbon shrub of medium vigour only, usually not over 4–5 ft (1·2–1·5 m.), growth rather slender. Flowers of similar shape to parent, globular, double, very pale silvery-pink, sometimes with a creamy flush, developing stronger colour in warm seasons, of medium size only up to 3 in. (7·6 cm.) across. Petals delicate, thin, rather shell-like, scented. Early to mid-June but recurrent. A very beautiful rose for the lovely water lily form of its flowers and its almost mother-of-pearl translucency and delicate flushed colour. **100**, p. 18.

'Mme Plantier'   A.
White, summer, 12 ft (3·7 m.) 1835
Raised by M. Plantier, France.
Parentage: possibly *R. × alba × R. moschata* seedling
Sometimes described as a Noisette rose. Shrub, pillar or climbing rose, up to 12 ft (3·7 m.) of good vigour. Flowers rather small, double, opening creamy-white, then becoming pure white, showing green button centre, strongly scented, flowers borne in large clusters and very free-flowering. Foliage with rather small soft olive-green leaflets. Mid to late June or early July but not recurrent. A great favourite of the late V. Sackville West who grew it around, up and over old apple trees in the orchard at Sissinghurst. Some of these trees have now collapsed under the weight of the roses.

'Mme Sancy de Parabère', *R. × l'heritierana*   Cl.
Deep pink, early summer, 15 ft (4·6 m.) 1874
Raised by A. Bonnet & Fils, France.
Parentage: *R. chinensis × ?R. blanda*
Vigorous climber with flowers of rather unusual shape but near to the hybrid tea type, up to 15 ft (4·6 m.). One of the group known as Boursault roses. Flowers large up to 5 in. (12·7 cm.) across, semi-double to double with numerous small petals in centre, clear deep pink, paler in outer petals, scented, free-flowering. Early flowering in June, not recurrent. Stems thornless. Rarely seen but an interesting rose. **214**, p. 39.

'Mme Zoetmans'   D.
Creamy-white, summer, 4 ft (1·2 m.) 1830
Raised by Marest, France.
Damask shrub rose of medium vigour up to 4 ft (1·2 m.). Flowers double, creamy-white, sometimes with very pale blush-purplish tinge towards centre, maturing to show small green button eye. Early to mid-June. Free-flowering. Foliage good, rich green. Origin unknown. Not very common in cultivation. **82**, p. 15.

'Magenta', 'Kordes' Magenta'   MSh.
Lilac-pink to deep mauve, recurrent, 4 ft (1·2 m.) 1954
Raised by W. Kordes, Germany.
Parentage: yellow Floribunda seedling × 'Lavender Pinnochio'
Although officially classed as a Floribunda, this has been placed with the modern shrubs and illustrated as such because of its open sprawling habit, caused by the weight of the large clusters of flowers which are so freely produced. The fully double, almost rosette type flowers vary from lilac-pink to soft deep mauve and have a delicious perfume. Usually grows to about 4 ft (1·2 m.) and has dark foliage. **181**, p. 34.

'Magic Wand'   Cl.Min.
Light red, 4 ft (1·2 m.) 1957
Raised by R. S. Moore, U.S.A.
Parentage: 'Eblouissant' × 'Zee'
An arching thorny grower, up to 4 ft (1·2 m.) high with clusters of
small, light red, semi-double flowers.

'Maid Marion' see **'Red Imp'**

'Maidens' Blush', 'Great Maidens' Blush', *R.* × *alba incarnata*   A.
Pale pink, summer, 8 ft (2·4 m.) before 1738
A vigorous shrub up to 8 ft (2·4 m.), usually thick and bushy.
Flowers semi-double, blush pink but variable, fading to a pale
creamy-pink near edges, but remaining pale blush pink in centre,
showing good boss of yellow stamens, of medium size about 3 in.
(7·6 cm.) across, strongly scented. Mid to late June. Free-flowering
but not recurrent. Foliage grey-green. An old rose whose origin is
unknown but it was certainly known in the fifteenth century and
probably earlier and is frequently seen in paintings. Very long-
lived and making probably the best garden shrub or informal hedge
in this group. Many names have been given to its forms since it is
variable. These include 'Cuisse de Nymphe', 'Cuisse de Nymphe
Emue' for a particularly well coloured but rather less vigorous form,
loosely translated as 'The Thigh of the Passionate Nymph', 'La
Royale', 'Incarnata', 'La Séduisante', 'La Virginale' and 'Small
Maidens' Blush' for a form with rather smaller flowers and slightly
less vigorous growth but still making a shrub 5 × 5 ft (1·5 × 1·5 m.)
when well cultivated. With its glaucous foliage and floriferous habit
it is a treasure. **67**, p. 12.

'Maigold'   MCl.Sh.
Bronzy-yellow, summer, 8–12 ft (2·4–3·7 m.) 1953
Raised by W. Kordes, Germany.
Parentage: 'Poulsen's Pink' × 'Frühlingstag'
A very vigorous branching grower, very thorny, attaining up to
12 ft (3·7 m.) on a wall as in the photograph, with a profusion of rich
glossy, healthy foliage. The large semi-double flowers are produced
early in the season, reddish in the bud, opening out to bronzy-
yellow, with golden stamens. Generally credited with being a recurrent flowerer but I have not found it so unless it is quickly dead-
headed. Then a second crop of lesser degree will be produced in the
autumn. May also be grown as a rather loose open shrub about 8
ft (2·4 m.) high. Powerfully fragrant, this rose is well worth a place
on a wall, pillar, fence or in the shrub border. **249**, p. 47; **251**, p. 48.
T.G.C., R.N.R.S. 1953.

'Mainzer Fastnacht', 'Blue Moon', 'Sissi'   HT.
Silvery-lilac, 3 ft (0·9 m.) 1964
Raised by M. Tantau, Germany.
Parentage: unnamed seedling × 'Sterling Silver'
A moderately vigorous grower with small, medium green semi-
glossy foliage. The fairly large, well formed, silvery-lilac flowers are
freely produced and have a strong lemon scent. Good for cutting
and delightful in combination with pale pink roses for artistic work.
May require protection from rust in some areas. **330**, p. 62.
C.M., R.N.R.S. 1964; R.G.M. 1964.

'Manning's Blush' see under *R. eglanteria*, **12**, p. 2.

'Manuela'   HT.
Cherry-pink, 2½–3 ft (0·8–0·9 m.) 1968
Raised by M. Tantau, Germany.
A vigorous, upright bushy grower with glossy foliage. The large
double flowers are shapely and well formed, cherry-pink in colour
and fragrant. This newcomer appears to be sufficiently free-
flowering to be a good bedding rose.

'Manx Queen', 'Isle of Man'   Fl.
Rich gold, 3 ft (0·9 m.) 1963
Raised by A. Dickson & Sons, Ltd, N. Ireland.
Parentage: 'Shepherd's Delight' × 'Circus'
A bushy compact grower, up to 3 ft (0·9 m.) high with plentiful
dark foliage. The medium sized flowers are produced on well spaced
trusses, rich gold, flushed bronze, red and pink, an attractive
combination. A very effective cultivar for bedding. Fragrant. **441**,
p. 82.
C.M., R.N.R.S. 1963.

'Maréchal Davoust'   Moss Sh.
Pinkish-crimson, summer, 5 ft (1·5 m.) 1853
Fairly vigorous shrub up to 5 ft (1·5 m.). Flowers large, semi-double,
bright crimson with tinges of purple, mauve and lilac and small
green eye in centre. Free-flowering. Mid to late June but not
recurrent. Bud well covered with browny-green moss. Makes a good
shrub with sumptuous flowering and bright effect.

'Maréchal Niel'   Cl.
Yellow, recurrent, 15 ft (4·6 m.) 1864
Raised by H. Pradel, France.
Parentage: said to be a seedling from the Noisette 'Chromatella'
A climber of moderate vigour, with probably both *R. chinensis* and
R. moschata in its ancestry. Buds long and pointed. Flowers large,
double, golden or copper-yellow, strongly scented, and tend to
droop as the stems are weak. Still worth growing for its strong
Tea rose fragrance, especially in warm climates; hardy in southern
states and on Pacific coast of the U.S.A. and on warm walls in
southern counties of England. Sometimes grown as greenhouse
climber for cut flowers, in which case root should be planted outside.

'Margaret' HT.
Bright pink and silver, 2½ ft (0·8 m.) 1954
Raised by A. Dickson & Sons Ltd, N. Ireland.
Parentage: 'May Wettern' seedling × 'Souvenir de Denier van der Gon'
A vigorous, tall branching grower, 2½ ft (0·8 m.) high, sometimes irregular in growth and with large mat, mid-green foliage. The scented, bright pink blooms have a silvery reverse, blueing off as they age, and are freely produced early. Form is good and full so that this cultivar is suitable for exhibition as well as bedding. Does not like rain. May require protection against black spot. **331**, p. 62.
G.M., R.N.R.S. 1954; A.M., R.H.S. 1954.

'Margo Koster' Fl.
Salmon, 1½ ft (0·5 m.) 1931
Discovered by D. A. Koster, Holland.
Parentage: 'Dick Koster' sport
A very short grower, really a Poly-pom, a class with a history of sporting, 15–18 in. (0·4–0·5 m.) in height. The flowers are globular of a delightful salmon colour and have a slight fragrance. Free-flowering, useful for small beds or edging and also good for forcing as a pot plant under glass. **446**, p. 83.

'Marguerite Hilling', 'Pink Nevada' MSh.
Pink, recurrent, 8 × 8 ft (2·4 × 2·4 m.) 1959
Discovered by Sleet, also by Sunningdale Nursery, England, and by Mrs Steen, New Zealand.
Parentage: 'Nevada' sport
Modern shrub rose of great vigour up to 8 ft (2·4 m.) and as much across and a tremendous flowerer, much resembling its parent except for colour. Flowers semi-double, up to 3 in. (7·6 cm.) across, light pink shading deeper. Mid to late June, slightly recurrent with odd flowers through summer. Its main value is its abundance of flower in June and its vigour. It occurred independently in three places and was introduced by T. Hilling Ltd, England, in 1959. **178**, p. 33.
A.M., R.H.S. 1960.

'Maria' Fl.
Orange-scarlet, 3 ft (0·9 m.) 1965
Raised by C. Gregory & Son Ltd, England.
Parentage: unknown seedling × 'Border Beauty'
A vigorous, upright grower, 3 ft (0·9 m.) high, with very large, dark, leathery foliage. The fairly large single flowers are freely produced in great clusters, orange-scarlet in colour. Slight fragrance.

'Maria Callas', 'Miss All-American Beauty' HT.
Dark carmine-pink, 3 ft (0·9 m.) 1965
Raised by M. L. Meilland, France.
Parentage: 'Chrysler Imperial' × 'Karl Herbst'
A vigorous bushy grower, 2½–3 ft (0·8–0·9 m.) high with dark green, glossy foliage. The large, double flowers are very full, cupped, without much form, dark carmine-pink with lighter shades, freely produced. **332**, p. 62.
A.A.R.S. 1968.

'Marita' Fl.
Coppery-red, 4 ft (1·2 m.) 1961
Raised by J. Mattock Ltd, England.
Parentage: 'Masquerade' × 'Serenade'
A tall, open growing cultivar, 3–4 ft (0·9–1·2 m.) high, with attractive coppery-red foliage. The medium sized, double flowers have quilled petals, giving an unusual starry appearance somewhat like a cactus dahlia. They are coppery-red shot with yellow and giving an overall orange appearance. Best in a border because of its habit. No scent. **442**, p. 82.

'Marlena' Fl.
Crimson-scarlet, 1½ ft (0·5 m.) 1964
Raised by R. Kordes, Germany.
Parentage: 'Gertrud Westphal' × 'Lilli Marleen'
A low compact grower 18 in. (0·5 m.) high, with very small, dark green foliage. The medium sized, semi-double flowers open out slightly cupped, crimson-scarlet in colour and in numerous clusters. Flowering profusely over a long period, this is an ideal cultivar for small gardens, for edging or for small beds. A forerunner in the development of compact growing roses, useful as a ground cover plant. **443**, p. 82.
G.T.A.B. 1966.

'Maryse Kriloff' see **'Lucy Cramphorn'**, **328**, p. 62.

'Masquerade' Fl.
Yellow to dark red, 3 ft (0·9 m.) 1949
Raised by E. S. Boerner, U.S.A.
Parentage: 'Goldilocks' × 'Holiday'
A vigorous, bushy grower which will attain 3 ft (0·9 m.) in height, with dark foliage. The medium sized, semi-double flowers are yellow, turning salmon-pink and eventually dark red. As all the variations occur in large trusses at the same time, this cultivar is most attractive when planted en masse. Requires efficient dead-heading to prevent seed pods from forming, otherwise little bloom will follow the first crop. Faint scent. **444**, p. 82.
G.M., R.N.R.S. 1952.

'Masquerade, Climbing' see **'Climbing Masquerade'**

'Master Hugh' see under *R. macrophylla*

'Maud Cole' Fl.
Deep mauve-purple, 2 ft (0·6 m) 1968
Raised by R. Harkness & Co. Ltd, England.
Parentage: 'Lilac Charm' × 'Africa Star'
A low bushy grower, about 2 ft (0·6 m.) high, with striking dark, glossy foliage. The medium sized, deep mauve-purple flowers are double with the petals held closely together and are freely produced. Slightly scented and generally healthy. Rather dull for general gardens but will delight floral arrangers who might appreciate the unusual colour.

'Max Graf', *R. × jacksonii* MSh. Trailer
Pink, early summer, 1 ft (0·3 m.) usually trailing 1919
Raised by G. Bowditch, U.S.A.
Parentage: *R. rugosa* × *R. wichuraiana*
Modern hybrid Rugosa shrub rose, usually making long growths which, unless trained upwards, tend to lie prostrate along the ground. Flowers single, pink paling to white at base and with good boss of yellow stamens, of medium size like a large dog rose. Mid to late June, but not recurrent. Scented. Foliage glossy. Recommended by many authors for use as ground cover. Its thick foliage will smother weeds in summer but it is difficult and prickly to weed among its long trailers in spring before foliage appears. *R. kordesii* was a tetraploid seedling of this.
A.M., R.H.S. 1964.

'McGredy's Yellow' HT.
Creamy-yellow, 2½ ft (0·8 m.) 1933
Raised by S. McGredy & Son Ltd, N. Ireland.
Parentage: 'Mrs Charles Lamplough' × ('The Queen Alexandra Rose' × 'J. B. Clark')
A cultivar which, in spite of its age, has retained its vigour; it is of medium height and upright growth. The dark green, glossy foliage

has bronze tints but it is somewhat sparse. The blooms are beautifully formed, creamy-yellow but have only a slight scent. Somewhat intolerant of rain, they are excellent for garden display if planted fairly closely. Blooms up to exhibition standard are occasionally produced if grown well. **333**, p. 63.

'McGredy's Yellow, Climbing' see **'Climbing McGredy's Yellow'**

'Meg' MCl.
Salmon-apricot, recurrent, 12 ft (3·7 m.) 1954
Raised by Dr A. C. V. Gosset, England.
Parentage: probably 'Paul's Lemon Pillar' × 'Mme Butterfly'
Vigorous climber with flowers of hybrid tea type. Flowers very large up to 5 in. (12·7 cm.) across, single or semi-double, pale salmon-apricot fading to pale blush-pink with some shadings of peach-pink, opening wide to show large boss of reddish-orange stamens, scented. Mid to late June and slightly recurrent. A very beautiful rose where there is ample space suitable for covering wall or growing up into an old tree. Growth rather stiff and brittle and so should be tied in as it grows. **250**, p. 47.
A.M., R.H.S. 1953; G.M., R.N.R.S. 1954.

'Meg Merrilies' see under **R. eglanteria, 13**, p. 3.

'Megiddo' Fl.
Bright scarlet-red, 2 ft (0·6 m) 1970
Raised by Gandy's Roses Ltd, England.
Parentage: 'Coup de Foudre' × 'S'Agaró'
A vigorous, upright grower, 2 ft (0·6 m.) high with dark green glossy foliage. The moderately full flowers are bright scarlet-red, borne in trusses, several together. Very spectacular when in full bloom. Repeats well. **447**, p. 84.
T.G.C., R.N.R.S. 1970.

'Mellow Yellow' HT.
Yellow, 2½ ft (0·8 m.) 1968
Discovered by Waterhouse Nurseries Ltd, England.
Parentage: 'Piccadilly' sport
Similar in growth to its parent but the blooms are yellow with pink edges. **334**, p. 63.
T.G.C., R.N.R.S. 1969.

'Memoriam' HT.
White, 2 ft (0·6 m.) 1960
Raised by G. J. Von Abrams, U.S.A.
Parentage: ('Blanche Mallerin' × 'Peace') × ('Peace' × 'Frau Karl Druschki')
A fairly vigorous upright, grower of 2 ft (0·6 m.) in height with semi-glossy, dark green foliage. The large full blooms are so well formed as to be ideal for exhibition and are white tinted in the heart with pastel pink. Really only an exhibitor's cultivar, it has an intense dislike of wet weather, is a delight in dry weather, otherwise insipid. P.G.M. 1960; C.M., R.N.R.S. 1961.

'Merlin' Fl.
Reddish-pink, 2 ft (0·6 m.) 1967
Raised by R. Harkness & Co. Ltd, England.
Parentage: 'Pink Parfait' × 'Circus'
A vigorous, upright grower, compact habit, 2 ft (0·6 m.) high with reddish-pink flowers, shading off to yellow at base but becoming reddish-pink all over as the blooms age. A very gay cultivar with abundant display during the summer and again in autumn. Resists wet weather well and has a slight scent. Seems to grow equally well in all areas. **448**, p. 84.
T.G.C., R.N.R.S. 1967.

'Mermaid' MCl.
Sulphur-yellow, recurrent, 25–30 ft (7·6–9·1 m.) 1918
Raised by W. Paul, England.
Parentage: *R. bracteata* × double yellow Tea rose
A very robust grower, once established and happy, with dark glossy foliage which may be evergreen or deciduous according to climatic conditions and the situation where planted. Generally it is not happy in cold situations; in the British Isles it is at its best on sunny walls, although in warm sites it will also do well on a north wall. The large, single flowers, pale sulphur-yellow with amber stamens which remain beautiful for some days after the petals fall, are of singular beauty. They consistently repeat during summer and especially during good weather in autumn, when the flowers are frequently in clusters. Delicately scented. 'Mermaid' is sterile, an advantage as far as the grower is concerned, no dead-heading being necessary, although I daresay some breeders might have wished it fertile. Generally regarded as being more difficult to propagate than the ordinary run of roses and it is generally supplied in pots as it does not like moving. Even then it is often a couple of seasons before getting away. Training is best applied while growths are young as they become somewhat brittle when older. Little pruning is required if sufficient space is allotted, merely the removal of dead or useless wood as the plant gets older. When suited, a supreme beauty. **252**, p. 48.
G.M., R.N.R.S. 1917; A.M., R.H.S. 1917; A.G.M., R.H.S. 1933.

'Message', 'White Knight' HT.
White, 2½ ft (0·8 m.) 1956
Raised by F. Meilland, France.
Parentage: ('Virgo' × 'Peace') × 'Virgo'

Abbreviations and Symbols used in the text

Rose classifications

A.	Alba	HT.	Hybrid Tea
B.	Bourbon	MCl.	Modern, large-flowered climber
C.	Centifolia	Min.	Miniature
Ch.	China	Moss	Centifolia muscosa
Cl.	Climber	MSh.	Modern shrub
D.	Damask	P.	Penzance Sweet Brier
Fl.	Floribunda	R.	Rambler
G.	Gallica	Rg.	Rugosa
HM.	Hybrid Musk	Sp.	Species and first hybrids
HP.	Hybrid Perpetual	Sw.	Sweet Brier

Rose Awards and Societies

A.A.R.S.	All-America Rose Selection
A.G.M.	Award of Garden Merit
A.M.	Award of Merit
A.R.S.	American Rose Society
B.B.G.M.	Baden Baden Gold Medal, Germany
B.G.M.	Bagatelle Gold Medal, Paris
C.C.V.	Clay Challenge Vase for scent
C.M.	Certificate of Merit
D.F.P.	David Fuerstenberg Prize
F.C.C.	First Class Certificate
G.G.M.	Geneva Gold Medal
G.M.	Gold Medal
G.M.C.B.	Gold Medal City of Belfast
G.M.H.G.M.	Gertrude M. Hubbard Gold Medal
G.R.H.	Golden Rose of The Hague
G.T.A.B.	Golden Thorn Award Belfast
H.E.M.M.	The Henry Edland Memorial Medal for the most fragrant rose of the year
H.G.M.	The Hague Gold Medal
L.G.M.	Lyon Gold Medal, France
M.G.M.	Madrid Gold Medal
N.G.M.C.	National Gold Medal Certificate
P.G.M.	Portland Gold Medal, Oregon, U.S.A.
P.I.T.	President's International Trophy
R.B.	Prize for the most fragrant rose, Roeulx, Belgium
R.B.G.M.	Roeulx, Belgium, Gold Medal
R.G.M.	Rome Gold Medal
R.H.S.	The Royal Horticultural Society, London
R.N.R.S.	The Royal National Rose Society, Great Britain*
T.G.C.	Trial Ground Certificate
U.A.B.	The 'Uladh' Award for fragrance, Belfast

*National Rose Society awards, before 1965, are included here under R.N.R.S.

The illustration numbers are in **bold type** and the page numbers in light type preceded by p.

Grows fairly vigorously to 2½ ft (0·8 m.), with mat, light green, small foliage. The blooms are full and shapely with long stems and are pure white with a suggestion of green at the base of petals, which enhances rather than detracts from their beauty. Unfortunately it is prone to mildew in some areas and dislikes rain.
A.M., R.H.S. 1956; A.A.R.S. 1958.

'Meteor'   Fl.
Bright orange-scarlet, 2 ft (0·6 m.) 1957
Raised by R. Kordes, Germany.
Parentage: 'Feurio' × 'Gertrud Westphal'
A moderate bushy grower, 2 ft (0·6 m.) high, with abundant light green foliage. The double flowers, cupped when young, open flat and are bright orange-scarlet in colour. Very freely produced. Useful for small gardens and edging.
C.M., R.N.R.S. 1958; A.M., R.H.S. 1959.

'Mevrouw Nathalie Nypels', 'Natalie Nypels'   Fl.
Clear pink, 2 ft (0·6 m.) 1919
Raised by M. Leenders & Co., Holland.
Parentage: 'Orléans Rose' × ('Comtesse du Cayla' × *R. foetida bicolor*)
A dwarf, spreading rose which still retains considerable vigour and produces its double, clear pink flowers over a long period. Sweetly scented and a favourite in many gardens. Classed as a Poly-pom.
449, p. 84.

'Michèle Meilland'   HT.
Soft pink, 2½ ft (0·8 m.) 1945
Raised by F. Meilland, France.
Parentage: 'Joanna Hill' × 'Peace'
A moderately vigorous grower, 2½ ft (0·8 m.) in height, with light green mat foliage. The soft pink blooms are flushed amber and salmon, deepening in the heart, and are moderately full. Freely produced and slightly scented. This is a delightful cultivar for cutting, associating well with 'Mainzer Fastnacht' ('Blue Moon'). Very good in autumn.
C.M., R.N.R.S. 1948.

'Michelle'   Fl.
Pale rose-pink, 3½ ft (1·1 m.) 1970
Raised by G. de Ruiter, Holland.
Parentage: seedling × 'Orange Sensation'
A vigorous grower, 3½ ft (1·1 m.) high, with light green mat foliage. The medium sized flowers are moderately full, porcelain-rose with a darker reverse, borne freely in trusses. An attractive new cultivar which is sweetly scented. **450**, p. 84.
C.M., R.N.R.S. 1969.

'Mignon' see **'Cécile Brunner'**

'Milord'   HT.
Crimson-scarlet, 3 ft (0·9 m.) 1962
Raised by S. McGredy IV, N. Ireland.
Parentage: 'Rubaiyat' × 'Karl Herbst'
A vigorous, tall upright grower, 3 ft (0·9 m.) high, with abundant, semi-glossy, medium green foliage, reddish when young. The full crimson-scarlet blooms are somewhat globular in shape and are produced freely, providing a good display but with little scent. Resists weather well.
C.M., R.N.R.S. 1962.

'Minnehaha'   R.
Pink, summer, 15 ft (4·6 m.) 1905
Raised by M. H. Walsh, U.S.A.

Parentage: *R. wichuraiana* × 'Paul Neyron'
Vigorous rambler up to 15 ft (4·6 m.). Flowers small, double, in large clusters, pink fading almost to white, slightly scented, free-flowering, late June to mid-July but not recurrent. Formerly much grown as a pergola rose, excellent as a weeping standard and now usually seen in old established gardens where recurrent-flowering climbers have not been planted. Foliage glossy but sensitive to mildew.

'Mischief'   HT.
Coral-salmon, 2½ ft (0·8 m.) 1960
Raised by S. McGredy IV, N. Ireland.
Parentage: 'Peace' × 'Spartan'
A vigorous branching grower, 2½ ft (0·8 m.) in height, with abundant light green, semi-glossy foliage which is reddish when young. The freely produced blooms are a pleasing coral-salmon in colour and have a sweet scent. Formation is in general good, but sometimes the flowers are small and quartered and borne in large trusses. If disbudded, good exhibition blooms can be produced but in general it is at its best as a bedding cultivar and few are better for this purpose. Weather resistance is very good indeed. Suspect if rust is prevalent in the area. **335**, p. 63.
G.M., R.N.R.S. 1961; P.I.T., R.N.R.S. 1961.

'Miss All-American Beauty' see **'Maria Callas'**, **332**, p. 62.

'Miss Ireland'   HT.
Coral-salmon, 2 ft (0·6 m.) 1961
Raised by S. McGredy IV, N. Ireland.
Parentage: 'Tzigane' × 'Independence'
A vigorous grower, 2 ft (0·6 m.) high, with mat dark green, crimson tinted foliage. The coral-salmon blooms have a peach reverse, which produces a delightful effect, although colour pales off with age. Well formed and reasonably full, the blooms are freely produced, making an effective bed and also useful for cutting. May require protection from mildew and black spot.
C.M., R.N.R.S. 1960.

'Mr Bluebird'   Min.
Lavender-blue, 15 in (38·1 cm.) 1960
Raised by R. S. Moore, U.S.A.
Parentage: 'Old Blush' × 'Old Blush'
A compact bushy grower, 12–15 in. (30·5–38·1 cm.) high with dark foliage. Small, semi-double flowers, lavender-blue in colour, varying somewhat in shade. Free-flowering. An interesting and rather unusual cultivar because of its origin from 'Old Blush', a well known garden plant often called 'Common Monthly'. This has pink flowers and grows about 3 ft (0·9 m.) high, more if placed against a wall. (It has also been claimed that this is the 'Last Rose of Summer', immortalized in song by Thomas Moore, the Irish poet.) Ralph S. Moore, famous in the rose world as a raiser of miniatures, obtained seedlings by sowing self-set seeds of 'Old Blush', many of these proving to be of miniature type. The only one introduced to cultivation was 'Mr Bluebird', which he found grew readily from cuttings. A plant so different in habit and colour from its parent must arouse some speculation amongst breeders.

'Mister Lincoln'   HT.
Dark crimson, 4 ft (1·2 m.) 1964
Raised by Swim and Weeks, U.S.A.
Parentage: 'Chrysler Imperial' × 'Charles Mallerin'
A vigorous, tall, upright grower with dark green, mat foliage which is generally healthy. The dark crimson-red blooms are well formed, of good size and open loosely as they age. Very fragrant, this is a useful cultivar for large beds and is good for cutting. Liable to mildew in some areas. **336**, p. 63.
A.A.R.S. 1965.

'Mrs Anthony Waterer'   Rg.
Magenta-crimson, summer, 5 ft (1·5 m.) 1898
Raised by Waterer, England.
Parentage: *R. rugosa* × 'Général Jacqueminot'
A vigorous bushy Rugosa hybrid up to 5 ft (1·5 m.). Flowers semi-double, a rather virulent magenta-crimson, about 3½ in. (8·9 cm.) across. Mid-June. Slightly recurrent. Free-flowering, scented. Difficult to place in the garden because of its colour and so needs to be grown on its own. **133**, p. 23.
A.G.M., R.H.S.

'Mrs Colville' see *R. spinosissima* **'Mrs Colville'**

'Mrs F. W. Flight'   Cl.
Pink, summer, 8 ft (2·4 m.) 1905
Raised by W. H. Cutbush & Son Ltd, England.
Parentage: 'Crimson Rambler' × unknown semi-double rose
Climber or pillar rose of moderate vigour, of Multiflora type. Flowers in large clusters, semi-double, carmine-pink with white centre, fading to light purplish-pink, very floriferous and giving a pretty bicolor effect of pink and white. Late June to mid-July but not recurrent and consequently has lost favour to more modern, recurrent climbers. **215**, p. 39.

'Mrs Herbert Stevens, Climbing' see **'Climbing Mrs Herbert Stevens'**

'Mrs John Laing'   HP.
Rose-pink, recurrent, 6 ft (1·8 m.) 1887
Raised by H. Bennett, England.
Parentage: 'François Michelon' seedling
Vigorous Hybrid Perpetual shrub up to 6 ft (1·8 m.). Flowers very large, double, cupped, clear rose-pink with a very faint purplish tone, strongly scented. Free-flowering and recurrent. One of the best and most vigorous roses in this group. The flowers are borne on stout stems and are excellent for cutting. **112**, p. 20.

'Mrs Jones' see **'Centenaire de Lourdes'**, **390**, p. 73.

'Mrs Oakley Fisher'   HT.
Deep orange-yellow, 2½ ft (0·8 m) 1921
Raised by B. R. Cant, England.
Still reasonably vigorous after half a century, this charming single rose has deep orange-yellow flowers which are fragrant and admirably complemented by the glossy bronzed foliage. Flowers over a long season. **337**, p. 63.

'Mrs Sam McGredy'   HT.
Coppery-scarlet, 2½ ft (0·8 m.) 1929
Raised by S. McGredy & Son Ltd. N. Ireland.
Parentage: ('Donald Macdonald' × 'Golden Emblem') × (seedling × 'The Queen Alexandra Rose')
This famous cultivar is now only of moderate vigour and has glossy, handsome bronze tinted, dark green foliage. The finely formed flowers are full, bright coppery-scarlet, on long slender stems and have some fragrance. Generous feeding is now required to make it worthwhile. If a suitable situation is available it is better grown in the climbing form introduced by Buisman, 1937, which has retained much of its vigour. Protection from black spot may be required.
G.M., R.N.R.S. 1929.

'Mrs Sam McGredy, Climbing' see **'Climbing Mrs Sam McGredy'**

'Mojave'   HT.
Orange, 3 ft (0·9 m.) 1954
Raised by H. C. Swim, U.S.A.
Parentage: 'Charlotte Armstrong' × 'Signora'
A vigorous tall upright grower with glossy, bronze-green foliage which is usually healthy. The medium sized blooms are moderately full and carried erect, frequently singly on long straight stems, so are useful for decorating purposes. Rich deep orange on opening, fading to pinkish-orange, the blooms are very freely produced. They are particularly good in autumn, resisting weather reasonably well. Not a great deal of scent. **338**, p. 63.
B.G.M. 1953; G.G.M. 1953; A.A.R.S. 1954; T.G.C., R.N.R.S. 1955.

'Molde'   Fl.
Geranium-red, 2 ft (0·6 m.) 1964
Raised by M. Tantau, Germany.
A low bushy grower, about 2 ft high, with dark glossy foliage. The medium sized, double flowers are geranium-red, produced in large clusters. A useful cultivar where low compact habit is required.
T.G.C., R.N.R.S. 1966.

'Molly McGredy'   Fl.
Cherry-red and silver, 3 ft (0·9 m.) 1969
Raised by S. McGredy IV, N. Ireland.
Parentage: 'Paddy McGredy' × ('Mme Léon Cuny' × 'Columbine')
An upright, bushy grower, up to 3 ft (0·9 m.) high, with dark green glossy foliage. The medium sized, double blooms are well formed

---

Abbreviations and Symbols used in the text

Rose classifications

A.	Alba	HT.	Hybrid Tea
B.	Bourbon	MCl.	Modern, large-flowered climber
C.	Centifolia	Min.	Miniature
Ch.	China	Moss	Centifolia muscosa
Cl.	Climber	MSh.	Modern shrub
D.	Damask	P.	Penzance Sweet Brier
Fl.	Floribunda	R.	Rambler
G.	Gallica	Rg.	Rugosa
HM.	Hybrid Musk	Sp.	Species and first hybrids
HP.	Hybrid Perpetual	Sw.	Sweet Brier

Rose Awards and Societies

A.A.R.S.	All-America Rose Selection
A.G.M.	Award of Garden Merit
A.M.	Award of Merit
A.R.S.	American Rose Society
B.B.G.M.	Baden Baden Gold Medal, Germany
B.G.M.	Bagatelle Gold Medal, Paris
C.C.V.	Clay Challenge Vase for scent
C.M.	Certificate of Merit
D.F.P.	David Fuerstenberg Prize
F.C.C.	First Class Certificate
G.G.M.	Geneva Gold Medal
G.M.	Gold Medal
G.M.C.B.	Gold Medal City of Belfast
G.M.H.G.M.	Gertrude M. Hubbard Gold Medal
G.R.H.	Golden Rose of The Hague
G.T.A.B.	Golden Thorn Award Belfast
H.E.M.M.	The Henry Edland Memorial Medal for the most fragrant rose of the year
H.G.M.	The Hague Gold Medal
L.G.M.	Lyon Gold Medal, France
M.G.M.	Madrid Gold Medal
N.G.M.C.	National Gold Medal Certificate
P.G.M.	Portland Gold Medal, Oregon, U.S.A.
P.I.T.	President's International Trophy
R.B.	Prize for the most fragrant rose, Roeulx, Belgium
R.B.G.M.	Roeulx, Belgium, Gold Medal
R.G.M.	Rome Gold Medal
R.H.S.	The Royal Horticultural Society, London
R.N.R.S.	The Royal National Rose Society, Great Britain*
T.G.C.	Trial Ground Certificate
U.A.B.	The 'Uladh' Award for fragrance, Belfast

National Rose Society awards, before 1965, are included here under R.N.R.S.

The illustration numbers are in **bold type** and the page numbers in light type preceded by p.

in early stages, opening out later, cherry-red with a silver reverse. They retain their colour and drop cleanly. Very freely produced in medium trusses. A spectacular cultivar for display purposes. **451**, p. 84.
P.I.T., R.N.R.S. 1968; G.M., R.N.R.S. 1968.

'Mon Petit' Min.
Light red, 6 in. (15·2 cm.) 1947
Raised by P. Dot, Spain.
Parentage: 'Merveille des Rouges' × 'Pompon de Paris'
Very dwarf and compact, 6 in. (15·2 cm.) high, with double very gay light red flowers, freely produced.

'Mon Tresor' see **'Red Imp'**

'Mona Ruth' Min.
Light rosy-crimson, 12 in. (30·5 cm.) 1959
Raised by R. S. Moore, U.S.A.
Parentage: (('Sœur Thérèse' × 'Wilhelm') × (seedling × 'Red Ripples')) × 'Zee'
A vigorous grower, 12 in. (30·5 cm.) high, with leathery foliage and small double flowers, beautiful light rosy-crimson in colour. Freely produced and slightly fragrant.

'Monique' HT.
Pink, 3 ft (0·9 m.) 1949
Raised by Paolino, France.
Parentage: 'Lady Sylvia' × seedling
A vigorous, tall grower with mat, light green pointed foliage. The rose-pink blooms, shading to silvery-pink, are fairly large. Though loose when fully opened, they are well formed when young and freely produced. Very free-flowering and very fragrant, this cultivar may require protection from mildew.
G.M., R.N.R.S. 1950.

'Mons. Paul Lédé, Climbing' see **'Climbing Mons. Paul Lédé'**, **267**, p. 50.

'Montezuma' HT.
Salmon-red, 3½ ft (1·1 m.) 1955
Raised by H. C. Swim, U.S.A.
Parentage: 'Fandango' × 'Floradora'
A very vigorous, tall upright grower with abundant semi-glossy, medium green foliage which, when young, is tinted red. The large, full blooms are well formed and with a high centre, making them much favoured for exhibition. Opening deep salmon-red, the flowers change to a pinker shade with purplish tones, quite a distinctive colour but with little scent. Flowers are freely produced, usually in clusters, so must be well disbudded if required for exhibition, and should be cut when young. Only happy in very good weather but could be protected for exhibition blooms. May require protection against mildew. **339**, p. 64
G.G.M. 1955; G.M., R.N.R.S. 1956; P.G.M. 1957.

'Moon Maiden' Fl.
Creamy-yellow, 2½ ft (0·8 m.) 1970
Raised by J. Mattock Ltd, England.
Parentage: 'Fred Streeter' × 'Allgold'
An open, spreading grower, 2½ ft (0·8 m.) high. The fairly large blooms are creamy-yellow, shaded deeper yellow, a cooler colour than most yellow Floribundas used for bedding purposes and associating well with purple, mauve or lilac roses. Slightly scented. **453**, p. 85.

'Moonlight' HM.
Pale lemon-cream, recurrent, 7 ft (2·1 m.) 1913
Raised by Rev. J. H. Pemberton, England.
Parentage: 'Trier' × 'Sulphurea'
Vigorous Hybrid Musk shrub rose, rather loose growing, up to 7 ft (2·1 m.) or more if left unpruned to scramble into a small tree or may be pruned harder to make shrub rose of 5 × 5 ft (1·5 × 1·5 m.). Flowers in large clusters, particularly in autumn, semi-double, a pale lemon-cream colour, of medium size, free-flowering. Late June to mid-July and recurrent throughout summer. Foliage with small leaflets, dark green, glossy, young branches dark reddish-brown. A valuable rose, showing up particularly well in the evening light, although not so widely grown as others of the Pemberton Hybrid Musk group. **121**, p. 21.

'Moonraker' Fl.
Creamy-white to flushed amber, 2½ ft (0·8 m.) 1968
Raised by R. Harkness & Co. Ltd, England.
Parentage: 'Pink Parfait' × 'Highlight'
A vigorous bushy grower, 2½ ft (0·8 m.) high, with mat light green foliage. The well formed, semi-double flowers vary in colour according to weather, creamy-white when hot, flushed amber when cool, and have a slight scent. Weather resistant.

'Morning Jewel' MCl.
Pink, recurrent, 8–10 ft (2·4–3 m.) 1968
Raised by J. Cocker & Sons Ltd, Scotland.
Parentage: 'New Dawn' × 'Red Dandy'
A free-growing cultivar with glossy foliage. The fairly large flowers are semi-double, rich glowing pink in colour and freely produced over a long period. Some fragrance. New basal growths are freely produced so this should be a useful rose for pillars and fences where space is restricted.

'Morsdag' see **'Mothersday'**

'Mothersday', 'Fête des Mères', 'Morsdag', Poly-pom
 'Muttertag'
Deep red, 1½ ft (0·5 m.) 1949
Introduced by F. J. Grootendorst, Holland.
Parentage: 'Dick Koster' sport
A dwarf plant with small, glossy foliage and medium sized globular deep red flowers which are freely produced. Much grown in Denmark and other European countries for market work, mainly for forcing as a pot plant.

'Mousseux de Japon' Moss Sh.
Pinkish-purple, summer, 4 ft (1·2 m.)
Moss rose distinguished by the heavy growth of moss which extends to young shoots and even leaf stalks and surface of leaves as well as surrounding buds. Shrub rose of only medium vigour, generally only 3–4 ft (0·9–1·2 m.). Flowers pinkish-purple with a magenta tinge, semi-double or double, but opening rather loose and untidy. Mid to late June, not recurrent. Foliage strongly tinted when young. Sometimes known as 'Moussu du Japon' and 'Japonica'. **75**, p. 14.

'Moussu du Japon' see **'Mousseux de Japon'**, **75**, p. 14.

'Mullard Jubilee', 'Electron' HT.
Deep rose-pink, 2½ (0·8 m.) 1969
Raised by S. McGredy IV, N. Ireland.
Parentage: 'Paddy McGredy' × 'Prima Ballerina'
A very vigorous, bushy grower, 2½ ft (0·8 m.) in height, with dark

green glossy foliage. The very full, deep rose-pink blooms are reasonably shapely, borne several together and have considerable fragrance. This cultivar comes into bloom somewhat later than the general run of bedding roses but makes a very impressive bed and would appear to have a future as an effective bedding rose. **340**, p. 64.
G.M., R.N.R.S. 1968; H.G.M. 1970; R.B. 1970.

'Munster'   MSh.
Pale pink, recurrent, 4 ft (1·2 m.) 1958
Raised by W. Kordes, Germany.
Modern shrub rose of medium vigour, up to 4 ft (1·2 m.). Floribunda type. Flowers semi-double, pale pink to terracotta-pink at first opening, paler near centre, about 3½ in. (8·9 cm.) across, in large clusters, free-flowering. Slightly scented. Mid-June, recurrent and good in the autumn. Valuable for its constant flowering and makes a good low hedge. **182**, p. 34.

Musk Rose see *R. moschata*

'Mutabilis', *R. chinensis mutabilis*, 'Tipo Ideale'   Ch.
Coppery-flame-pink to pale crimson, 5–20 ft (1·5–6·1 m.)
Shrub rose of medium vigour but variable in this character, sometimes up to 8 ft (2·4 m.) as an old woody, open shrub. Also grows as a wall climber up to 20 ft (6·1 m.). Flowers single with petals not overlapping, of medium size, changing colour as they mature, buds pointed and coppery-flame in colour, fading as they open to a paler copper then to pink and finally darkening to pale crimson, about 3 in. (7·6 cm.) across, in small clusters. Mid-June but recurrent and sometimes showing flowers at Christmas. A very beautiful rose but best in warm gardens where wood can get well ripened. Usually slow to establish from young plants and at first weak in growth. Very long lived. Young foliage coppery-red. A very magnificent specimen on a wall of Kiftsgate Court, Gloucestershire, England, which grows up to the roof, is about 20 ft (6·1 m.) high and as much wide. In June 1970 this plant was one of the finest rose spectacles I have ever seen, absolutely covered with flowers of varying colour and maturity. It is best seen in the morning when the new flowers open. Well worth trying as a wall plant. In the early stages prune only lightly. Origin unknown but it is certainly an old rose in cultivation.
A.M., R.H.S. 1957.

'Muttertag' see 'Mothersday'

'My Choice'   HT.
Pink and buff, 2½ ft (0·8 m.) 1959
Raised by E. B. LeGrice, England.
Parentage: 'Wellworth' × 'Ena Harkness'
A vigorous, tall branching grower, 2½ ft (0·8 m.) high with abundant, light green, semi-glossy, healthy foliage. The large, beautifully formed flowers are somewhat globular, light carmine to salmon-pink inside, pale creamy-buff on the outside, fading slightly with age and are frequently borne singly. A good weather resister with rich lemon scent, this cultivar is sufficiently floriferous to be a good bedder and if cut when young, is also useful for exhibition. **341**, p. 64.
G.M., R.N.R.S. 1958; C.C.V., R.N.R.S. 1958; A.M., R.H.S. 1959.

'Natalie Nypels' see 'Mevrouw Nathalie Nypels', **449**, p. 84.

'National Trust'   HT.
Deep crimson, 2½ ft (0·8 m.) 1969
Raised by S. McGredy IV, N. Ireland.
Parentage: 'Evelyn Fison' × 'King of Hearts'
A vigorous, upright, bushy grower of medium height and abundant

mat green foliage. The well formed blooms are of good size, deep crimson-red and very freely produced well into the autumn. This appears to be an excellent cultivar for bedding purposes. Little scent. **342**, p. 64.
T.G.C., R.N.R.S. 1969.

'Nestor'   G.
Deep lilac-pink, summer, 4 ft (1·2 m.) *c.* 1846
Gallica shrub rose up to 4 ft (1·2 m.). Flowers cupped on opening, double, deep lilac-pink with darker purplish colouring in centre, quartered. Foliage rather bright green.

'Nevada'   MSh.
Creamy-white, recurrent, 8 × 8 ft (2·4 × 2·4 m.) 1927
Raised by P. Dot, Spain.
Modern shrub rose of great vigour and abundant flowering, up to 8 ft (2·4 m.) and as much across. Parentage doubtful, but claimed to have been raised from *R. moyesii*, a tetraploid form such as *fargesii* × 'La Giralda' (a hybrid from 'Frau Karl Druschki'). Flowers semi-double, large up to 5 in. (12·7 cm.) across, creamy-white, rather loose and untidy on maturing. Not scented. Early to mid-June with flowers all along arching sprays and giving solid mass of white. Slightly recurrent throughout summer. One of the most valuable shrub roses we have for its freedom of flower and vigour. In some areas may get black spot. **179**, p. 33.
F.C.C., R.H.S. 1954.

'New Dawn'   Cl.R. sport
Pale pink, recurrent, 7–12 ft (2·1–3·7 m.) or 20 ft (6·1 m.) 1930
Introduced by H. A. Dreer, U.S.A.
Parentage: 'Dr W. Van Fleet' sport

Abbreviations and Symbols used in the text

Rose classifications

A.	Alba	HT.	Hybrid Tea
B.	Bourbon	MCl.	Modern, large-flowered climber
C.	Centifolia	Min.	Miniature
Ch.	China	Moss	Centifolia muscosa
Cl.	Climber	MSh.	Modern shrub
D.	Damask	P.	Penzance Sweet Brier
Fl.	Floribunda	R.	Rambler
G.	Gallica	Rg.	Rugosa
HM.	Hybrid Musk	Sp.	Species and first hybrids
HP.	Hybrid Perpetual	Sw.	Sweet Brier

Rose Awards and Societies

A.A.R.S.	All-America Rose Selection
A.G.M.	Award of Garden Merit
A.M.	Award of Merit
A.R.S.	American Rose Society
B.B.G.M.	Baden Baden Gold Medal, Germany
B.G.M.	Bagatelle Gold Medal, Paris
C.C.V.	Clay Challenge Vase for scent
C.M.	Certificate of Merit
D.F.P.	David Fuerstenberg Prize
F.C.C.	First Class Certificate
G.G.M.	Geneva Gold Medal
G.M.	Gold Medal
G.M.C.B.	Gold Medal City of Belfast
G.M.H.G.M.	Gertrude M. Hubbard Gold Medal
G.R.H.	Golden Rose of The Hague
G.T.A.B.	Golden Thorn Award Belfast
H.E.M.M.	The Henry Edland Memorial Medal for the most fragrant rose of the year
H.G.M.	The Hague Gold Medal
L.G.M.	Lyon Gold Medal, France
M.G.M.	Madrid Gold Medal
N.G.M.C.	National Gold Medal Certificate
P.G.M.	Portland Gold Medal, Oregon, U.S.A.
P.I.T.	President's International Trophy
R.B.	Prize for the most fragrant rose, Roeulx, Belgium
R.B.G.M.	Roeulx, Belgium, Gold Medal
R.G.M.	Rome Gold Medal
R.H.S.	The Royal Horticultural Society, London
R.N.R.S.	The Royal National Rose Society, Great Britain*
T.G.C.	Trial Ground Certificate
U.A.B.	The 'Uladh' Award for fragrance, Belfast

National Rose Society awards, before 1965, are included here under R.N.R.S.

The illustration numbers are in **bold type** and the page numbers in light type preceded by p.

Vigorous rambler up to 12 ft (3·7 m.) or climber spanning 20 ft (6·1 m.) on a fence or wall. May also be grown as a sprawling bush against a wall some 7 ft (2·1 m.) high and 12 ft (3·7 m.) across. Flowers semi-double to double, of medium size, in clusters, pale blush-silvery-pink, deeper in centre, in hot sun fading almost to blush-white, scented and very free-flowering. Mid to late June but recurrent although its main effect is at midsummer. Foliage glossy green. It has superseded its parent in most gardens because of its recurrence in flowering. One of the most popular and useful climbing roses which hardly ever fails to make a fine effect. Suitable for most uses a climber or rambler may be put to, including growing up into a small tree. Much used now in the breeding of recurrent flowering climbers. **216**, p. 40.

'New Dawn Rouge' see **'Etendard', 204**, p. 38.

'New Penny' Min.
Coppery-salmon-pink, 10 in. (25·4 cm.) 1962
Raised by R. S. Moore, U.S.A.
Parentage: (*R. wichuraiana* × 'Floradora') × unnamed seedling
A bushy grower, up to 10 in. (25·4 cm.) high, with glossy foliage. The semi-double, open flowers are an unusual and beautiful shade of coppery-salmon-pink, freely produced and slightly fragrant.

'News' Fl.
Purple, 2½ ft (0·8 m.) 1969
Raised by E.B. LeGrice, England.
Parentage: 'Lilac Charm' × 'Tuscany Superb'
A compact, bushy grower about 2½ ft (0·8 m.) high with medium green mat foliage and a robust constitution. This cultivar extends the colour range in Floribunda roses, being beetroot-red in the bud stage, opening to purple which deepens with age. The flowers are enhanced by bright golden anthers. Very free-flowering over a long season. Makes a magnificent picture when combined with pale yellow roses or grey foliage plants. **454**, p. 85.
C.M., R.N.R.S. 1969; G.M., R.N.R.S. 1970.

'Nordia' Fl.
Light crimson-scarlet, 2½–3 ft (0·8–0·9 m.) 1967
Raised by D. T. Poulsen, Denmark.
Parentage: ('Pinocchio' × 'Pinocchio') × 'Elsinore'
A free growing, free blooming cultivar, with double, medium sized light crimson-scarlet flowers. In cool climates may be too tender for the garden but makes a successful cool greenhouse plant. **452**, p. 84.

'Norman Hartnell' HT.
Crimson-red, 3 ft (0·9 m.) 1964
Raised by R. Kordes, Germany.
Parentage: 'Ballet' × 'Detroiter'
A very vigorous, upright grower, 3 ft (0·9 m.) high, with medium green foliage. The large blooms are crimson-red, of good formation, useful for exhibition as well as garden display. Slightly fragrant. **343**, p. 64.
T.G.C., R.N.R.S. 1962.

'Normandica' see **'Petite de Hollande', 70**, p. 13.

'Northern Lights' HT.
Canary-yellow, 2½ ft (0·8 m.) 1969
Raised by J. Cocker & Sons Ltd, Scotland.
Parentage: 'Duftwolke' × 'Kingcup'
A vigorous upright grower with medium, mid-green mat foliage, 2½ ft (0·8 m.) high, possibly more when established. The very full

flowers are beautifully formed with high pointed centres, canary-yellow in colour with a suffusion of rosy-pink on the outer petals. They are borne several together and in trusses later in the season and are very fragrant. When it becomes available, exhibitors will welcome this new cultivar. **344**, p. 64.

'Norwich Pink' MCl.
Cerise-pink, recurrent, 10 ft (3 m.) 1962
Raised by W. Kordes, Germany.
Vigorous Kordesii climber or pillar rose. Flowers semi-double, of medium size, bright cerise-pink, opening darker cerise, free-flowering, scented. Mid to late June and recurrent. Foliage dark glossy green. A useful rose but not very frequently grown. **253**, p. 48.
T.G.C., R.N.R.S. 1961

'Norwich Salmon' MCl.
Pale salmon-pink, recurrent, 8 ft (2·4 m.) 1962
Raised by W. Kordes, Germany.
Kordesii climber or pillar rose of moderate vigour. The flowers are of hybrid tea type, semi-double or double, large pale salmon-pink, yellow at base. Mid to late June and recurrent. Foliage deep glossy green. **254**, p. 48.
T.G.C., R.N.R.S. 1961

'Nova Zembla' see under **'Conrad F. Meyer'**

'Nozomi' Cl.Min.
Pearly pink, 1½–4 ft (0·4–1·2 m.) 1968
Raised by T. Onodera, Japan.
Parentage: 'Fairy Princess' × 'Sweet Fairy'
If allowed to grow without support, this plant has a low arching habit 1½ ft (0·4 m.) high, with very small pointed, glossy foliage and spreading 2 ft (0·6 m.) across. Supported, attains a height of 4 ft (1·2 m.). The small, single, 5-petalled flowers are freely produced in trusses, pale pearly-pink in colour. An attractive cultivar which appears to do well on its own roots but not recurrent.
T.G.C., R.N.R.S. 1970.

'Nuage Parfumé' see **'Duftwolke', 296**, p. 56.

'Nuits de Young' Moss Sh.
Dark maroon-purple, summer, 4 ft (1·2 m.) 1845
Raised by M. Laffay, France.
Shrub of medium vigour only, usually making rather a thin, sparse bush. Flowers double, very dark maroon-purple, of medium size only, maturing to purplish-mauve and falling loosely apart showing deep yellow stamens. Free-flowering. Mid to late June but not recurrent. Bud mossy. A distinctive shrub for its unusual deep colour. Mr G. Thomas suggests that it was presumably named after the poem 'Night Thoughts' by Edward Young, an eighteenth-century poet. This is certainly an ingenious and possible solution of a problem that has puzzled many.

'Nymphenburg' MSh.Cl.
Salmon-pink, recurrent, 8 ft (2·4 m.) 1954
Raised by W. Kordes, Germany.
Parentage: 'Sangerhausen' × 'Sunmist'
Modern shrub or pillar rose, vigorous up to 8 ft (2·4 m.) or more, rather upright in habit. Flowers of floribunda type in small clusters or singly. Flowers apricot-pink in bud, them salmon with pale cerise-pink towards outer edges, with yellow centre, paler as they age and in bright sun; semi-double to almost double, slightly quartered, large, up to 4 in. (10·2 cm.) across. Finely scented. Mid to late June, recurrent and free-flowering. Valuable for its vigour, abundance of flower and good glossy foliage. **183**, p. 34.
T.G.C., R.N.R.S. 1954; A.M., R.H.S. 1960.

'Oakington Ruby'   Min.
Pale crimson, 12 in. (30·5 cm.) 1933
Introduced by C.R. Bloom, England.
This rose came from the garden of an old lady who lived in Oakington and it is said to have come there from the garden of the cathedral
at Ely. It has been suggested that this rose may be the result of
crossing 'Rouletii' with a red Poly-pom. It grows about 12 in.
(30·5 cm.) high, with small, double pale crimson flowers with a
white eye. It has long been popular in the British Isles.
A.M., R.H.S. 1934.

'Officinalis', *R. gallica officinalis, R. gallica maxima*,   G.
   Rose of Provins, Apothecary's Rose, Red Rose of Lancaster
Crimson, summer, 4 ft (1·2 m.)
Shrub rose of medium size, up to 4 ft (1·2 m.), usually less, of
medium vigour. Flowers semi-double, bright crimson-red with a
slight purplish hue, and good boss of golden stamens in centre,
3½–4½ in. (8·9–11·4 cm.) across. Hips rounded, small, but quite
ornamental. Mid to late June and early July. Flowering branches
are erect and hold flowers upright clear of the foliage. Bushes tend
to sucker freely and in time will make small thickets. This is
probably the oldest rose in cultivation and its history is discussed in
the introductory chapter. Although sometimes called 'Red
Damask' this name is undesirable and it should not be confused
with the Damask roses. It is the parent of 'Versicolor' (**92**, p. 17),
which sported from it. It is well featured by Redouté in Vol. I,
Plate 73, as 'Le Rosier de Provins ordinaire'. **86**, p. 16.

'Olala'   Fl.
Crimson-scarlet, 3 ft (0·9 m.) 1956
Raised by M. Tantau, Germany.
Parentage: 'Fanal' × 'Crimson Glory'
A very vigorous spreading grower, 3 ft (0·9 m.) high, sometimes
more, with an abundance of large, glossy, dark green foliage. The
large, semi-double flowers are crimson-scarlet, paling slightly
towards the centre which can be seen after they open. Flowers
mainly in huge trusses, especially in autumn making a spectacular
cultivar which, for several years, impressed many at the main
entrance to Queen Mary's Garden, Regent's Park, London.
Resists wet weather well. Little scent. **455**, p. 86.

'Old Velvet Moss' see **'William Lobb'**, **76**, p. 14.

'Old Velvet Rose' see **'Tuscany'**

'Olé'   Fl.
Vermilion-red, 2 ft + (0·6 m.) 1964
Raised by D.L. Armstrong, U.S.A.
Parentage: 'Roundelay' × 'El Capitan'
A vigorous grower, just over 2 ft (0·6 m.) high, with glossy foliage.
The medium sized, double flowers are well shaped and vermilion-
red in colour with ruffled petals. Very free-flowering. **456**, p. 86.

'Omar Khayyam'   D.
Bluish-pink, summer, 3½ ft (1·1 m.)
Damask type shrub of only medium vigour up to 3½ ft (1·1 m.).
Straggly and prickly growth. Flowers double, slightly bluish-pink,
not very large, rather irregular and formless, but slightly quartered.
Foliage grey-green with small leaflets. This rose was propagated by
seed from one said to have been growing on Omar Khayyam's
grave at Nashipur in Persia and was planted on the grave in Suffolk
of Edward Fitzgerald, his translator. Chiefly of interest to lovers of
Omar Khayyam's verse rather than as a rose of beauty, otherwise
not worth a place in the garden. Other history unknown.

'Ophelia'   HT.
Pale blush, 3 ft (0·9 m.) 1912
Raised by W. Paul & Son Ltd, England.
This famous rose continues to be reasonably vigorous, upright in
growth with mat, mid-green foliage. Long pointed buds open into
pale blush flowers, tinted light yellow in the centre, very fragrant.
Large bushes are frequently seen in gardens where they flower
profusely, especially in autumn, and are particularly useful for
cutting (see 'Mme Butterfly' and 'Lady Sylvia'). The blooms are
liable to damage by thrips.

'Orange Sensation'   Fl.
Bright vermilion, 2 ft (0·6 m.) 1961
Raised by G. de Ruiter, Holland.
A vigorous bushy grower, 2 ft (0·6 m.) high with light green,
rather dull foliage. The large semi-double flowers are bright
vermilion, fading slightly towards the edges of the petals. They are
freely produced over a long season in medium sized clusters. Very
weather resistant and strongly scented. One of the best bedding
cultivars but requires protection from mildew in some areas and
may have to be watched for black spot also. **457**, p. 86.
G.M., R.N.R.S. 1961; G.R.H. 1968.

'Orange Silk'   Fl.
Orange-vermilion, 2½ ft (0·8 m.) 1968
Raised by S. McGredy IV, N. Ireland.
Parentage: 'Orangeade' × ('Ma Perkins' × 'Independence')
A vigorous bushy grower, 2½ ft (0·8 m.) high, with semi-glossy dark
green foliage. The large flowers are full, of hybrid tea form while
young, opening loosely, orange-vermilion in colour which changes

---

Abbreviations and Symbols used in the text

Rose classifications

A.	Alba	HT.	Hybrid Tea
B.	Bourbon	MCl.	Modern, large-flowered climber
C.	Centifolia	Min.	Miniature
Ch.	China	Moss	Centifolia muscosa
Cl.	Climber	MSh.	Modern shrub
D.	Damask	P.	Penzance Sweet Brier
Fl.	Floribunda	R.	Rambler
G.	Gallica	Rg.	Rugosa
HM.	Hybrid Musk	Sp.	Species and first hybrids
HP.	Hybrid Perpetual	Sw.	Sweet Brier

Rose Awards and Societies

A.A.R.S.	All-America Rose Selection
A.G.M.	Award of Garden Merit
A.M.	Award of Merit
A.R.S.	American Rose Society
B.B.G.M.	Baden Baden Gold Medal, Germany
B.G.M.	Bagatelle Gold Medal, Paris
C.C.V.	Clay Challenge Vase for scent
C.M.	Certificate of Merit
D.F.P.	David Fuerstenberg Prize
F.C.C.	First Class Certificate
G.G.M.	Geneva Gold Medal
G.M.	Gold Medal
G.M.C.B.	Gold Medal City of Belfast
G.M.H.G.M.	Gertrude M. Hubbard Gold Medal
G.R.H.	Golden Rose of The Hague
G.T.A.B.	Golden Thorn Award Belfast
H.E.M.M.	The Henry Edland Memorial Medal for the most fragrant rose of the year
H.G.M.	The Hague Gold Medal
L.G.M.	Lyon Gold Medal, France
M.G.M.	Madrid Gold Medal
N.G.M.C.	National Gold Medal Certificate
P.G.M.	Portland Gold Medal, Oregon, U.S.A.
P.I.T.	President's International Trophy
R.B.	Prize for the most fragrant rose, Roeulx, Belgium
R.B.G.M.	Roeulx, Belgium, Gold Medal
R.G.M.	Rome Gold Medal
R.H.S.	The Royal Horticultural Society, London
R.N.R.S.	The Royal National Rose Society, Great Britain*
T.G.C.	Trial Ground Certificate
U.A.B.	The 'Uladh' Award for fragrance, Belfast

National Rose Society awards, before 1965, are included here under R.N.R.S.

The illustration numbers are in **bold type** and the page numbers
in light type preceded by p.

little as it ages. A good bedding cultivar, which repeats quickly and always gives a good display. **458**, p. 86.

'Orangeade'   Fl.
Brilliant vermilion, 2½ ft (0·8 m.) 1959
Raised by S. McGredy IV, N. Ireland.
Parentage: 'Orange Sweetheart' × 'Independence'
A robust, branching grower, 2½ ft (0·8 m.) high, with handsome glossy, bronze tinted, dark green foliage. The semi-double flowers are brilliant vermilion when young, turning reddish-orange as they age and soon open to show their centres. They are freely produced in large trusses. A fine bedding rose which repeats quickly. Slight scent. **459**, p. 86.
G.M., R.N.R.S. 1959; A.M., R.H.S. 1959.

'Oskar Scheerer'   MSh.
Dark red, recurrent, 4 ft (1·2 m.) 1961
Raised by R. Kordes, Germany.
Modern shrub rose of medium vigour up to 4 ft (1·2 m.), of floribunda type. Flowers semi-double, in small clusters, very dark garnet-red with prominent yellow centre of stamens. No scent. Mid-June, recurrent, with good autumn flowering. A promising new rose which shows up well after bad weather. **184**, p. 34.

'Paddy McGredy'   Fl.
Deep carmine-pink, 2 ft (0·6 m.) 1962
Raised by S. McGredy IV, N. Ireland.
Parentage: 'Spartan' × 'Tzigane'
A compact, bushy grower, 2 ft (0·6 m.) high, with abundant glossy, dark green foliage. The deep carmine-pink flowers sometimes have a salmon flush and have a paler reverse. Full, excellently formed and slightly fragrant. Produced so freely and in such large trusses as to hide the foliage, with a gap before the second, also good, crop. May require protection from black spot. **460**, p. 86.
G.M., R.N.R.S. 1961; A.M., R.H.S. 1961.

'Paint Box'   Fl.
Red and golden-yellow, 3 ft (0·9 m.) 1963
Raised by A. Dickson & Sons Ltd, N. Ireland.
Parentage: seedling × 'St Pauli'
A vigorous, upright grower, 3 ft high (0·9 m.) with medium green foliage. The large flowers vary from single to semi-double, opening flat, red and golden-yellow which becomes dark red as they age. Very freely produced in clusters and reasonably weather resistant. An effective bedder. **461**, p. 87.
C.M., R.N.R.S. 1963.

'Panachée à fleur double' see *R.* × *centifolia* **'Variegata'**

'Panachée d'Angers' see **'Commandant Beaurepaire'**

'Papa Meilland'   HT.
Dark crimson, 2½ ft (0·8 m.) 1963
Raised by A. Meilland, France.
Parentage: 'Chrysler Imperial' × 'Charles Mallerin'
A cultivar of medium vigour, upright in growth, 2½ ft (0·8 m.) high with glossy dark green foliage. Full flowers, dark velvety crimson, full of fragrance, a joy when clean but very prone to mildew in some districts. Worth growing under glass by amateur growers, where mildew is more easily controlled.

'Paprika'   Fl.
Bright geranium-red, 2½ ft (0·8 m.) 1958
Raised by M. Tantau, Germany.

Parentage: 'Märchenland' × 'Red Favorite'
A vigorous, bushy grower, 2½ ft (0·8 m.) high, with handsome, very glossy dark green foliage. The semi-double flowers are bright geranium-red with a distinctive bluish zone at the base of the petals and are borne in large trusses. A profuse cropper in summer and also in autumn, resisting wet weather well. This cultivar has for several years been a most attractive and reliable bedder, holding its own with more recent introductions. Makes a good standard. **462**, p. 87.
A.M., R.H.S. 1957; G.M., R.N.R.S. 1959; G.R.H. 1961.

'Para Ti', 'For You', 'Pour Toi', 'Wendy'   Min.
Cream, 10 in. (25·4 cm.) 1946
Raised by P. Dot, Spain.
Parentage: 'Eduardo Toda' × 'Pompon de Paris'
Very bushy, 8–10 in. (20·3–25·4 cm.) high with glossy foliage. The semi-double flowers are beautiful in the bud stage, then they open cream and turn white with a green tint at the base. Beautifully formed. One of the favourite miniatures.

'Parade'   MCl.
Deep carmine, recurrent, 10–12 ft (3–3·7 m.) 1953
Raised by E. S. Boerner, U.S.A.
Parentage: 'New Dawn' seedling × 'Climbing World's Fair'
Vigorous climber or pillar rose with flowers of hybrid tea type. Flowers double, quite large, deep carmine and scented, the heavy heads tending to droop slightly. Mid-June and recurrent later. Foliage glossy, dark green with reddish tints. **255**, p. 48.

'Paris-Match'   HT.
Carmine to rose, 2½ ft (0·8 m.) 1956
Raised by F. Meilland, France.
Parentage: 'Independence' × 'Grand'mère Jenny'
A vigorous grower, 2½ ft (0·8 m.) high with abundant, semi-glossy dark green foliage. The large full blooms are well formed, slightly scented, carmine to rose-pink in colour and are freely produced. **345**, p. 65.
B.G.M. 1956.

'Pariser Charme' see **'Charm of Paris'**, **395**, p. 74.

'Parkdirektor Riggers'   MCl.
Deep crimson, recurrent, 12 ft (3·7 m.) 1957
Raised by W. Kordes, Germany.
Parentage: *R. kordesii* × 'Our Princess'
Vigorous Kordesii climber or pillar rose. Flowers semi-double, in large clusters, quite large, up to 3 in. (7·6 cm.) across, unfading deep crimson, velvety with small centre of yellow stamens and a little white and purple at the base of the petals. Slight fragrance. Mid to late June and recurrent. Free-flowering. Foliage dark green, glossy. One of the most reliable of the Kordesii climbers for its freedom of flower. When grown against a wall may be sensitive to mildew and black spot. **256**, p. 48.
A.M., R.H.S. 1961.

'Park's Yellow Tea-scented China' see under *R.* × *odorata*

'Parson's Pink China' see under *R.* × *odorata*

'Pascali'   HT.
White, 3½ ft (1·1 m.) 1963
Raised by L. Lens, Belgium.
Parentage: 'Queen Elizabeth' × 'White Butterfly'
A tall upright grower, 3½ ft (1·1 m.) high with dark green, glossy

foliage. Medium sized, the moderately full flowers are white, shaded cream in the centre, produced freely, generally one flower on a stem. Apt to spot with pink in wet weather but the best bedder of present day white Hybrid Tea roses. Almost scentless. **346**, p. 65. H.G.M. 1963; C.M., R.N.R.S. 1963

'Paul Neyron'   HP.
Deep pink, recurrent, 6 ft (1·8 m.) 1869
Raised by A. Levet, France.
Parentage: 'Victor Verdier' × 'Anna de Diesbach'
Vigorous Hybrid Perpetual shrub up to 6 ft (1·8 m.). Flowers very large, 5 in. (12·7 cm.) or more across, double, deep rose-pink with a purple flush, globular, quartered when fully open. Paeony-like. Scent slight. Free-flowering. Mid to late June and recurrent. Foliage broad with glossy green leaflets. Appears slightly blowsy in flower but a useful shrub for its floriferousness and its vigour and its size of flower. **113**, p. 20.

'Paul Ricault'   C.
Deep pink, summer, 5 ft (1·5 m.) 1845
Raised by Portemer, France.
Centifolia rose of unknown parentage, of medium vigour up to 5 ft (1·5 m.). Flowers large, deep pink, fully double, rather globular, heavy with recurved outer petals, slightly quartered centre and tending to droop, strongly scented. Mid to late June, free-flowering but not recurrent. Raised about 1845, but not very common in cultivation. **69**, p. 13.

'Paul Transon'   R.
Coppery-buff, recurrent, 15 ft (4·6 m.) 1900
Raised by Barbier, France.
Parentage: *R. wichuraiana* × 'L'Idéal'
Vigorous rambler with dark green, glossy foliage and pointed leaflets, young stems purplish-red and bronze. Flowers double, opening flat, of medium size, about 2½ in. (6·4 cm.) across. Buds orange-copper with some deep coppery or terracotta-pink, flowers coppery-buff, scented, free-flowering, borne singly. Mid to late June, recurrent. Rather subject to mildew. **217**, p. 40.

'Paul's Lemon Pillar'   Cl.
Pale lemon-yellow, early summer, 12 ft (3·7 m.) 1915
Raised by W. Paul & Son Ltd, England.
Parentage: 'Frau Karl Druschki' × 'Maréchal Niel'
Vigorous climber with flowers of the hybrid tea type and foliage with large leaflets. Flowers large, double, creamy-lemon, tinged green towards base and opening almost white, petals rolled at edges, strongly scented, free-flowering, mid to late June but not recurrent. A very fine rose with large heavy blooms like those of 'Frau Karl Druschki' (**111**, p. 20), frequently up to exhibition standard, though they tend to droop slightly like those of its other parent. Rather subject to black spot. **218**, p. 40.
G.M., R.N.R.S. 1915; A.M., R.H.S. 1915.

'Paul's Scarlet Climber'   Cl.
Crimson, summer, 10 ft (3 m.) 1916
Raised by W. Paul & Son Ltd, England.
Parentage: 'Paul's Carmine Pillar' seedling × probably 'Rêve d'Or'
Climber or pillar rose of medium vigour only up to 10 ft (3 m.). Flowers bright reddish-crimson, in small clusters, semi-double, of medium size, slightly scented. Blooms profusely in mid to late June with little recurrence, the later flowering being better if it is only pruned very lightly after first flowering. One of the most popular roses for many years and still widely grown but in colour it is now superseded by others with stronger, clearer red with practically no tinge of purplish-blue in the red. Some stocks seem to have deteriorated in vigour in recent years. **219**, p. 40.
A.M., R.H.S. 1915; A.G.M., R.H.S. 1931.

'Pax'   HM.
Creamy-white, recurrent, 6 ft (1·8 m.) 1918
Raised by Rev. J. H. Pemberton, England.
Parentage: 'Trier' × 'Sunburst'
Fairly vigorous Hybrid Musk making a large loose-growing shrub with arching branches up to 6 ft (1·8 m.) or even more. Flowers in large, rather drooping clusters, or sprays, semi-double, creamy-yellow in bud opening to creamy-white, of medium size, scented. Late June to mid-July and recurrent, often with finest sprays in early autumn. Valuable as a large shrub. Foliage dark green, glossy; branches dark brown. Growth rather like that of 'Felicia' (**120**, p. 21).

'Peace', 'Gioia', 'Gloria Dei', 'Mme A. Meilland'   HT.
Yellow, 4 ft + (1·2 m.) 1945
Raised by F. Meilland, France.
Parentage: (('George Dickson' × 'Souvenir de Claudius Pernet') × ('Joanna Hill' × 'Charles P. Kilham')) × 'Margaret McGredy'
A cultivar of exceptional vigour which has achieved great success and is consequently well known all over the world, this is indeed a giant amongst roses. Tall and branching, upwards of 4 ft (1·2 m.) in height, it will make quite a large shrub if lightly pruned. If pruned severely, apt to produce 'blind' shoots, especially at the first time of blooming; these will break, however, and flower later. Foliage is healthy, glossy, deep green, seldom troubled by disease. The flowers are very large and full, yellow with flushes of pink, which pales slightly with age, but somewhat variable in depth of colouring according to the season. Form is generally good, therefore suitable for exhibition. Most beautiful for garden display when the flowers are fully expanded. Blooms profusely summer and autumn, with

---

Abbreviations and Symbols used in the text

Rose classifications

A.	Alba	HT.	Hybrid Tea
B.	Bourbon	MCl.	Modern, large-flowered climber
C.	Centifolia	Min.	Miniature
Ch.	China	Moss	Centifolia muscosa
Cl.	Climber	MSh.	Modern shrub
D.	Damask	P.	Penzance Sweet Brier
Fl.	Floribunda	R.	Rambler
G.	Gallica	Rg.	Rugosa
HM.	Hybrid Musk	Sp.	Species and first hybrids
HP.	Hybrid Perpetual	Sw.	Sweet Brier

Rose Awards and Societies

A.A.R.S.	All-America Rose Selection
A.G.M.	Award of Garden Merit
A.M.	Award of Merit
A.R.S.	American Rose Society
B.B.G.M.	Baden Baden Gold Medal, Germany
B.G.M.	Bagatelle Gold Medal, Paris
C.C.V.	Clay Challenge Vase for scent
C.M.	Certificate of Merit
D.F.P.	David Fuerstenberg Prize
F.C.C.	First Class Certificate
G.G.M.	Geneva Gold Medal
G.M.	Gold Medal
G.M.C.B.	Gold Medal City of Belfast
G.M.H.G.M.	Gertrude M. Hubbard Gold Medal
G.R.H.	Golden Rose of The Hague
G.T.A.B.	Golden Thorn Award·Belfast
H.E.M.M.	The Henry Edland Memorial Medal for the most fragrant rose of the year
H.G.M.	The Hague Gold Medal
L.G.M.	Lyon Gold Medal, France
M.G.M.	Madrid Gold Medal
N.G.M.C.	National Gold Medal Certificate
P.G.M.	Portland Gold Medal, Oregon, U.S.A.
P.I.T.	President's International Trophy
R.B.	Prize for the most fragrant rose, Roeulx, Belgium
R.B.G.M.	Roeulx, Belgium, Gold Medal
R.G.M.	Rome Gold Medal
R.H.S.	The Royal Horticultural Society, London
R.N.R.S.	The Royal National Rose Society, Great Britain*
T.G.C.	Trial Ground Certificate
U.A.B.	The 'Uladh' Award for fragrance, Belfast

*National Rose Society awards, before 1965, are included here under R.N.R.S.

The illustration numbers are in **bold type** and the page numbers in light type preceded by p.

some intermittent flowers. Weather resistance is good. Only faintly scented. **347**, p. 65.
P.G.M. 1944; A.A.R.S. 1946; N.G.M.C., A.R.S. 1947; G.M., R.N.R.S. 1947; A.M., R.H.S. 1947.

'Peachy'   Min.
Light peach-pink, 10 in. (25·4 cm.) 1964
Raised by R. S. Moore, U.S.A.
Parentage: 'Golden Glow' × 'Zee'
A bushy grower, 9–10 in. (20·3–25·4 cm.) high, with soft light green foliage. The small double flowers are a light peach-pink. Free flowering.

'Pearl of Canada' see **'Perla de Alcanada'**

'Peer Gynt'   HT.
Canary-yellow, 3 ft (0·9 m.) 1968
Raised by R. Kordes, Germany.
Parentage: 'Königin der Rosen' × 'Golden Giant'
A vigorous compact, bushy grower, about 3 ft (0·9 m.) high, with large mat, light green leaves. The full, somewhat globular flowers are canary-yellow, tinged pink on outer petal edges, intensifying with age and in the autumn. Petal edges slightly fringed. A free flowering cultivar, good for display purposes and slightly fragrant. May require protection against mildew in some areas, but looks very promising. **348**, p. 65.
C.M., R.N.R.S. 1967.

'Penelope'   HM.
Salmon-apricot-pink, recurrent, 5 × 6 ft (1·5 × 1·8 m.) 1924
Raised by Rev. J. H. Pemberton, England.
Parentage: 'Ophelia' × 'William Allen Richardson'
Vigorous Hybrid Musk shrub rose of spreading dense habit usually up to about 5 ft (1·5 m.) and even more across. Old bushes build up into massive densely twiggy bushes. Flowers in large clusters or sprays, semi-double, pale salmon-pink with a slight apricot tinge, fading to blush-pink, strongly scented. Very free-flowering. Late June to mid-July and recurrent, usually with a good display in early autumn. Hips pink. Leaves rather large for this group. One of the most valuable roses for general garden purposes for its constancy of flower, its delicate colouring and for the vigour of the growth. Makes a good hedge. Probably the most popular of Mr Pemberton's Hybrid Musks. **122**, p. 22.
A.G.M., R.H.S.

Penzance Sweet Briers see under **R. eglanteria**

'Peon' see **'Tom Thumb'**

'Percy Thrower'   HT.
Pink, 3 ft (0·9 m.) 1964
Raised by L. Lens, Belgium.
Parentage: 'La Jolla' × 'Karl Herbst'
A fairly vigorous grower about 3 ft (0·9 m.) high, which is apt to sprawl, a habit which can be improved by pruning to an inside eye. Foliage is dark green and glossy. The clear pink flowers are well formed when young, opening loosely, and are long lasting when cut; consequently useful for decoration. Fragrance is slight and protection against black spot may be required.
T.G.C., R.N.R.S. 1962.

'Perfecta' see **'Kordes' Perfecta', 324**, p. 61.

'Perla de Alcanada', 'Baby Crimson', 'Pearl of Canada',   Min.
  'Titania', 'Wheatcroft's Baby Crimson'
Reddish-carmine, 12 in. (30·5 cm.) 1944
Raised by P. Dot, Spain.
Parentage: 'Perle des Rouges' × 'Rouletii'
A very hardy cultivar which grows and flowers well, 10–12 in. (25·4–30·5 cm.) high with dark glossy foliage. The small buds are charming and develop into semi-double, open flowers, reddish-carmine in colour, touched white at the base.

'Perla de Monserrat'   Min.
Warm rose-pink, 12 in. (30·5 cm.) 1945
Raised by P. Dot, Spain.
Parentage: 'Cécile Brunner' × 'Rouletii'
A dwarf, compact grower, 12 in. (30·5 cm.) high, with dainty, shapely buds. This must be one of the most beautiful miniatures, a tiny mimic of the Hybrid Tea 'Lady Sylvia' (**327**, p. 61). Warm rose-pink flowers with paler edges. Blooms profusely.

'Perle d'Or'   Ch.
Apricot-yellow, recurrent, 3 ft (0·9 m) 1883
Raised by Rambaud, France.
Parentage: possibly R. multiflora form × 'Mme Falcot'
Dwarf shrub, usually not over 3 ft (0·9 m.). Flowers are rather like those of 'Cécile Brunner' but slightly larger, buds buff-apricot, pointed and tightly rolled, opening pale apricot – almost white, in clusters. This rose is difficult to classify. It is almost a small Floribunda but owing to the small flowers and pointed buds is usually placed with the China roses. Useful in groups or as a bedding rose but a single specimen does not make much effect.

'Pernille Poulsen'   Fl.
Salmon-pink, 2½ ft (0·8 m.) 1965
Raised by N. D. Poulsen, Denmark.
Parentage: 'Ma Perkins' × 'Columbine'
A vigorous, branching grower, 2½ ft (0·8 m.) high with medium green, semi-glossy foliage. The semi-double flowers open quickly, a salmon-pink colour which lightens with age. Very freely produced. This is an attractive cultivar for bedding, especially in sheltered gardens, and blooms earlier than most Floribundas. Scented. **463**, p. 87.
T.G.C., R.N.R.S. 1965.

'Persian Yellow' see **R. foetida persiana**

'Peter Frankenfeld'   HT.
Deep rose pink, 3 ft (0·9 m.) 1966
Raised by R. Kordes, Germany.
A strong, upright plant with dark green foliage. The large, high centred flowers are deep rose pink and are slightly fragrant. Long strong stems provide ideal material for cutting and the flowers last well. Appears to be healthy.

'Petite de Hollande'   C.
Pale pink, summer 4 ft (1·2 m.)
Centifolia Provence Rose. Compact shrub, not often over 4 ft (1·2 m.). Flowers double, pale blush pink, but deeper bright rose pink towards centre, rather small about 2½ in. (6·4 cm.) across, free-flowering, scented. Mid-late June. Miniature but larger in growth and flower than 'De Meaux' and intermediate between this and R. × centifolia, a delightful rose, especially where space is limited. Also known as 'Petite Junon de Hollande' or 'Pompon des Dames', 'Normandica', or 'Le Petit Rosier à cent feuilles', R. centifolia minor. An old rose, origin not known. **70**, p. 13.

'Petite Junon de Hollande' see **'Petite de Hollande', 70**, p. 13.

'Petite Orléanaise'   G.
Deep pink, summer, 5 ft (1·5 m.)
Vigorous Gallica shrub, about 5 ft (1·5 m.). Flowers rather small to medium, double, deep pink with a slight purplish tinge, but showing small centre with white eye when mature, numerous, late June to early July, not recurrent. Somewhat resembles a Damask rose in habit and fruit. **87**, p. 16

'Pharaoh', 'Pharaon'   HT.
Vivid crimson-scarlet, 3 ft (0·9 m.) 1967
Raised by M. L. Meilland, France.
Parentage: ('Happiness' × 'Independence') × 'Suspense'
A vigorous upright grower, up to 3 ft (0·9 m.) with semi-glossy dark green foliage. The scentless flowers are fairly large, regular in form but do not reflex and are vivid crimson-scarlet with a velvety sheen. They present a striking appearance as they retain their colour until they fall and last a long time on the plants. Mainly produced singly. Requires protection against black spot. **349**, p. 65.
T.G.C., R.N.R.S. 1967; M.G.M. 1967; G.G.M. 1967; H.G.M. 1967.

'Pharaon' see **'Pharaoh', 349**, p. 65.

'Picasso'   Fl.
Cherry-red, 2½ ft (0·8 m.) 1971
Raised by S. McGredy IV, N. Ireland.
Parentage: ('Marlena' × 'Evelyn Fison') × ('Orange Sweetheart' × 'Frühlingsmorgen')
A compact, bushy grower, up to 2½ ft (0·8 m.) high with small, distinctive, mahonia like, mat mid-green foliage. This unique cultivar represents a further extension to the range of Floribunda roses, particularly because of its colour. This bears a strong resemblance to some Regal Pelargoniums; the medium sized, semi-double open flowers are two shades of cherry-red on the inside of the petals, flecked and streaked with white and with a white base and reverse. Colouring becomes more pronounced with age and in autumn. The flowers are freely produced over a long season, right into November in mild weather. This rose has already aroused much interest amongst rosarians, particularly as further developments on similar lines are coming along for trial. **464**, p. 87.
C.M., R.N.R.S. 1970.

'Piccadilly'   HT.
Scarlet and yellow, 2½ ft (0·8 m.) 1959
Raised by S. McGredy IV, N. Ireland.
Parentage: 'McGredy's Yellow' × 'Karl Herbst'
A vigorous, upright, bushy grower, about 2½ ft (0·8 m.) high, with abundant glossy, coppery-green foliage. The flowers are of medium size, moderately full, opening quickly, scarlet in colour, merging into yellow and with a pale yellow reverse. Loses colour in hot weather and should be planted where some shade can be obtained part of the day. Resists weather well and is particularly free-flowering, repeating quickly. A fine bicolor and a remarkable sight when weather is not too hot. **350**, p. 65.
C.M., R.N.R.S. 1959; M.G.M. 1960; R.G.M. 1960; A.M., R.H.S. 1960

'Pike's Peak'   MSh.
Cerise-pink, early summer, 6 ft (1·8 m.) 1940
Raised by Dr N. C. Gunter, U.S.A.
Parentage: reputedly *R. acicularis* × 'Hollywood'
Modern shrub rose of medium vigour up to 6 ft (1·8 m.). Flowers single or semi-double, deep cerise-pink with prominent white or pale yellow centre, of medium size up to 3½ in. (8·9 cm.) across, in small clusters. Slightly scented. Mid-June, not recurrent.

'Pineapple Poll'   Fl.
Brilliant orange, 2 ft (0·6 m.) 1970
Raised by J. Cocker & Sons Ltd, Scotland.
Parentage: 'Orange Sensation' × 'Circus'
A short, bushy grower, 2 ft (0·6 m.) high, with glossy foliage. Smallish but very showy flowers, brilliant orange with red shadings in a neat formation. May require protection against mildew. Unusual sharp fruity scent. **465**, p. 87.

'Pink Cameo', 'Climbing Cameo'   Cl.Min.
Rich rose-pink, 5 ft (1·5 m.) 1954
Raised by R. S. Moore, U.S.A.
Parentage: ('Sœur Thérèse' × 'Wilhelm') × 'Zee'
Grows from 3–5 ft (0·9–1·5 m.) high with small, glossy foliage. The small double, rich rose-pink flowers are produced in clusters. Has a long flowering season.

'Pink Elizabeth Arden' see **'Geisha'**

'Pink Favorite'   HT.
Rose-pink, 2½ ft (0·8 m.) 1956
Raised by G. J. Von Abrams, U.S.A.
Parentage: 'Juno' × ('George Arends' × 'New Dawn')
A vigorous upright spreading bush, 2½ ft (0·8 m.) high, with very healthy, handsome, very glossy bright green foliage. Large, full shapely blooms. clear rose-pink, deeper on outside of petals, fading slightly as they get older. The slightly fragrant flowers are generally borne 3 or more to the stem; if disbudded, this is one of the finest

---

Abbreviations and Symbols used in the text

Rose classifications

A.	Alba	HT.	Hybrid Tea
B.	Bourbon	MCl.	Modern, large-flowered climber
C.	Centifolia	Min.	Miniature
Ch.	China	Moss	Centifolia muscosa
Cl.	Climber	MSh.	Modern shrub
D.	Damask	P.	Penzance Sweet Brier
Fl.	Floribunda	R.	Rambler
G.	Gallica	Rg.	Rugosa
HM.	Hybrid Musk	Sp.	Species and first hybrids
HP.	Hybrid Perpetual	Sw.	Sweet Brier

Rose Awards and Societies

A.A.R.S.	All-America Rose Selection
A.G.M.	Award of Garden Merit
A.M.	Award of Merit
A.R.S.	American Rose Society
B.B.G.M.	Baden Baden Gold Medal, Germany
B.G.M.	Bagatelle Gold Medal, Paris
C.C.V.	Clay Challenge Vase for scent
C.M.	Certificate of Merit
D.F.P.	David Fuerstenberg Prize
F.C.C.	First Class Certificate
G.G.M.	Geneva Gold Medal
G.M.	Gold Medal
G.M.C.B.	Gold Medal City of Belfast
G.M.H.G.M.	Gertrude M. Hubbard Gold Medal
G.R.H.	Golden Rose of The Hague
G.T.A.B.	Golden Thorn Award Belfast
H.E.M.M.	The Henry Edland Memorial Medal for the most fragrant rose of the year
H.G.M.	The Hague Gold Medal
L.G.M.	Lyon Gold Medal, France
M.G.M.	Madrid Gold Medal
N.G.M.C.	National Gold Medal Certificate
P.G.M.	Portland Gold Medal, Oregon, U.S.A.
P.I.T.	President's International Trophy
R.B.	Prize for the most fragrant rose, Roeulx, Belgium
R.B.G.M.	Roeulx, Belgium, Gold Medal
R.G.M.	Rome Gold Medal
R.H.S.	The Royal Horticultural Society, London
R.N.R.S.	The Royal National Rose Society, Great Britain*
T.G.C.	Trial Ground Certificate
U.A.B.	The 'Uladh' Award for fragrance, Belfast

*National Rose Society awards, before 1965, are included here under R.N.R.S.

The illustration numbers are in **bold type** and the page numbers in light type preceded by p.

exhibition cultivars and is certainly one of the best bedding roses. Resistant to disease. **351**, p. 66.
P.G.M. 1957; A.M., R.H.S. 1962.

'Pink Grootendorst' Rg.
Bright pink, recurrent, 4–5 ft (1·2–1·5 m.)
Introduced by F. J. Grootendorst & Sons, Holland.
Parentage: 'F. J. Grootendorst' sport
Flowers are a bright cerise-pink, fading rather in the sun, double and fringed. A little less vigorous than the parent, but strong enough for most gardens and very floriferous. Excellent for cutting. **134**, p. 24.
A.M., R.H.S. 1953.

'Pink Heather' Min.
Lavender-pink, 10 in. (25·4 cm.) 1959
Raised by R. S. Moore, U.S.A.
Parentage: (*R. wichuraiana* × 'Floradora') × ('Violette' × 'Zee')
A bushy grower, 8–10 in. (20·3–25·4 cm.) high, with small glossy foliage. The very small double flowers are produced in clusters, clear lavender-pink. A profuse bloomer with some scent.

'Pink Nevada' see **'Marguerite Hilling', 178**, p. 33.

'Pink Parfait' Fl.
Pink, 2½ ft (0·8 m.) 1960
Raised by H. C. Swim, U.S.A.
Parentage: 'First Love' × 'Pinocchio'
A vigorous, healthy grower about 2½ ft (0·8 m.) in height with abundant semi-glossy foliage. Medium to light pink with pale yellow base, and some veining in petals, a little variable in colour according to the season, but charming at all times. Beautiful in form until half expanded when it opens out, with heads of several blooms. Prolific to the point of abundance from summer to autumn, and very weather resistant. A cultivar which has few prickles, a slight fragrance, and not prone to disease. **466**, p. 87.
P.G.M. 1959; A.A.R.S. 1961; G.M., R.N.R.S. 1962; A.M., R.H.S. 1963.

'Pink Perpétue' MCl.
Bright rose-pink, recurrent, 6–8 ft (1·8–2·4 m.) 1965
Raised by C. Gregory & Sons Ltd, England.
Parentage: 'Danse du Feu' × 'New Dawn'
A vigorous grower of restrained height with plentiful dark green glossy foliage. The medium sized double flowers are bright rose-pink, the reverse somewhat inclined to carmine. Slight fragrance. Freely produced in medium sized clusters. This is a recurrent blooming cultivar, exceptional in the autumn and excellent for low pillars or fences. **257**, p. 49.
C.M., R.N.R.S. 1964; B.G.M. 1964; A.M., R.H.S. 1966.

'Pink Peace' HT.
Deep pink, 3½ ft (1·1 m.) 1959
Raised by F. Meilland, France.
Parentage: ('Peace' × 'Monique') × ('Peace' × 'Mrs John Laing')
A vigorous, tall grower, at least 3½ ft (1·1 m.) high, with semi-glossy bronzy-green foliage. The large, somewhat cupped flowers are deep pink, sweetly scented but bear no resemblance to 'Peace' in shape. A useful cultivar for large beds, growing and flowering freely. **352**, p. 66.
G.G.M. 1959; R.G.M. 1959; A.M., R.H.S. 1959.

'Pink Sensation' HT.
Pink, 2½ ft + (0·8 m.) 1958
Discovered by H. Bos, U.S.A.
Parentage: 'Pink Lady' sport
A vigorous and bushy greenhouse cultivar with glossy foliage, 2½ ft (0·8 m.) and more in height. Flowers large, double, pink and fragrant. An excellent and popular rose for cutting.

'Pink Supreme' HT.
Bright pink, 3½ ft (1·1 m.) 1964
Raised by G. de Ruiter, Holland.
Parentage: 'Amor' × 'Peace'
A very vigorous, branching grower, 3½ ft (1·1 m.) high, with glossy light green foliage. The medium sized flowers are moderately full, rounded in shape, opening quickly, particularly in hot weather, are bright pink in colour and fragrant. Flowers are frequently borne in large trusses and are so freely produced that sometimes support is required after heavy rain. A few forked hazel branches or something akin are adequate and will not spoil a spectacular bed. Repeats quickly but may require protection where black spot is prevalent. **353**, p. 66.
C.M., R.N.R.S. 1963; A.M., R.H.S. 1967.

'Pink Wonder', 'Kalinka' Fl.
Glowing salmon, 2½ ft (0·8 m.) 1970
Raised by A. Meilland, France.
Parentage: 'Zambra' × ('Sarabande' × ('Goldilocks' × 'Fashion'))
An open, branching grower, 2½ ft (0·8 m.) high, with semi-glossy dark green foliage. The medium sized flowers are nicely shaped, glowing salmon in colour, freely produced usually singly, especially in autumn. Useful for bedding. Lightly scented. **467**, p. 88.

'Pixie', 'Little Princess', 'Princesita' Min.
White, 9 in. (22·9 cm.) 1940
Raised by J. de Vink, Holland.
Parentage: 'Ellen Poulsen' × 'Tom Thumb'
A dwarf compact plant, up to 9 in. (22·9 cm.) high, with very small, soft foliage. The small double flowers are white, tinted with shell-pink and are freely produced. Lightly scented.

'Pixie Rose' Min.
Glowing pink, 12 in. (30·5 cm.) 1961
Raised by P. Dot, Spain.
Parentage: 'Perla de Montserrat' × 'Coralín'
A dwarf, much branched plant, 9–12 in. (22·9–30·5 cm.) high, with very small, dark foliage. The small double flowers are glowing pink, deepening in the centre, and abundantly produced.

'Plentiful' Fl.
Deep pink, 2 ft (0·6 m.) 1960
Raised by E. B. LeGrice, England.
A short, branching grower, 2 ft (0·6 m.) high with medium green, glossy foliage. The flat, fully double, quartered flowers are a strong deep pink and so freely produced as to cause the stems to bend. Repeating quickly, this cultivar appeals to many with a preference for old fashioned roses allied to the performance of the moderns. Unfortunately unscented. **468**, p. 88.

'Polly Flinders' Min.
Cream, 8 in. (20·3 cm.) 1954
Raised by T. Robinson, England.
Parentage: 'Little Princess' (Poly) × 'Fashion'
A small bushy grower, 6–8 in. (15·2–20·3 cm.) high, with small double flowers, which are cream tinted coppery-pink, a variable shade. The slightly fragrant flowers last well.

'Polyantha Grandiflora' see *R. gentiliana*, **18**, p. 3.

'Pompom de Paris, Climbing' see **'Climbing Pompon de Paris', 268**, p. 50

'Pompon des Dames' see **'Petite de Hollande', 70**, p. 13.

'Pour Toi' see **'Para Ti'**

'Premier Amour' see **'First Love', 304**, p. 57.

'Première Ballerine' see **'Prima Ballerina', 354**, p. 66.

'Président de Sèze'   G.
Purplish-crimson, summer, 4 ft (1·2 m.) c. 1836
Introduced by Mme Hébert, France.
Shrub rose of medium vigour up to 4 ft (1·2 m.). Flowers large,
double, deep pinkish-purple to purplish-crimson, paler around the
edges, up to 4 in. (10·2 cm.) across, quartered. Scented. One of the
best of the Gallica roses for garden effect. Probably raised before
1836. **88**, p. 16.

'Prestige'   MSh.
Scarlet-red, recurrent, 6 ft (1·8 m.) 1957
Raised by R. Kordes, Germany.
Parentage: 'Rudolf Timm' × 'Fanal'
A moderately vigorous shrub up to 6 ft (1·8 m.). Flowers semi-
double, quite large and of hybrid tea type, up to 4 in. (10·2 cm.)
across, very bright scarlet-red, slightly scented. Mid-June, recur-
rent with good autumn flowering. A variety with attractive bronzy
foliage but may require protection from disease. **185**, p. 34.
C.M., R.N.R.S. 1957.

'Prima Ballerina', 'Première Ballerine'   HT.
Cherry-pink, 3 ft (0·9 m.) 1958
Raised by M. Tantau, Germany.
Parentage: seedling × 'Peace'
A very vigorous, upright grower, 3 ft (0·9 m.) high, with very
abundant, semi-glossy, coppery-green foliage. The flowers are of
exquisite shape when young, deep cherry-pink, paling slightly with
age and richly scented. Blooms profusely summer and autumn, with
a few between, very resistant to wet weather, a very fine bedding
rose which took some years to receive recognition. **354**, p. 66.
T.G.C., R.N.R.S. 1957; A.M., R.H.S. 1965.

'Prince Camille de Rohan'   HP.
Deep maroon, recurrent, 4 ft (1·2 m.) 1861
Raised by E. Verdier, France.
A bushy Hybrid Perpetual shrub of medium vigour only, usually
not over 4 ft (1·2 m.). Flowers double, deep velvety maroon with
deep red towards edge; scented. Free-flowering. Mid to late June
and recurrent. Stems not very strong and flowers tend to droop.
Interesting for its deep colour.

'Prince Charles'   B.
Dark purplish-crimson, early summer, 5 ft (1·5 m.) 1842
Vigorous Bourbon shrub up to 5 ft (1·5 m.). Flowers large dark
velvety purplish-crimson, double, fading to grey-violet, up to 4 in.
(10·2 cm.) across. Slight scent. Petals veined and rather crumpled.
Mid to late June but usually not recurrent. Leaves large with 7
leaflets. Nearly thornless. **101**, p. 18.

'Prince Charming'   Min.
Scarlet-crimson, 12 in. (30·5 cm.) 1953
Raised by J. de Vink, Holland.
Parentage: 'Ellen Poulsen' × 'Tom Thumb'
A dwarf compact plant, 8–12 in. (20·3–30·5 cm.) high, with red
tinted foliage. Small flowers, double; attractive in bud and opening
to rich scarlet-crimson. One of the best in this colour.

'Princesita' see **'Pixie'**

'Princess'   HT.
Vermilion, 2 ft (0·6 m.) 1964
Raised by Ets J. Laperrière, France.
Parentage: ('Peace' × 'Magicienne') × ('Independence' ×
'Radar')
A moderately vigorous grower, 2 ft (0·6 m.) high, with mat,
medium green foliage. The large blooms are produced singly, are
fully double with high pointed centres, vermilion but not so bright
as 'Super Star'. Fragrance faint. A good cultivar for exhibition
though not free enough in bloom for garden display. **355**, p. 66.

'Princess Chichibu'   Fl.
Pink, 2 ft + (0·6 m.) 1971
Raised by R. Harkness & Co. Ltd, England.
Parentage: ('Vera Dalton' × 'Highlight') × 'Merlin'
A fairly vigorous, branching grower, just over 2 ft (0·6 m.) high,
with dark green glossy foliage. The flowers are a combination of
rose-madder and soft porcelain-rose, with a light orange reverse, a
lively combination giving a general effect of deep rose with a light
salmon centre.

'Princess Margaret of England'   HT.
Bright rose-pink, 3 ft (0·9 m.) 1968
Raised by M. L. Meilland, France.
Parentage: 'Queen Elizabeth' × ('Peace' × 'Michèle Meilland')
A vigorous upright grower, 3 ft (0·9 m.) high with luxuriant medium
green foliage. The large double, high centred flowers, bright rose-

---

Abbreviations and Symbols used in the text

Rose classifications

A.	Alba	HT.	Hybrid Tea
B.	Bourbon	MCl.	Modern, large-flowered climber
C.	Centifolia	Min.	Miniature
Ch.	China	Moss	Centifolia muscosa
Cl.	Climber	MSh.	Modern shrub
D.	Damask	P.	Penzance Sweet Brier
Fl.	Floribunda	R.	Rambler
G.	Gallica	Rg.	Rugosa
HM.	Hybrid Musk	Sp.	Species and first hybrids
HP.	Hybrid Perpetual	Sw.	Sweet Brier

Rose Awards and Societies

A.A.R.S.	All-America Rose Selection
A.G.M.	Award of Garden Merit
A.M.	Award of Merit
A.R.S.	American Rose Society
B.B.G.M.	Baden Baden Gold Medal, Germany
B.G.M.	Bagatelle Gold Medal, Paris
C.C.V.	Clay Challenge Vase for scent
C.M.	Certificate of Merit
D.F.P.	David Fuerstenberg Prize
F.C.C.	First Class Certificate
G.G.M.	Geneva Gold Medal
G.M.	Gold Medal
G.M.C.B.	Gold Medal City of Belfast
G.M.H.G.M.	Gertrude M. Hubbard Gold Medal
G.R.H.	Golden Rose of The Hague
G.T.A.B.	Golden Thorn Award Belfast
H.E.M.M.	The Henry Edland Memorial Medal for the most fragrant rose of the year
H.G.M.	The Hague Gold Medal
L.G.M.	Lyon Gold Medal, France
M.G.M.	Madrid Gold Medal
N.G.M.C.	National Gold Medal Certificate
P.G.M.	Portland Gold Medal, Oregon, U.S.A.
P.I.T.	President's International Trophy
R.B.	Prize for the most fragrant rose, Roeulx, Belgium
R.B.G.M.	Roeulx, Belgium, Gold Medal
R.G.M.	Rome Gold Medal
R.H.S.	The Royal Horticultural Society, London
R.N.R.S.	The Royal National Rose Society, Great Britain*
T.G.C.	Trial Ground Certificate
U.A.B.	The 'Uladh' Award for fragrance, Belfast

*National Rose Society awards, before 1965, are included here under R.N.R.S.

The illustration numbers are in **bold type** and the page numbers
in light type preceded by p.

pink in colour, do not fade. Repeats very quickly and has some scent. Should be useful for massed beds. **356**, p. 66.

'Princess Michiko'   Fl.
Bright coppery-orange, 2½ ft (0·8 m.) 1966
Raised by A. Dickson & Sons Ltd, N. Ireland.
Parentage: 'Circus' × 'Spartan'
A vigorous, upright grower, 2½ ft (0·8 m.) high, with somewhat handsome coppery foliage. The semi-double flowers are bright coppery-orange becoming duller with age, sometimes assuming salmon shades. May require protection against black spot. **469**, p. 88.
T.G.C., R.N.R.S. 1965.

'Prominent', 'Korp'   HT.
Signal-red, 3 ft (0·9 m.) 1971
Raised by R. Kordes, Germany.
Parentage: 'Königen der Rosen' × 'Zorina'
A strong, very upright grower with dark green foliage. The medium sized flowers are a startling shade of signal-red with orange-scarlet reverse, very striking. Flowers are produced freely, mostly single with good stems, so should be useful for cut flowers and for growing under glass for that purpose. Holds its colour well but has little scent. A cross between a Hybrid Tea and a Floribunda and illustrated in the latter group, this has now been classified as HT. Though exhibited in 1970 at the Chelsea Show, England, as 'Prominent', it is understood that this name may be changed. **470**, p. 88.
C.M., R.N.R.S. 1970.

'Prosperity'   HM.
White, recurrent, 5 ft (1·5 m.) 1919
Raised by Rev. J. H. Pemberton, England.
Parentage: 'Marie-Jeanne' × 'Perle des Jardins'
Vigorous Hybrid Musk shrub rose with upright growth up to 5 ft (1·5 m.) and sprays of flowers like a large Polyantha rose. Flowers semi-double, small to medium in size, in bud creamy-white flushed pale pink, opening to ivory-white, slightly flushed with pale lemon-yellow towards centre, strongly scented. Free-flowering. Late June to mid-July, recurrent. Not so commonly grown as 'Penelope' (**122**, p. 22) but still a fine garden shrub. **123**, p. 23.

Provence Rose see *R.* × *centifolia*

'Purity'   Cl.
White, recurrent, 12 ft (3·7 m.) 1917
Raised by Hoopes, Bro. & Thomas Co., U.S.A.
Parentage: unnamed seedling × 'Mme Caroline Testout'
Vigorous climber with long, very thorny, rambler stems and light green, glossy foliage, indicating *R. wichuraiana* in its ancestry. Flowers semi-double, rather loose and open, large, pure white, free-flowering, scented; late June to mid-July and only slightly recurrent. Now rarely planted but still useful for growing up into an old tree for its abundance of pure white flowers.

'Purple Elf'   Min.
Crimson-purple, 10 in. (25·4 cm.) 1963
Raised by R. S. Moore, U.S.A.
Parentage: 'Violette' × 'Zee'
A dwarf, bushy grower, 8–10 in. (20·3–25·4 cm.) high with glossy foliage. The small double open flowers are crimson-purple.

Quatre Saisons Rose see *R. damascena semperflorens*

'Queen Elizabeth'   Fl.
Clear pink, 5 ft (1·5 m.) 1954
Raised by Dr W. E. Lammerts, U.S.A.
Parentage: 'Charlotte Armstrong' × 'Floradora'
A cultivar of exceptional vigour, usually 5 ft (1·5 m.) high but frequently more, almost thornless growths and abundant dark green glossy foliage. The well formed flowers have high centres when young, becoming cupped later, and are good clear pink, paling slightly with age. A profuse bloomer in summer and autumn, sometimes as single flowers, frequently in trusses. Good weather resistance but little scent. Frequently used for cutting. Tends to produce a few blind shoots early in the year, these however break and flower normally. An exceptionally popular cultivar which can be seen in many public and private gardens and at the headquarters of the R.N.R.S., where the photograph was taken, it is used as a hedge. **471**, p. 88.
A.A.R.S. 1955; P.I.T. and G.M., R.N.R.S. 1955; G.M.H.G.M., A.R.S. 1957; N.G.M.C., A.R.S. 1960; G.R.H. 1968.

'Queen of Denmark' see **'Königin von Dänemark', 66**, p. 12.

'Queen of Roses' see **'Königin der Rosen', 323**, p. 61.

'Radway Sunrise'   MSh.
Flame-cerise, recurrent, 5 ft (1·5 m.) 1962
Raised by Waterhouse Nurseries Ltd, England.
Parentage: 'Masquerade' seedling
Modern shrub rose, of medium vigour, up to 5 ft (1·5 m.). Of floribunda type. Flowers in large clusters, single, deep flame-cerise, with buff-yellow centre, outside flecked with terracotta-pink, slightly scented. Mid-June, recurrent with good autumn flowering. A flower of unusual and striking colouring. **186**, p. 35.

'Raubritter'   MSh.Cl.
Purplish-pink, summer, 8 ft (2·4 m.) 1936
Raised by W. Kordes, Germany.
Parentage: 'Daisy Hill' × 'Solarium'
Modern shrub or pillar rose of hybrid 'Macrantha' origin, vigorous up to 8 ft (2·4 m.) of loose sprawling habit. Flowers semi-double, rather globular with incurved petals, clear purplish-pink, singly or in small clusters. Slightly scented, very free-flowering. Rather late flowering, in late June to mid-July but not recurrent. Can be used as a trailer for covering old trees, stumps or low walls.

'Raymond Chenault'   MCl.
Scarlet-red, recurrent, 10 ft (3 m.) 1960
Raised by W. Kordes, Germany.
Parentage: *R. kordesii* × 'Montezuma'
Kordesii climber of medium vigour. The flowers are of hybrid tea type, semi-double, quite large, up to 4 in. (10·2 cm.) across, in clusters, bright scarlet-red, scented and free-flowering. Mid-June and recurrent. Foliage dark green, glossy.
T.G.C., R.N.R.S. 1961.

'Red Dandy'   Fl.
Scarlet, 3 ft (0·9 m.) 1959
Raised by A. Norman, England.
Parentage: 'Ena Harkness' × 'Karl Herbst'
A vigorous, upright grower, 3 ft (0·9 m.) high with slightly glossy, mid-green foliage. The medium sized flowers are well formed, full, velvety-scarlet in colour, deepening to crimson. Freely produced in large trusses over a long season. Resists wet weather well and also appears to be disease resistant. Slight scent. **472**, p. 88.
C.M., R.N.R.S. 1960; A.M., R.H.S. 1963.

'Red Devil', 'Cœur d'Amour'   HT.
Scarlet, 3½ ft (1·1 m.) 1967
Raised by A. Dickson & Sons Ltd, N. Ireland.

Parentage: 'Silver Lining' × 'Prima Ballerina'
A very strong, vigorous grower, 3½ ft (1·1 m.) high, with handsome, abundant, glossy foliage, with crimson tints especially when young. The deep glowing scarlet blooms have a lighter reverse, are very full, with high pointed centres and ideal for exhibition. Fragrance is good and this would be a good garden rose also were it not so intolerant of rain, a climatic hazard which does not occur in all countries. **357**, p. 67.
C.M., R.N.R.S. 1965; G.M., Japan 1967; G.M.C.B. 1969.

'Red Dorothy Perkins' see **'Excelsa'**

'Red Imp', 'Maid Marion', 'Mon Tresor'   Min.
Scarlet-crimson, 9 in. (22·9 cm.) 1951
Raised by J. de Vink, Holland.
Parentage: 'Ellen Poulsen' × 'Tom Thumb'
An upright, bushy grower, 9 in. (22·9 cm.) high with small double flowers which become very flat on opening, rich velvety scarlet-crimson with good texture.

'Red Lion'   HT.
Rose-red, 4 ft (1·2 m.) 1965
Raised by S. McGredy IV, N, Ireland.
Parentage: 'Kordes' Perfecta' × 'Detroiter'
A vigorous grower, somewhat slender in habit, about 4 ft (1·2 m.) high with bronzy-green, glossy foliage. The large double flowers have a high centre and are produced on good stems, and consequently are useful for exhibition. Rose-red, they retain colour well and have a good fragrance. This variety has been found suitable for growing under glass. **358**, p. 67.
T.G.C., R.N.R.S. 1964.

'Red New Dawn' see **'Etendard'**, **204**, p. 38.

'Red Planet'   HT.
Crimson, 3½ ft (1·1 m.) 1970
Raised by A. Dickson & Sons Ltd, N. Ireland.
Parentage: 'Red Devil' × ('Detroiter' × seedling)
A vigorous, upright grower, 3½ ft (1·1 m.) high, with dark green, glossy foliage. The large, full, crimson flowers have a paler reverse, are frequently borne singly, occasionally in trusses. This cultivar was impressive on trial in 1969 but less so in the following year.
P.I.T., R.N.R.S. 1969; G.M., R.N.R.S. 1969.

'Red Queen', 'Liebestraum'   HT.
Cherry-red, 3 ft (0·9 m.) 1968
Raised by W. Kordes, Germany.
Parentage: 'Königin der Rosen' × 'Liberty Bell'
A very tall, vigorous upright growing cultivar with medium green foliage and large, very full, cherry red blooms, borne several together. May be useful for exhibition, but some of the larger flowers are inclined to be top heavy. **359**, p. 67.
T.G.C., R.N.R.S. 1968.

Red Rose of Lancaster see **'Officinalis'**, **86**, p. 16.

'Redgold', 'Rouge et Or'   Fl.
Bright yellow and red, 2½ ft (0·8 m.) 1966
Raised by A. Dickson & Sons Ltd, N. Ireland.
Parentage: ('Karl Herbst' × 'Masquerade') × ('Faust' × 'Piccadilly')
A vigorous, branching grower, 2½ ft (0·8 m.) high with small, slightly glossy, medium green foliage. The moderately full flowers are bright yellow flushed cherry-red, very bright when young, dulling off to pinkish-orange. A prolific bloomer in summer and autumn, resists wet reasonably well and has a slight scent. **473**, p. 89.
C.M., R.N.R.S. 1966.

'Reine Blanche' see **'Hebe's Lip'**, **79**, p. 14.

'Reine des Neiges' see **'Frau Karl Druschki'**, **111**, p. 20.

'Reine des Roses' see **'Königin der Rosen'**, **323**, p. 61.

'Reine des Violettes'   HP.
Violet-purple, recurrent, 6 ft (1·8 m.) 1860
Raised by Millet-Malet, France.
Parentage: 'Pius IX' seedling
Vigorous Hybrid Perpetual up to 6 ft (1·8 m.). Flowers deep violet-purple, fading to Parma violet, petals paler on the underside, velvety, double, of medium size, opening flat and quartered but with a small button eye, resembling a Gallica in shape of flower and in its colour, scented. Mid to late June, recurrent in summer and early autumn. Foliage rather grey-green. **114**, p. 20.

'Rêve d'Or'   Cl.
Buff-yellow, recurrent, 10 ft (3 m.) 1869
Raised by Veuve Ducher, France.
Parentage: 'Mme Schultz' seedling
Vigorous climber with flowers of hybrid tea type and glossy deep green foliage, tinted reddish when young. Flowers double, large, well-shaped, buff-yellow fading to butter-yellow with outward rolled petals on outside buds with some red. Slightly scented. Mid to late June but recurrent. A rose which grows best on a warm wall. **220**, p. 40.

Abbreviations and Symbols used in the text

Rose classifications

A.	Alba	HT.	Hybrid Tea
B.	Bourbon	MCl.	Modern, large-flowered climber
C.	Centifolia	Min.	Miniature
Ch.	China	Moss	Centifolia muscosa
Cl.	Climber	MSh.	Modern shrub
D.	Damask	P.	Penzance Sweet Brier
Fl.	Floribunda	R.	Rambler
G.	Gallica	Rg.	Rugosa
HM.	Hybrid Musk	Sp.	Species and first hybrids
HP.	Hybrid Perpetual	Sw.	Sweet Brier

Rose Awards and Societies

A.A.R.S.	All-America Rose Selection
A.G.M.	Award of Garden Merit
A.M.	Award of Merit
A.R.S.	American Rose Society
B.B.G.M.	Baden Baden Gold Medal, Germany
B.G.M.	Bagatelle Gold Medal, Paris
C.C.V.	Clay Challenge Vase for scent
C.M.	Certificate of Merit
D.F.P.	David Fuerstenberg Prize
F.C.C.	First Class Certificate
G.G.M.	Geneva Gold Medal
G.M.	Gold Medal
G.M.C.B.	Gold Medal City of Belfast
G.M.H.G.M.	Gertrude M. Hubbard Gold Medal
G.R.H.	Golden Rose of The Hague
G.T.A.B.	Golden Thorn Award Belfast
H.E.M.M.	The Henry Edland Memorial Medal for the most fragrant rose of the year
H.G.M.	The Hague Gold Medal
L.G.M.	Lyon Gold Medal, France
M.G.M.	Madrid Gold Medal
N.G.M.C.	National Gold Medal Certificate
P.G.M.	Portland Gold Medal, Oregon, U.S.A.
P.I.T.	President's International Trophy
R.B.	Prize for the most fragrant rose, Roeulx, Belgium
R.B.G.M.	Roeulx, Belgium, Gold Medal
R.G.M.	Rome Gold Medal
R.H.S.	The Royal Horticultural Society, London
R.N.R.S.	The Royal National Rose Society, Great Britain*
T.G.C.	Trial Ground Certificate
U.A.B.	The 'Uladh' Award for fragrance, Belfast

*National Rose Society awards, before 1965, are included here under R.N.R.S.

The illustration numbers are in **bold type** and the page numbers in light type preceded by p.

'Réveil Dijonnais'   Cl.Sh.
Scarlet-crimson, recurrent, 8 ft (2·4 m.) 1931
Raised by Buatois, France.
Parentage: 'Eugène Fürst' × 'Constance'
Climber or pillar rose of medium vigour only, with *R. foetida* blood through the Hybrid Tea 'Constance'. Featured as a shrub in the public gardens of The Hague, Holland, with brilliant effect. Flowers of hybrid tea type, semi-double, large up to 5 in. (12·7 cm.) across, bright scarlet-crimson with yellow centre giving bicolor effect, scented, free-flowering. Mid to late June and recurrent. A very striking rose for its colour that usually does best in a warm summer or against a warm wall. Foliage deep glossy green but subject to black spot. **221**, p. 40.
P.G.M. 1929.

'Ripples'   Fl.
Pale lilac-purple, 2¼ ft (0·7 m.) 1971
Raised by E. B. LeGrice, England.
Parentage: ('Tantau's Triumph' × 'Marjorie LeGrice') × 'Africa Star'
A bushy grower, about 2¼ ft (0·7 m.) high with small, light green, mat foliage. The frilled open flowers are a combination of pansy-violet and rose, the effect being of pale lilac-purple. This very free-flowering cultivar may require protection against mildew.

'Ritter von Barmstede'   MCl.
Cerise-pink, recurrent, 10 ft (3 m.) 1959
Raised by W. Kordes, Germany.
Vigorous Kordesii climber or pillar rose. Flowers semi-double in clusters, deep cerise-pink with small white eye, scented. Mid to late June and recurrent throughout summer. Foliage glossy, rather light green, particularly disease-resistant. Probably the deepest pink climber in the recurrent Kordesii group. **258**, p. 49.
A.M., R.H.S. 1963.

'Roaming'   Fl.
Reddish-pink, 3½ ft (1·1 m.) 1970–71
Raised by J. Sanday Ltd, England.
Parentage: 'Vera Dalton' × 'Super Star'
A bushy, compact grower, 3½ ft (1·1 m.) high with dark green, mat foliage. The moderately full flowers are reddish-pink in colour, either borne singly or in trusses. No scent.
T.G.C., R.N.R.S. 1970.

'Rob Roy'   Fl.
Scarlet-crimson, 3½ ft (1·1 m.) 1971
Raised by J. Cocker & Sons Ltd, Scotland.
Parentage: 'Evelyn Fison' × 'Wendy Cussons'
A tall fairly upright vigorous grower, with dark green, semi-glossy foliage. The moderately full flowers are a rich scarlet-crimson in colour, slightly fragrant and are produced freely over a long season, several together. **474**, p. 89.
T.G.C., R.N.R.S. 1969.

'Robert le Diable'   C.
Dark purplish-crimson, summer, 4 ft (1·2 m.)
Shrub of medium vigour and rather loose growth, not often over 4 ft (1·2 m), usually needing support. Flowers dark purplish-crimson, maturing to a slaty-purple flushed with deeper purple, fully double with outer petals recurved, fading to Parma violet, medium-large and free-flowering. Scented. Mid to late June. A flower of so many tints, changing so much as it matures that it is difficult to describe, it is thought to have been a hybrid between a Provence and Gallica but origin not known.

'Robin'   Min.
Deep cherry-red, 12 in. (30·5 cm.) 1956
Raised by P. Dot, Spain.
Parentage: 'Perla de Montserrat' × 'Perla de Alcanada'
A vigorous, dwarf 12 in. (30·5 cm.) high, with dull green foliage. The small double flowers are deep cherry-red, produced in clusters and recurrent flowering. A gay, pleasing cultivar.

'Roger Lambelin'   HP.
Deep crimson-red, recurrent, 5 ft (1·5 m.) 1890
Discovered by Veuve Schwartz, France.
Parentage: 'Fisher Holmes' sport
A Hybrid Perpetual rose up to 5 ft (1·5 m.), generally not very vigorous. Flowers full-petalled, reminiscent of a dark carnation, deep crimson-red without a purple tinge, with white edge sometimes extending into the flower, fairly large, scented. Mid to late June and slightly recurrent. A more open flower than in 'Baron Girod de l'Ain' (**106**, p. 19) and a slightly richer colour. It needs good cultivation to produce good flowers but then they are very lovely and worth the effort. Rather subject to black spot and often with a weak stalk. A very distinct flower, no modern rose is quite like it. **115**, p. 20.

ROSA

R. × ***alba***, White Rose of York   A.
White or blush-pink, summer, 8 ft (2·4 m.)
Parentage: probably *R. corymbifera* × *R. gallica*
The parent of the great race of Alba roses, which have given us some of the finest of all midsummer flowering shrubs. Alba roses are distinguished by the erect, very thorny growth and the rather glaucous foliage, being sometimes known as Tree roses. The flowers are mostly semi-double with pointed buds and do not include the dark dusky purple or the striped roses of some of the other groups. *R.* × *alba* is one of the oldest of all garden roses, having been known both to the Greeks and Romans and its origin is unknown although Dr C. C. Hurst recorded that it had been found growing wild in the U.S.S.R. in the Crimea and thought that the hybrid may have originated there as a natural hybrid. Later chromosomal evidence suggests the parentage given above. They are very persistent in growth under conditions of neglect and very long-lived but, like most other shrubs, will repay good cultivation and some pruning with more vigorous healthy growth and larger flowers. The semi-double form has been distinguished as the variety *semiplena*, a pale pink double form as *incarnata*, and a semi-double white as *suaveolens*. This is one of the roses grown at Kazanlik in Bulgaria for distilling the perfume Attar of Roses but hardly differs from the variety *semiplena* with which it may be synonymous. *R.* × *alba* may then be described as follows:

Vigorous shrub up to 8 ft (2·4 m.) making thickset bushes with prickly growth. Flowers semi-double, white or pale blush-pink, medium in size, 2½–3 in. (6·4–7·6 cm.) across, showing good boss of golden stamens in centre, scented. Mid to late June but usually not recurrent. Foliage grey-green or glaucous with 5–7 leaflets, broadly oval or ovate, toothed, wrinkled. Hips bright red, oblong, about ¾ in. (1·9 cm.) long.

R. × ***alba incarnata*** see **'Maidens' Blush'**, **67**, p. 12.

R. alpina see ***R. pendulina***

R. altaica see ***R. spinosissima altaica***, **52**, p. 10.

R. × ***anemonoides***, *R. sinica* 'Anemone'   Cl.
Pale pink, early summer, 15 ft (4·6 m.) 1895
Raised by J. C. Schmidt, Germany.

Parentage: *R. laevigata* × possibly *R.* × *odorata*

Vigorous climber up to 15 ft (4·6 m.) but best grown on a south facing warm wall. Flowers single, clear shell-pink with overlapping petals, about 4 in. (10·2 cm.) across. Early-flowering, late May to late June, floriferous over a long season but not recurrent. Slightly scented. Foliage rather sparse on long shoots which require to be carefully tied in. Rather sensitive to mildew. There is a wonderful specimen against the big wall in the Savill Garden, Windsor Great Park, England, and it is such a beautiful rose that it should be grown where there is a suitable site, such as against a wall or over an old tree. **196**, p. 36.

A.M., R.H.S. 1900.

R. × **anemonoides 'Ramona'** is a sport with deeper carmine-pink flowers which originated in California, U.S.A. in 1913, otherwise similar in growth. **197**, p. 36.

A.M., R.H.S. 1950.

R. banksiae   Sp:Cl.

Creamy-white or pale yellow, early summer, 30 ft (9·1 m.)

Country of origin: W. China.

Climbing rose, very vigorous, best on a south facing wall, reaching up to 30 ft (9·1 m.). Flowers white or pale yellow, single or double, small but borne in large clusters of hanging sprays. Early-flowering late May to mid-June but not recurrent. Stems almost thornless, foliage fresh yellow-green.

Flowers are produced on the second or third year of growth off older trailing shoots so pruning should consist only of removal of very old or dead branches and some thinning out of surplus shoots since it is important to get good ripening of wood to secure good flowering. Young plants need not be pruned at all until they have reached the top of their support. In the Riviera, and warmer climates than Britain, they are excellent, covering old trees and may have thousands of blooms. The following are grown.

R. banksiae alba-plena see **R. banksiae banksiae, 1**, p. 1.

R. banksiae banksiae   Sp.Cl.

White, early summer

Better known as variety *alba-plena* and the first form to be introduced in 1803 by William Kerr from a Canton garden and named after Lady Banks. This is the type although almost certainly not a wild plant. Flowers double, pure white, strongly scented as of violets, globular, about 1 in. (2·5 cm.) across like round buttons in large clusters. **1**, p. 1.

R. banksiae lutea   Sp.Cl.

Yellow, early summer

Flowers small, double, deep butter-yellow, scented, although not so strongly as the double white. Introduced by J. D. Parks for Horticultural Society of London and first flowered in Britain in 1824. Probably the most free-flowering form. Recommended for planting with pink forms of *Clematis montana*. **2**, p. 1.

R. banksiae lutescens   Sp.Cl.

Pale yellow, early summer

Flowers single, pale creamy-yellow. Strongly scented. Probably introduced to England only in 1870 from La Mortola, a famous Riviera garden. **3**, p. 1.

R. banksiae normalis   Sp.

Flowers single, white, strongly scented. The original wild plant from W. China where it is native to mountain ranges 5,000 ft

(1524 m.) high in Yunnan, Shensi and Hupeh. Mr G. Thomas gives a possible record of its introduction to a Scottish castle garden in 1796 where it never flowered and it was only recognized when a cutting from it flowered in a Riviera garden.

R. berberifolia see **Hulthemia persica**

R. × **bifera** see **R. damascena semperflorens**

R. × **borboniana**   B.Sh.

Pink shades, 4–6 ft (1·2–1·8 m.)

Country of origin: Isle of Réunion

Parentage: (*R. chinensis semperflorens* × *R. gigantea*) × hybrids of *R. gallica* and *R. moschata*

A group hybrid name for the older crosses of *R. chinensis semperflorens* and *R. gigantea* with hybrids of *R. gallica* and *R. moschata*, a complicated parentage for a very varying group. It is said that the first Bourbon rose originated in the Isle of Réunion (then known as Bourbon), from a cross between the Pink autumn Damask rose and the Parsons pink China form of *R. chinensis* and had deep rosy-red semi-double flowers. Seeds from these were sent to France in 1819 and from them and subsequent crosses the group was raised. It is characterized by its late summer and autumn flowering as well as in early summer and formed the parents of the Hybrid Perpetuals and through them the Hybrid Teas. The flowers are mostly globular, scented and with infolding petals and the stems with stout prickles.

R. bracteata, The Macartney Rose   Sp.Cl.R.
White 12 ft (3·7 m.)
Country of origin: E. China.
Vigorous rambler or climber, sometimes grown as a large loose
shrub up to 8 ft (2·4 m.) with hard pruning. Flowers large, single,
up to 4 in. (10·2 cm.) across, pure white, silky, with large golden
boss of stamens, scented. Flowers borne singly on short stalks. Bracts
large and leafy around buds. Rather late flowering, early July and
occasionally throughout summer. Stems stout, downy, prickly.
Foliage light green, glossy, resistant to black spot; almost evergreen,
in warmer countries quite evergreen, up to 9 leaflets. Tender
and needs to be grown against a warm wall in most counties, but
along south coast of Britain it can be grown successfully as a large
shrub. In warmer countries it is rampant and has naturalized over
parts of the south-east United States. Introduced from China in
1793 by Lord Macartney, head of the British mission then in China
and collected by Sir George Staunton, from one of the coastal
provinces at a time when very few Europeans were able to botanize
in China. A parent of 'Mermaid' (**252**, p. 48).

R. brunonii see **R. moschata nepalensis**

R. brunonii 'La Mortola' see **R. moschata nepalensis
'La Mortola', 29**, p. 6.

R. californica   Sp.
Deep pink, 8 ft (2·4 m.)
Country of origin: U.S.A.
A vigorous shrub with single flowers, deep pink, 1½ in. (3·8 cm.)
across, in clusters. Mid-June to early July. Foliage delicate. Stems
with hooked spines. A variable species. More often grown is *R.
californica* 'Plena', a form with abundant semi-double flowers of deep
pink. It makes a bush 8 ft (2·4 m.) high and as much across covered
with pleasantly scented flowers cascading downwards on the long
pendulous shoots. As they mature they become a bit untidy and
assume a pale purplish-tinge but the abundance of flowers makes
up for this fault. A valuable plant where there is plenty of space.
Foliage small and delicate. **4**, p. 1.
A.M., R.H.S. 1958.

R. canina, Dog Rose   Sp.
Pink, summer, 12 ft (3·7 m.)
Countries of origin: N. Europe including Britain.
Vigorous shrub, very prickly with stout stems, very variable and
widespread throughout Britain and N. Europe as well as W. Asia.
Some botanists have considered *R. canina* as aggregate name for a
large group which they have split into numerous species but since this
is not of horticultural interest they are all considered here under
the name *canina*. Flowers single, pale blush to deeper pink, 1½–2 in.
(3·8–5·1 cm.) across, in clusters, scented. Foliage toothed all round
margin; hips oval, scarlet, conspicuous. In gardens chiefly used as
understock for budding or grafting other roses but tending to sucker
freely and now partly superseded by multiflora and other stocks.
Parent of such hybrids as *R. × hibernica* (**22**, p. 5) and *R. × collina*
'Andersonii', sometimes known as *R. × andersonii*, with deeper pink
flowers, very free-flowering.

R. × centifolia, 'Rose des Peintres', The Provence   C.
or Cabbage Rose
Deep pink, 5 ft (1·5 m.)
Considered to be a complex hybrid which arose between the 16th
and 18th centuries, possibly containing in its parentage the four
species, *R. gallica*, *R. phoenicia*, *R. moschata* and *R. canina*. Its forms
were raised in Holland from many crosses over a long period.
  The typical *R. centifolia* is a loose-growing shrub of medium vigour
only, generally not over 5 ft (1·5 m.). The long shoots bear large
prickles of varying sizes, some being big hooked thorns. Flower large,

fully double, deep pink with a slight purplish hue towards centre,
rather globular and fully petalled, strongly scented, with long
projecting sepals. Mid-June to early July, not recurrent. Foliage
with large leaflets, broadly toothed. Flowers are heavy and with
foliage tend to droop, a pose well shown by the Old Dutch painters.
Strongly scented. *R. × centifolia* is sterile and most of the cultivars
have arisen as sports. The Centifolia roses need good cultivation
and flower best in a warm season.

R. × centifolia alba see **'Mme Hardy'**

R. × centifolia 'Bullata'   C.
Deep pink, summer, 4 ft (1·2 m.)
Distinguished by the large, bullate leaflets puckered like the leaves
of a Cos lettuce or a primrose and bronze-tinted when young.
Thought to have originated about 1801 and portrayed by Redouté,
also known as 'Rose à Feuilles de Laitue'. An interesting curiosity
for its distinct foliage, otherwise no more beautiful than *R. × centifolia* from which it probably arose as a sport. Mid-June to early July,
not recurrent.

R. × centifolia 'Cristata', 'Chapeau de Napoléon',   C.
  'Crested Moss'
Deep pink, summer, 4 ft (1·2 m.)
Distinguished by the great crested wings to the calyx which give
the buds the appearance of a three-cornered cockaded hat; the
wings are so large that the bud seems almost enveloped in greenery.
Flower pink as in *R. × centifolia*, but slightly smaller. Usually not
quite so vigorous a grower; this is recorded as being noticed first
about 1820. Worth growing for the fantastic buds. This is not
regarded as a true Moss rose and Bunyard described its crests as 'an
exaggerated development of the sepal margins'.

R. × centifolia minor see **'Petite de Hollande', 70**, p. 13.

R. × centifolia 'Muscosa', Common Moss   Moss Sh.
Pink, summer, 4 ft (1·2 m.)
Moss rose of *centifolia* type, a sport from *R. × centifolia*. Shrub of
medium vigour, usually not much over 4 ft (1·2 m.). Flower clear
pink and scented as in its parent but buds well mossed with long
calyx and some reddish colouring in the moss. Mid to late June,
not recurrent. One of the most interesting and charming of the old
shrub roses as well as being very fragrant. Too rarely seen now, this
rose was known probably at the end of the seventeenth century.

R. × centifolia 'Muscosa Alba'   Moss Sh.
White, summer, 4 ft (1·2 m.)
Moss rose of *centifolia* type and probably a direct sport from it.
Shrub of medium vigour not often over 4 ft (1·2 m.). Flower pure
white, but with slight blush towards centre and with thinner petals
than type. Buds very mossy as in the Common Moss. An old rose
known possibly at the end of the seventeenth century. Also known
and listed as 'Shailer's White Moss' but the sport from which this is
grown did not originate till 1788. It is possible, however, for two
similar sports to have occurred and this may have happened in this
case.

R. × centifolia pomponia see **'De Meaux'**

R. × centifolia 'Variegata'   C.
White and lilac-pink, summer, 4 ft (1·2 m.)
Sometimes known as 'Village Maid'. A sport from *R. × centifolia*
distinguished by the creamy white flowers streaked with pale lilac-
pink. Thought to have arisen near Angers, France about 1825 and
also known according to Mr G. Thomas as 'Belle des Jardins', 'La

Rubanée', 'Cottage Maid', 'Panachée à fleur double', 'La Belle Villageoise', 'Dometil Beccard', 'Dominic Boccardo', but not very often grown now although it is quite a vigorous and free-flowering bush. The petals are thinner than in *R.* × *centifolia* and the flowers do not last so long. Mid-June to early July, not recurrent.

R. chinensis, China Rose   Sp.Cl.
Blush-pink, recurrent, 20 ft (6·1 m.)
Country of origin: China.
Vigorous climber originally introduced from China in the form of garden varieties which were important parents of our modern group of roses for their introduction of perpetual flowering. The wild species is probably unknown in cultivation. Its flowers are single, blush-pink, pink or crimson, about 2 in. (5·1 cm.) across, but larger in cultivars and hybrids, leaflets rather small, shining, ovate to oblong with up to 5 leaflets.

Varieties known from Chinese gardens and early introduced include 'Blush China', flowers small, rose-pink, introduced possibly during the 1750's; 'Crimson China', flowers bright crimson, early introduced, possibly dates from 1733; 'Slater's Crimson China', dwarf, flowers semi-double, deep crimson, strongly scented, perpetual-flowering, introduced by G. Slater of Leytonstone, England, about 1792. This last rose was reproduced in Curtis's Bot. Mag. t.286 of 1894 as *Rosa semperflorens*, the 'Ever-Blooming Rose', when it was grown as a greenhouse plant not over 3 ft (0·9 m.) tall. For further hybrids see under *R.* × *odorata*.

R. chinensis minima 'Rouletii' see 'Rouletii'

R. chinensis mutabilis see 'Mutabilis'

R. chinensis viridiflora see 'Viridiflora', **127**, p. 22.

R. cooperi, Cooper's Burmese Rose   Sp.Cl.
White, summer, 30 ft (9·1 m.)
Countries of origin: N.E. Burma, S.W. China.
Very vigorous climber, but slightly tender in colder areas, up to 30 ft (9·1 m.) and as much across. Flowers large, borne singly, white with slightly pointed broad wedge-shaped petals, overlapping only slightly at base, single with good boss of yellow stamens in centre, up to 4 in. (10·2 cm.) across. Formerly considered as a variety of *R. gigantea* and possibly a natural hybrid. The plant sometimes suffers damage in very cold winters but it is slightly hardier than *R. gigantea*. Collected by Mr R. E. Cooper, it is recorded as having grown first at the then National Rose Society's Trial Ground, at Haywards Heath, and was received there about 1931. **5**, p. 1.

R. × *coryana* see 'Coryana', **154**, p. 28.

R. damascena, Damask Rose   D.Sh.
White to deep pink, 5 ft (1·5 m.)
Dr Hurst, the famous rose geneticist, considered that the Summer Damask roses were derived from *R. gallica* × *R. phoenicia*, a strong climber with white flowers in clusters from Turkey and Syria, while the Autumn Damask *R.* × *bifera* came from *R. gallica* crossed with *R. moschata*. They are obviously as a group closely related to the Centifolias and probably had at least one parent in common. They do not include the deep crimson-purples of the Gallica roses but have flowers more in shades of white and pink, mostly large and fragrant. Their foliage is usually a soft grey-green, downy beneath, the leaflets oval and simply toothed, usually 5 to a leaf. The branches are very prickly with hooked spines as well as prickly bristles and the hips are pear-shaped and bristly.

The original *R. damascena* is a vigorous shrub up to 8 ft (2·4 m.). Flowers are borne in large clusters, semi-double, variable in colour, blush-white to deep pink, the pedicels being long and covered with

glandular bristles and small prickles; fragrant. This is still a good garden rose but is generally surpassed by that known as 'Blush Damask'. For history of the Damasks see the introductory chapter.

R. damascena semperflorens, *R.* × *bifera*   D.
Deep pink, summer and autumn, 4 ft (1·2 m.)
Quatre Saisons Rose. Shrub rose of medium vigour up to 4 ft (1·2 m.). Flowers deep pink, double, slightly quartered, mid-June but also recurrent in autumn up to October. A very old rose, possibly the original Autumn Damask rose.

R. damascena trigintipetala   D.
Deep rose-pink, summer, 6 ft (1·8 m)
The rose from which Attar of Roses is derived, and widely grown for this purpose in Bulgaria. Shrub rose of medium vigour and bushy habit up to 6 ft (1·8 m.). Flowers semi-double, deep rose-pink rather loose, heavily scented, the petals retaining the scent after picking. Mid to late June. Foliage light apple-green. The rose 'Kazanlik' named after the chief Bulgarian rose growing town is considered synonymous with this or may be a related form of it.

R. damascena variegata   D.
White and purplish-pink, summer, 5 ft (1·5 m.)
'York and Lancaster Rose'. Shrub rose of only medium vigour up to 5 ft (1·5 m.). Flowers rather small, rounded, white streaked irregularly with purplish-pink, often almost entirely pink, scented. Mid to late June. Foliage light green. Often branches with entirely pink flowers which have sported back to original *R. damascena* are found on bushes. If it is desired to retain the variegated variety, these must be cut out. A very old rose.

Abbreviations and Symbols used in the text

Rose classifications

A.	Alba	HT.	Hybrid Tea
B.	Bourbon	MCl.	Modern, large-flowered climber
C.	Centifolia	Min.	Miniature
Ch.	China	Moss	Centifolia muscosa
Cl.	Climber	MSh.	Modern shrub
D.	Damask	P.	Penzance Sweet Brier
Fl.	Floribunda	R.	Rambler
G.	Gallica	Rg.	Rugosa
HM.	Hybrid Musk	Sp.	Species and first hybrids
HP.	Hybrid Perpetual	Sw.	Sweet Brier

Rose Awards and Societies

A.A.R.S.	All-America Rose Selection
A.G.M.	Award of Garden Merit
A.M.	Award of Merit
A.R.S.	American Rose Society
B.B.G.M.	Baden Baden Gold Medal, Germany
B.G.M.	Bagatelle Gold Medal, Paris
C.C.V.	Clay Challenge Vase for scent
C.M.	Certificate of Merit
D.F.P.	David Fuerstenberg Prize
F.C.C.	First Class Certificate
G.G.M.	Geneva Gold Medal
G.M.	Gold Medal
G.M.C.B.	Gold Medal City of Belfast
G.M.H.G.M.	Gertrude M. Hubbard Gold Medal
G.R.H.	Golden Rose of The Hague
G.T.A.B.	Golden Thorn Award Belfast
H.E.M.M.	The Henry Edland Memorial Medal for the most fragrant rose of the year
H.G.M.	The Hague Gold Medal
L.G.M.	Lyon Gold Medal, France
M.G.M.	Madrid Gold Medal
N.G.M.C.	National Gold Medal Certificate
P.G.M.	Portland Gold Medal, Oregon, U.S.A.
P.I.T.	President's International Trophy
R.B.	Prize for the most fragrant rose, Roeulx, Belgium
R.B.G.M.	Roeulx, Belgium, Gold Medal
R.G.M.	Rome Gold Medal
R.H.S.	The Royal Horticultural Society, London
R.N.R.S.	The Royal National Rose Society, Great Britain*
T.G.C.	Trial Ground Certificate
U.A.B.	The 'Uladh' Award for fragrance, Belfast

National Rose Society awards, before 1965, are included here under R.N.R.S.

The illustration numbers are in **bold type** and the page numbers in light type preceded by p.

R. davidii   Sp.

Bright pink to pale crimson, summer, 9 ft (2·7 m.)

Countries of origin: W. China, S.E. Tibet.

Vigorous shrub rose with rather erect prickly growth. Flowers in large, loose clusters, single, bright rose-pink to pale crimson, about 2 in. (5·1 cm.) across, each with downy gland under stalk, scented. Rather late-flowering, early to mid-July. Leaflets up to 11, ovate or oval, toothed, in leaves 6 in. (15·2 cm.) long or more. Hips bright orange-red, narrowly flask shaped, conspicuous. From W. China and S.E. Tibet, introduced by E. H. Wilson in 1903. Related to R. macrophylla but not so vigorous. This rose is usually grown for its bright bunches of hips but in a garden of limited size it is not the equivalent of R. moyesii. The variety elongata has rather larger, longer hips and longer leaflets but fewer flowers in the clusters.

R. × dupontii   Sp.

White, summer, 7 ft (2·1 m.) c. 1817

Raised by M. Dupont, France.

Parentage: probably R. moschata × R. damascena

Vigorous shrub up to 7 ft (2·1 m.) and as much across. Flowers large, 3–3½ in. (7·6–8·9 cm.) across, single or sometimes semi-double with 8 petals, well rounded and overlapped, white with slight flush on first opening, in clusters of 5 or more, scented. Mid-June to early July. Foliage mat, grey-green, downy below. Stems with few thorns. Raised possibly at La Malmaison, featured in Botanical Register under the name R. moschata nivea and in Redouté as R. damascena subalba. A valuable shrub where there is space. The flowers are a good clear white. Mr G. Thomas suggests growing with R. rubrifolia. **6**, p. 1.

A.M., R.H.S. 1954.

R. ecae   Sp.

Bright golden-yellow, late spring to early summer, 5 ft (1·5 m.)

Country of origin: Afghanistan.

Shrub up to 5 ft (1·5 m.) or more on a wall. Flowers bright golden-yellow, probably the strongest yellow of any rose, single, small 1 in. (2·5 cm.) across, but numerous. Early-flowering late May to early June. Stems upright, thorny; foliage delicate, grey-green. A very beautiful rose but only suitable for a warm position and usually best against a wall where I have seen it up to 7 ft (2·1 m) and nearly as much across. Not usually a vigorous grower and needs care to establish. Collected in 1880 by Dr Aitchison, the name is derived from his wife's initials 'E.C.A.'. One parent of the very promising 'Golden Chersonese' (**167**, p. 31). **7**, p. 2.

A.M., R.H.S. 1933.

R. eglanteria, R. rubiginosa, Sweet Brier   Sp.

Pink, 8 ft (2·4 m.)

Country of origin: N. Europe including Britain.

Vigorous shrub with dense prickly branches and small leaflets, scented spicily, especially when wet, from glands in underside. Variable and widely distributed in N. Europe including Britain. Flowers single, in clusters, blush-pink to brighter pink, 1½–2 in. (3·8–5·1 cm.) across. Hips bright red, more rounded with more persistent sepals than in R. canina from which it is also distinguished by less vigorous growth, deeper pink but slightly smaller flowers and smaller leaflets. Sometimes planted to make an informal hedge. More often seen are the Penzance and other briers introduced about 1894–5 by Lord Penzance by crossing R. eglanteria, probably the double form (duplex) with Hybrid Perpetual and Bourbon roses as well as R. foetida. Amongst the best are the following.

R. eglanteria 'Amy Robsart'   P.

Pink, summer, 10 ft (3 m.) c. 1893

Very vigorous shrub up to 10 ft (3 m.) with small leaflets and scented foliage. Flowers semi-double, deep clear pink with good golden centres, paler at base – almost white. Free-flowering in clusters. Mid to late June but not recurrent. Good scarlet hips in

late summer and autumn. One of the most vigorous of the Penzance group raised from R. eglanteria × a hybrid Perpetual or Bourbon Rose. Suitable for a hedge or back of large border or semi-wild garden. The scent of the foliage is not so strong as in 'Lord' or 'Lady Penzance'. **8**, p. 2.

A.M., R.H.S. 1893.

R. eglanteria 'Anne of Geierstein'   P.

Crimson, summer, 10 ft (3 m.) c. 1894

Very vigorous shrub up to 10 ft (3 m.) with small leaflets and scented foliage. Flowers single, dark crimson-red with good golden centre. Mid to late June but not recurrent. Free-flowering. Good scarlet hips in late summer and autumn. Raised by Lord Penzance about 1894 from R. eglanteria × a hybrid Perpetual or Bourbon Rose.

R. eglanteria 'Flora McIvor'   P.

Pink, summer, 10 ft (3 m.) c. 1894

Very vigorous shrub up to 10 ft (3 m.) with small leaflets and slightly scented foliage. Flowers single, rose-pink fading to blush-pink with a white centre. Mid to late June but not recurrent. Raised from R. eglanteria × a Hybrid Perpetual or Bourbon rose. **9**, p. 2.

R. eglanteria 'Julia Mannering'   P.

Pink, summer, 1895

Very vigorous shrub with small leaflets and scented foliage. Flowers single or semi-double, pale pink with darker veining, rather large, like a Dog rose. Not very common in cultivation. Mid to late June, but not recurrent. **10**, p. 2.

R. eglanteria 'Lady Penzance'   P.

Coppery-pink, summer, 6 ft (1·8 m.) c. 1894

Vigorous, very prickly, shrub with small leaflets and quite strongly scented foliage, especially when wet, up to 6 ft (1·8 m.) but not so vigorous as other Penzance Briers. Flowers single, coppery-salmon-pink with large centre of yellow stamens. Mid to late June but not recurrent. Raised about 1894 from R. eglanteria × R. foetida bicolor, the Austrian Copper and susceptible to black spot.

R. eglanteria 'Lord Penzance'   P.

Rosy-yellow, summer, 6 ft (1·8 m.) c. 1894

Vigorous, very prickly shrub with small leaflets and quite strongly scented foliage, especially when wet, up to 6 ft (1·8 m.). Not so vigorous as other Penzance Briers. Flowers single, soft rosy-yellow, paler than 'Lady Penzance' with pale lemon-yellow centre. Mid to late June, not recurrent. Raised from R. eglanteria × R. × harisonii. **11**, p. 2.

R. eglanteria 'Manning's Blush'   Sw.

Blush, summer, 5 ft (1·5 m.)

Shrub rose, making a dense bush up to 5 ft with small leaflets, in bud pale blush-pink opening to white with a faint pink flush. Mid to late June but not recurrent. An old rose raised earlier than 1799 when it was portrayed in Miss Lawrance's book of rose pictures. **12**, p. 2.

R. eglanteria 'Meg Merrilies'   P.

Crimson, summer, 10 ft (3 m.) c. 1894

Very vigorous and prickly shrub rose up to 10 ft (3 m.). Foliage scented. Flowers bright crimson, semi-double, free-flowering. Mid to late June but not recurrent. Good bright red hips. Raised about 1894 from R. eglanteria × a hybrid Perpetual or Bourbon. One of the best of this series, with both flowers and foliage scented. Suitable for making a tall hedge, but liable to black spot. **13**, p. 3.

R. ernestii see **R. rubus**

R. farreri   Sp.
Pale-pink, early summer, 5 ft (1·5 m.)
Countries of origin: W. China, S. Kansu.
Shrub up to 5 ft (1·5 m.) and often more across. Flowers small, about ¾–1 in. (1·9–2·5 cm.) across, pale pink or white or shell-pink in the form *persetosa*, which open deeper pink with a white centre, slightly scented, very numerous. Early-flowering, early to mid-June. Foliage very delicate with up to 9 leaflets. Stems bristly, often arching over with abundance of flowers. Introduced by R. Farrer in 1915 from S. Kansu. Forma *persetosa* was selected by Mr E. A. Bowles among his seedlings and is the form now usually grown, the type has almost disappeared from cultivation. It is distinguished by deeper pink flowers. A very beautiful rose at all seasons owing to its delicate growth and often called the 'Threepenny-bit' rose because of the size of its flowers. It also shows some autumn colour and small coral-red hips. **14**, p. 3.

R. fedtschenkoana   Sp.
White, summer–autumn, 8 ft (2·4 m.)
Countries of origin: U.S.S.R., Turkestan.
Large shrub rose with very dark older wood, bristly and with straight prickles. Flowers singly or in small clusters, single, white or occasionally pale pink, about 2 in. (5·1 cm.) across. Scent described as unpleasant. Foliage distinctly glaucous on both sides and this is a distinguishing character, leaflets finely toothed, oval or obovate. Hips about ¾ in. (1·9 cm.) long, pear-shaped, bright red with persistent sepals and very hairy. From Turkestan, discovered by the Russian traveller after whom it is named during his journey of 1868–71. Close to *R. webbiana* but distinct in its bristly stem and usually white flowers. It was introduced to Kew, England, in 1890 from a nursery in Ireland. In the wild it is variable and Regel, the famous botanist, described four separate forms. **15**, p. 3.

R. ferruginea see **R. rubrifolia, 47, 48**, p. 9.

R. filipes   Sp.Cl.R.
White, early summer, 20 ft (6·1 m.)
Country of origin: W. China.
Rampant and very vigorous climber up to 20 ft (6·1 m.), suitable for growing over shed or old trees, making new young shoots up to 10 ft (3 m.) or more, somewhat prickly with hooked spines. Flowers in very large corymbose clusters, single, white with prominent centre of yellow stamens, creamy in bud; scented, early to mid-July, not recurrent. Foliage, grey-green, with up to 7 leaflets. Introduced from W. China by E. H. Wilson in 1908. One of the finest of our climbing roses of *moschata* group. The most vigorous cultivar is **'Kiftsgate'**, named after the famous Cotswold garden and the specimen there is probably the largest climbing rose in England: in 1970 it was 20 yards (18·3 m.) long by 15 yards (13·7 m.) wide; its owner has recorded 428 flowers in one corymb. In its rampageousness it seems that the sky is the limit and other roses should be planted where there is only a small space. With plenty of room, however, it is superb, cascading down in great white showers and no other rose can surpass it. **19**, p. 4.

R. foetida, *R. lutea*   Sp.
Golden-yellow, early summer, 5 ft (1·5 m.)
Country of origin: N. Iran, Kurdistan.
Often misnamed as the Austrian Brier. In cultivation usually of rather sparse growth, with stiff, erect, prickly stems. Flowers single, about 2–2½ in. (5·1–6·4 cm.) across, bright golden-yellow, with heavy not very agreeable scent. Early to mid-June, not recurrent. Foliage delicate, often very susceptible to black spot which may cause total defoliation early in season. It grows best in warm situations during a hot summer and for garden purposes is usually discarded for the yellow *spinosissima* rose.

R. foetida bicolor, *R. lutea punicea*   Sp.
Orange and coppery-red, summer, 5 ft (1·5 m.)
Parentage: *R. foetida* sport
Shrub rose, not usually very vigorous or over 5 ft (1·5 m.). Flowers very strong orange and coppery-red with golden-yellow centre, in sprays along arching branches. Mid to late June, not recurrent. When well grown one of the most striking roses and almost unique in its brilliant colour. Very susceptible to black spot but worth spraying and growing for its marvellous colour, best planted on its own but it shows up well against copper beech. Often called the 'Austrian Copper Brier' this old rose is said to have been introduced before 1590. **16**, p. 3.

R. foetida persiana, 'Persian Yellow'   Sp.
Bright golden-yellow, summer, 5 ft (1·5 m.)
Country of origin: probably Iran.
Parentage: probably *R. foetida* sport
Shrub rose, not usually very vigorous except in warmer countries than Britain. Flowers semi-double or double, bright golden-yellow. Only successful in a warm climate, I have seen it in the Elburz Mts of Iran and in Spain making a hedge 4–5 ft (1·2–1·5 m.) high and covered with flowers, unforgettable sights. Introduced about 1838. Parent of many of our yellow and bicolor roses.

R. forrestiana   Sp.
Rosy-crimson, summer, 7 ft (2·1 m.)
Country of origin: S. W. China.
Shrub rose of medium size, but may reach up to 7 ft (2·1 m.) by 6 ft (1·8 m.) across according to Mr G Thomas, but usually less. Flowers in rather dense clusters, singly, rosy-crimson with creamy-

yellow boss of stamens up to 1½ in. (3·8 cm.) across, scented, free-flowering, the flowers bearing large leafy bracts. Late June to mid-July. Foliage rather bright fresh green with up to 7 rounded leaflets. Hips ovoid, bright orange-red, flask-shaped, and slightly bristly with persistent green bracts. Close to *R. multibracteata* but with fewer flowers. **17**, p. 3.

R. gallica   Sp.
Shrub rose of medium size and parent of the large group of Gallica roses and so indirectly of our modern roses. Gallica roses are distinguished by comparative thornlessness but an abundance of small prickles; leaves which are rounded or blunt pointed at the end, darkish green above and downy beneath. The original species has single, purplish-crimson flowers in small clusters, about 2½ in. (6·4 cm.) across, and is usually described as native to central and south-east Europe, but it is probably not now in cultivation and I do not know of any wild populations. The rose usually grown as *R. gallica* is the semi-double variety 'Officinalis' (**86**, p. 16) and this is of very ancient origin, probably a sport of the original single-flowered species. Also rarely seen, but still in cultivations is *R. gallica haplodonta* with single flowers.

R. gallica maxima see 'Officinalis', **86**, p. 16.

R. gallica officinalis see 'Officinalis', **86**, p. 16.

R. gallica versicolor see 'Versicolor', **92**, p. 17.

R. gentiliana, 'Polyantha Grandiflora'   Sp.R.,Sh.
White, summer, 15 ft (4·6 m.) 1886
Country of origin: probably China.
A vigorous rambler distinguished by red, glandular branches, or large shrub up to 7 ft (2·1 m.) if hard pruned. Flowers in large clusters, single, white with yellow centre, and each about 1 in. (2·5 cm.) across, buds pale yellow, strongly scented. Late June to mid-July but not recurrent. Foliage bright glossy green, bronze-tinted on first opening. Hips plentiful, orange-red, long lasting. It was introduced in 1886 by Bernaix of France but its wild origin is not known and it may be a hybrid of *R. multiflora* and *R. moschata*. The name *gentiliana*, although adopted here and accepted in the International Rose Register, has been a source of confusion since it has been used for two separate roses, the use by Léveillé and Vaniot being the first one and that referred to here. Syn. *R. wilsonii* hort. but not Borrer. Probably the name *R. multiflora* var. *catheyensis* also belongs here. It is at any rate a valuable and beautiful garden plant still frequently listed as 'Polyantha Grandiflora' which is an invalid name. **18**, p. 3.
A.G.M. & F.C.C., R.H.S. 1888

R. gigantea   Sp.Cl.
Cream or pale yellow, summer, 30 ft (9·1 m.) 1889
Country of origin: W. China, Upper Burma (Shan States).
Very vigorous but tender, climber up to 30 ft (9·1 m.) or more when grown under glass or in warmer countries than in Britain, where it flowers freely instead of sparsely. Flowers large, single, up to 5 in. (12·7 cm.) across, pale yellow, cream or white with broad, silky petals overlapping for most of their length, like a single *Paeonia wittmanniana* and with a good boss of yellow stamens in centre, scented. Mid to late June. Foliage dark glossy green, almost evergreen. In its native Shan States in Upper Burma, *R. gigantea* is reputed to grow truly gigantic with woody stems up to 4 in. (10·2 cm.) in diameter at the base and straight prickles about ¼ in. (6·4 mm.) long with leaves 9 in. (22·9 cm.) long and flowers 6 in. (15·2 cm.) across, white, more or less tinged with yellow, almost golden in bud, flowering branchlets usually without thorns. It first flowered in England in 1904 at Albury Park, Surrey. This

flowering antedated that in the Temperate House at Kew where it had grown 50 ft (15·2 m.) without flowering. Hips large, globose, smooth, about 1½ in. (3·8 cm.) across, described in Burma like 'a small bright yellow apple' and sold for eating in the bazaars of Manipur State. Some records of its flowering outside in Great Britain are doubtful and may refer to *R. cooperi* which is close. In warmer countries, however, it must be one of the finest roses that can be grown. Its hybrids with *R. chinensis* are described under *R. × odorata*. In Manipur it was discovered by Sir George Watt in 1882 at 7,000 ft (2,134 m.) and introduced by Sir Henry Collet in 1889 from the Shan States. Mr F. G. Preston, who flowered it in the corridor of the greenhouses at the University Botanic Garden, Cambridge England, recommended that 'it should be planted in a well-drained position with not too much root run' and that it should be left on the dry side during the late summer and autumn. *R. gigantea erubescens* is a form with blush-pink flowers and may have been one of the parents of *R. × odorata* and thence of our Hybrid Tea roses.

R. gigantea 'Cooperi' see *R. cooperi*, **5**, p. 1.

R. giraldii   Sp.
Pink, summer, 8 ft (2·4 m.) *c.* 1897
Country of origin: N. and Central China.
Vigorous shrub of rather upright growth. Flowers singly or in small clusters, pink with white centre, up to 1 in. (2·5 cm.) across. Late June to mid-July but not recurrent. Foliage with fine leaflets as in *R. webbiana*, to which it is related. Hips globular, red, about ¾ in. (1·9 cm.) long. Thought to have been introduced about 1897 but it has never become a popular or widely grown rose.

R. glauca see *R. rubrifolia*, **47**, **48**, p. 9.

R. glaucophylla see *R. hemisphaerica*

R. grandiflora see *R. spinosissima altaica*, **52**, p. 10.

R. × hardii see × **Hulthemosa hardii**

R. × harisonii, 'Harison's Yellow'   Sh.
Bright yellow, early summer, 4 ft (1·2 m.) *c.* 1830
Raised by G. Harison, U.S.A.
Parentage: *R. foetida persiana* × *R. spinosissima*
Shrub rose, only of medium vigour, probably raised by George Harison of New York about 1830. Flowers double, globular, very bright yellow, 2½–3 in. (6·4–7·6 cm.) across, showing a few yellow stamens in centre, free-flowering. Early, late May to mid-June, but not recurrent. Foliage grey-green, delicate. Usually a rather sparse but erect grower and always striking for the very bright yellow of its flowers. Widely planted in the U.S.A. in the pioneer days and still found in California. **20**, p. 5.
A.M., R.H.S. 1949.

R. helenae   Sp.R.,Sh.
White, summer, 18 ft (5·5 m.)
Country of origin: W. and Central China, Szechwan, Hupeh.
Vigorous rose forming a loose rambler up to 18 ft (5·5 m.) or if pruned a large shrub as much through as high with pubescent stems and small hooked prickles. Flowers in large clusters, 6 in. (15·2 cm.) across, single, creamy white, each about 1½ in. (3·8 cm.) across, scented. Early to mid-July but not recurrent. Foliage dark green with up to 9 pointed leaflets. Discovered by E. H. Wilson in 1900 and introduced by him in 1907. A fine rose of the same type as *R. longicuspis* or *R. filipes* (**19**, p. 4), but not quite so vigorous, still it will cover quite a large tree in time. Hips decorative, orange-red, egg-shaped, drooping gracefully and distinctively in bunches as seen in the photograph. **21**, p. 5.

R. hemisphaerica, *R. glaucophylla, R. sulphurea,*   Sp.
  The Sulphur Rose

Sulphur-yellow, summer, 6 ft (1·8 m.) before 1625.
Loose growing shrub or climber up to 6 ft (1·8 m.) tender and best grown against a south-facing wall in warm situations. Named from the double cultivar which is thought to have been derived from the single wild species discovered much later and named *R. hemisphaerica rapinii. R. hemisphaerica* is the Sulphur Rose of the old Dutch flower painters and Redouté. Introduced before 1625 but unfortunately now very rarely seen and seldom satisfactory now as a garden plant for it lacks vigour and only opens its flowers perfectly in very warm weather. Flowers large, 3 in. (7·6 cm.) across, fully double and heavy, tending to droop, pale sulphur-yellow, rather late-flowering, early to mid-July. Foliage slightly glaucous. Until *R. foetida* was introduced this was the only cultivated yellow rose.

R. × hibernica, Irish Rose   Sh.

Pale pink, summer, 6–9 ft (1·8–2·7 m.) 1802
Raised by J. Templeton, near Belfast, N. Ireland.
A hybrid of *R. canina* and *R. spinosissima* which occurred near Belfast, prior to 1802 when it was discovered by a Mr John Templeton who won a prize from Botanical Society of Dublin of 5 or 50 guineas, according to different authors. It was then described as a new indigenous plant. Shrub rose 6–9 ft (1·8–2·7 m.) with erect stems and arching branches. Flowers single, pale pink, white near base, about 1½ in. (3·8 cm.) across, singly or in small clusters. Leaflets grey-green, downy below. Hips red, about ½ in. (1·3 cm.) across. Rarely seen now in cultivation. **22**, p. 5.

R. × highdownensis, 'Highdownensis'   Sh.

Crimson, early summer, 12 ft (3·7 m.) *c.* 1928
Parentage: *R. moyesii* seedling
A seedling selected at Highdown, England, for its lighter flowers which are a good crimson with a white centre and borne in larger clusters than the type. A very vigorous grower forming a very large bush. Hips are orange-red and among the finest of the *moyesii* group. **23, 24**, p. 5.
A.M., R.H.S. 1928.

R. × hillieri see **R. × pruhoniciana**, **40**, p. 8.

R. holodonta   Sp.

Deep pink, early summer.
Country of origin: W. China.
Very close to *R. moyesii* and considered by some botanists to be a variety of it under the name *R. moyesii rosea.* Flowers deep rose-pink, hips orange-red, narrowly flask-shaped, bristly, up to 2¼ in. (5·7 cm.) long and often abundant. Perhaps the best rose for hips in this group and hardly surpassed in this character by any other species. It is well worth growing for this characteristic. Some less thorny varieties have been raised from seed. Usually not quite so vigorous as *R. moyesii.* **25**, p. 5.
A.M., R.H.S. 1936.

R. hugonis   Sp.

Pale canary-yellow, early summer, 8 × 8 ft (2·4 × 2·4 m.) 1899
Country of origin: W. China.
Shrub rose, vigorous up to 8 ft (2·4 m.) and as much across, but subject to die-back in branches. Flowers single, of medium size, saucer-shaped, 1½–2 in. (3·8–5·1 cm.) across, pale creamy-yellow with good boss of yellow stamens in centre, deeper near base on first opening, very numerous on arching branches. Early flowering late May to early June. Foliage delicate with up to 11 leaflets. Introduced in 1899 from seed sent to Kew, England, by Father Hugh Scanlon, a missionary known as Pater Hugo. A beautiful rose valuable for its early flowering, in some seasons as early as mid-May, but flowers do not always open wide and as a garden plant its hybrid *R. × pteragonis* 'Cantabrigiensis' (**41**, p. 8) is to be preferred. **26**, p. 6.
A.M., R.H.S. 1917; A.G.M. 1925.

R. humilis see **R. virginiana**

R. × jacksonii see **'Max Graf'**

R. kordesii   Sh.,Cl.

Deep pink, 6 ft (1·8 m.) 1952
Country of origin: Germany.
Parentage: *R. rugosa* × *R. wichuraiana*
A hybrid which arose in W. Kordes' nursery in Germany derived from 'Max Graf', a usually infertile hybrid of *R. rugosa* × *R. wichuraiana,* by the spontaneous doubling of the chromosomes making a fertile tetraploid. This was the parent of the great race of recurrent-flowering *kordesii* climbers and shrubs such as 'Dortmund' (**241**, p. 45) and thus made one of the great contributions of this century to our modern roses.

Shrub with arching branches up to 6 ft (1·8 m.) which can be grown as a climber. Flowers semi-double, cup-shaped, deep pink. Mid to late June but not recurrent. This is seldom grown but is of great historical interest now as a parent.

R. laevigata, Cherokee Rose   Sp.R.,Sh.

White, summer, 20 ft (6·1 m.)
Country of origin: China.
Very vigorous climber or large shrub of loose growth, almost evergreen, rather tender. In Britain only suitable for warm and sheltered positions usually against a south wall, but in the southern states of U.S.A. it grows abundantly and has become naturalized so widely that it has become the State flower of Georgia and is given the

---

Abbreviations and Symbols used in the text

Rose classifications

A.	Alba	HT.	Hybrid Tea
B.	Bourbon	MCl.	Modern, large-flowered climber
C.	Centifolia	Min.	Miniature
Ch.	China	Moss	Centifolia muscosa
Cl.	Climber	MSh.	Modern shrub
D.	Damask	P.	Penzance Sweet Brier
Fl.	Floribunda	R.	Rambler
G.	Gallica	Rg.	Rugosa
HM.	Hybrid Musk	Sp.	Species and first hybrids
HP.	Hybrid Perpetual	Sw.	Sweet Brier

Rose Awards and Societies

A.A.R.S.	All-America Rose Selection
A.G.M.	Award of Garden Merit
A.M.	Award of Merit
A.R.S.	American Rose Society
B.B.G.M.	Baden Baden Gold Medal, Germany
B.G.M.	Bagatelle Gold Medal, Paris
C.C.V.	Clay Challenge Vase for scent
C.M.	Certificate of Merit
D.F.P.	David Fuerstenberg Prize
F.C.C.	First Class Certificate
G.G.M.	Geneva Gold Medal
G.M.	Gold Medal
G.M.C.B.	Gold Medal City of Belfast
G.M.H.G.M.	Gertrude M. Hubbard Gold Medal
G.R.H.	Golden Rose of The Hague
G.T.A.B.	Golden Thorn Award Belfast
H.E.M.M.	The Henry Edland Memorial Medal for the most fragrant rose of the year
H.G.M.	The Hague Gold Medal
L.G.M.	Lyon Gold Medal, France
M.G.M.	Madrid Gold Medal
N.G.M.C.	National Gold Medal Certificate
P.G.M.	Portland Gold Medal, Oregon, U.S.A.
P.I.T.	President's International Trophy
R.B.	Prize for the most fragrant rose, Roeulx, Belgium
R.B.G.M.	Roeulx, Belgium, Gold Medal
R.G.M.	Rome Gold Medal
R.H.S.	The Royal Horticultural Society, London
R.N.R.S.	The Royal National Rose Society, Great Britain*
T.G.C.	Trial Ground Certificate
U.A.B.	The 'Uladh' Award for fragrance, Belfast

National Rose Society awards, before 1965, are included here under R.N.R.S.

The illustration numbers are in **bold type** and the page numbers in light type preceded by p.

American vernacular name of 'Cherokee Rose'. Flowers single, pure white with petals which do not overlap, up to 4 in. (10·2 cm.) across, borne singly or in pairs, scented. Mid to late June, but not recurrent. Foliage, very fine, glossy bright green with red petioles, almost evergreen in warm gardens. Stem very prickly with hooked spines. It grows well at Highdown in Sussex, and in a hot dry position has made a large shrub there, about 6 ft (1·8 m.) high and as much across. Parent of R. × anemonoides and 'Ramona' (**196**, **197**, p. 36).

R. × **l'heritierana** see **'Mme Sancy de Parabère', 214**, p. 39.

R. longicuspis, R. lucens   Sp.Cl.
Creamy-white, summer, 25 ft (7·6 m.)
Country of origin: W. China.
Climbing rose of great vigour, related to R. moschata and R. filipes (**19**, p. 4) but not quite so wide spreading as the latter. Flowers single, white or creamy-white with good yellow centre of stamens, 1½ in. (3·8 cm.) across, in very large sprays of up to 150 flowers, strongly scented. Late flowering, late June to mid-July. Foliage bright shining green with reddish leaflets when young. Young shoots of great length. Hips tiny, deep orange-red, decorative. Introduced prior to 1904. Valuable for its late flowering, it is an excellent climber for covering an old tree and its shining foliage is decorative all summer. **27**, p. 6.
A.M., R.H.S. 1964.

R. lucens see **R. longicuspis, 27**, p. 6.

R. luciae see **R. wichuraiana**

R. lucida see **R. virginiana**

R. lutea see **R. foetida**

R. macrantha see under **'Macrantha'**

R. macrophylla   Sp.
Bright cerise-pink, summer, 10 ft (3 m.)
Countries of origin: N. India, Himalaya, W. China.
Vigorous upright-growing shrub up to 10 ft (3 m.) or more, with dark reddish branches, not very prickly. One of the common shrub roses of the Himalaya. Flowers single, deep rose or bright cerise-pink up to 3 in. (7·6 cm.) across, in small clusters or singly. Late June to early July but not recurrent. Foliage finely divided with up to 11 leaflets in leaves up to 8 in. (20·3 cm.) long. Hips, bottle-shaped, in drooping clusters, bright red, bristly. Not very often grown in gardens, its place being taken largely by R. moyesii (**30**, p. 6) to which there is some resemblance, but still it is a fine plant for flower, foliage and fruit. Widely distributed and variable, probably first introduced about 1818. A.M., R.H.S. 1897, and to clone 'Master Hugh' 1966 in fruit, well illustrated in colour in R.H.S. Journal Fig. 252, Dec. 1966, where hips were 3 in. (7.6 cm.) long and 1 in. (2·5 cm.) across. This was an exceptional form collected in Nepal and given an A.M., R.H.S. 1966.

R. microphylla see **R. roxburghii, 45, 46**, p. 9.

R. × **micrugosa**   Rg.Sh.
Pale lilac-pink, early summer, 10 × 10 ft (3 × 3 m.)
Parentage: R. rugosa × R. roxburghii
Very vigorous shrub, 10 ft (3 m.) high and as much across. Flowers single, large, pale lilac-pink with a slight purplish tinge, 4 in. (10·2 cm.) across. Early to mid-June. Hips rounded, orange-green, conspicuous, covered with stiff bristles. Foliage a good dark green, of rugosa type. Stems prickly, making vigorous growth each year,

but it is usually not very floriferous for the size of bush. Forms vary in colour. There is also one with deep purplish-pink, rather small flowers, which is grown at the Roserie de L'Haÿ, Paris, a pleasant white form 'Alba', and a deeper rose form 'Walter Butt'. The name R. microphylla, from which part of this hybrid's name was taken, is now regarded as a synonym of R. roxburghii. **28**, p. 6.

R. moschata, Musk Rose   Sp.
White, late summer, 10 ft (3 m.)
Country of origin: believed unknown in the wild.
There has been much confusion over the true R. moschata, the plant supposed to have been introduced in about 1651 and grown subsequently till about 1830 and used as a parent of many good roses imparting its unique musk scent and autumn flowering. Since about 1830 the rose grown under this name was quite different from the original and was probably a form or hybrid of R. moschata nepalensis more often grown under the name R. brunonii (see below). The true R. moschata was, however, recently discovered by Mr G. Thomas growing in the garden of the late Mr E. A. Bowles at Enfield, England, and having the true musk scent. It is unique also in its late-flowering, not till August but then repeatedly till autumn. It is a rather lax-growing shrub up to 10 ft (3 m.) with reddish, sparsely prickly stems, flowers in small clusters, usually semi-double but sometimes single, white with reflexed rather untidy petals and intensely sweet musk scent. Foliage dark green with purplish flush on first opening and up to 7 leaflets, greyish below. It is now a rare and not very effective garden plant but is of great historical interest for the part it has played in the breeding of our modern roses. It was accurately portrayed by Redouté.

R. moschata nepalensis, R. brunonii,   Sp.Cl.Sh.
  Himalayan Musk Rose
White, summer, 30 ft (9·1 m)
Countries of origin: N. India, Nepal and westwards to Afghanistan.
Very vigorous climber, or if pruned, a large bush. Flowers white or creamy-white, single, with good boss of yellow stamens in centre, 1–2 in. (2·5–5·1 cm.) across, in large clusters, scented. Late June to mid-July. Foliage grey-green, downy below; leaflets rather narrow; stems with stout hooked thorns. Western and central Himalaya from Afghanistan to Nepal. One of the finest white-flowered climbing roses where it can be given a large space and is best in a warm situation; in a cold place its young growth may not ripen sufficiently to stand the winter.
'La Mortola' is a fine and very vigorous form to 30 ft (9·1 m.) high and 40 ft (12·2 m.) across. Introduced from the Riviera garden of that name. **29**, p. 6.

R. moyesii   Sp.
Deep blood-red, early summer, 10 ft (3 m.) 1903
Country of origin: N.W. China.
Vigorous shrub rose with erect stems armed with stout thorns then arching over. Flowers deep blood-red, slightly variable in seedlings, single about 2½–3 in. (6·4–7·6 cm.) across, petals overlapping, singly or in pairs, numerous. Early to mid-June, unscented. Foliage delicate with up to 13 leaflets; hips, broad at base, flask shaped, 1–1½ in. (2·5–3·8 cm.) long, bright orange-red and persistent for quite a long period from late August to October but birds tend to take them. This rose is as valuable for its hips as its flowers. Hardy and quick growing. Some old canes should be cut out completely after flowering each year. Collected first by A. E. Pratt near the Tibetan frontier in 1890 but not introduced till 1903 when collected by E. H. Wilson. Named after the Reverend E. J. Moyes, a missionary in China. **30**, p. 6.
A.M., R.H.S. 1908; F.C.C., R.H.S. 1916; A.G.M., R.H.S. 1925.

R. moyesii 'Eos'   MSh.
Parentage: R. moyesii × 'Magnifica'
Cerise-pink, early summer, 12 ft (3·7 m.)

Vigorous but rather gaunt in habit. Flowers deep cerise-pink, white at centre, with large boss of stamens, free-flowering. **31**, p. 6.

R. moyesii fargesii   Sp.
Vivid carmine, early summer
A tetraploid variety said to have been a parent of 'Nevada', otherwise botanically little distinguishable from the type.
A.M., R.H.S. 1922.

R. moyesii 'Geranium'   MSh.
Bright crimson-red, early summer
Slightly dwarfer than the type and flowers brighter red. One of the best for the abundance of its orange-red hips and compact growth, making it valuable for the average sized garden. **32**, **33**, p. 7.
A.M., R.H.S. 1950.

R. moyesii holodonta see **R. holodonta, 25**, p. 5.

R. moyesii rosea see **R. holodonta, 25**, p. 5.

R. multibracteata   Sp.
Bright pink, summer, 7 ft (2·1 m.) 1908
Country of origin: China.
Shrub rose of rather delicate, widely arching growth and moderate vigour. Flowers bright pink, single, about 1–1½ in. (2·5–3·8 cm.) across, in small clusters or singly. Late June to mid-July. Foliage finely divided, almost fern-like with up to 9 small leaflets to a leaf. Flower stalks downy and glandular. Hips round, orange-red, not very large. Discovered in W. Szechwan by Dr E. H. Wilson and introduced by him in 1908. Close to *R. willmottiae* (**60**, p. 11) and *R. webbiana* and not very widely grown but parent of the distinctive 'Cerise Bouquet' (**146**, p. 26).
A.M., R.H.S. 1936.

R. multiflora   Sp.Sh.,Cl.
White, summer, 10 ft (3 m.) before 1868
Countries of origin: N. China, Korea, Japan.
Vigorous large shrub or climber making annually long arching stems, up to 10 × 6 ft (3·0 × 1·8 m.) across or more, a beautiful shrub when in flower but now largely used as stock for budding Hybrid Teas and Floribundas. Cuttings root very easily but seed raised plants are more usual now. Flowers in large branching clusters of about 6 in. (15·2 cm.) across, single, white with golden centre of stamens, each about 1 in. (2·5 cm.) across, scented. Late June to mid-July. Foliage with up to 9 leaflets thus distinguishing it from the other roses budded on it as stock. Hips small, red, oval. *R. multiflora* was part parent of the Poly-poms and the Polyantha roses and has probably been introduced from China and Japan in various hybrid coloured forms as well as in the species which is probably variable. Makes a useful hedge.

R. nitida   Sp.
Deep pink, summer, 2 ft (0·6 m.)
Countries of origin: Canada, U.S.A., N.E. States.
Dwarf shrub, suckering freely with numerous dwarf prickly branches usually not over 2 ft (0·6 m.). It is grown chiefly for its very striking autumn foliage colour which is probably the brightest of any rose, a deep scarlet-crimson. Flowers single, deep pink, unfading, up to 2 in. (5·1 cm.) across, early to mid-July. Foliage shining, deep green with up to 9 leaflets, early in autumn assuming very bright tints. Hips bright red, round, slightly bristly, not very large. *R. nitida* is not usually a very vigorous grower and takes time to establish after moving but once established it makes a good foreground for the rose border.

R. × odorata   Sp.Cl.
Pink, crimson or pale yellow, summer, 15 ft (4·6 m.)
Introduced by R.H.S., England.
Parentage: *R. chinensis* × *R. gigantea*
Vigorous climbers raised in China in very early times, a few of which were introduced towards the end of the eighteenth century and have been important in rose history. The early introductions include: 'Fortune's Double Yellow', also known as 'Beauty of Glazenwood' and *R. × odorata pseudindica*. It was found by Robert Fortune, the great plant collector, in a Mandarin's garden at Ningpo, E. China in 1845. He described it as 'glowing yellow and salmon' and it was known to the Chinese as 'Wang-jang-ve' or yellow rose. Climber of moderate vigour with purplish-red prickly stems up to 8 ft (2·4 m.), tender and best grown in sheltered position against a wall. Flowers slightly drooping, large, double, bright gamboge-yellow overlaid with crimson-lake, 3–4 in. (7·6–10·2 cm.) across. Strongly scented. Mid to late June. It can also be grown as a standard but since it flowers on wood of the previous year, it should only be lightly pruned. Popular during latter part of the last century but now very rarely seen.

'Hume's Blush Tea-scented China'. Flowers blush-pink, strongly scented, climber. Introduced in 1809 by Sir A. Hume from the East Indies (probably from China) and also painted by Redouté in 1817.

'Parson's Pink China'. Flowers pale pink, semi-double. Climber. Probably sent by Lord Macartney's commission in China to Sir Joseph Banks about 1789 and later sent by Parsons to Colville, the nurseryman, in 1793 and also to France about the same time, where it was painted by Redouté in 1817.

'Park's Yellow Tea-scented China'. Flowers double, large, yellow, climber. Introduced by J. D. Parks for the Horticultural

Society of London in 1824 and painted by Redouté in 1835 but not now known in cultivation.

R. omeiensis see **R. sericea**

R. omeiensis pteracantha see **R. sericea pteracantha, 50**, p. 10.

R. × paulii   Trailing Sp.,Sh.
White or pink, summer, 3 × 6 ft (0·9 × 1·8 m.) before 1903
Raised by G. Paul, England.
Parentage: *R. arvensis* × *R. rugosa*
Vigorous trailing rose or, if pruned hard, forming shrub about 3 ft (0·9 m.) high and 6 ft (1·8 m.) across, very thorny and usually with long shoots. Flowers single, white, with wedge-shaped petals, not overlapping appreciably, 3 in. (7·6 cm.) across. Very free-flowering, slightly scented. Mid to late June. Recommended for ground cover and said to smother weeds. A valuable plant for its abundance of beautiful flowers and trailing habit. **34**, p. 7.

R. × paulii 'Rosea'   Sp.
A very beautiful cultivar with deep pink notched petals and white centres around mass of gold stamens. Scented. Usually slightly less vigorous than the white form, from which it is considered to be a sport. **35**, p. 7.

R. pendulina, *R. alpina*   Sp.
Deep pink, late summer, 4 ft (1·2 m.)
Countries of origin: Central and S. Europe, subalpine regions.
Dwarf shrub usually suckering freely up to 4 ft (1·2 m.) but usually less, branches almost without prickles. Flowers single, deep pink or purplish-pink but variable, about 2 in. (5·1 cm.) across, usually singly. Late June to August depending on altitude. Foliage finely divided with up to 9 leaflets. Hips pear-shaped, bright red, up to 1 in. (2·5 cm.) long, conspicuous. Although lovely in its native regions, collected plants seldom establish well in England. Sometimes known as the 'Rose without a thorn'. *R. pendulina pyrenaica* is a form with more thorny, glaucous branches and glandular bristles on the flower stalks and tubes of the calyces.

R. persica see **Hulthemia persica**

R. pimpinellifolia see under **R. spinosissima**

R. pisocarpa   Sp.
Rose-purple, summer, 5 ft (1·5 m.)
Countries of origin: U.S.A., Canada.
Small shrub usually not over 5 ft (1·5 m.) with rather straggling growth, branches slender with few prickles. Some plants in gardens under this name are much more vigorous, up to 10 ft (3 m.) and with larger leaves and hips but probably these are hybrids with *R. rugosa*. Flowers single, rose-purple or deep purplish-pink about 1½ in. (3·8 cm.) across, solitary or in small clusters. Mid-June to early July. Foliage finely downy below. Hips round, bright red, but not very large. **36**, p. 7.

R. polyantha grandiflora see **R. gentiliana, 18**, p. 3.

R. pomifera, *R. villosa*, The Apple Rose   Sp.
Pink, summer, 7 × 7 ft (2·1 × 2·1 m.)
Countries of origin: Central Europe.
A large shrub rose, vigorous up to 7 ft (2·1 m.) and as much across with long arching branches and large, downy, grey-green leaflets.

Flowers single, large, up to 2½ in. (6·4 cm.) across, clear rosy-pink, in small clusters or singly, slightly crinkled, scented. Hips large, variable in colour from orange-red to purplish-crimson, bristly. **37**, p. 7.

R. pomifera 'Duplex', *R. villosa* 'Duplex',   Sh.
  'Wolley-Dod's Rose'
Rosy-pink, summer, 10 × 12 ft (3 × 3·7 m.)
Probably a hybrid between *R. pomifera* and a tetraploid garden rose. Flowers semi-double, clear rosy-pink, about 2½–3 in. (6·4–7·6 cm.) across, only slightly scented. Foliage grey-green, downy. Hips dark-red, flask-shaped, contrasting well with the foliage. This is the form usually grown in gardens and is a very fine plant for its delightful combination of flower and foliage. Probably raised before 1797 on the evidence of early plates although the plant now usually grown was probably derived from the Reverend Wolley-Dod's garden much later. As vigorous as *R. pomifera* and in Savill Garden, Windsor, England, about 10 ft (3 m.) high and 12 ft (3·7 m.) across. **38**, p. 8.

R. pomponia see **'De Meaux'**

R. primula   Sp.
Creamy-yellow, spring, 8 × 8 ft (2·4 × 2·4 m.) 1911
Country of origin: Turkestan.
A vigorous shrub up to 8 ft (2·4 m.) and as much through. Flowers early in long arching sprays, slightly scented but its chief distinction is the scent of incense, which is carried on the wind, from its delicate foliage. One of the earliest bush roses to flower. Discovered near Samarkand in 1911 by F. N. Meyer, an American collector. Flowers open wider but are slightly smaller than in *R. hugonis* (**26**, p. 6), to which it is close, and prickles rather longer, straight and wide at base. **39**, p. 8.
A.M., R.H.S. 1962.

R. × pruhoniciana, *R. × hillieri*   Sh.
Parentage: *R. willmottiae* × *R. moyesii*
Crimson-maroon, early summer, 12 × 8 ft (3·7 × 2·4 m.) 1924
Raised by Hillier & Sons, England.
Flowers very dark crimson-maroon, otherwise like typical *moyesii*. A very vigorous shrub up to 12 ft (3·7 m.) and 8 ft (2·4 m.) across. Hips dark red, narrow flask-shaped, usually less abundant than in *R. moyesii*. **40**, p. 8.

R. pseudindica see under **R. × odorata**

R. × pteragonis
A group hybrid name now slowly coming into use but not yet widely adopted for a very valuable group of early flowering and vigorous shrub roses, raised by crossing *R. hugonis* with forms of *R. sericea*. As might be expected, they are somewhat variable. Among the finest are those described below.

R. × pteragonis 'Cantabrigiensis'   Sh.
Pale yellow, early summer, 10 × 10 ft (3 × 3 m.) 1931
Raised by Dr C. C. Hurst, England.
Parentage: *R. hugonis* × *R. sericea hookeri*
A very vigorous and free-flowering shrub rose growing up to 10 ft (3 m.) and as much through; in my opinion it is a distinct improvement on both its parents and the best garden plant in this group. Flowers creamy-yellow, single, bowl-shaped, opening flat, up to 2½ in. (6·4 cm.) across, fading to pale cream as they mature, showing central boss of buff-yellow stamens, petals broad and overlapping. Flowers are borne singly but very freely on long sprays, rather vertical but arching outwards slightly as flowers open. Very faint scent. Early flowering in late May and early June, usually one of the first roses to flower. Season about three weeks but non-recurrent.

Foliage fine, rather fern-like with 5–9 leaflets. Prune after flowering by cutting out older flowering shoots, or in winter. A rose which requires plenty of space to give its best result, lovely against a blue sky or against a darker green background. In late summer bears small, orange-red, round hips. Raised at the University Botanic Garden, Cambridge, England, by Dr C. C. Hurst, a famous scientific rosarian to whom we owe much of our knowledge of the genetics of roses. **41**, p. 8.

R. × pteragonis 'Earldomensis'   Sh.
Creamy-yellow, early summer, 6 × 6 ft (1·8 × 1·8 m.) 1934
Raised by Courtney Page, England.
Parentage: *R. hugonis × R. sericea pteracantha*
Vigorous shrub up to 6 ft (1·8 m.) and as much across, twigs thorny and with some reddish colour in prickles as in *pteracantha*. Flowers single, creamy-yellow, about 2 in. (5·1 cm.) across, very free-flowering. Early May to early June. Foliage delicate. Raised by Mr Courtney Page, late Secretary of the R.N.R.S., in his garden at Earldom, near Haywards Heath, England. Its garden value is close to that of 'Cantabrigiensis' but it is now rarely seen in cultivation but grown at the R.N.R.S. **42**, p. 8.

R. × pteragonis 'Headleyensis'   Sh.
Creamy-yellow, early summer, 9 × 9+ ft (2·7 × 2·7+ m.) *c.* 1920
Raised by Sir O. Warburg, England.
Another good seedling of this group. It has creamy-yellow, single flowers, slightly larger than 'Cantabrigiensis'. Hips deep maroon, globular, and also larger than in 'Cantabrigiensis'. Very rare and not generally available, which is unfortunate. Mr G. Thomas wrote in his book *Shrub Roses of Today* that he considered it 'The most ornamental of all the hybrids of *R. hugonis* that I have seen so far'. **43**, p. 8; **44**, p. 9.

R. rapinii see under **R. hemisphaerica.**

R. × richardii, R. sancta, Abyssinian Rose, Holy Rose,   Sp.
St John's Rose
Pale pink, summer, 3 ft (0·9 m.)
Country of origin: probably Asia Minor but introduced from Ethiopia.
A dwarf shrub, a natural hybrid between *R. gallica* and *R. phoenicia*, thus including it in group of Damask roses. Flowers single, pale rose-pink up to 3 in. (7·6 cm.) across, in small clusters, sepals unusually large and glandular. Mid-June to early July. Foliage with up to 5 leaflets, hairy beneath. Hips usually not formed. The history of this rose is intriguing. It was introduced by Messrs Paul, the rose nurserymen of Cheshunt, England, about 1902 and was collected from courtyards of churches in Tigre Province of Ethiopia, where it had apparently been long cultivated. Mr G. Thomas, in his book *The Old Shrub Roses*, speculates that it may have been taken there by St Frumentius in the fourth century and that it may also have been the rose portrayed in Egyptian tombs and in a Minoan fresco. Unfortunately, it is rarely now seen in gardens. It is not the *R. sancta* described by Andrews and hence this name has had to be discarded although formerly widely used for this rose.

R. roxburghii, R. microphylla, Burr Rose, Chestnut Rose,   Sp.
Chinquapin Rose
Pink, summer, 7 ft (2·1 m.)
Countries of origin: China, Japan.
Vigorous shrub rose up to 7 ft (2·1 m.) and as much across, with rather stiff horizontal branches, very prickly and, in old specimens, with flaking, light brown bark. Flowers usually solitary, of medium size up to 3 in. (7·6 cm.) across, single, pale clear pink fading to white around a central mass of gold stamens. A white form is also recorded. Late June to mid-July. Foliage rather distinct with up to

15 leaflets, regularly arranged and decorative. Hips large, up to 1¼ in. (3·2 cm.) across, broadly flask-shaped, bristly, green with persistent calyx; they fall early while still green. Introduced in 1908 although the double form with a central mass of small petals was introduced from a Chinese garden in 1824, and so is considered as the type plant. **45, 46**, p. 9.

R. rubiginosa see **R. eglanteria**

R. rubrifolia, R. glauca, R. ferruginea   Sp.
Pink, summer, 7 × 7 ft (2·1 × 2·1 m.)
Countries of origin: Central Europe.
Vigorous shrub up to 7 ft (2·1 m.) and as much through, distinguished for its blue-grey foliage; probably the finest rose for foliage in cultivation. Flowers rather small, cerise-pink on opening fading to deep blush-pink with a slight purplish tinge, white in centre around stamens, about 2 in. (5·1 cm.) across, singly or in small clusters with long sepals. A blush-white flowered form is also known. June over quite a long season. Foliage with long pointed leaflets, grey-green with a slight bluish-purple glaucous bloom which also covers young stems, in autumn red-tinted. Hips rather globular, bright red complementing foliage and giving a beautiful effect of arching branches in September and October. Central Europe, subalpine regions of Alps and Pyrenees up to about 6,600 ft (2,000 m.). Curiously, *R. rubrifolia* has not been used much by hybridists. It adds distinction to any border of mixed shrub and herbaceous planting and looks particularly well against the warm stone walls of the Cotswolds, England. **47, 48**, p. 9.

Abbreviations and Symbols used in the text

Rose classifications

A.	Alba	HT.	Hybrid Tea
B.	Bourbon	MCl.	Modern, large-flowered climber
C.	Centifolia	Min.	Miniature
Ch.	China	Moss	Centifolia muscosa
Cl.	Climber	MSh.	Modern shrub
D.	Damask	P.	Penzance Sweet Brier
Fl.	Floribunda	R.	Rambler
G.	Gallica	Rg.	Rugosa
HM.	Hybrid Musk	Sp.	Species and first hybrids
HP.	Hybrid Perpetual	Sw.	Sweet Brier

Rose Awards and Societies

A.A.R.S.	All-America Rose Selection
A.G.M.	Award of Garden Merit
A.M.	Award of Merit
A.R.S.	American Rose Society
B.B.G.M.	Baden Baden Gold Medal, Germany
B.G.M.	Bagatelle Gold Medal, Paris
C.C.V.	Clay Challenge Vase for scent
C.M.	Certificate of Merit
D.F.P.	David Fuerstenberg Prize
F.C.C.	First Class Certificate
G.G.M.	Geneva Gold Medal
G.M.	Gold Medal
G.M.C.B.	Gold Medal City of Belfast
G.M.H.G.M.	Gertrude M. Hubbard Gold Medal
G.R.H.	Golden Rose of The Hague
G.T.A.B.	Golden Thorn Award Belfast
H.E.M.M.	The Henry Edland Memorial Medal for the most fragrant rose of the year
H.G.M.	The Hague Gold Medal
L.G.M.	Lyon Gold Medal, France
M.G.M.	Madrid Gold Medal
N.G.M.C.	National Gold Medal Certificate
P.G.M.	Portland Gold Medal, Oregon, U.S.A.
P.I.T.	President's International Trophy
R.B.	Prize for the most fragrant rose, Roeulx, Belgium
R.B.G.M.	Roeulx, Belgium, Gold Medal
R.G.M.	Rome Gold Medal
R.H.S.	The Royal Horticultural Society, London
R.N.R.S.	The Royal National Rose Society, Great Britain*
T.G.C.	Trial Ground Certificate
U.A.B.	The 'Uladh' Award for fragrance, Belfast

National Rose Society awards, before 1965, are included here under R.N.R.S.

The illustration numbers are in **bold type** and the page numbers in light type preceded by p.

R. rubus, *R. ernestii*   Sp.Sh., Semi-cl.
White, summer, 15 ft (4·6 m.)
Country of origin: W. China.
Vigorous large shrub or semi-climber up to 15 ft (4·6 m.) of *moschata* group. Buds yellow, flowers white, single, each about 1½ in. (3·8 cm.) across, strongly scented, in large panicles of up to 40. Late June to August but not recurrent. Leaflets ovate, toothed, purplish below when young. Hips rather small, globose, dark red. Originally discovered by A. Henry about 1886 and later collected by E. H. Wilson in 1907 and later again by R. Farrer. Farrer praised it strongly and described it in China as 'A most glorious bush making shoots 12 ft (3·7 m.) long in a season . . . the blossom of such a fragrance that all the air is drunk with its sweetness'; he noted that the fragrance is only noticeable after midday.

R. rugosa, The Ramanas Rose   Sp.
Purplish-rose or carmine, 8 ft (2·4 m.) *c.* 1845
Introduced by Dr von Siebold.
Countries of origin: China, Japan, Korea.
Vigorous, up to 8 × 8 ft (2·4 × 2·4 m.) distinguished for strong, sturdy growth and bright apple-green rugulose foliage. Stems very prickly. Flowers in small clusters, single, large, purplish-rose to violet-carmine, 3½–4 in. (8·9–10·2 cm.) across, slightly scented. Variable in colour. Leaflets large, 5–9, hairy beneath, turning yellow in autumn. Hips, large, rounded, orange-scarlet, up to 1 in. (2·5 cm.) across and very decorative. In China, ladies are said to have prepared a pot-pouri from its petals mixed with camphor and musk. *R. rugosa* is little grown now as a garden plant but has been used much as a stock for budding and sometimes large bushes of this stock survive. Various forms and hybrids, with very distinct *rugosa* characteristics, have been named and these form some of our finest and most floriferous shrub roses. They include 'Alba', 'Blanc Double de Coubert', 'Roseraie de l'Haÿ', 'Rubra' and 'Scabrosa'. All may be pruned hard in winter to make compact shrubs or even hedges or allowed to grow into larger bushes up to 5 ft (1·5 m.) and as much through.

R. rugosa alba see **'Alba', 129**, p, 23.

R. rugosa plena see **'Roseraie de l'Haÿ', 135**, p. 24.

R. rugosa rosea see **'Frau Dagmar Hartopp', 132**, p. 23.

R. rugosa rubra see **'Rubra', 136**, p. 24.

R. rugosa scabrosa see **'Scabrosa', 138**, p. 24.

R. sancta see **R. × richardii**

R. sericea   Sp.
White, early summer, 10 ft (3 m.)
Countries of origin: N. India, Himalaya, N. Burma, W. China.
Vigorous shrub rose with stout very thorny stems up to 10 ft (3 m.), distinguished for the bright red colour of thorns in the variety *pteracantha*, the form usually grown and usually, but not invariably, having only 4 petals. Flowers white, single, petals wedge-shaped and often not overlapping, 1½–2 in. (3·8–5·1 cm.) across; very early flowering, late May to early June. Often the first rose to flower, free-flowering but flowers are not large enough to make it a very effective shrub in bloom. Foliage finely divided with up to 17 leaflets to a leaf. Stem grey-brown. Hips small, pear-shaped, bright red. Widely spread along Himalayan range and into China. *R. omeiensis* has sometimes been separated but it is now more often regarded as a synonym of *R. sericea* and for garden purposes, there is no appreciable difference.

R. sericea 'Heather Muir'   Sp.
Cream, early summer 15 ft (4·6 m.)
Named after the former owner of a great rose garden at Kiftsgate in the Cotswolds, England. Probably raised or selected originally by E. A. Bunyard. Flowers larger than type, creamy-white with overlapping petals, up to 3 in. (7·6 cm.) across, free-flowering over long season, late May to early July. Hips orange-red. A great improvement on *R. sericea* and a very beautiful, large shrub rose. An old specimen at Hidcote, England, is now about 15 ft (4·6 m.) high and 10 ft (3 m.) across. **49**, p. 9.

R. sericea pteracantha, *R. omeiensis pteracantha*   Sp.
White, early summer, 8 ft (2·4 m.)
Distinguished by the very large triangular bright crimson, translucent thorns, up to ¾ in. (1·9 cm.) across at base and borne on the the one-year-old branches. Very conspicuous over a long season when sun shines through them. As the branches age, the thorns turn brownish-grey and so this rose should be pruned hard after flowering, cutting out the old flowering branches to encourage plentiful new growth. Flowers white. **50**, p. 10.
F.C.C., R.H.S. 1905 to form 'Aux grandes Epines', presumably this rose.

R. setipoda   Sp.
Purplish-pink, summer, 10 ft (3 m.)
Country of origin: Central China.
Vigorous bushy shrub up to 10 ft (3 m.) with arching branches and large thorns, distinguished by its handsome foliage with large leaves up to 7 in. (17·9 cm.) long and 9 leaflets of glaucous green borne along the purplish-crimson rachis (axis), slightly scented as a sweet brier. Flowers rather pale purplish-pink with large white centre around stamens, 2½–3 in. (6·4–7·6 cm.) across in small clusters, and with distinct bristly purple flower stalks. Mid to late June. Hips bottle-shaped, bristly with persistent sepals, orange-red and rather decorative. From Hupeh Province, Central China, introduced by E. H. Wilson and first flowered in England in 1909. Rarely seen but worth cultivation for its distinctive foliage. **51**, p. 10.

R. sibirica see **R. spinosissima altaica, 52**, p. 10.

R. sinica 'Anemone' see **R. × anemonoides, 196**, p. 36.

R. sinowilsonii   Sp.Cl.
White, summer, 1904
Flowers white, single, in large clusters, with buds more rounded that in *R. longicuspis* with which some botanists consider it synonymous. Foliage dark shining green with leaves up to 1 ft (0·3 m.) long; purplish below when young. A very fine and vigorous climber which usually does better in warm climates.

R. soulieana   Sp.Cl.
White, summer, 12 ft (3·7 m.)
Country of origin: W. China.
Vigorous climber up to 12 ft (3·7 m.) or may be grown as a large, loose-growing shrub, with long arching stems. Distinguished by its grey foliage and stems, and stout yellowish clawed spines. Flowers single, white, about 1½ in. (3·8 cm.) across, in clusters, about 6 in. (15·2 cm.) across, free-flowering, scented, sepals downy. Early to mid-July. Foliage grey with up to 9 leaflets. Hips orange-red, egg-shaped, numerous but not very large. Discovered by Père Soulié in W. China and sometimes known as 'Père Soulié's Rose', introduced from France to Kew, England, in 1899. A beautiful rose, especially when in flower and best suited to the wild garden where it will form a thick tangle of silvery-grey and where it does not need much pruning. In cold gardens, it may prove slightly tender, young

shoots being killed to the ground after severe winters but it is likely to sprout again.

R. spinosissima, Scotch or Burnet Rose, Scotch Brier   Sp.
White, pale yellow or pale pink, to 6 ft (1·8 m.)
Countries of origin: N. Europe, U.S.S.R., Siberia.
Dwarf bush of varying height, usually only 2–3 ft (0·6–0·9 m.) but occasionally reaching to 6 ft (1·8 m.), stems covered with stiff bristles and slender spines, usually suckering freely. Leaflets small and delicate. Flowers single or semi-double, numerous along stems, 2–3 in. (5·1–7·6 cm.) across. Some double forms are known in cultivation only. Very variable in colour from creamy-white, through pink and yellow to deep purplish-crimson, usually followed by striking hips. A rose of very wide distribution through N. Europe including Britain and stretching through N. Russia and Altai Mts. It is usually a rose of sandy soils, growing almost on the beaches in some parts of Scotland and in cultivation grows well in light sandy soils. May be kept tidy by trimming with shears.

By some botanists *R. pimpinellifolia* has been treated as a separate species with varieties *altaica*, *lutea* and *ochroleuca* on basis of gland-free pedicels but for garden purposes as well as by such authorities as Rehder and Bean they are considered best as merged together under *R. spinosissima* in its broadest sense and this arrangement is followed here. There is a dwarf form, with very fine hips, widespread on the curious Burren formation on the coast of Co. Clare, W. Ireland.

There is a good account of 'The Scotch Rose and its Garden descendants' by Mr G. Rowley in the R.H.S. Journal 86, 433 (1961). He refers to a list by G. Don of 1832 with no fewer than 25 doubles and 149 singles but now only a sprinkling of these survive. Their contribution, however, to modern gardening as parents of Herr W. Kordes' Frühlings series (**162**, **163**, **164**, p. 29; **165**, p. 3) is very great.

R. spinosissima altaica, *R. altaica*, *R. grandiflora*, *R. sibirica*   Sp.
Creamy-white, late spring, 6 × 6 ft (1·8 × 1·8 m.)
Vigorous shrub rose up to 6 ft (1·8 m.) tall and broad. Flowers single, very pale yellow on opening, then creamy-white with good boss of golden stamens, about 2½–3 in. (6·4–7·6 cm.) across, early flowering, late May to early June, in sprays along arching branches and very free-flowering but not recurrent. Distinguished by smooth flower stalks (pedicels). Foliage pinnate, delicate, slightly grey-green, stems dark brown. A valuable shrub for its freedom and earliness of flower. Hips dark maroon-purple, rather globular. **52**, p. 10.

R. spinosissima hispida   Sp.
White, late spring, 4 ft (1·2 m.)
Shrub rose of moderate vigour, usually not over 4 ft, but suckering freely. Flowers single, white or creamy-white with large yellow centre of stamens, 2½ in. (6·4 cm.) across, free-flowering and early; late May to early June, but not recurrent. Stems bristly but not very prickly, foliage delicate, bluish-green; hips rounded. Described by Mr W. J. Bean as 'one of the most lovely of single roses' and deserves to be more widely planted. **53**, p. 10.

R. spinosissima lutea   Sp.
Yellow, late spring, 4 ft (1·2 m.)
Vigorous shrub rose, usually not over 3–4 ft (0·9–1·2 m.) high but suckering freely and quickly forming a prickly thicket. Flowers single, strong buttercup-yellow, 2–2½ in. (5·1–6·4 cm.) across, free-flowering, early, late May to early June, but not recurrent. Foliage downy below, leaflets up to 1 in. (2·5 cm.) long. Hips maroon, almost black, rather globular. This rose has nearly as bright a yellow colour as the Persian *R. foetida*, with which it may be a hybrid, and on its own roots is usually a much better grower. The oldest shoots should be cut out each year right down to the base after

flowering or during the winter. The cultivar 'Lutea Maxima' is slightly larger in flower but usually not such a vigorous grower.

R. spinosissima 'Double White', 'Scotch White'   Sh.
White, late spring, 5 ft (1·5 m.)
Vigorous spreading shrub, usually suckering freely and if left growing makes a dense thicket. Flowers double, creamy-white, with yellow towards centre and on first opening, 2½–3 in. (6·4–7·6 cm.) across. Scented. An old rose of unknown origin. There is also a cultivar with bluish-pink flowers known as 'Double Blush' but it is not seen so often. **54**, p. 10.

R. spinosissima 'Double Yellow', 'Scotch Yellow',   Sh.
  'Old Yellow Scotch'
Yellow, late spring, 5 ft (1·5 m.)
Vigorous shrub, usually suckering freely. Flowers double or semi-double, deep yellow in centre, paling towards edge, about 2½ in. (6·4 cm.) across, free-flowering, slightly scented. An old rose of unknown origin. **55**, p. 10.

R. spinosissima 'Duke of Argyll'   Sh.
Cerise, late spring to summer, 4 ft (1·2 m.)
Vigorous shrub up to 4 ft (1·2 m.). Flowers single, deep cerise-pink with white centre and good boss of yellow stamens. **56**, p. 11.

R. spinosissima 'Mrs Colville'   Sh.
Crimson-purple, early summer, 2½ ft (0·8 m.)
Dwarf shrub rose, usually not over 2½ ft (0·8 m.), possibly hybrid

between *R. spinosissima* and *R. pendulina*. Flowers single, deep crimson-purple with white centre around boss of yellow stamens. Early flowering, late May to early June, but not recurrent. Shoots rather smooth and reddish-brown, foliage delicate, grey-green. Hips purplish-red, less globular than in most Spinosissimas. A beautiful rose which will sucker freely when on its own roots.

R. spinosissima 'Stanwell Perpetual'   Sh.
Blush, recurrent, 7 ft (2·1 m.) 1838
Introduced by J. Lee, England.
Parentage: *R. damascena semperflorens* × *R. spinosissima*
Large shrub or pillar rose up to 7 ft (2·1 m.) but often with rather loose, straggling growth. Flowers semi-double, very pale blush-pink, fading to white with buff-yellow stamens, 3½ in. (8·9 cm.) across, in small clusters; scented; flower is pleasing on first opening but as it fades tends to be rather untidy. Early to mid-June, recurrent into November in a mild autumn. Floriferous. Stems very prickly with numerous small red thorns on young growth. Foliage grey-green or slightly glaucous with up to 9 small leaflets. Prune by taking out weaker growth after flowering and in winter. It should occasionally be pruned quite hard by taking out older growth entirely. 'Stanwell Perpetual' occurred as a chance seedling in a garden at Stanwell, Essex and was first marketed in 1838. **57**, p. 11.

R. spinosissima 'William III'   Sh.
Purplish-crimson, late spring, 2 ft (0·6 m.)
Dwarf shrub rose, usually not over 2 ft (0·6 m.), but usually spreading freely by suckers. Flowers small, semi-double, purplish-crimson, fading to pinkish-lilac, paler on outside, about 2 in. (5·1 cm.) across, rather globular. Early flowering, late May to early June. Foliage delicate, grey-green; hips nearly black, round.

R. sulphurea see R. hemisphaerica

R. sweginzowii   Sp.
Rose-pink, 10 × 10 ft (3 × 3 m.) 1909
Country of origin: N.W. China.
Vigorous shrub, similar to *R. moyesii*, up to 10 ft (3 m.) and as much through, very prickly. Flowers rose-pink with white centre around stamens, single, rather small, 1½–2 in. (3·8–5·1 cm.) across, in small clusters. Foliage with up to 11 leaflets, doubly toothed. Hips flask-shaped, 1–1¼ in. (2·5–3·2 cm.) long, bristly, orange-red, ripening early. Not a widely grown plant; requires much space. **58, 59**, p. 11.

R. villosa see R. pomifera, **37**, p. 7.

R. villosa 'Duplex' see R. pomifera, 'Duplex', **38**, p. 8.

R. virginiana, R. lucida, R. humilis   Sp.
Deep pink, summer, 6 ft (1·8 m.)
Countries of origin: U.S.A., Canada.
Dense growing shrub forming a thick mass of shoots from the base, usually over 6 ft (1·8 m.) or slightly less, distinguished by very brilliant autumn colouring of foliage with scarlet hips and throughout summer by shining glossy foliage. Flowers pale cerise-pink, paler in centre, rather small, with long pointed buds, scented; late flowering, late June continuing to early August but not very floriferous. Foliage tinted bronze when young, bright glossy green all summer and in autumn fiery orange-red and deep yellow. Stems reddish-brown with few thorns. Hips round, of medium size, bright red, persistent. Useful for making a rounded mass in the wild garden. A.G.M., R.H.S.; A.M., R.H.S., for autumn foliage 1970.

R. virginiana 'Alba'
Flowers white, more numerous than in *R. virginiana*, possibly a hybrid with *R. carolina*.

R. virginiana 'Plena'
Flowers double pink. Here possibly belongs the form known as 'Rose d'Amour' which has more numerous double pink flowers and taller growth up to 7 ft (2·1 m.). Buds long pointed and among the most beautiful of rose buds. Possibly a hybrid with *R. carolina*. Late flowering, late June to early September.

R. webbiana   Sp.
Pale pink, early summer, 6 × 6 ft (1·8 × 1·8 m.)
Country of origin: India, Himalaya.
Dense vigorous bush with rather slender growth up to 6 ft (1·8 m.) and as much through with purplish-red stem and finely divided leaves with up to 9 leaflets to a leaf. Flowers single, pale pink or lilac-pink, about 2 in. (5·1 cm.) across, borne singly on short lateral twigs of long arching sprays. Early flowering, early to mid-June and not recurrent. Hips flask shaped, bright scarlet-red, about ¾ in. (1·9 cm.) long. Closely resembling *R. willmottiae* (**60**, p. 11) which is probably the more eastern Chinese counterpart. A rose with a large mountain range from 6,000–18,000 ft (1,800–5,500 m.). Rarely seen in cultivation but a beautiful rose.

R. wichuraiana   Sp. R. Trailer
White, late summer, 20 ft (6·1 m.)
Country of origin: Japan, E. China, Korea, Taiwan.
Vigorous rambler, naturally growing prostrate as a trailer with annual shoots 10 ft (3 m.) long but it may be trained up a pergola or into an old tree, where it will easily grow up to 20 ft (6·1 m.). Flowers single, in large clusters, white with yellowish centre, each up to 1½–2 in. (3·8–5·1 cm.) across. Scented. Late flowering, mid-July to mid-August. Foliage bright green, glossy, semi-evergreen. Hips small, ovoid, dark red. Although now rarely grown *R. wichuraiana* has been most valuable as a parent of the race of garden ramblers which included 'Dorothy Perkins' and 'Crimson Rambler'. It is however valuable for covering banks in the wild garden or small dead trees. Probably not distinct from *R. luciae,* which is the earlier name.

R. willmottiae   Sp.
Pale pink, early summer, 8 × 6 ft (2·4 × 1·8 m.)
Country of origin: China.
Vigorous twiggy and bristly shrub of up to 8 ft (2·4 m.) and 6 ft (1·8 m.) across with finely divided almost fern-like foliage. Flowers pale pink to pale purplish-rose, variable in colour, single, 1½–2 in. (3·8–5·1 cm.) across, with creamy stamens in centre. Early flowering, early to mid-June with an occasional flower later. Hips small, round, bright orange-red. Introduced from W. China near Tibetan border by Dr E. H. Wilson and collected at quite a high altitude, 9,500–11,000 ft (2,900–3,400 m.), so the plant is quite hardy. Distinguished from *R. webbiana* by the absence of glands on the calyx while the hips lack the persistent remains of the calyx. Slightly more vigorous, in colour and with flowers tending to be slightly pinker. **60**, p. 11.

R. wilsonii see R. gentiliana, **18**, p. 3.

R. × wintoniensis   Sh.
Rose-pink, summer, 1935
Raised by Hillier & Sons, England.
Parentage: *R. moyesii* × *R. setipoda*
In general appearance closer to *R. setipoda* (**51**, p. 10) than to *R. moyesii* (**30**, p. 6). Flowers deeper rose-pink than *R. setipoda*. Fine orange-red, bristly hips. Foliage has some sweet brier fragrance.

R. woodsii   Sh.
Pink or white, 6 ft (1·8 m.)
Countries of origin: N. America, Central and Western States,

Canada, Saskatchewan and British Colombia to Kansas and Utah. Shrub of medium vigour with reddish stems when young, becoming grey as they age. Flowers pink or occasionally white, single, about 1½ in. across, in small clusters or singly. Hips bright red, round. The variety *fendleri* is more often grown than the type and has a more southerly distribution down the western states, U.S.A. to New Mexico but which is still quite hardy. Distinguished by its glandular leaflets, petioles and stipules and slightly larger bright scarlet shiny hips which last well through autumn and hang in clusters; also by its strongly scented, lilac-pink flowers but chiefly grown for its hips. **61**, p. 11.

R. xanthina spontanea see **'Canary Bird'**, **143, 144**, p. 25.

'Rosa Mundi' see **'Versicolor'**, **92**, p. 17.

Rose à Feuilles de Laitue see *R.* × *centifolia* **'Bullata'**

'Rose d'Amour' see under *R. virginiana* **'Plena'**

'Rose des Maures' see **'Sissinghurst Castle'**, **90**, p. 16.

Rose des Peintres see *R.* × *centifolia*

'Rose du Maître d'Ecole'　　　　　　　　　　　　　G.
Pale purplish-pink, summer, 4 ft (1·2 m.)
Gallica shrub rose of medium vigour up to 4 ft (1·2 m.). Flowers large, fully double, opening deep rose, then maturing to pale purplish-pink, veined with purple and with a green eye, slightly quartered and opening flat. Up to 4½ in. (11·4 cm.) across, sometimes shaded with mauve and coppery-pink. Now rarely seen in gardens but it used to be a favourite. It tends to fade in strong sun as illustrated. **89**, p. 16.

'Rose Gaujard'　　　　　　　　　　　　　　　　　HT.
White flushed carmine, 3½ ft (1·1 m.) 1957
Raised by J. Gaujard, France.
Parentage: 'Peace' × 'Opera' seedling
A very vigorous, upright grower which spreads to make a large plant, 3½ ft (1·1 m.) high, with handsome glossy, dark green, bronze tinted foliage. The large, full flowers have a white ground flushed and veined with carmine, outer petals somewhat paler than centre and with silvery reverse. Sometimes split but frequently blooms of sufficiently good form for exhibition are produced. In general, this is an outstanding cultivar for the garden, a prolific bloomer, very healthy and especially good in autumn. Ideal for the beginner, unless the slightly garish colour of the flowers is disliked. **360**, p. 67.
G.M., R.N.R.S. 1958; A.M., R.H.S. 1963.

'Rose Marie Viaud'　　　　　　　　　　　　　　　R.
Purple-violet, summer, 15 ft (4·6 m.) 1924
Raised by Igoult, France.
Parentage: 'Veilchenblau' seedling
Vigorous rambler with rather coarse foliage and almost thornless stems. Flowers in large clusters, double, rather small, rosette-like, purplish-violet on opening, changing to Parma violet as flower matures with a slight dusky pale green sheen. Late June to mid-July. Unscented. Distinct for its colour. A better rose than its parent, the more frequently grown 'Veilchenblau', with slightly more blue and worth growing over an old tree where it looks well with a white flowered rambler. Sometimes also hard pruned and grown as a

bush, but this is less effective. Subject to mildew, particularly on pedicels of flowers. **222**, p. 41.

Rose of Persia see *Hulthemia persica*

Rose of Provins see **'Officinalis'**, **86**, p. 16.

'Rose of Tralee'　　　　　　　　　　　　　　　　Fl.
Warm deep pink, 3 ft (0·9 m.) 1964
Raised by S. McGredy IV, N. Ireland.
Parentage: 'Leverkusen' × 'Korona'
A vigorous, shrubby grower, 3 ft (0·9 m.) high, with dark, glossy, rather small foliage. The large double flowers are produced in small clusters, a deep warm pink colour, flushed with salmon. Very freely produced. Usually healthy. **475**, p. 89.

'Rosemary Rose'　　　　　　　　　　　　　　　　Fl.
Rosy-red, 2½ ft (0·8 m.) 1954
Raised by G. de Ruiter, Holland.
Parentage: 'Gruss an Teplitz' × a floribunda seedling
A vigorous, branching grower, 2–2½ ft (0·6–0·8 m.) high, with medium green, mat foliage, coppery-red when young. The full, double flowers are rosette shaped, rosy-red in colour and borne in large clusters. Slightly fragrant. A unique rose for bedding with the charm of the old garden roses but unfortunately subject to mildew.
G.M., R.N.R.S. 1954; R.G.M. 1954.

Abbreviations and Symbols used in the text

Rose classifications

A.	Alba	HT.	Hybrid Tea
B.	Bourbon	MCl.	Modern, large-flowered climber
C.	Centifolia	Min.	Miniature
Ch.	China	Moss	Centifolia muscosa
Cl.	Climber	MSh.	Modern shrub
D.	Damask	P.	Penzance Sweet Brier
Fl.	Floribunda	R.	Rambler
G.	Gallica	Rg.	Rugosa
HM.	Hybrid Musk	Sp.	Species and first hybrids
HP.	Hybrid Perpetual	Sw.	Sweet Brier

Rose Awards and Societies

A.A.R.S.	All-America Rose Selection
A.G.M.	Award of Garden Merit
A.M.	Award of Merit
A.R.S.	American Rose Society
B.B.G.M.	Baden Baden Gold Medal, Germany
B.G.M.	Bagatelle Gold Medal, Paris
C.C.V.	Clay Challenge Vase for scent
C.M.	Certificate of Merit
D.F.P.	David Fuerstenberg Prize
F.C.C.	First Class Certificate
G.G.M.	Geneva Gold Medal
G.M.	Gold Medal
G.M.C.B.	Gold Medal City of Belfast
G.M.H.G.M.	Gertrude M. Hubbard Gold Medal
G.R.H.	Golden Rose of The Hague
G.T.A.B.	Golden Thorn Award Belfast
H.E.M.M.	The Henry Edland Memorial Medal for the most fragrant rose of the year
H.G.M.	The Hague Gold Medal
L.G.M.	Lyon Gold Medal, France
M.G.M.	Madrid Gold Medal
N.G.M.C.	National Gold Medal Certificate
P.G.M.	Portland Gold Medal, Oregon, U.S.A.
P.I.T.	President's International Trophy
R.B.	Prize for the most fragrant rose, Roeulx, Belgium
R.B.G.M.	Roeulx, Belgium, Gold Medal
R.G.M.	Rome Gold Medal
R.H.S.	The Royal Horticultural Society, London
R.N.R.S.	The Royal National Rose Society, Great Britain*
T.G.C.	Trial Ground Certificate
U.A.B.	The 'Uladh' Award for fragrance, Belfast

*National Rose Society awards, before 1965, are included here under R.N.R.S.

The illustration numbers are in **bold type** and the page numbers in light type preceded by p.

'Rosenresli' see **'Horstmann's Rosenresli', 428**, p. 80.

'Roseraie de l'Hay', *R. rugosa plena*　　　　　Rg.
Purplish-crimson, recurrent, 8 × 8 ft (2·4 × 2·4 m.) 1901
Raised by Cochet-Cochet, France.
Vigorous shrub rose up to 8 ft (2·4 m.) high and as much across.
Flowers very large, semi-double, loosely formed, deep purplish-crimson fading to paler purple with violet tinge, up to 4½ in. (11·4 cm.) across. Velvety. Richly scented. Early June, recurrent throughout season. A unique colour among shrub roses which lights up like wine with the light behind, a wonderful shot blend of deep purples and crimson, rich and sumptuous. Foliage good and luxuriant. Hips rarely produced. A group of three shrubs of this in the garden makes a grand feature. **135**, p. 24.
A.G.M., R.H.S.

'Rosina', 'Josephine Wheatcroft', 'Yellow Sweetheart'　　Min.
Bright yellow, 12 in. (30·5 cm.) 1951
Raised by P. Dot, Spain.
Parentage: 'Eduardo Toda' × 'Rouletii'
A dwarf, compact plant, 8–12 in. (20·3–30·5 cm.) high with light glossy foliage. The small, semi-double flowers are clear bright yellow, have a slight fragrance and are produced freely. A very popular cultivar which may require protection against black spot.

'Rosmarin'　　　　　　　　　　　　　　Min.
Soft light pink, 12 in. (30·5 cm.) 1965
Raised by R. Kordes, Germany.
Parentage: 'Tom Thumb' × 'Dacapo'
A very compact, free-flowering plant with glossy light green foliage. The small, somewhat globular, double flowers are soft light pink with light red reverse. Slightly fragrant. An attractive cultivar. Grows well as a standard on a 1 ft (0·3 m.) stem. **505**, p. 96.

'Rouge Eblouissante' see **'Assemblage des Beautés'**

'Rouge et Or' see **'Redgold', 473**, p. 89.

'Rosy Mantle'　　　　　　　　　　　　MCl.
Light rose-pink, 8–10 ft (2·4–3 m.) 1968
Raised by J. Cocker & Sons Ltd, Scotland.
Parentage: 'New Dawn' × 'Prima Ballerina'
A vigorous climber with glossy dark green foliage. The moderately full flowers are of hybrid tea form, light rose-pink in colour with deeper shadings and sweetly fragrant. Flowering freely, this new cultivar is very good in autumn, and appears to be a useful addition to the new climbers which have an extended flowering season.
T.G.C., R.N.R.S. 1970.

'Rouletii', *R. chinensis minima* 'Rouletii'　　　Min.
Rose-pink, 10 in. (25·4 cm.)
Discovered by Major Roulet
A dwarf hardy plant 8–10 in. (20·3–25·4 cm.) high, with a long flowering season, found, it is believed, by Major Roulet growing in pots on the window ledges of Swiss cottages. It was introduced or possibly reintroduced, to cultivation by Henri Correvon, a Swiss nurseryman living in Geneva, and is generally regarded as the forebear of the Miniature roses. Small double rose-pink flowers. A very dainty plant.

'Royal Gold'　　　　　　　　　　　　MCl.
Deep yellow, recurrent, 10 ft (3 m.) 1957
Raised by D. Morey, U.S.A.

Parentage: 'Climbing Goldilocks' × 'Lydia'
Climber or pillar rose of moderate vigour with flowers of hybrid tea type. Flowers large, double, deep golden-yellow, singly or in small clusters, scented. Mid-June and recurrent. Foliage glossy. This rose does best in a warm and sheltered situation and may suffer from die back after a severe winter in cold areas.

'Royal Highness', 'Königliche Hoheit'　　　　HT.
Light pink, 3 ft (0·9 m.) 1962
Raised by Swim and Weeks, U.S.A.
Parentage: 'Virgo' × 'Peace'
A vigorous, branching grower, 3 ft (0·9 m.) high, with glossy, healthy, dark green foliage. The large, high centred flowers are soft, light pink, very full and shapely, ideal for exhibition. They are fragrant, freely produced but do not like wet weather. **361**, p. 67.
P.G.M. 1960; M.G.M. 1962; A.A.R.S. 1963.

'Rubra', *R. rugosa rubra*　　　　　　　　Rg.
Deep purplish-crimson, recurrent, 7 × 7 ft (2·1 × 2·1 m.)
Very vigorous form, making large shrub up to 7 × 7 ft (2·1 × 2·1 m.). Flowers large, up to 4 in. (10·2 cm.) across, single, deep purplish or wine-crimson, free-flowering. Mid to late June and recurrent. Foliage bright green, rugulose. Hips large, shaped like a flat flask, orange-red, probably the finest hips in the *rugosa* group, if not among all roses. **136**, p. 24.
A.M., R.H.S. 1955.

'Rubrotincta' see **'Hebe's Lip', 79**, p. 14.

'Rudolph Timm'　　　　　　　　　　　Fl.
Pale pink, 2 ft (0·6 m.) 1951
Raised by W. Kordes, Germany.
Parentage: ('Johannes Boettner' × 'Magnifica') × ('Baby Château' × 'Else Poulsen')
A cultivar which still retains some of its vigour, 2 ft (0·6 m.) high, with glossy, light green foliage. The flowers are semi-double and soon open an attractive pale pink, edged deeper pink, slightly reminiscent of apple blossom. Scented. **476**, p. 89.
C.M., R.N.R.S. 1951.

'Rumba'　　　　　　　　　　　　　　Fl.
Bright yellow to orange, 2 ft (0·6 m.) 1958
Raised by S. Poulsen, Denmark.
Parentage: 'Masquerade' × ('Poulsen's Bedder' × 'Floradora')
An upright, dense bush, 2 ft (0·6 m.) high, with abundant yellowish-green glossy foliage. The small, full flowers are in tight rosette formation, bright yellow to orange with red edges, very bright and distinctive when young, becoming paler with age. Resists weather well and would be a good bedder if the old faded flowers did not adhere so tightly to the stems, necessitating regular trimming. **477**, p. 89.

St John's Rose see *R. × richardii*

'St Nicholas'　　　　　　　　　　　　D.
Pink, summer, 7 ft (2·1 m.) 1950
A vigorous Damask × Gallica shrub rose up to 7 ft (2·1 m.) and as much across which originated in the garden of a great plantsman, the Hon. Robert James at St Nicholas, Richmond, Yorkshire, England, during this century. Flowers semi-double, deep rose-pink, saucer-shaped, with fine boss of central golden stamens. A deeper stronger pink than 'Céleste', 3 in. (7·6 cm.) across. Very slightly scented. Free-flowering in clusters up to 5, but not recurrent. Mid-season, mid to late June. Stem very prickly with

short red prickles. Foliage good, 5 leaflets, bright green. Hips large, bright orange-red in autumn. A vigorous and usually trouble-free rose of much beauty that is deserving of being more widely grown; unless well supported, tends to arch over and be weighed down with the abundance of flower. Prune out some older flowering wood and weaker shoots after flowering but main pruning should be delayed till winter for the sake of the hips.

'Samourai', 'Scarlet Knight'　　　　　　　　　　　HT.
Crimson-scarlet, 4 ft + (1·2 m.) 1966
Raised by M. L. Meilland, France.
Parentage: ('Happiness' × 'Independence') × 'Sutter's Gold'
A tall, vigorous, upright grower, over 4 ft (1·2 m.) high, with thick, leathery foliage. The flowers are medium to large in size, double and cupped, crimson-scarlet with undertones in a lighter shade. Slight fragrance. **362**, p. 67.
M.G.M. 1966; A.A.R.S. 1968.

'Sanders' White Rambler'　　　　　　　　　　　R.
White, summer, 12 ft (3·7 m.) 1912
Raised by Sanders & Sons, England.
Vigorous rambler of hybrid *wichuraiana* type with glossy foliage. Suitable for pergola or pillar or can be grown effectively as a weeping umbrella standard as at the Roserie de l'Haÿ, Paris. Flowers in large clusters, small semi-double, clear white with gold centre, produced very freely. Mid-June to early July but not recurrent. One of the most beautiful ramblers and most fragrant of the *wichuraiana* group.

'Santa Catalina'　　　　　　　　　　　MCl.
Soft warm pink, recurrent 6–8 ft (1·8–2·4 m.) 1970
Raised by S. McGredy IV, N. Ireland.
Parentage: 'Paddy McGredy' × 'Heidelberg'
A robust grower of restricted height with dark green semi-glossy foliage. The large semi-double flowers are a soft warm pink and open wide to reveal the stamens. Plenty of basal growths, ideal for pillars. This promises to be a beautiful new rose of delicate and unusual colouring among the climbers. **259**, p. 49.

'Sante Fé'　　　　　　　　　　　HT.
Salmon-rose, 3 ft (0·9 m.) 1967
Raised by S. McGredy IV, N. Ireland.
Parentage: 'Mischief' × 'Super Star'
A vigorous, upright grower, 3 ft (0·9 m.) high, with small, dark green, mat foliage. The large full blooms are salmon-rose-pink with lighter reverse, somewhat globular in form, freely produced; a useful bedding cultivar, at its best in the autumn. **363**, p. 68.
C.M., R.N.R.S. 1967.

'Santa Maria'　　　　　　　　　　　Fl.
Deep scarlet, 2½ ft (0·8 m.) 1969
Raised by S. McGredy IV, N. Ireland.
Parentage: 'Evelyn Fison' × ('Ma Perkins' × 'Moulin Rouge')
A very free-flowering bedding rose, deep scarlet, slightly fragrant, open flowers in trusses. Small foliage. About 2½ ft (0·8 m.) high. **478**, p. 89.

'Sarabande'　　　　　　　　　　　Fl.
Bright orange-red, 2½ ft (0·8 m.) 1957
Raised by F. Meilland, France.
Parentage: 'Cocorico' × 'Moulin Rouge'
A low, bushy grower, about 2–2½ ft (0·6–0·8 m.) high, with semi-glossy, abundant foliage. The medium sized semi-double flowers open quickly to show bright yellow stamens, a wonderful contrast to the brilliant orange-red flowers which hold their colour well.

Fragrance is slight. A good bedding rose. **482**, p. 92.
B.G.M. 1957; G.G.M. 1957; R.G.M. 1957; P.G.M. 1958; A.A.R.S. 1960.

'Sarah Arnot'　　　　　　　　　　　HT.
Rose-pink, 2½ ft (0·8 m.) 1957
Raised by D. & W. Croll Ltd, Scotland.
Parentage: 'Ena Harkness' × 'Peace'
A vigorous grower, 2½ ft (0·8 m.) high, with semi-glossy, medium green foliage. The large, fairly full flowers are warm rose-pink, very freely produced and fragrant. Weather resistant, this is a useful bedding rose which seems to produce better results in the cooler weather conditions of northern gardens. **364**, p. 68.
G.M., R.N.R.S. 1958.

'Sarah Van Fleet'　　　　　　　　　　　Rg.
Pink, recurrent, 8 ft (2·4 m.) 1926
Raised by Dr W. Van Fleet, U.S.A.
Parentage: reputedly *R. rugosa* × 'My Maryland'
Vigorous Rugosa hybrid shrub or pillar rose up to 8 ft (2·4 m.). Flowers semi-double, china-pink with good yellow centre, large, up to 3½ in. (8·9 cm.) across, in clusters. Flowers somewhat resemble those of 'New Dawn' (**216**, p. 40) but are deeper pink and larger. Mid-June but recurrent throughout summer, very floriferous. Highly recommended for its vigour and freedom of flower combined with its long season; it is useful for making a dense screen or informal hedge. **137**, p. 24.
A.M., R.H.S. 1962.

'Saratoga'   Fl.
White, 2½ ft + (0·8 m.) 1963
Raised by E.S. Boerner, U.S.A.
Parentage: 'White Bouquet' × 'Princess White'
A vigorous, upright, bushy grower, 2½ ft (0·8 m.) and upwards in
height with glossy dark green foliage. The white flowers are large,
freely produced in somewhat irregular clusters and distinctly
fragrant.
A.A.R.S. 1964.

'Satchmo'   Fl.
Crimson-scarlet, 2½ ft (0·8 m.) 1969
Raised by S. McGredy IV, N. Ireland.
Parentage: 'Evelyn Fison' × 'Diamant'
A short, compact grower, just over 2½ ft (0·8 m.) high, with mid-
green foliage. The bright crimson-scarlet flowers present a dazzling
piece of colour and are produced in trusses, occasionally single. No
scent. Weather resistant.
H.G.M. 1970; R.B.G.M. 1970.

'Scabrosa', *R. rugosa scabrosa*   Rg.
Purplish-crimson, recurrent, 6 × 6 ft (1·8 × 1·8 m.)
Introduced by R. Harkness & Co. Ltd, England.
Vigorous shrub up to 6 ft (1·8 m.) and as much across. Probably a
fine form of *R. rugosa rubra*. Flowers very large, single, rich crimson-purple with a slight violet tinge or deep purplish-pink, up to
5½ in. (14 cm.) across. Mid to late June main flowering but slightly
recurrent. Hips large, broadly flask-shaped with persistent calyx,
orange-red or tomato-red. Foliage good, light green, very rugulose.
'Scabrosa' makes a large, widespreading bush, usually of great
vigour and is one of the best for its hips. Worth planting in the
larger garden. **138**, p. 24.
A.M., R.H.S. 1964.

'Scania'   Fl.
Deep rich red, 2½ ft (0·8 m.) 1965
Raised by G. de Ruiter, Holland.
Parentage: 'Cocorico' × seedling
A bushy low grower, 2½ ft (0·8 m.) high, with dull, reddish-green
foliage. The large double flowers are well formed, of hybrid tea
shape, eventually opening wide, deep rich velvety red in colour,
which is retained until the end. Resists weather well but may
require protection against black spot. **483**, p. 92.

'Scarlet Fire' see **'Scharlachglut'**, **187**, p. 35.

'Scarlet Gem', 'Scarlet Pimpernel'
Bright scarlet, 12 in. (30·5 cm.) 1961
Raised by A. Meilland, France.
Parentage: ('Moulin Rouge' × 'Fashion') × ('Perla de Montserrat'
× 'Perla de Alcanada')
A dwarf bushy grower, 10–12 in. (25·4–30·5 cm.) high with dark
glossy foliage. The small, very double flowers are a bright scarlet,
which does not fade. An attractive plant and one of the popular
cultivars. Useful as a standard on a 12 in. (30·5 cm.) stem.

'Scarlet Knight' see **'Samourai'**, **362**, p. 67.

'Scarlet Pimpernel' see **'Scarlet Gem'**

'Scarlet Queen Elizabeth'   Fl.
Bright scarlet, 4 ft (1·2 m.) 1963
Raised by A. Dickson & Sons Ltd, N. Ireland.
Parentage: ('Korona' × seedling) × 'Queen Elizabeth'

A very vigorous, upright grower about 4 ft (1·2 m.) high, with dark
green healthy foliage. The flowers are somewhat globular, showing
reverse side of petals in the centre, bright scarlet, fading slightly with
age. Weather resistance is good. Slight scent. Freely produced. A
good and attractive cultivar for large beds or back of borders.
479, p. 90.
T.G.C., R.N.R.S. 1963.

'Scented Air'   Fl.
Deep salmon-pink, 3 ft (0·9 m.) 1965
Raised by A. Dickson & Sons Ltd, N. Ireland.
Parentage: 'Spartan' seedling × 'Queen Elizabeth'
A vigorous, bushy grower, at least 3 ft (0·9 m.) high, with very
large, glossy dark green foliage. The large, well formed flowers are
moderately full, deep salmon-pink in colour and produced in
clusters. Fragrant. A very reliable cultivar. **480**, p. 80.
C.C.V., R.N.R.S. 1965; C.M., R.N.R.S. 1965.

'Scharlachglut', 'Scarlet Fire'   MSh.Cl.
Scarlet-crimson, early summer, 8 ft (2·4 m.) 1952
Raised by W. Kordes, Germany.
Parentage: 'Poinsettia' × 'Alika' (*R. gallica* 'Grandiflora')
Very vigorous and thorny modern shrub or pillar rose up to 8 ft
(2·4 m.). Flowers large, single, in large clusters or singly, up to 4 in.
(10·2 cm.) across, bright clear velvety scarlet-crimson with conspicuous yellow boss of stamens, not scented, very free-flowering.
Mid to late June, but not recurrent. Hips large, pear-shaped,
orange-scarlet in heavy clusters and usually lasting well into
winter. One of the finest red shrub roses of recent introduction and
unusual in its very large hips and fine arching growth. **187**, p. 35.
A.M., R.H.S. 1960.

'Schlösser's Brilliant' see **'Detroiter'**

'Schneewittchen', 'Fée des Neiges', 'Iceberg'   Fl.
White, 4 ft (1·2 m.) 1958
Raised by R. Kordes, Germany.
Parentage: 'Robin Hood' × 'Virgo'
A vigorous, upright grower, producing many shoots which spread
into a shapely, graceful plant, well furnished with glossy light
green foliage. The medium sized flowers are moderately full,
opening flat, generally pure white, sometimes flushed pale pink,
especially in late autumn, some pink spots developing as the flowers
age. Flowering profusely in clusters, sometimes in large trusses all
over the plant. Resists weather well and has a slight but pleasant
scent. Has been, for several years, one of the great Floribunda roses.
Pruned lightly, will develop into a shrub; is ideal for a hedge and
outstanding as a bedder or a standard and consequently has become
very popular. Protection against mildew and black spot may be
necessary in some areas. **481**, p. 91.
G.M., R.N.R.S. 1958; A.M., R.H.S. 1961; F.C.C., R.H.S. 1962.

'Schneewittchen, Climbing' see **'Climbing Iceberg'**

'Schneezwerg', 'Snow Dwarf'   Rg.
White, recurrent, 5 × 5 ft (1·5 × 1·5 m.) 1912
Raised by P. Lambert, Germany.
Parentage: possibly *R. rugosa* × *R. bracteata* or a white polyantha
Shrub up to 5 ft (1·5 m.) and as much across. Flowers ice-white,
semi-double with pale yellow stamens, of medium size, 3–3½ in. (7·6–
8·9 cm.) across, opening flat. Mid-June and recurrent throughout
season. Slight scent. Hips smaller than in other Rugosas, orange-
red. A pleasing shrub with good *rugosa* type foliage of deep apple-
green, leaflets slightly smaller than in other forms. Distinct for the
shining whiteness of its flowers which contrast well with the early
hips. Makes a fine hedge which may be clipped with shears. **139**, p.24.
A.M., R.H.S. 1948.

'Schoolgirl' MCl.
Apricot-orange, recurrent, 8–10 ft (2·4–3 m.) 1964
Raised by S. McGredy IV, N. Ireland.
Parentage: 'Coral Dawn' × 'Belle Blonde'
A vigorous grower with dark green glossy foliage. The full shapely flowers are freely produced, a bright apricot-orange colour, a most attractive shade but fading to salmon-pink. Fragrant. Grows freely but is apt to become bare at the base if not pruned and trained to correct.

'Schwanensee' see **'Swan Lake', 261**, p. 49.

'Scintillation' MSh.Cl.
Blush-pink, summer, 10 ft (3 m.) 1966
Raised by D. Austin, England.
Parentage: 'Macrantha' × 'Vanity'
Large shrub or climbing rose, very vigorous, of sprawling growth up to 10 ft (3 m.). Flowers semi-double, blush-pink with conspicuous stamens, in large clusters. Free-flowering, scented. Late June to mid-July with long flowering season but not recurrent. Valuable for covering old stumps or small trees. Foliage grey-green.

Scotch Briers see *R. spinosissima* varieties, **52-55**, p. 10; **56, 57**, p. 11.

Scotch Rose see *R. spinosissima*

'Sea Foam' MSh.Cl.
White and cream, recurrent, 3 × 6 ft across (0·9 × 1·8 m.) 1964
Raised by E. W. Schwartz, U.S.A.
Parentage: (('White Dawn' × 'Pinocchio') × ('White Dawn' × 'Pinocchio')) × ('White Dawn' × 'Pinocchio')
A semi-prostrate, vigorous grower with small, glossy dark green foliage. The small double flowers are white, touched with cream, shaded pink as they age, and are freely produced in clusters. Would seem to be most useful as a ground cover plant when grown naturally but could be trained on a wall or fence to attain limited height. Has impressed as a ground cover rose in U.S.A. where it appears to be more vigorous than in the U.K. where it has been disappointing as the flowers become untidy very quickly in damp weather. Very healthy foliage and some scent.
R.G.M. 1963; D.F.P., A.R.S. 1968.

'Sea Pearl', 'Flower Girl' Fl.
Orange and salmon-pink, 3½ ft (1·1 m.) 1964
Raised by A. Dickson & Sons Ltd, N. Ireland.
Parentage: 'Kordes' Perfecta' × 'Montezuma'
A very upright, vigorous grower with glossy, coppery dark green foliage, generally 3½ ft (1·1 m.) high. The moderately full flowers have a decided hybrid tea shape in the early stages, opening wide later. Variable in colour, a blend of orange and salmon-pink with a peach-pink reverse, paling off as they age, when the blooms become flecked with red. Flowers are produced in large trusses on strong growths and resist wet well. Some scent. **484**, p. 92.
C.M., R.N.R.S. 1964.

'Seagull' R.
White, early summer, 12 ft (3·7 m.) 1907
Raised by Pritchard, England.
Parentage: probably derived from *R. multiflora*
Very vigorous rambler up to 12 ft (3·7 m.). Flowers in large clusters, single, white with yellow centre, scented, very free-flowering. Mid-June. Not recurrent. Excellent for climbing into a small tree or on a large pergola as in the photograph. A good clear white rambler that can be used in place of *R. filipes* 'Kiftsgate' (**19**, p. 4) where there is insufficient space for the latter. **223**, p. 41.

'Sénateur Amic' Cl.
Cerise-pink, early summer, 20 ft (6·1 m.) 1924
Raised by P. Nabonnand, France.
Parentage: *R. gigantea* × 'General MacArthur'
A vigorous and free-flowering climber for the warmer garden, flowering early. Most spectacular in Riviera gardens, however it grows well enough in cooler but not cold areas, especially if planted on a south or west wall. Flowers bright cerise-pink, semi-double and showing boss of yellow stamens when fully open, petals rather loose and irregular, bud long pointed, flower up to 4½ in. (11·4 cm.) across when fully open; as the flower matures it becomes a warmer pink with shades of terracotta. The flowers are borne singly or in clusters of 2–3. Scent slight. Early June but in south Europe March to April to early May. Foliage light green with 3–5 leaflets, rather susceptible to mildew and black spot but still worth its place where it can be grown well, since its sumptuous effect is unrivalled in its colour early in the rose season. Like other *gigantea* hybrids, it makes strong young shoots after the flowers are over and to encourage these the old flowering shoots should be pruned out as soon as the flowers are over. **224**, p. 42.

'Serenade' HT.
Coral-orange, 3 ft (0·9 m.) 1949
Raised by E.S. Boerner, U.S.A.
Parentage: 'Sonata' × 'Mev. H.A. Verschuren'

Abbreviations and Symbols used in the text

Rose classifications

A.	Alba	HT.	Hybrid Tea
B.	Bourbon	MCl.	Modern, large-flowered climber
C.	Centifolia	Min.	Miniature
Ch.	China	Moss	Centifolia muscosa
Cl.	Climber	MSh.	Modern shrub
D.	Damask	P.	Penzance Sweet Brier
Fl.	Floribunda	R.	Rambler
G.	Gallica	Rg.	Rugosa
HM.	Hybrid Musk	Sp.	Species and first hybrids
HP.	Hybrid Perpetual	Sw.	Sweet Brier

Rose Awards and Societies

A.A.R.S.	All-America Rose Selection
A.G.M.	Award of Garden Merit
A.M.	Award of Merit
A.R.S.	American Rose Society
B.B.G.M.	Baden Baden Gold Medal, Germany
B.G.M.	Bagatelle Gold Medal, Paris
C.C.V.	Clay Challenge Vase for scent
C.M.	Certificate of Merit
D.F.P.	David Fuerstenberg Prize
F.C.C.	First Class Certificate
G.G.M.	Geneva Gold Medal
G.M.	Gold Medal
G.M.C.B.	Gold Medal City of Belfast
G.M.H.G.M.	Gertrude M. Hubbard Gold Medal
G.R.H.	Golden Rose of The Hague
G.T.A.B.	Golden Thorn Award Belfast
H.E.M.M.	The Henry Edland Memorial Medal for the most fragrant rose of the year
H.G.M.	The Hague Gold Medal
L.G.M.	Lyon Gold Medal, France
M.G.M.	Madrid Gold Medal
N.G.M.C.	National Gold Medal Certificate
P.G.M.	Portland Gold Medal, Oregon, U.S.A.
P.I.T.	President's International Trophy
R.B.	Prize for the most fragrant rose, Roeulx, Belgium
R.B.G.M.	Roeulx, Belgium, Gold Medal
R.G.M.	Rome Gold Medal
R.H.S.	The Royal Horticultural Society, London
R.N.R.S.	The Royal National Rose Society, Great Britain*
T.G.C.	Trial Ground Certificate
U.A.B.	The 'Uladh' Award for fragrance, Belfast

National Rose Society awards, before 1965, are included here under R.N.R.S.

The illustration numbers are in **bold type** and the page numbers in light type preceded by p.

A fairly vigorous grower, 3 ft (o·9 m.) high, with mat, coppery-green foliage. The flowers of medium size, coral-orange with deeper shadings, are very freely produced over a long season. **365**, p. 68.

'Shailer's White Moss' see *R.* × *centifolia* **'Muscosa Alba'**

'Shannon'   HT.
Bright pink, 3 ft (o·9 m.) 1965
Raised by S. McGredy IV, N. Ireland.
Parentage: 'Queen Elizabeth' × 'McGredy's Yellow'
A tall, upright grower, at least 3 ft (o·9 m.) high, with glossy, medium green foliage and very round leaflets. The full flowers are somewhat globular, but on occasions an exhibition type bloom is produced. Bright pink in colour and somewhat later coming into flower than most, this is a useful cultivar for large beds, particularly in good weather.

'Shepherdess'   Fl.
Yellow, 2½ ft (o·8 m.) 1967
Raised by J. Mattock Ltd, England.
Parentage: 'Allgold' × 'Peace'
A vigorous, branching grower with dark glossy bronze-tinted foliage, 2½ ft (o·8 m.) high. The hybrid tea shaped flowers become semi-double as they open, are freely produced over a long season and are yellow with reddish-salmon flushes. Slightly fragrant. A useful bedding rose. **485**, p. 92.
T.G.C., R.N.R.S. 1966.

'Shepherd's Delight'   Fl.
Rich deep orange, 3 ft (o·9 m.) 1956
Raised by A. Dickson & Sons Ltd, N. Ireland.
Parentage: 'Masquerade' seedling × 'Joanna Hill'
A very upright, vigorous grower, 3 ft (o·9 m.) high with handsome glossy dark green foliage. The fairly large blooms are produced in clusters, open rich deep orange with yellow and carmine showing up as the flowers age, when they open somewhat untidily. Slight fragrance and reasonably weather resistant. Better as a border cultivar than as a bedder. May require protection against mildew. **486**, p. 92.
G.M., R.N.R.S. 1958; A.M., R.H.S. 1958.

'Shot Silk'   HT.
Salmon-pink, 2½ ft (o·8 m.) 1924
Raised by A. Dickson & Sons Ltd, N. Ireland.
Parentage: 'Hugh Dickson' seedling × 'Sunstar'
An old favourite, still fairly vigorous in northern gardens. I saw it in good form in Saughton Park, Edinburgh in 1970. The glossy, mid-green foliage is very attractive and the salmon-pink flowers which are shaded yellow, soon open but resist wet and are richly scented. The climbing form, discovered by C. Knight and introduced in 1931, is still very vigorous and well worth growing. No rose has been produced since in this attractive, sparkling shade.
G.M., R.N.R.S. 1923.

'Shot Silk, Climbing' see **'Climbing Shot Silk'**

'Silva'   HT.
Pale apricot and yellow, 2½ ft (o·8 m.) 1964
Raised by A. Meilland, France.
Parentage: 'Peace' × 'Confidence'
A vigorous, upright grower, 2½ ft (o·8 m.) high, with glossy, dark bronze-green foliage. The flowers are of medium size, pale apricot, flushed pink with yellow reverse, and are full with a slight fragrance.

A very free-flowering cultivar over a long season and very useful as a garden plant or for cutting for decorative purposes. **366**, p. 68.
H.G.M. 1964; T.G.C., R.N.R.S. 1967.

'Silver Lining'   HT.
Silvery-rose-pink, 2½ ft (o·8 m.) 1958
Raised by A. Dickson & Sons Ltd, N. Ireland.
Parentage: 'Karl Herbst' × 'Eden Rose' seedling
A fairly vigorous grower, 2½ ft (o·8 m.) high, with glossy, dark green foliage which is generally very healthy. The blooms are large, of ideal shape and therefore much favoured by exhibitors, and are silvery-rose-pink in colour with a silvery reverse. Very fragrant. This cultivar will only appeal to lovers of pastel shades.
C.C.V., R.N.R.S. 1957; G.M., R.N.R.S. 1958.

'Silver Moon'   Cl.
Creamy-white, summer, 20 ft + (6·1 m.) 1910
Raised by Dr W. Van Fleet, U.S.A.
Parentage: reputedly (*R. wichuraiana* × 'Devoniensis') × *R. laevigata*
Vigorous climber up to 20 ft (6·1 m.) or more. Flowers large, single or semi-double, creamy-white with large boss of deep yellow stamens, strongly scented. Buds creamy-yellow. Mid to late June, but not recurrent. Foliage dark green, glossy as in *R. laevigata*. **225**, p. 42.

'Sir Lancelot'   Fl.
Apricot-yellow, 2½ ft (o·8 m.) 1967
Raised by R. Harkness & Co. Ltd, England.
Parentage: 'Vera Dalton' × 'Woburn Abbey'
A fairly vigorous, branching grower with small, mat light green foliage. Beautiful in the bud stage, the apricot-yellow flowers pale off as they age. They have a slight scent. Continues to flower until late in the season if weather is fine but may require protection against black spot. **487**, p. 92.

'Sissi' see **'Mainzer Fastnacht', 330**, p. 62.

'Sissinghurst Castle', 'Rose des Maures'   G.
Purplish-crimson, summer, 4 ft (1·2 m.)
Shrub rose of medium vigour, but often suckering freely to make a small thicket, up to 4 ft (1·2 m.). Flowers semi-double, up to 3½ in. (8·9 cm.) across, deep purplish-crimson with a gold centre, sometimes slightly flecked with white towards base and on petals; free flowering in mid to late June. Reintroduced in 1947 this old Gallica was rediscovered by V. Sackville-West at Sissinghurst Castle where a large bed of it is grown. It also makes a good low hedge. **90**, p. 16.

'Skyrocket' see **'Wilhelm', 191**, p. 35.

'Slater's Crimson China' see under *R. chinensis*

'Small Maidens' Blush' see under **'Maidens' Blush', 67**, p. 12.

'Snow Dwarf' see **'Schneezwerg', 139**, p. 24.

'Snow Queen' see **'Frau Karl Druschki', 111**, p. 20.

'Snowline'   Fl.
White, 2 ft (o·6 m.) 1969
Raised by N. D. Poulsen, Denmark.

A compact bushy grower, 2 ft (0·6 m.) high with glossy dark green foliage. The full flowers are white, produced freely in trusses. Looks like being a good bedding cultivar.
T.G.C., R.N.R.S. 1970.

'Soldier Boy'   MCl.
Scarlet, recurrent, 12 ft (3·7 m.) 1953
Raised by E.B. LeGrice, England.
Parentage: unnamed seedling × 'Guinée'
Vigorous climber or pillar rose. Flowers large, single, up to 5 in. (12·7 cm.) across, bright scarlet-red, velvety, with golden stamens, singly or in clusters, free-flowering. Slight scent. Early June and recurrent to.early autumn. **260**, p. 49.
T.G.C., R.N.R.S. 1953.

'Soraya'   HT.
Orange-flame, 2½ ft (0·8 m.) 1956
Raised by F. Meilland, France.
Parentage: ('Peace' × 'Floradora') × 'Grand'mère Jenny'
A fairly vigorous, upright grower, 2½ ft (0·8 m.) high, with glossy, dark green, red tinted foliage which is crimson in its youth. The medium sized flowers are full, somewhat cupped in shape, vivid orange-flame with blackish shadings, becoming bluish-mauve when old. A useful cultivar for cutting, having long stems and many of the flowers being produced singly, except in autumn. Only slight fragrance. A good weather rose which must be dead-headed before flowers are too old if garden effect is to be maintained. May require protection from black spot.

'Souvenir d'Alphonse Lavallée'   HP.
Crimson-maroon, recurrent, 4 ft (1·2 m.) 1884
Introduced by C. Verdier, France.
A Hybrid Perpetual rose of only medium vigour, not often over 4 ft (1·2 m.). Flowers double, of medium size, very dark velvety crimson-maroon, which appear almost black in the shade, shaped like a Hybrid Tea with closely packed petals, strongly scented. Fading to a deep plum-purple. Flowers in rather tight clusters. Mid to late June, recurrent. Foliage of Hybrid Tea type. In wet weather sometimes the tightly packed petals tend to rot before the flower opens fully and for this reason it cannot be recommended for small collections.

'Souvenir de Claudius Denoyel'   Cl.
Deep crimson, recurrent, 15 ft (4·6 m.) 1920
Raised by C. Chambard, France.
Parentage: 'Château de Clos Vougeot' × 'Commandeur Jules Gravereaux'
Climber of medium vigour with flowers of hybrid tea type. Flowers large, semi-double, bright crimson-red, velvety, retaining colour well; rather a loose open flower when mature and slightly drooping. Strongly scented. Mid-June and recurrent. Foliage rather sparse. A lovely climber for its intense and bright red colour, suitable for a pillar, pergola or for growing against a wall. **226**, p. 42.

'Souvenir de la Malmaison'   B.
Pale pink, recurrent, 10 ft (3 m.) 1843
Raised by J. Béluze, France.
Parentage: 'Mme Desprez' × a Tea rose
Bourbon shrub or pillar rose, vigorous, up to 10 ft (3 m.). Flowers large, cup-shaped on opening, pale blush-pink, fading to almost white, maturing flat and quartered, up to 5 in. (12·7 cm.) across, strongly scented. Mid to late June, but recurrent, usually with a good flowering in September. Named in memory of the Empress Josephine's garden.

'Souvenir de la Princesse de Lamballe' see **'Bourbon Queen'**, **93**, p. 17.

'Souvenir de l'Impératrice Josephine' see **'Francofurtana'**

'Souvenir de St Anne's'   B.
Blush-pink, recurrent, 6 ft (1·8 m.) 1950
Discovered in the garden of Lady Ardilaun, Eire, introduced by G. Thomas, England.
Parentage: 'Souvenir de la Malmaison' sport
Bourbon rose. Vigorous shrub up to 6 ft (1·8 m.) This arose as a sport from 'Souvenir de la Malmaison' in the garden of the late Lady Ardilaun at St Anne's near Dublin, Eire. Flowers single, blush-pink to almost white. Otherwise close to her parent. **102**, p. 18.

'Souvenir du Docteur Jamain'   HP.
Deep purplish-crimson, recurrent, 6–8 ft (1·8–2·4 m.) 1865
Raised by F. Lacharme, France.
Parentage: 'Charles Lefèbvre' or 'Général Jacqueminot' seedling
Hybrid Perpetual shrub up to 6 ft (1·8 m.) or wall rose up to 8 ft (2·4 m.) not over vigorous but the finest rose I know for scent, which is strong, sweet and deep. Flowers deep crimson-maroon, maturing to deep purplish-crimson, full double and well-formed, opening flat and quartered like many of the old roses, of medium size, 3–3½ in. (7·6–8·9 cm.) across, velvety. Its colour is rich and subtle and lights up in the sunlight. Early to mid-June with some flowers later throughout the season. Foliage deep green with 5

leaflets, but susceptible to black spot and rust. Hips large, orange-red. It is well worth some care and attention and seems to grow best as a wall plant out of the strongest morning sun since the flowers tend to fade in strong sun. Prune some of the older flowering shoots out after flowering and again in winter. **116**, p. 21.

'Spanish Beauty' see **'Mme Grégoire Staechelin', 213**, p. 39.

'Sparkie'   Min.
Brilliant light crimson, 12 in. (30·5 cm.) 1957
Raised by R. S. Moore, U.S.A.
Parentage: (*R. wichuraiana* × 'Floradora') × 'Little Buckaroo'
A vigorous plant, 10–12 in. (25·4–30·5 cm.) high with glossy foliage. The single flowers are brilliant light crimson and are produced in clusters.

'Sparrieshoop'   MSh.Cl.
Apricot-pink, recurrent, 10 ft (3 m.) 1953
Raised by W. Kordes, Germany.
Parentage: ('Baby Château' × 'Else Poulsen') × 'Magnifica'
Very vigorous modern shrub or pillar rose up to 10 ft (3 m.) with large red thorns on reddish stems of young growth. Flowers large, 4 in. (10·2 cm.) across, single to semi-double, salmon-apricot-pink, paler in centre, scented, very free-flowering in clusters or singly. Mid to late June and recurrent. Popular and valuable for its abundance of flower and great vigour. **188**, p. 35.

'Spectacular' see **'Danse du Feu', 240**, p. 45.

'Spek's Yellow', 'Golden Scepter'   HT.
Golden-yellow, 3 ft (0·9 m.) 1947
Raised by J. Verschuren-Pechtold, Holland.
Parentage: 'Golden Rapture' × unnamed seedling
A tall, leggy grower, some 3 ft (0·9 m.) high, with dark green, glossy foliage. The small to medium sized flowers are full, shapely, deep golden-yellow in colour, very free. In autumn large candelabra like trusses of bloom are produced, more like a Floribunda. Most useful for cutting as the colour remains consistent and the flowers are fragrant.
A.M., R.H.S. 1947; T.G.C., R.N.R.S. 1947.

'Stanwell Perpetual' see *R. spinosissima* **'Stanwell Perpetual', 57**, p. 11.

'Starina'   Min.
Vivid orange-scarlet, 10 in. (25·4 cm.) 1965
Raised by M. L. Meilland, France.
Parentage: ('Dany Robin' × 'Fire King') × 'Perla de Montserrat'
A vigorous dwarf, 10 in. (25·4 cm.) high with glossy foliage. The fully double flowers are beautifully formed, vivid orange-scarlet in colour and last several days when cut without losing form. Highly thought of in the U.S.A. but considered difficult to propagate. **506**, p. 96.
G.M., Japan 1968.

'Stella'   HT.
Cream flushed pink, 3 ft (0·9 m.) 1958
Raised by M. Tantau, Germany.
Parentage: 'Horstmann's Jubiläumsrose' × 'Peace'
A vigorous grower, about 3 ft (0·9 m.) high, with abundant, glossy mid-green, bronze tinted foliage. The large, full blooms are seldom produced singly but are frequently in large heads of up to 7 blooms, which when disbudded are ideal for exhibition. The well shaped

flowers are cream in the centre, flushed pink, deeper towards the outside fading somewhat when old. This cultivar resists weather exceptionally well and is worth growing as a garden plant. Slight fragrance.
G.M., R.N.R.S. 1960; A.M., R.H.S. 1961.

'Stephen Langdon'   Fl.
Deep crimson, 3 ft (0·9 m.) 1969
Raised by J. Sanday Ltd, England.
Parentage: 'Karl Herbst' × 'Sarabande'
A vigorous, upright grower, 2½–3 ft (0·8–0·9 m.) high, with dark green mat foliage. The large, moderately full flowers are deep crimson, borne in trusses. A very healthy cultivar and looks like being a good bedder.
T.G.C., R.N.R.S. 1970.

'Sterling Silver'   HT.
Silvery-lilac, 2 ft (0·6 m.) 1957
Raised by G. Fisher, U.S.A.
Parentage: seedling × 'Peace'
A poorish grower outside in the U.K., not suitable for the garden and better for growing under glass where it is much happier and more attractive. The medium sized flowers are silvery-lilac with deeper shadings, becoming paler with age. Most useful for decoration when disbudded to one flower per stem. Pleasantly scented, this cultivar impresses me most when arranged in combination with a light pink variety such as 'Lady Sylvia', when it is really beautiful.

'Stroller'   Fl.
Cerise and gold, 2½ ft (0·8 m.) 1968
Raised by A. Dickson & Sons Ltd, N. Ireland.
Parentage: 'Manx Queen' × 'Happy Event'
A vigorous bushy grower, 2½ ft (0·8 m.) high, with dark green glossy foliage. The moderately full flowers are an unusual shade of cerise with a gold reverse, a likeable combination enhanced by its free-flowering qualities. A good bedding cultivar. Flowers borne several together and in trusses. **489**, p. 94.
C.M., R.N.R.S. 1969.

Sulphur Rose see *R. hemisphaerica*

'Summer Holiday'   HT.
Orange-red, 3 ft (0·9 m.) 1968
Raised by C. Gregory & Son Ltd, England.
Parentage: 'Super Star' × unknown
A vigorous, spreading grower, some 3 ft (0·9 m.) high, with semi-glossy medium green foliage. The full vivid orange-red flowers have a paler reverse, are freely produced and have a slight fragrance. Borne singly or in trusses. This is a most promising cultivar for effect in the garden. **367**, p. 68.
T.G.C., R.N.R.S. 1968.

'Summer Meeting'   Fl.
Bright yellow, 2½ ft (0·8 m.) 1968
Raised by R. Harkness & Co. Ltd, England.
Parentage: 'Allgold' × 'Circus'
A bushy compact grower, about 2½ ft (0·8 m.) high, with glossy foliage, which is generally healthy. The large flowers are bright yellow on opening, becoming cream with age, and are very freely produced. Slight fragrance.
T.G.C., R.N.R.S. 1968.

'Summer Song', 'Chanson d'Eté'   Fl.
Orange and yellow, 2½ ft (0·8 m.) 1962
Raised by A. Dickson & Sons Ltd, N. Ireland.

Parentage: seedling × 'Masquerade'
A fairly vigorous grower, 2½ ft (0·8 m.) high, with glossy bronze-tinted foliage. The moderately sized flowers are freely produced in trusses, a blend of orange and yellow, and slightly fragrant. Precautions against mildew may be required in some areas.

'Summer Sunshine' HT.
Deep yellow, 2½ ft (0·8 m.) 1962
Raised by H. C. Swim, U.S.A.
Parentage: 'Buccaneer' × 'Lemon Chiffon'
A fairly vigorous, spreading grower, 2½ ft (0·8 m.) high, with semi-glossy, mid-green foliage. The medium sized flowers are rich deep yellow, opening rather quickly, and profusely produced. A striking cultivar because of its colour and good weather resistance but possibly not of very strong constitution. Slightly fragrant.

'Sunday Times' Fl.
Bright pink, 2 ft (0·6 m.) 1971
Raised by S. McGredy IV, N. Ireland.
Parentage: ('Little Darling' × 'Goldilocks') × 'München'
A short, fairly compact grower with small dark green semi-glossy foliage and very thorny growths. Deep pink in bud, opening into medium sized, semi-double flowers, bright phlox-pink with rose reverse, enhanced by yellow base and stamens. No hips are formed so appears to be sterile. Flowers very freely over a very long season, indeed seldom out of flower. This is another unusual cultivar which will have many uses for garden decoration, underplanting shrub roses and ground cover planting. It will probably be possible to trim with shears as a substitute for pruning. **488**, p. 93.
C.M., R.N.R.S. 1970.

'Super Star', 'Tropicana' HT.
Vermilion, 3 ft (0·9 m.) 1960
Raised by M. Tantau, Germany.
Parentage: (seedling × 'Peace') × (seedling × 'Alpine Glow')
A distinctive cultivar which brought an entirely new colour into roses, a pure light vermilion of luminous brilliance and also a distinctive, slightly top heavy type of growth. On good soils a very vigorous grower, with fairly abundant, mat, medium green foliage. Flowering usually commences with a single terminal bloom, followed by the side shoots, often 5 to a stem, frequently more in autumn when quite large trusses are formed. Very free-flowering summer and autumn, with several intermittent blooms between. Blooms resist wet weather well but assume purplish edges to the petals when they become old. They are full, with a distinctive if light fragrance and are sufficiently well formed to be useful for exhibition. Appreciated as a cut flower, it is grown under glass commercially for this purpose. Generally healthy, it does require protection in some gardens against mildew. Tall grower, over 3 ft (0·9 m.), rather small foliage and somewhat later than many cultivars in commencing blooming. **369**, p. 69.
G.M., R.N.R.S. 1960; P.I.T., R.N.R.S. 1960; B.G.M. 1960; G.G.M. 1960; P.G.M. 1960; A.M., R.H.S. 1960; F.C.C., R.H.S. 1963; G.R.H. 1963; A.A.R.S. 1963; N.G.M.C., A.R.S. 1967.

'Super Star, Climbing' see **'Climbing Super Star'**

'Super Sun' HT.
Orange, 2½ ft (0·8 m.) 1967
Distributed by W. Bentley & Sons Ltd, England.
Parentage: 'Piccadilly' sport
This cultivar is one of several sports from 'Piccadilly' with all the good qualities of that cultivar. The blooms are orange with scarlet shading and paler reverse. **368**, p. 68.
T.G.C., R.N.R.S. 1968.

'Sutter's Gold' HT.
Light orange-yellow, 3 ft (0·9 m.) 1950
Raised by H. C. Swim, U.S.A.
Parentage: 'Charlotte Armstrong' × 'Signora'
A vigorous, upright grower, 3 ft (0·9 m.) high, with many side shoots of spindly appearance but producing good flowers when established. Glossy, dark green, bronzy foliage. The orange-red buds develop into light orange-yellow flowers flushed pink and veined scarlet, paling slightly with age. Most profuse in production of its very shapely flowers, both in summer and again in autumn, with reasonably good weather resistance. A very fine bedding rose when well grown, excellent for cutting and very fragrant. One of the few roses which disperses its scent for yards around. **370**, p. 69.
P.G.M. 1946; B.G.M. 1948; G.G.M. 1949; A.A.R.S. 1950; C.M., R.N.R.S. 1951.

'Swan Lake', 'Schwanensee' MCl.
White, recurrent, 7–8 ft (2·1–2·4 m.) 1968
Raised by S. McGredy IV, N. Ireland.
Parentage: 'Memoriam' × 'Heidelberg'
A strong free growing rose with an abundance of medium green foliage. The large, fully double flowers are well formed, white tinged pink in centre, freely produced several together. Resists weather well and has a slight fragrance. Ideal for pillars. A promising new rose. **261**, p. 49.

Sweet Briers see *R. eglanteria* varieties, **8-12**, p. 2; **13**, p. 3.

Abbreviations and Symbols used in the text

Rose classifications

A.	Alba	HT.	Hybrid Tea
B.	Bourbon	MCl.	Modern, large-flowered climber
C.	Centifolia	Min.	Miniature
Ch.	China	Moss	Centifolia muscosa
Cl.	Climber	MSh.	Modern shrub
D.	Damask	P.	Penzance Sweet Brier
Fl.	Floribunda	R.	Rambler
G.	Gallica	Rg.	Rugosa
HM.	Hybrid Musk	Sp.	Species and first hybrids
HP.	Hybrid Perpetual	Sw.	Sweet Brier

Rose Awards and Societies

A.A.R.S.	All-America Rose Selection
A.G.M.	Award of Garden Merit
A.M.	Award of Merit
A.R.S.	American Rose Society
B.B.G.M.	Baden Baden Gold Medal, Germany
B.G.M.	Bagatelle Gold Medal, Paris
C.C.V.	Clay Challenge Vase for scent
C.M.	Certificate of Merit
D.F.P.	David Fuerstenberg Prize
F.C.C.	First Class Certificate
G.G.M.	Geneva Gold Medal
G.M.	Gold Medal
G.M.C.B.	Gold Medal City of Belfast
G.M.H.G.M.	Gertrude M. Hubbard Gold Medal
G.R.H.	Golden Rose of The Hague
G.T.A.B.	Golden Thorn Award Belfast
H.E.M.M.	The Henry Edland Memorial Medal for the most fragrant rose of the year
H.G.M.	The Hague Gold Medal
L.G.M.	Lyon Gold Medal, France
M.G.M.	Madrid Gold Medal
N.G.M.C.	National Gold Medal Certificate
P.G.M.	Portland Gold Medal, Oregon, U.S.A.
P.I.T.	President's International Trophy
R.B.	Prize for the most fragrant rose, Roeulx, Belgium
R.B.G.M.	Roeulx, Belgium, Gold Medal
R.G.M.	Rome Gold Medal
R.H.S.	The Royal Horticultural Society, London
R.N.R.S.	The Royal National Rose Society, Great Britain*
T.G.C.	Trial Ground Certificate
U.A.B.	The 'Uladh' Award for fragrance, Belfast

National Rose Society awards, before 1965, are included here under R.N.R.S.

The illustration numbers are in **bold type** and the page numbers in light type preceded by p.

'Sweet Fairy'   Min.
Apple-blossom-pink, 10 in. (25·4 cm.) 1946
Raised by J. de Vink, Holland.
Parentage: 'Tom Thumb' × unnamed seedling
A vigorous dwarf grower, 8–10 in. (20·3–25·4 cm.) high, with small dark foliage. The delicate apple-blossom-pink flowers are double with pointed petals and are deliciously scented. Highly rated in the U.S.A.

'Sweet Repose' see **'The Optimist', 492**, p. 94.

'Sweet Sultan'   MCl.
Deep scarlet-crimson, recurrent, 10 ft (3 m.) 1958
Raised by S. Eacott, England.
Parentage: 'Independence' × 'Honour Bright'
One of the deepest red climbers which also has brightness in its flowers. Moderately vigorous and with deep green, red-tinted foliage. Flowers singly or in clusters, single, large up to 5 in. (12·7 cm.) across, very deep scarlet-crimson with some maroon shading. Rich scent. Recurrent from mid-June. **262**, p. 49.

'Sweetheart Rose' see **'Cécile Brunner'**

'Sympathie'   MCl.
Dark red, recurrent, 9–10 ft (2·7–3 m.) 1964
Raised by R. Kordes, Germany.
This showy climber appears to have some *R. kordesii* in its breeding. A healthy, vigorous grower with glossy dark green foliage. The flowers are of hybrid tea type, carried in medium clusters, velvety dark red in colour and with a pleasing scent. Rain resistant and freely produced with a good repeat performance.

'Telstar'   Fl.
Orange-buff and yellow, 3 ft (0·9 m.) 1962
Raised by Gandy's Roses Ltd, England.
Parentage: 'Rosemary Gandy' × 'Masquerade'
A vigorous, bushy grower, up to 3 ft (0·9 m.) high with dark green, semi-glossy foliage. The fairly large flowers are semi-double, opening quickly but last well, orange-buff and yellow changing to red as they age. Free flowering. **490**, p. 94.
C.M., R.N.R.S. 1963.

'The Dawson Rose' see **'Dawson', 202**, p. 37.

'The Fairy'   Fl.
Soft pink, 3 ft (0·9 m.) 1932
Discovered by J. A. Bentall, England.
Parentage: 'Lady Godiva' sport
A vigorous, spreading grower, up to 3 ft (0·9 m.) high, with small, very deep green, glossy foliage, almost like box in character, and very healthy. The double flowers, produced in large trusses, are a pretty rosette shape, soft pink in colour, which fades in hot weather. Abundant. Strictly a Poly-pom, it begins to flower rather later than most Floribundas but makes up for it afterwards. Resists weather well. Very effective beside the fountain at the R.N.R.S. Headquarters. **491**, p. 94.

'The Garland', 'Wood's Garland'   R.
Pale salmon-pink, summer, 15 ft (4·6 m.) 1835
Raised by Wells, England.
Parentage: *R. moschata* × *R. multiflora*
Vigorous old rambler up to 15 ft (4·6 m.), but sometimes hard pruned and grown as a large bush. Flowers small, in large clusters, always facing upwards, semi-double, opening with pale creamy-salmon tint and fading to almost white with very faint buff-yellow

tinge, petals slightly quilled, strongly scented, very free-flowering. Mid to late June but not recurrent. May be grown into small trees with great effect. **227**, p. 42.

'The Knight'   MSh.
Deep crimson, recurrent, 4 ft (1·2 m.) 1969
Raised by D. Austin, England.
Parentage: 'Chianti' × unnamed seedling
Shrub rose of *gallica* type, of medium vigour up to 4 ft (1·2 m.). Flowers double, opening deep but bright crimson, ball shaped about 3 in. (7·6 cm.) across, in clusters but well separated, like a Floribunda, maturing to dusky purplish-crimson, the colour of 'Zigeunerknabe' (**105**, p.19); scent very strong. Bud rounded like 'Cardinal de Richelieu' (**83**, p. 15) but larger. Mid-June and then recurrent flowering. Described by raiser 'as perpetual as a hybrid tea'. Foliage dark, of *gallica* type with prickly growth. This rose should be a very valuable addition to our shrub roses since it is probably the only rose of *gallica* type and this colouring which is recurrent-flowering.

The Macartney Rose see *R. bracteata*

'The Optimist', 'Sweet Repose'   Fl.
Pale creamy-pink, 3 ft (0·9 m.) 1955
Raised by G. de Ruiter, Holland.
Parentage: 'Golden Rapture' × Floribunda seedling
A tall, vigorous grower, about 3 ft (0·9 m.) high, with abundant bronze tinted, dark green foliage. The full, well formed hybrid tea type flowers are produced in small clusters, sometimes singly, opening pale creamy-pink with salmon base changing to dull crimson as the flowers age. A very effective and excellent bedding cultivar which has a sweet fragrance. **492**, p. 94.
G.M., R.N.R.S. 1955.

The Ramanas Rose see *R. rugosa*

'The Wife of Bath'   MSh.
Pink, recurrent, 3 ft (0·9 m.) 1969
Raised by D. Austin, England.
Parentage: 'Mme Caroline Testout' × ('Ma Perkins' × 'Constance Spry')
Shrub rose, rather dwarf and making a small twiggy bush. Flowers double, cupped, warm pink, the colour of 'Constance Spry' (**153**, p. 28). Scented. Mid-June and then recurrent. Described by raiser as 'very perpetual'. **189**, p. 35.

'The Yeoman'   MSh.
Salmon-pink, recurrent, 4 ft (1·2 m.) 1969
Raised by D. Austin, England.
Parentage: 'Ivory Fashion' × ('Constance Spry' × 'Monique')
Shrub rose of medium vigour making an open bush up to 4 ft (1·2 m.). Flowers cup-shaped on opening, double, warm salmon or terracotta-pink, paler in outer petals, almost colour of 'Elizabeth of Glamis' (**407**, p. 76), with melting tones, in large clusters, 3 in. (7·6 cm.) across, strongly scented, slightly acrid, reminiscent of myrrh. Very free-flowering. Mid-June and then recurrent. Foliage neat, rather like that of a small Floribunda. A beautiful flower. Described by raiser as 'best performer in his series'. **190**, p. 35.

'Thisbe'   HM.
Buff-yellow, recurrent, 4 ft (1·2 m.) 1918
Raised by Rev. J. H. Pemberton, England.
Hybrid Musk shrub rose of moderate vigour and rather erect growth. Flowers semi-double, buds deep buff-yellow, then fading to

a creamy-buff, of medium size in clusters, strongly scented with musk fragrance. Late June to mid-July and recurrent with best sprays often in early autumn. Not very commonly grown but still valuable for its scent. **124**, p. 22.

'Tiffany' HT.
Rose-salmon, 3 ft (0·9 m.) 1954
Raised by R. V. Lindquist, U.S.A.
Parentage: 'Charlotte Armstrong' × 'Girona'
An upright, vigorous grower, about 3 ft (0·9 m.) high, with large mat, deep green foliage. The large full flowers have petals with serrated edges, a soft rosy-salmon with golden-yellow shadings at base of petals and a pronounced fragrance. A distinctive rose in fine weather but intolerant of rain. **371**, p. 70.
A.A.R.S. 1955.

'Timothy Eaton' HT.
Deep coral-salmon, 2½ ft (0·8 m.) 1968
Raised by S. McGredy IV, N. Ireland.
Parentage: 'Radar' × 'Mischief'
A vigorous upright grower with light green, semi-glossy foliage. The medium sized flowers are coral-salmon in colour and are very freely produced over a long period. Very good for bedding display; fragrance is slight. **372**, p. 70.

'Tip Top' Fl.
Salmon, under 2 ft (0·6 m.) 1963
Raised by M. Tantau, Germany.
A vigorous bushy, low growing cultivar, under 2 ft (0·6 m.) in height, with large double, well formed warm salmon shaded pink flowers borne in large clusters. Flowers almost continuously over a long season and ideal for edging or for small beds.

'Tipo Ideale' see **'Mutabilis'**

'Titania' see **'Perla de Alcanada'**

'Tivoli' Fl.
Rose-pink, 3 ft (0·9 m.) 1955
Raised by S. Poulsen, Denmark.
Parentage: 'Poulsen's Supreme' × ('Souvenir de Claudius Denoyel' × 'Hvissinge-Rose')
A fairly vigorous grower with dark green glossy foliage, about 3 ft (0·9 m.) high. The medium sized blooms are well formed, produced in clusters, warm rose-pink shading to yellow at the base and have some fragrance. Not seen very often in gardens, this still flowers well in Queen Mary's Garden, Regent's Park, London.

'Tom Thumb', 'Peon' Min.
Deep crimson, 6 in. (15·2 cm.) 1936
Raised by J. de Vink, Holland.
Parentage: 'Rouletii' × 'Gloria Mundi'
Very dwarf, 4–6 in. (10·2–15·2 cm.) high with light green foliage and free-flowering. The flowers are deep crimson with a white base. The first of the modern Miniatures and still a favourite which has been much used for breeding.

'Tombola' Fl.
Deep salmon and carmine, 3 ft (0·9 m.) 1967
Raised by G. de Ruiter, Holland.
Parentage: 'Amor' × ('Ena Harkness' × 'Peace')
A vigorous, upright bushy grower, about 3 ft (0·9 m.) high with glossy dark green leaves. The large double flowers are somewhat camellia-like in shape, deep salmon with a suffusion of carmine,

shaded gold towards the base. Very free flowering with a longish interval between. Scented. **493**, p. 94.
T.G.C., R.N.R.S. 1966.

'Tour de Malakoff' C.
Bright purplish-crimson, 6 ft (1·8 m.) 1856
Raised by Soupert & Notting, Luxembourg.
Vigorous shrub up to 6 ft (1·8 m.), sometimes of rather lax habit. Flowers large, double, bright purplish-crimson with a magenta tinge, lighter outside as they mature becoming more blue and almost parma violet, heavily veined violet, about 4 in. (10·2 cm.) across, rather loose petalled paeony-like, sumptuous. Scent medium. Floriferous. Mid-late June but not recurrent. Growth tends to be horizontal in old bushes and may need support but this is one of the finest and most vigorous roses of this group. Sometimes used as a pillar rose. **71**, p. 13.

'Tradition' HT.
Rich scarlet-crimson, 2½ ft (0·8 m.) 1964
Raised by R. Kordes, Germany.
Parentage: 'Detroiter' × 'Don Juan'
A fairly vigorous grower with mat, medium green foliage. The moderately full flowers are a rich, non-fading scarlet-crimson which lasts well. Very free-flowering and repeats quickly, but lacking in scent.

'Traumland', 'Dreamland' Fl.
Soft peach-pink, 2 ft (0·6 m.) 1958
Raised by M. Tantau, Germany.
Parentage: 'Cinnabar Improved' × 'Fashion'

A vigorous bushy grower, about 2 ft (0·6 m.) high, with dark leathery foliage. The large, semi-double flowers are well formed in clusters, soft peach-pink in colour and showing attractive golden stamens as they open. Slightly fragrant. A good cultivar for bedding.
T.G.C., R.N.R.S. 1959.

'Travesti'   Fl.
Yellow and orange, 2 ft (0·6 m.) 1965
Raised by G. de Ruiter, Holland.
Parentage: 'Orange Sensation' × 'Circus'
A vigorous, bushy, branching grower, just over 2 ft (0·6 m.) high, with small, semi-glossy dark green leaves. Flowers are rather small in early stages, opening semi-double, yellow and orange, flushed carmine-red, with yellow reverse, an attractive and bright combination which fades slightly with age. Slightly fragrant. A good cultivar for bedding because of its compact habit. Seems to be disease resistant. **494**, p. 94.
C.M., R.N.R.S. 1966.

'Tropicana' see **'Super Star', 369**, p. 69.

'Tropicana, Climbing' see **'Climbing Super Star'**

'Tuscany'   G.
Crimson-maroon, summer, 5 ft (1·5 m.)
Shrub rose of fair vigour up to 5 ft (1·5 m.) but often of rather loose growth. Flowers large, semi-double, opening flat, dark crimson-maroon with some white flecks towards centre and flush of purple, with large centre of golden stamens, up to 4 in. (10·2 cm.) across. Scent slight. Mid to late June. Foliage grey-green. One of the finest Gallica roses and an effective garden plant. Sometimes known as the 'Old Velvet Rose' from the texture of its petals, this pre-1800 rose may be Gerard's Velvet Rose of 1596.

'Tuscany Superb'   G.
Crimson-maroon, summer, 5 ft (1·5 m.)
Gallica rose of moderate vigour up to 5 ft (1·5 m.). Close to 'Tuscany' but with slightly larger flowers with smaller centres, and broader leaves. Probably a sport from 'Tuscany' which occurred prior to 1848. **91**, p. 16.

'Tzigane'   HT.
Scarlet and yellow, 2 ft (0·6 m.) 1951
Raised by F. Meilland, France.
Parentage: 'Peace' × 'J. B. Meilland'
A moderate grower in my experience, 2 ft (0·6 m.) high, with glossy, very dark green foliage. The flowers are full, slightly globular, scarlet-red with yellow reverse. Where suited, can be a useful bedding rose but may have to be protected against mildew. Fragrant.

'Ulrich Brunner' see **'Ulrich Brunner Fils'**

'Ulrich Brunner Fils', 'Ulrich Brunner'   HP.
Carmine, recurrent, 6 ft (1·8 m.) 1882
Raised by A. Levet, France.
Hybrid Perpetual shrub or pillar rose of considerable vigour, making very long shoots up to 6 ft (1·8 m.) which will flower freely along their length if pegged down near the tips. Flowers bright carmine, double, of medium size, cupped on opening, scented. Free-flowering. Mid to late June and recurrent. A rose of such strong colour that it is best grown on its own and then it is very effective.

'Uncle Walter'   HT.
Scarlet, 6 ft (1·8 m.) 1963
Raised by S. McGredy IV, N. Ireland.
Parentage: 'Detroiter' × 'Heidelberg'
Really a shrub, reaching 6 ft (1·8 m.) in height and grown in New Zealand, I understand, as a climber. The dark green, glossy foliage is crimson when young. The medium sized flowers are borne in clusters and are scarlet with crimson shadings; fragrance is slight. Most effective grown as a shrub.
C.M., R.N.R.S. 1963.

'Vanity'   HM.
Strong pink, recurrent, 8 ft (2·4 m.) 1920
Raised by Rev. J. H. Pemberton, England.
Parentage: 'Château de Clos Vougeot' × unrecorded seedling
Fairly vigorous Hybrid Musk with upright growth and long shoots particularly in autumn, up to 8 ft (2·4 m.) but not very dense growth. Flowers in large open clusters, single, strong crimson-pink but with some blue tone in it, quite large, scented, very floriferous. Late June to mid-July and recurrent, often with finest flowering in autumn. Always a conspicuous rose, especially when grown in a group, but unfortunately the colour is rather a hard pink at first but softer in the autumn. **125**, p. 22.
F.C.C., R.H.S. 1958.

'Variegata di Bologna'   B.
White, streaked with pale purple, recurrent, 5 ft (1·5 m.) 1909
Raised by A. Bonfiglioli, Italy.
Vigorous Bourbon shrub making wide bush up to 5 ft (1·5 m.). Flowers large or medium in size, rounded and nearly globular, double, white well streaked with pale purple, showing more colour in the open buds, markings irregular in size, some as splashes or flecks of colour, about 3½ in. (8·9 cm.) across. Free-flowering. Mid to late June, slightly recurrent. One of the most striking of the old striped roses and usually making a well foliaged and thick shrub, but sometimes sensitive to black spot. **103**, p. 18.

'Variety Club'   Fl.
Pink, cream and yellow, 3 ft (0·9 m.) 1965
Raised by S. McGredy IV, N. Ireland.
Parentage: 'Columbine' × 'Circus'
A vigorous cultivar, up to 3 ft (0·9 m.) high, with plenty of dark green glossy foliage. Flowers are full, of hybrid tea shape in the early stages, opening as they get older; a cheerful mixture of pink, cream and yellow which varies according to weather. Produces plenty of basal growth and slightly fragrant flowers.
T.G.C., R.N.R.S. 1965.

'Veilchenblau', 'Violet Blue'   R.
Purple-violet, 12 ft + (3·7 m.) 1909
Raised by J. C. Schmidt, Germany.
Parentage: 'Crimson Rambler' × 'Souvenir de Brod'
Vigorous rambler, 12 to 15 ft (3·7–4·6 m.), of *multiflora* type, sometimes referred to as the 'blue' rose. Flowers in large clusters, rather small, about 1¼ in. (3·2 cm.) across, semi-double, purplish-violet with some white in centre, maturing to dark bluish-violet, then lilac-grey, scented. Late June to mid-July, but not recurrent. Valuable and distinctive for giving purplish-blue colour among ramblers. In hot sun this colour tends to fade and is usually better preserved in some shade. It is not quite so bright a colour as 'Rose Marie Viaud' (**222**, p. 41) but has more violet than 'Violette'.

Velvet Rose see under **'Tuscany'**

'Vera Dalton' Fl.
Pink, 3½ ft (1·1 m.) 1961
Raised by A. Norman, England.
Parentage: 'Paul's Scarlet Climber' self-set seedling × ('Mary' × 'Queen Elizabeth')
A vigorous grower with abundant semi-glossy, dark green foliage which may, in some gardens, require protection from black spot and mildew but in my own experience, always healthy. Blooms are a beautiful soft pink and most attractive when fully open. Very free-flowering in large, well spaced trusses which resist weather well but spot slightly as they age. A pleasantly scented cultivar which has not attained the popularity it deserves. **495**, p. 95.
C.M., R.N.R.S. 1961; A.M., R.H.S. 1964.

'Versicolor', *R. gallica versicolor*, 'Rosa Mundi' G.
Pale pink striped purple, summer, 4 ft (1·2 m.)
Sport from 'Officinalis', originated before the sixteenth century when it is first recorded. Shrub rose of medium size up to 4 ft (1·2 m.). Flowers semi-double, pale blush-pink, almost white, liberally splashed and irregularly striped with deep pinkish-purple, up to 4½ in. (11·4 cm.) across with good boss of yellow stamens in centre. Others describe it as rose-red splashed with white and the two colours are about equal in amount. A very striking flower and usually a very floriferous plant and a great favourite of many lovers of shrub roses. Foliage abundant, a good green. Branches with few thorns. This rose can be pruned or even clipped quite hard and has been grown very successfully as a thick hedge about 3 ft (0·9 m.) high which is covered with flowers for about four weeks from mid-June. Should not be confused with the York and Lancaster roses which are forms of *R. damascena*. There is a famous plate of it by Redouté which portrays it very clearly. **92**, p. 17.

'Vesper' Fl.
Pale orange-brown, 2½ ft (0·8 m.) 1966
Raised by E. B. LeGrice, England.
A fairly vigorous branching grower, 2½ ft (0·8 m.) high, with small, semi-glossy bronze-green foliage. The full, medium sized flowers are an unusual pastel shade of orange-brown, inclined to fade in hot weather. Trusses larger in the autumn. Useful as a foil to other cultivars. Fragrance slight. **496**, p. 95.
T.G.C., R.N.R.S. 1967.

'Vick's Caprice' HP.
Rose-pink flecked white, recurrent, 4 ft (1·2 m.) 1891
Discovered by J. Vick, U.S.A.
Parentage: 'Archiduchesse Elizabeth d'Autriche' sport
Hybrid Perpetual shrub of medium vigour, generally not over 3–4 ft (0·9–1·2 m.). Flowers large, double, deep pink in bud, then rose-pink variously striped and flecked with white and carmine-pink. Mid to late June and recurrent. Occurred as sport from 'Archiduchesse Elizabeth d'Autriche', a self pink rose in Mr Vick's garden at Rochester, New York, but branches tend to revert back. **117**, p. 21.

'Vienna Charm' see **'Wiener Charme'**, **375**, p. 70.

'Village Maid' see *R. × centifolia* 'Variegata'

'Ville de Chine' see **'Chinatown'**, **148**, p. 26.

'Violet Blue' see **'Veilchenblau'**

'Violet Carson' Fl.
Peach, 2½ ft (0·8 m.) 1964
Raised by S. McGredy IV, N. Ireland.
Parentage: 'Mme Léon Cuny' × 'Spartan'
A vigorous grower of spreading habit, foliage reasonably abundant, semi-glossy, dark green with bronze tints which harmonize with the light peach-pink flowers. A refined cultivar which fades in very hot weather but produces blooms very freely in large trusses from the stronger growths. Resists wet fairly well and has a pleasing light scent. 2½ ft (0·8 m.) high. **497**, p. 95.
C.M., R.N.R.S. 1963.

'Violette' R.
Purplish-mauve, summer, 15 ft (4·6 m.) 1921
Raised by E. Turbat & Co., France.
Rambler of moderate vigour of *multiflora* type. Flowers in large clusters, small, semi-double, purplish-mauve with some touch of maroon-crimson, slightly scented, free-flowering. Late June to mid-July but not recurrent. Growth long and almost thornless; best grown out of strong sun so that the colour is retained.

'Virgo', 'Virgo Liberationem' HT.
White, 2 ft (0·6 m.) 1947
Raised by C. Mallerin, France.
Parentage: 'Blanche Mallerin' × 'Neige Parfum'
A moderate grower, 2 ft (0·6 m.) high, with mat, dark green foliage. The medium sized flowers are shapely, white, occasionally flushed very pale pink, with long stems and excellent for cutting. Is intolerant of rain and requires protection against mildew.
G.M., R.N.R.S. 1949.

Abbreviations and Symbols used in the text

Rose classifications

A.	Alba	HT.	Hybrid Tea
B.	Bourbon	MCl.	Modern, large-flowered climber
C.	Centifolia	Min.	Miniature
Ch.	China	Moss	Centifolia muscosa
Cl.	Climber	MSh.	Modern shrub
D.	Damask	P.	Penzance Sweet Brier
Fl.	Floribunda	R.	Rambler
G.	Gallica	Rg.	Rugosa
HM.	Hybrid Musk	Sp.	Species and first hybrids
HP.	Hybrid Perpetual	Sw.	Sweet Brier

Rose Awards and Societies

A.A.R.S.	All-America Rose Selection
A.G.M.	Award of Garden Merit
A.M.	Award of Merit
A.R.S.	American Rose Society
B.B.G.M.	Baden Baden Gold Medal, Germany
B.G.M.	Bagatelle Gold Medal, Paris
C.C.V.	Clay Challenge Vase for scent
C.M.	Certificate of Merit
D.F.P.	David Fuerstenberg Prize
F.C.C.	First Class Certificate
G.G.M.	Geneva Gold Medal
G.M.	Gold Medal
G.M.C.B.	Gold Medal City of Belfast
G.M.H.G.M.	Gertrude M. Hubbard Gold Medal
G.R.H.	Golden Rose of The Hague
G.T.A.B.	Golden Thorn Award Belfast
H.E.M.M.	The Henry Edland Memorial Medal for the most fragrant rose of the year
H.G.M.	The Hague Gold Medal
L.G.M.	Lyon Gold Medal, France
M.G.M.	Madrid Gold Medal
N.G.M.C.	National Gold Medal Certificate
P.G.M.	Portland Gold Medal, Oregon, U.S.A.
P.I.T.	President's International Trophy
R.B.	Prize for the most fragrant rose, Roeulx, Belgium
R.B.G.M.	Roeulx, Belgium, Gold Medal
R.G.M.	Rome Gold Medal
R.H.S.	The Royal Horticultural Society, London
R.N.R.S.	The Royal National Rose Society, Great Britain*
T.G.C.	Trial Ground Certificate
U.A.B.	The 'Uladh' Award for fragrance, Belfast

National Rose Society awards, before 1965, are included here under R.N.R.S.

The illustration numbers are in **bold type** and the page numbers in light type preceded by p.

'Virgo Liberationem' see **'Virgo'**

'Viridiflora', *R. chinensis viridiflora*   Ch.
Green and purplish-brown, recurrent, 4 ft (1·2 m.)
Parentage: probably *R. chinensis* sport
In cultivation for over 100 years, this is a shrub of medium vigour, usually not over 4 ft (1·2 m.). Flowers fully double with green petals, twisted with some purplish-brown colouring towards base and centre, opening jade-green, then turning to apple-green, in clusters of medium size. This plant is sometimes grown as a curiosity but it is not of great beauty. Foliage rather blue-green. **127**, p. 22.

'Vison Blanc' see **'Ice White', 429**, p. 80.

'Wedding Day'   R.
White, summer, 25 ft (7·6 m.) 1950
Raised by F. C. Stern, England.
Parentage: seedling of *R. sinowilsonii* × unknown rose
One of the most rampant ramblers, in a class with *R. filipes* 'Kiftsgate' (**19**, p. 4), very vigorous, thorny, and ideal for covering or hiding old buildings, up to 25 ft (7·6 m.). Flowers in large clusters, single, buds apricot, opening pale creamy-yellow turning to white and dying off with some pink. Given its name because it just opened in its raiser's garden, at Highdown, on the anniversary of his Wedding Day, 26 June. **228**, p. 42.
A.M., R.H.S. 1950.

'Wendy' see **'Para Ti'**

'Wendy Cussons'   HT.
Cerise-scarlet, 3 ft (0·9 m.) 1959
Raised by C. Gregory & Son Ltd, England.
Parentage: probably 'Independence' × 'Eden Rose'
An outstanding cultivar of vigorous growth which branches out into a large bush. Foliage is dark green, leathery and glossy, generally very healthy but may require protection from black spot in some gardens. The blooms are full, rosy-scarlet when young becoming cerise-scarlet as they grow older, appearing almost scarlet in artificial light. They resist wet weather well and are suitable for exhibition if selected carefully as on occasions split flowers occur. Although a tall grower, around 3 ft (0·9 m.), this cultivar is of such good habit that it is one of the best for standards, flowering very freely in summer and again in autumn; strongly fragrant. **373**, p. 70.
G.M., R.N.R.S. 1959; P.I.T., R.N.R.S. 1959; A.M., R.H.S. 1959; G.R.H. 1964; P.G.M. 1964; F.C.C., R.H.S. 1965.

'Wheatcroft's Baby Crimson' see **'Perla de Alcanada'**

'Whisky Mac'   HT.
Gold, 3 ft (0·9 m.) 1967
Raised by M. Tantau, Germany.
A fairly vigorous grower, 2½–3 ft (0·8–0·9 m.) high, well furnished with glossy dark green, holly like foliage, tinted bronze when young. The full shapely blooms are gold, overlaid tangerine and bronze and are freely produced. Unusually fragrant for a rose in this colour, this cultivar is already in demand and may prove a spectacular bedder. In some Continental countries 'Mac' is dropped from the name but as 'Whisky', a Floribunda, already exists, this is not permissible. **374**, p. 70.

'White American Beauty' see **'Frau Karl Druschki', 111**, p. 20.

'White Cockade'   MCl.Sh.
White, 6–8 ft (1·8–2·4 m.) 1969
Raised by J. Cocker & Sons Ltd, Scotland.
Parentage: 'New Dawn' × 'Circus'
A short growing climber or shrub with glossy foliage. The medium sized flowers are double, of good hybrid tea form, freely produced well into autumn and have a pleasant scent. Useful for low pillars if trained or as a shrub which requires little pruning.

'White Knight' see **'Message'**

White Rose of York see *R.* × *alba*

'White Spray'   Fl.
Pure white, 3 ft (0·9 m.) 1968
Raised by E. B. LeGrice, England.
Parentage: seedling × 'Schneewittchen'
An upright, free grower, 2½–3 ft (0·8–0·9 m.) high, with attractive foliage. The small, well formed flowers are pure white, buds creamy-white, and have some scent. Good for cutting. May require protection against mildew.

'Wiener Charme', 'Charme de Vienne',   HT.
   'Charming Vienna', 'Vienna Charm'
Coppery-orange, 3½ ft (1·1 m.) 1963
Raised by R. Kordes, Germany.
Parentage: 'Golden Sun' × 'Chantre'
A vigorous, tall grower up to 3½ ft (1·1 m.) high, with a somewhat gawky appearance, unsuitable for bedding, but useful in a border. The full flowers are pleasing in shape, a gorgeous coppery-orange, paling towards the edges of the petals and with some fragrance. Requires careful protection against mildew and black spot in areas where these diseases prevail. **375**, p. 70.
T.G.C., R.N.R.S. 1963.

'Wilhelm', 'Skyrocket'   MSh.
Crimson, recurrent, 6 ft (1·8 m.) 1934
Raised by W. Kordes, Germany.
Parentage: 'Robin Hood' × 'J. C. Thornton'
Vigorous modern Hybrid Musk shrub rose up to 6 ft (1·8 m.). Flowers in large clusters, semi-double, crimson with good boss of gold stamens in centre, about 3½ in. (8·9 cm.) across, paler near base, paling as it matures to mauvish-crimson, slightly scented, free-flowering. Mid to late June, recurrent. Good glossy foliage. Makes a large and vigorous bush. Better, clearer colour has now been reached in more modern varieties and it is becoming superseded, but being a tetraploid, it has been widely used as a parent. Hips large and colouring late, persistent. **191**, p. 35.

'Will Scarlet'   MSh.
Crimson, recurrent, 6 ft (1·8 m.) 1950
Introduced by T. Hilling Ltd, England.
Parentage: 'Wilhelm' sport
Modern Hybrid Musk shrub rose. Vigorous up to 6 ft (1·8 m.). Flowers scarlet-crimson, but with a little purplish-blue tint, and paler in centre, less deep in colour than 'Wilhelm' (**191**, p. 35), semi-double, in large clusters, slightly scented, free-flowering. Mid-June and recurrent. Good orange-red hips in late autumn and winter. In bright sun it tends to fade with lilac-red, especially in centre and like its parent is now superseded by the stronger crimson of more modern varieties, but it makes a strong, well-foliaged free-flowering bush for a long season. Named after one of Robin Hood's merry men.
A.M., R.H.S. 1954.

'William III' see *R. spinosissima* **'William III'**

'William Allen Richardson'   Cl.
Orange-yellow, recurrent, 8 ft + (2·4 m.) 1878
Raised by Veuve Ducher, France.
Parentage: 'Rêve d'Or' sport or seedling
Climber of medium vigour with flowers of hybrid tea type, growing
to 8 ft (2·4 m.) or more. Flowers quite large, semi-double to
double, bright orange-yellow, tinted with orange-red towards
centre, but the colour bleaches in strong sunlight. Strongly scented.
Mid to late June, recurrent. Foliage dark glossy green, but subject
to black spot. Best grown on a warm wall, this is an old favourite,
but seems in recent years to have lost some of its former vigour and
good specimens are rarely seen now although we found one to
photograph. Mr W. A. Richardson was an American grower of
roses, who sent the original yellow seedling from which this rose
sported to Mme Ducher of Lyons. Needs protection in northern
states of the U.S.A. **229**, p. 42.

'William Lobb'   Moss Sh.
Dark purplish-crimson, summer, 6 ft (1·8 m.) 1855
Raised by M. Laffay, France.
Vigorous shrub up to 6 ft (1·8 m.) or more. Flowers semi-double,
crimson in bud, dark purplish-crimson fading as they mature to
paler purplish-lavender with lighter base, scented. Mid-late June
but not recurrent. Buds and also pedicels well mossed with green and
in large clusters. A group of three plants at Sissinghurst Castle,
England of this distinctive old rose measures 10 × 10 ft (3 × 3 m.)
but it is exceptional. It is much the most vigorous of the Moss roses
with young shoots covered with small reddish thorns. Also known as
'Duchesse d'Istrie' and 'Old Velvet Moss'. **76**, p. 14.

'Willie Winkie'   Min.
Light rose-pink, 10 in. (25·4 cm.) 1955
Raised by J. de Vink, Holland.
Parentage: 'Katharina Zeimet' × 'Tom Thumb'
Dwarf, 6–10 in. (15·2–25·4 cm.) high with very double, globular,
light rose-pink flowers.

'Winefred Clarke'   HT.
Yellow, 3½ ft (1·1 m.) 1965
Raised by H. Robinson, England.
Parentage: 'Peace' × 'Lydia'
A vigorous branching grower, 3½ ft (1·1 m.) high, with glossy
medium green foliage. The slightly fragrant flowers are full, well
formed and lasting, yellow fading to cream. Free-flowering. This
cultivar seems to be at its best in the autumn and in northern
gardens. **376**, p. 70.
T.G.C., R.N.R.S. 1965.

Wolley-Dod's Rose see *R. pomifera* **'Duplex'**, **38**, p. 8.

'Wood's Garland' see **'The Garland'**, **227**, p. 42.

'Yellow Cushion'   Fl.
Clear yellow, 2 ft (0·6 m.) 1966
Raised by D. L. Armstrong, U.S.A.
Parentage: 'Fandango' × 'Pinocchio'
A short bushy grower, about 2 ft (0·6 m.) high, with well formed
double flowers, clear yellow becoming cream. Very free-flowering.
Slightly scented. Very useful for small gardens. **498**, p. 95.

'Yellow Doll'   Min.
Soft yellow, 12 in. (30·5 cm.) 1962
Raised by R. S. Moore, U.S.A.
Parentage: 'Golden Glow' × 'Zee'

A vigorous bushy grower, 10–12 in. (25·4–30·5 cm.) high with
leathery glossy foliage. The small double flowers have narrow petals,
soft yellow in colour and have some fragrance.

'Yellow Queen Elizabeth'   Fl.
Creamy-yellow, 4 ft + (1·2 m.) 1964
Discovered by Vlaeminck, Belgium.
Parentage: 'Queen Elizabeth' sport
A creamy-yellow sport, not quite so tall and vigorous as its parent.
Useful where a tall cultivar is required in this colour, for large beds
or a hedge. Little scent.

'Yellow Sweetheart' see **'Rosina'**

York and Lancaster Rose see *R. damascena variegata*

'Youki San', 'Mme Neige'   HT.
White, 2½ ft (0·8 m.) 1965
Raised by Meilland, France.
Parentage: 'Lady Sylvia' × 'Message'
A moderate grower with small, light green foliage. The flowers are
fairly full, white with a greenish tinge, showing red stamens when
fully open and with a dainty appearance. Does not like rain and
requires protection against mildew in some areas, but is sweet
scented.

Abbreviations and Symbols used in the text

Rose classifications

A.	Alba	HT.	Hybrid Tea
B.	Bourbon	MCl.	Modern, large-flowered climber
C.	Centifolia	Min.	Miniature
Ch.	China	Moss	Centifolia muscosa
Cl.	Climber	MSh.	Modern shrub
D.	Damask	P.	Penzance Sweet Brier
Fl.	Floribunda	R.	Rambler
G.	Gallica	Rg.	Rugosa
HM.	Hybrid Musk	Sp.	Species and first hybrids
HP.	Hybrid Perpetual	Sw.	Sweet Brier

Rose Awards and Societies

A.A.R.S.	All-America Rose Selection
A.G.M.	Award of Garden Merit
A.M.	Award of Merit
A.R.S.	American Rose Society
B.B.G.M.	Baden Baden Gold Medal, Germany
B.G.M.	Bagatelle Gold Medal, Paris
C.C.V.	Clay Challenge Vase for scent
C.M.	Certificate of Merit
D.F.P.	David Fuerstenberg Prize
F.C.C.	First Class Certificate
G.G.M.	Geneva Gold Medal
G.M.	Gold Medal
G.M.C.B.	Gold Medal City of Belfast
G.M.H.G.M.	Gertrude M. Hubbard Gold Medal
G.R.H.	Golden Rose of The Hague
G.T.A.B.	Golden Thorn Award Belfast
H.E.M.M.	The Henry Edland Memorial Medal for the most fragrant rose of the year
H.G.M.	The Hague Gold Medal
L.G.M.	Lyon Gold Medal, France
M.G.M.	Madrid Gold Medal
N.G.M.C.	National Gold Medal Certificate
P.G.M.	Portland Gold Medal, Oregon, U.S.A.
P.I.T.	President's International Trophy
R.B.	Prize for the most fragrant rose, Roeulx, Belgium
R.B.G.M.	Roeulx, Belgium, Gold Medal
R.G.M.	Rome Gold Medal
R.H.S.	The Royal Horticultural Society, London
R.N.R.S.	The Royal National Rose Society, Great Britain*
T.G.C.	Trial Ground Certificate
U.A.B.	The 'Uladh' Award for fragrance, Belfast

National Rose Society awards, before 1965, are included here under R.N.R.S.

The illustration numbers are in **bold type** and the page numbers
in light type preceded by p.

'Yvonne Rabier'   Fl.
White, 3 ft (0·9 m.) 1910
Raised by F. Turbat & Co., France.
Parentage: *R. wichuraiana* × a Polyantha
A vigorous, bushy grower which, if lightly pruned, will attain 3 ft
(0·9 m.) in height, with deep green, slender foliage, often retained
well into the winter. The medium sized flowers are semi-double,
rosette shaped, white with a slight tint of sulphur-yellow at the base
and freely produced over a long season in small trusses. This is one of
the roses frequently called Poly-pom at the present time but which
for convenience can be included in a Floribunda section. Very
sweetly scented and still a favourite of mine. **499**, p. 95.

'Zambra'   Fl.
Orange and yellow, 2 ft + (0·6 m.) 1961
Raised by M. L. Meilland, France.
Parentage: ('Goldilocks' × 'Fashion') × ('Golidlocks' × 'Fashion')
A fairly vigorous grower, just over 2 ft (0·6 m.), with glossy, mid-
green foliage. The semi-double flowers are medium sized, produced
in small trusses, orange with yellow reverse, a very striking combina-
tion. Liable to get black spot in certain areas. **500**, p. 95.
B.G.M. 1961; R.G.M. 1961; C.M., R.N.R.S. 1961.

'Zéphirine Drouhin'   B.
Cerise-carmine, recurrent, 10 ft (3 m.) 1868
Raised by Bizot, France.

A famous Bourbon rose. Vigorous shrub or climber up to 10 ft
(3 m.). Flowers very bright, cerise-carmine, semi-double, of
medium size but borne in large clusters. Strongly scented. Free-
flowering, mid to late June and recurrent throughout summer if old
heads are pruned off. Young growth is tinted bronzy red. Distinct
by absence of thorns from main stems. One of the most popular old
roses for this character and for its freedom of flower. Rather
susceptible to black spot and mildew. Sometimes used as a hedge
and will stand heavy pruning. **104**, p. 19.

'Zigeunerknabe', 'Gypsy Boy'   B.
Bright purplish-crimson, summer, 9 ft (2·7 m.) 1909
Raised by P. Lambert, Germany.
Parentage: probably seedling from 'Russelliana'
Bourbon rose. Very vigorous shrub or climber, up to 9 ft (2·7 m.).
Flowers in clusters, semi-double, opening bright purplish-crimson,
becoming violet-crimson as they mature, showing central golden
stamens, 2½–3 in. (6·4–7·6 cm.) across. Nearly scentless. Very free-
flowering but not recurrent. Mid to late June. Foliage good, with 3–5
leaflets. Hips large, round, orange-red. This is by far the most
vigorous of the dark purplish-crimson Bourbon roses and is a
wonderful sight when grown up into an old tree or supported,
making 6 ft (1·8 m.) vigorous growths in season. By pruning it may
be kept to a large shrub, but is better allowed to grow freely with
old wood cut out from time to time. Very prickly. **105**, p. 19.

'Zwergkönig' see **'Dwarfking'**, **503**, p. 96.